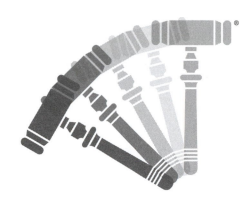

Casenote® Legal Briefs

BANKRUPTCY

Keyed to Courses Using

Warren, Bussel, and Skeel's
Bankruptcy

Ninth Edition

Wolters Kluwer
Law & Business

Copyright © 2013 CCH Incorporated. All Rights Reserved.

Published by Wolters Kluwer Law & Business in New York.

Wolters Kluwer Law & Business serves customers worldwide with CCH, Aspen Publishers, and Kluwer Law International products. (www.wolterskluwerlb.com)

No part of this publication may be reproduced or transmitted in any form or by any means, electronic or mechanical, including photocopy, recording, or utilized by any information storage and retrieval system, without written permission from the publisher. For information about permissions or to request permission online, visit us at wolterskluwerlb.com or a written request may be faxed to our permissions department at 212-771-0803.

To contact Customer Service, e-mail customer.service@wolterskluwer.com, call 1-800-234-1660, fax 1-800-901-9075, or mail correspondence to:

Wolters Kluwer Law & Business
Attn: Order Department
P.O. Box 990
Frederick, MD 21705

Printed in the United States of America.

1 2 3 4 5 6 7 8 9 0

ISBN 978-1-4548-2458-9

About Wolters Kluwer Law & Business

Wolters Kluwer Law & Business is a leading global provider of intelligent information and digital solutions for legal and business professionals in key specialty areas, and respected educational resources for professors and law students. Wolters Kluwer Law & Business connects legal and business professionals as well as those in the education market with timely, specialized authoritative content and information-enabled solutions to support success through productivity, accuracy and mobility.

Serving customers worldwide, Wolters Kluwer Law & Business products include those under the Aspen Publishers, CCH, Kluwer Law International, Loislaw, Best Case, ftwilliam.com and MediRegs family of products.

CCH products have been a trusted resource since 1913, and are highly regarded resources for legal, securities, antitrust and trade regulation, government contracting, banking, pension, payroll, employment and labor, and healthcare reimbursement and compliance professionals.

Aspen Publishers products provide essential information to attorneys, business professionals and law students. Written by preeminent authorities, the product line offers analytical and practical information in a range of specialty practice areas from securities law and intellectual property to mergers and acquisitions and pension/benefits. Aspen's trusted legal education resources provide professors and students with high-quality, up-to-date and effective resources for successful instruction and study in all areas of the law.

Kluwer Law International products provide the global business community with reliable international legal information in English. Legal practitioners, corporate counsel and business executives around the world rely on Kluwer Law journals, looseleafs, books, and electronic products for comprehensive information in many areas of international legal practice.

Loislaw is a comprehensive online legal research product providing legal content to law firm practitioners of various specializations. Loislaw provides attorneys with the ability to quickly and efficiently find the necessary legal information they need, when and where they need it, by facilitating access to primary law as well as state-specific law, records, forms and treatises.

Best Case Solutions is the leading bankruptcy software product to the bankruptcy industry. It provides software and workflow tools to flawlessly streamline petition preparation and the electronic filing process, while timely incorporating ever-changing court requirements.

ftwilliam.com offers employee benefits professionals the highest quality plan documents (retirement, welfare and non-qualified) and government forms (5500/PBGC, 1099 and IRS) software at highly competitive prices.

MediRegs products provide integrated health care compliance content and software solutions for professionals in healthcare, higher education and life sciences, including professionals in accounting, law and consulting.

Wolters Kluwer Law & Business, a division of Wolters Kluwer, is headquartered in New York. Wolters Kluwer is a market-leading global information services company focused on professionals.

Format for the Casenote® Legal Brief

Nature of Case: This section identifies the form of action (e.g., breach of contract, negligence, battery), the type of proceeding (e.g., demurrer, appeal from trial court's jury instructions), or the relief sought (e.g., damages, injunction, criminal sanctions).

Fact Summary: This is included to refresh your memory and can be used as a quick reminder of the facts.

Rule of Law: Summarizes the general principle of law that the case illustrates. It may be used for instant recall of the court's holding and for classroom discussion or home review.

Facts: This section contains all relevant facts of the case, including the contentions of the parties and the lower court holdings. It is written in a logical order to give the student a clear understanding of the case. The plaintiff and defendant are identified by their proper names throughout and are always labeled with a (P) or (D).

Palsgraf v. Long Island R.R. Co.

Injured bystander (P) v. Railroad company (D)

N.Y. Ct. App., 248 N.Y. 339, 162 N.E. 99 (1928).

NATURE OF CASE: Appeal from judgment affirming verdict for plaintiff seeking damages for personal injury.

FACT SUMMARY: Helen Palsgraf (P) was injured on R.R.'s (D) train platform when R.R.'s (D) guard helped a passenger aboard a moving train, causing his package to fall on the tracks. The package contained fireworks which exploded, creating a shock that tipped a scale onto Palsgraf (P).

🏛 RULE OF LAW
The risk reasonably to be perceived defines the duty to be obeyed.

FACTS: Helen Palsgraf (P) purchased a ticket to Rockaway Beach from R.R. (D) and was waiting on the train platform. As she waited, two men ran to catch a train that was pulling out from the platform. The first man jumped aboard, but the second man, who appeared as if he might fall, was helped aboard by the guard on the train who had kept the door open so they could jump aboard. A guard on the platform also helped by pushing him onto the train. The man was carrying a package wrapped in newspaper. In the process, the man dropped his package, which fell on the tracks. The package contained fireworks and exploded. The shock of the explosion was apparently of great enough strength to tip over some scales at the other end of the platform, which fell on Palsgraf (P) and injured her. A jury awarded her damages, and R.R. (D) appealed.

ISSUE: Does the risk reasonably to be perceived define the duty to be obeyed?

HOLDING AND DECISION: (Cardozo, C.J.) Yes. The risk reasonably to be perceived defines the duty to be obeyed. If there is no foreseeable hazard to the injured party as the result of a seemingly innocent act, the act does not become a tort because it happened to be a wrong as to another. If the wrong was not willful, the plaintiff must show that the act as to her had such great and apparent possibilities of danger as to entitle her to protection. Negligence in the abstract is not enough upon which to base liability. Negligence is a relative concept, evolving out of the common law doctrine of trespass on the case. To establish liability, the defendant must owe a legal duty of reasonable care to the injured party. A cause of action in tort will lie where harm,

though unintended, could have been averted or avoided by observance of such a duty. The scope of the duty is limited by the range of danger that a reasonable person could foresee. In this case, there was nothing to suggest from the appearance of the parcel or otherwise that the parcel contained fireworks. The guard could not reasonably have had any warning of a threat to Palsgraf (P), and R.R. (D) therefore cannot be held liable. Judgment is reversed in favor of R.R. (D).

DISSENT: (Andrews, J.) The concept that there is no negligence unless R.R. (D) owes a legal duty to take care as to Palsgraf (P) herself is too narrow. Everyone owes to the world at large the duty of refraining from those acts that may unreasonably threaten the safety of others. If the guard's action was negligent as to those nearby, it was also negligent as to those outside what might be termed the "danger zone." For Palsgraf (P) to recover, R.R.'s (D) negligence must have been the proximate cause of her injury, a question of fact for the jury.

▶ ANALYSIS

The majority defined the limit of the defendant's liability in terms of the danger that a reasonable person in defendant's situation would have perceived. The dissent argued that the limitation should not be placed on liability, but rather on damages. Judge Andrews suggested that only injuries that would not have happened but for R.R.'s (D) negligence should be compensable. Both the majority and dissent recognized the policy-driven need to limit liability for negligent acts, seeking, in the words of Judge Andrews, to define a framework "that will be practical and in keeping with the general understanding of mankind." The Restatement (Second) of Torts has accepted Judge Cardozo's view.

Quicknotes

FORESEEABILITY A reasonable expectation that change is the probable result of certain acts or omissions.

NEGLIGENCE Conduct falling below the standard of care that a reasonable person would demonstrate under similar conditions.

PROXIMATE CAUSE The natural sequence of events without which an injury would not have been sustained.

Party ID: Quick identification of the relationship between the parties.

Concurrence/Dissent: All concurrences and dissents are briefed whenever they are included by the casebook editor.

Analysis: This last paragraph gives you a broad understanding of where the case "fits in" with other cases in the section of the book and with the entire course. It is a hornbook-style discussion indicating whether the case is a majority or minority opinion and comparing the principal case with other cases in the casebook. It may also provide analysis from restatements, uniform codes, and law review articles. The analysis will prove to be invaluable to classroom discussion.

Issue: The issue is a concise question that brings out the essence of the opinion as it relates to the section of the casebook in which the case appears. Both substantive and procedural issues are included if relevant to the decision.

Holding and Decision: This section offers a clear and in-depth discussion of the rule of the case and the court's rationale. It is written in easy-to-understand language and answers the issue presented by applying the law to the facts of the case. When relevant, it includes a thorough discussion of the exceptions to the case as listed by the court, any major cites to the other cases on point, and the names of the judges who wrote the decisions.

Quicknotes: Conveniently defines legal terms found in the case and summarizes the nature of any statutes, codes, or rules referred to in the text.

Wolters Kluwer Law & Business is proud to offer *Casenote® Legal Briefs*—continuing thirty years of publishing America's best-selling legal briefs.

Casenote® Legal Briefs are designed to help you save time when briefing assigned cases. Organized under convenient headings, they show you how to abstract the basic facts and holdings from the text of the actual opinions handed down by the courts. Used as part of a rigorous study regimen, they can help you spend more time analyzing and critiquing points of law than on copying bits and pieces of judicial opinions into your notebook or outline.

Casenote® Legal Briefs should never be used as a substitute for assigned casebook readings. They work best when read as a follow-up to reviewing the underlying opinions themselves. Students who try to avoid reading and digesting the judicial opinions in their casebooks or online sources will end up shortchanging themselves in the long run. The ability to absorb, critique, and restate the dynamic and complex elements of case law decisions is crucial to your success in law school and beyond. It cannot be developed vicariously.

Casenote® Legal Briefs represents but one of the many offerings in Legal Education's Study Aid Timeline, which includes:

- *Casenote® Legal Briefs*
- *Emanuel® Law Outlines*
- Emanuel® *Law in a Flash* Flash Cards
- Emanuel® *CrunchTime®* Series
- *Siegel's Essay and Multiple-Choice Questions and Answers Series*

Each of these series is designed to provide you with easy-to-understand explanations of complex points of law. Each volume offers guidance on the principles of legal analysis and, consulted regularly, will hone your ability to spot relevant issues. We have titles that will help you prepare for class, prepare for your exams, and enhance your general comprehension of the law along the way.

To find out more about Wolters Kluwer Law & Business' study aid publications, visit us online at *www.wolterskluwerlb.com* or email us at *legaledu@wolterskluwer.com*. We'll be happy to assist you.

A. Decide on a Format and Stick to It

Structure is essential to a good brief. It enables you to arrange systematically the related parts that are scattered throughout most cases, thus making manageable and understandable what might otherwise seem to be an endless and unfathomable sea of information. There are, of course, an unlimited number of formats that can be utilized. However, it is best to find one that suits your needs and stick to it. Consistency breeds both efficiency and the security that when called upon you will know where to look in your brief for the information you are asked to give.

Any format, as long as it presents the essential elements of a case in an organized fashion, can be used. Experience, however, has led *Casenote* ® *Legal Briefs* to develop and utilize the following format because of its logical flow and universal applicability.

NATURE OF CASE: This is a brief statement of the legal character and procedural status of the case (e.g., "Appeal of a burglary conviction").

There are many different alternatives open to a litigant dissatisfied with a court ruling. The key to determining which one has been used is to discover *who is asking this court for what*.

This first entry in the brief should be kept as *short as possible*. Use the court's terminology if you understand it. But since jurisdictions vary as to the titles of pleadings, the best entry is the one that addresses who wants what in this proceeding, not the one that sounds most like the court's language.

RULE OF LAW: A statement of the general principle of law that the case illustrates (e.g., "An acceptance that varies any term of the offer is considered a rejection and counteroffer").

Determining the rule of law of a case is a procedure similar to determining the issue of the case. Avoid being fooled by red herrings; there may be a few rules of law mentioned in the case excerpt, but usually only one is *the* rule with which the casebook editor is concerned. The techniques used to locate the issue, described below, may also be utilized to find the rule of law. Generally, your best guide is simply the chapter heading. It is a clue to the point the casebook editor seeks to make and should be kept in mind when reading every case in the respective section.

FACTS: A synopsis of only the essential facts of the case, i.e., those bearing upon or leading up to the issue.

The facts entry should be a short statement of the events and transactions that led one party to initiate legal proceedings against another in the first place. While some cases conveniently state the salient facts at the beginning of the decision, in other instances they will have to be culled from hiding places throughout the text, even from concurring and dissenting opinions. Some of the "facts" will often be in dispute and should be so noted. Conflicting evidence may be briefly pointed up. "Hard" facts must be included. Both must be *relevant* in order to be listed in the facts entry. It is impossible to tell what is relevant until the entire case is read, as the ultimate determination of the rights and liabilities of the parties may turn on something buried deep in the opinion.

Generally, the facts entry should not be longer than three to five *short* sentences.

It is often helpful to identify the role played by a party in a given context. For example, in a construction contract case the identification of a party as the "contractor" or "builder" alleviates the need to tell that that party was the one who was supposed to have built the house.

It is always helpful, and a good general practice, to identify the "plaintiff" and the "defendant." This may seem elementary and uncomplicated, but, especially in view of the creative editing practiced by some casebook editors, it is sometimes a difficult or even impossible task. Bear in mind that the *party presently* seeking something from this court may not be the plaintiff, and that sometimes only the cross-claim of a defendant is treated in the excerpt. Confusing or misaligning the parties can ruin your analysis and understanding of the case.

ISSUE: A statement of the general legal question answered by or illustrated in the case. For clarity, the issue is best put in the form of a question capable of a "yes" or "no" answer. In reality, the issue is simply the Rule of Law put in the form of a question (e.g., "May an offer be accepted by performance?").

The major problem presented in discerning what is *the* issue in the case is that an opinion usually purports to raise and answer several questions. However, except for rare cases, only one such question is really the issue in the case. Collateral issues not necessary to the resolution of the matter in controversy are handled by the court by language known as *"obiter dictum"* or merely *"dictum."* While dicta may be included later in the brief, they have no place under the issue heading.

To find the issue, ask *who wants what* and then go on to ask *why did that party succeed or fail in getting it*. Once this is determined, the "why" should be turned into a question.

The complexity of the issues in the cases will vary, but in all cases a single-sentence question should sum up the issue. *In a few cases,* there will be two, or even more rarely, three issues of equal importance to the resolution of the case. Each should be expressed in a single-sentence question.

Since many issues are resolved by a court in coming to a final disposition of a case, the casebook editor will reproduce the portion of the opinion containing the issue or issues most relevant to the area of law under scrutiny. A noted law professor gave this advice: "Close the book; look at the title on the cover." Chances are, if it is Property, you need not concern yourself with whether, for example, the federal government's treatment of the plaintiff's land really raises a federal question sufficient to support jurisdiction on this ground in federal court.

The same rule applies to chapter headings designating sub-areas within the subjects. They tip you off as to what the text is designed to teach. The cases are arranged in a casebook to show a progression or development of the law, so that the preceding cases may also help.

It is also most important to remember to *read the notes and questions* at the end of a case to determine what the editors wanted you to have gleaned from it.

HOLDING AND DECISION: This section should succinctly explain the rationale of the court in arriving at its decision. In capsulizing the "reasoning" of the court, it should always include an application of the general rule or rules of law to the specific facts of the case. Hidden justifications come to light in this entry: the reasons for the state of the law, the public policies, the biases and prejudices, those considerations that influence the justices' thinking and, ultimately, the outcome of the case. At the end, there should be a short indication of the disposition or procedural resolution of the case (e.g., "Decision of the trial court for Mr. Smith (P) reversed").

The foregoing format is designed to help you "digest" the reams of case material with which you will be faced in your law school career. Once mastered by practice, it will place at your fingertips the information the authors of your casebooks have sought to impart to you in case-by-case illustration and analysis.

B. Be as Economical as Possible in Briefing Cases

Once armed with a format that encourages succinctness, it is as important to be economical with regard to the time spent on the actual reading of the case as it is to be economical in the writing of the brief itself. This does not mean "skimming" a case. Rather, it means reading the case with an "eye" trained to recognize into which "section" of your brief a particular passage or line fits and having a system for quickly and precisely marking the case so that the passages fitting any one particular part of the brief can be easily identified and brought together in a concise and accurate manner when the brief is actually written.

It is of no use to simply repeat everything in the opinion of the court; record only enough information to trigger your recollection of what the court said. Nevertheless, an accurate statement of the "law of the case," i.e., the legal principle applied to the facts, is absolutely essential to class preparation and to learning the law under the case method.

To that end, it is important to develop a "shorthand" that you can use to make marginal notations. These notations will tell you at a glance in which section of the brief you will be placing that particular passage or portion of the opinion.

Some students prefer to underline all the salient portions of the opinion (with a pencil or colored underliner marker), making marginal notations as they go along. Others prefer the color-coded method of underlining, utilizing different colors of markers to underline the salient portions of the case, each separate color being used to represent a different section of the brief. For example, blue underlining could be used for passages relating to the rule of law, yellow for those relating to the issue, and green for those relating to the holding and decision, etc. While it has its advocates, the color-coded method can be confusing and time-consuming (all that time spent on changing colored markers). Furthermore, it can interfere with the continuity and concentration many students deem essential to the reading of a case for maximum comprehension. In the end, however, it is a matter of personal preference and style. Just remember, whatever method you use, underlining must be used sparingly or its value is lost.

If you take the marginal notation route, an efficient and easy method is to go along underlining the key portions of the case and placing in the margin alongside them the following "markers" to indicate where a particular passage or line "belongs" in the brief you will write:

N   (NATURE OF CASE)
RL   (RULE OF LAW)
I   (ISSUE)
HL   (HOLDING AND DECISION, relates to the RULE OF LAW behind the decision)
HR   (HOLDING AND DECISION, gives the RATIONALE or reasoning behind the decision)
HA   (HOLDING AND DECISION, APPLIES the general principle(s) of law to the facts of the case to arrive at the decision)

Remember that a particular passage may well contain information necessary to more than one part of your brief, in which case you simply note that in the margin. If you are using the color-coded underlining method instead of marginal notation, simply make asterisks or checks in the margin next to the passage in question in the colors that indicate the additional sections of the brief where it might be utilized.

The economy of utilizing "shorthand" in marking cases for briefing can be maintained in the actual brief writing process itself by utilizing "law student shorthand" within the brief. There are many commonly used words and phrases for which abbreviations can be substituted in your briefs (and in your class notes also). You can develop abbreviations that are personal to you and which will save you a lot of time. A reference list of briefing abbreviations can be found on page xii of this book.

C. Use Both the Briefing Process and the Brief as a Learning Tool

Now that you have a format and the tools for briefing cases efficiently, the most important thing is to make the time spent in briefing profitable to you and to make the most advantageous use of the briefs you create. Of course, the briefs are invaluable for classroom reference when you are called upon to explain or analyze a particular case. However, they are also useful in reviewing for exams. A quick glance at the fact summary should bring the case to mind, and a rereading of the rule of law should enable you to go over the underlying legal concept in your mind, how it was applied in that particular case, and how it might apply in other factual settings.

As to the value to be derived from engaging in the briefing process itself, there is an immediate benefit that arises from being forced to sift through the essential facts and reasoning from the court's opinion and to succinctly express them in your own words in your brief. The process ensures that you understand the case and the point that it illustrates, and that means you will be ready to absorb further analysis and information brought forth in class. It also ensures you will have something to say when called upon in class. The briefing process helps develop a mental agility for getting to the *gist* of a case and for identifying, expounding on, and applying the legal concepts and issues found there. The briefing process is the mental process on which you must rely in taking law school examinations; it is also the mental process upon which a lawyer relies in serving his clients and in making his living.

Abbreviations for Briefs

acceptance	acp	offer	O
affirmed	aff	offeree	OE
answer	ans	offeror	OR
assumption of risk	a/r	ordinance	ord
attorney	atty	pain and suffering	p/s
beyond a reasonable doubt	b/r/d	parol evidence	p/e
bona fide purchaser	BFP	plaintiff	P
breach of contract	br/k	prima facie	p/f
cause of action	c/a	probable cause	p/c
common law	c/l	proximate cause	px/c
Constitution	Con	real property	r/p
constitutional	con	reasonable doubt	r/d
contract	K	reasonable man	r/m
contributory negligence	c/n	rebuttable presumption	rb/p
cross	x	remanded	rem
cross-complaint	x/c	res ipsa loquitur	RIL
cross-examination	x/ex	respondeat superior	r/s
cruel and unusual punishment	c/u/p	Restatement	RS
defendant	D	reversed	rev
dismissed	dis	Rule Against Perpetuities	RAP
double jeopardy	d/j	search and seizure	s/s
due process	d/p	search warrant	s/w
equal protection	e/p	self-defense	s/d
equity	eq	specific performance	s/p
evidence	ev	statute	S
exclude	exc	statute of frauds	S/F
exclusionary rule	exc/r	statute of limitations	S/L
felony	f/n	summary judgment	s/j
freedom of speech	f/s	tenancy at will	t/w
good faith	g/f	tenancy in common	t/c
habeas corpus	h/c	tenant	t
hearsay	hr	third party	TP
husband	H	third party beneficiary	TPB
injunction	inj	transferred intent	TI
in loco parentis	ILP	unconscionable	uncon
inter vivos	I/v	unconstitutional	unconst
joint tenancy	j/t	undue influence	u/e
judgment	judgt	Uniform Commercial Code	UCC
jurisdiction	jur	unilateral	uni
last clear chance	LCC	vendee	VE
long-arm statute	LAS	vendor	VR
majority view	maj	versus	v
meeting of minds	MOM	void for vagueness	VFV
minority view	min	weight of authority	w/a
Miranda rule	Mir/r	weight of the evidence	w/e
Miranda warnings	Mir/w	wife	W
negligence	neg	with	w/
notice	ntc	within	w/i
nuisance	nus	without	w/o
obligation	ob	without prejudice	w/o/p
obscene	obs	wrongful death	wr/d

Table of Cases

CHAPTER 2

The Bankruptcy Estate

Quick Reference Rules of Law

Butner v. United States

Mortgagee (P) v. Federal government (D)

440 U.S. 48 (1979).

NATURE OF CASE: Appeal from court of appeal's reversal of district court's reversal of bankruptcy court's denial of motion claiming a security interest in rents.

FACT SUMMARY: Butner (P), a second mortgagee of property mortgaged by Golden Enterprises, Inc. (Golden) (D) in Chapter 11 arrangement proceedings, contended that state law should govern his rights to rents collected during the period between Golden's (D) bankruptcy and the foreclosure sale of the mortgaged property.

> 🏛 **RULE OF LAW**
> State law governs a mortgagee's rights to rents collected during the period between the mortgagor's bankruptcy and the foreclosure sale of the mortgaged property.

FACTS: In Chapter 11 arrangement proceedings under the Bankruptcy Act, Butner (P) acquired a second mortgage from Golden Enterprises, Inc. (Golden) (D) on certain real estate to secure a $360,000 indebtedness but received no express security interest in the rents earned by the property. The bankruptcy judge thereafter appointed an agent to collect the rents and apply them to the payment of taxes, insurance, interest, and principal payments due on the first and second mortgages. Golden (D) was later adjudicated a bankrupt, at which time the first and second mortgages were in default, and the trustee was ordered to collect and retain all rents. Golden's (D) properties were ultimately sold to Butner (P) for $174,000, that price being paid by reduction of the estate's indebtedness to Butner (P) from $360,000 to $186,000. At the sale date, the trustee had accumulated almost $163,000 in rents which Butner (P) unsuccessfully sought to have applied to the balance of the second mortgage indebtedness, since the bankruptcy judge ruled that the $186,000 balance due Butner (P) should be treated as a general unsecured claim. The district court reversed. Though recognizing that under state law a mortgagor is deemed the owner of the land subject to the mortgage and during his possession is entitled to rents and profits, even after default, the court viewed the agent's appointment during the arrangement proceedings as tantamount to the appointment of a receiver which satisfied the state-law requirement of a change of possession, giving Butner (P) an interest in the rents which no further action after the bankruptcy adjudication was required to preserve. The court of appeals reversed, reinstating the bankruptcy court's disposition, based on its conclusion that the bankruptcy adjudication had terminated the state-court receivership status arising out of the appointment of the agent to collect rents, and that because Butner (P) had made no request

during the bankruptcy for a sequestration of rents or for the appointment of a receiver, Butner (P) had not taken the kind of action state law required to give a mortgagee a security interest in the rents collected after the bankruptcy adjudication. The United States Supreme Court granted certiorari.

ISSUE: Does state law govern a mortgagee's rights to rents collected during the period between the mortgagor's bankruptcy and the foreclosure sale of the mortgaged property?

HOLDING AND DECISION: (Stevens, J.) Yes. State law governs a mortgagee's rights to rents collected during the period between the mortgagor's bankruptcy and the foreclosure sale of the mortgaged property. The Court granted certiorari in this case to resolve a conflict between the Third and Seventh Circuits on the one hand, and several other circuits on the other, concerning the proper approach to the issue presented. The majority of the circuits regard the question whether a security interest in property extends to rents and profits derived from the property as one that should be resolved by reference to state law. The Third and Seventh Circuits, which have adopted a federal rule of equity that affords the mortgagee a secured interest in the rents even if state law would not recognize any such interest until after foreclosure, reason that since the bankruptcy court has the power to deprive the mortgagee of his state-law remedy, equity requires that the right to rents not be dependent on state-court action that may be precluded by federal law. Under this approach, no affirmative steps are required by the mortgagee—in state or federal court—to acquire or maintain a right to the rents. The approach adopted by the majority of the circuits is correct, and the approach taken by the Third and Seventh Circuits is rejected. Apart from certain special provisions, Congress in the Bankruptcy Act generally left the determination of property rights in the assets of a bankrupt's estate to state law. Property interests are created and defined by state law, so that unless some federal interest requires a different result, there is no reason why such interests should be analyzed differently simply because an interested party is involved in a bankruptcy proceeding. The approach taken by the Third and Seventh Circuits is based on their perception of the demands of equity. However, undefined considerations of equity provide no basis for adoption of a uniform federal rule affording mortgagees an automatic interest in the rents as soon as the mortgagor is declared bankrupt. The Third and Seventh Circuits have emphasized that while the mortgagee may pursue various

Continued on next page.

state-law remedies prior to bankruptcy, the adjudication leaves the mortgagee "only such remedies as may be found in a court of bankruptcy in the equitable administration of the bankrupt's assets." It does not follow, however, that "equitable administration" requires that all mortgagees be afforded an automatic security interest in rents and profits when state law would deny such an automatic benefit and require the mortgagee to take some affirmative action before his rights are recognized. Instead, the law of the State where the property is located governs a mortgagee's right to rents during bankruptcy, and a federal bankruptcy court should take whatever steps are necessary to ensure that a mortgagee is afforded in federal bankruptcy court the same protection he would have under state law had no bankruptcy ensued. Although the lower courts in this case took the correct approach in applying state law, they disagreed about whether the requirements of state law had been met. However, that state-law issue as such will not be reviewed by this Court, as it is best left to the lower courts that regularly deal with state law and determine how local courts would dispose of comparable issues. Affirmed.

▶ ANALYSIS

The result of the United States Supreme Court's decision in this case was that the outcome in bankruptcy proceedings as to the state-law issue would vary from state to state. In a few states, sometimes referred to as "title states," the mortgagee is automatically entitled to possession of the property, and to a secured interest in the rents. In most states, the mortgagee's right to rents is dependent upon his taking actual or constructive possession of the property by means of a foreclosure, the appointment of a receiver for his benefit, or some similar legal proceeding. Because of such state-to-state variations, and the confusion and lack of uniformity that resulted therefrom, in 1994 Congress promulgated § 552(b)(2) of the Bankruptcy Code, which treats real property rents as "cash collateral" without regard to state law, thus rendering a uniform federal bankruptcy rule as to the scope of the mortgagee's rights to rents.

■■■■

Quicknotes

CERTIORARI A discretionary writ issued by a superior court to an inferior court in order to review the lower court's decisions; the United States Supreme Court's writ ordering such review.

CHAPTER 11 BANKRUPTCY A legal proceeding whereby a debtor, who is unable to pay his debts as they become due, is relieved of his obligation to pay his creditors through reorganization and payment from future income.

DEFAULT Failure to carry out a legal obligation.

SECURITY INTEREST An interest in property that may be sold upon a default in payment of the debt.

■■■■

In re Silveira

Judicial lienholder (D) v. Debtor property owner (P)

141 F.3d. 34 (1st Cir. 1998).

NATURE OF CASE: Appeal of an order of the bankruptcy court permitting avoidance of a judicial lien.

FACT SUMMARY: Silveira (P) filed for bankruptcy and was allowed to avoid a bank's judicial lien in its entirety.

🏛 RULE OF LAW
A judicial lien impairs an exemption to the extent that the targeted lien, in combination with other liens and the value of the debtor's exemption, exceeds the value of the debtor's property.

FACTS: Silveira (P) owned as his primary residence a property with a fair market value of $157,000. The property was subject to a mortgage of $117,680, and East Cambridge Savings Bank (Bank) (D) held a $209,500 judicial lien on the property. When Silveira (P) filed a voluntary petition under Chapter 7 of the Bankruptcy Code, he claimed an exemption of $15,000 in the property pursuant to Bankruptcy Code § 522(d)(1) and filed a motion to avoid the Bank's (D) judicial lien pursuant to § 522(f). The bankruptcy court granted the motion. The Bank (D) appealed to the district court, arguing that § 522(f) permitted only a partial avoidance of its judicial lien, based on the facts of this case. The district court affirmed and the Bank (D) appealed again.

ISSUE: Does a judicial lien impair an exemption to the extent that the targeted lien, in combination with other liens and the value of the debtor's exemption, exceeds the value of the debtor's property?

HOLDING AND DECISION: (Stahl, J.) Yes. A judicial lien impairs an exemption to the extent that the targeted lien, in combination with other liens and the value of the debtor's exemption, exceeds the value of the debtor's property. In this case the Bank's (D) judicial lien clearly does impair an exemption of the debtor, but Silveira (P) is entitled to avoid only so much of the Bank's (D) lien as necessary to prevent impairment of the debtor's exemption, not the entire amount of the Bank's (D) lien. The language of § 522(f)(1) and § 522(f)(2)(A) support the Bank's (D) position. The words of the statute are that a debtor may avoid the fixing of a lien "to the extent that" the lien impairs an exemption. This means that impairment is not only a precondition of avoidability, but also a proportional measurement of the scope of the debtor's avoidance power. Reversed and remanded.

▶ *ANALYSIS*

Prior to the 1994 amendment of § 522(f), there was a split among jurisdictions as to the meaning of "impairment." The problem was whether to interpret the statute to mean that the debtor could avoid a lien impairing an exemption to which the debtor is entitled or to one he would have been entitled to but for the lien itself. The avoiding power given to the debtor by the statute provides a fresh start.

■■■

Quicknotes

EXEMPTION Colloquial term usually used to refer to a deduction not keyed to actual expenditures.

■■■

Norwest Bank Nebraska v. Tveten

Creditor (P) v. Real estate investor (D)

848 F.2d 871 (8th Cir. 1988).

NATURE OF CASE: Appeal in action to prevent the discharge of debts.

FACT SUMMARY: Dr. Tveten (D) petitioned for Chapter 11 bankruptcy after converting almost $700,000 of his personal property into exempt property that could not be reached by his creditors.

RULE OF LAW
Absent extrinsic evidence of fraud, mere conversion of non-exempt property to exempt property is not fraudulent as to creditors, even if the motivation behind the conversion is to place those assets beyond the reach of creditors.

FACTS: Dr. Tveten (D) invested in various real estate developments that were initially quite successful. By mid-1985, as the investments began to sour, Tveten (D) was personally liable to creditors, including Norwest Bank (Norwest) (P), for approximately $19,000,000. Before filing for bankruptcy, Tveten (D) converted his non-exempt property worth $700,000 into life insurance or annuity contracts with the Lutheran Brotherhood, a fraternal benefit organization, which, under Minnesota law, could not be attached by creditors. Unlike similar exemptions in other states, the Minnesota exemption has no monetary limit. Tveten (D) then sought a discharge with respect to $18,920,000 of his debts. Norwest (P) and other creditors (P) attempted to prevent the discharge and argued that Tveten (D) had acted with intent to defraud, delay, and hinder their efforts to collect from him. The bankruptcy court concluded that although Tveten's (D) conversion of non-exempt property to exempt property just before petitioning for bankruptcy, standing alone, would not justify denial of a discharge, his inferred intent to defraud would. The court further stated that Tveten's (D) awareness of the lawsuits pending against him, his rapidly deteriorating business investments, and his exposure to liability well beyond his ability to pay were all evidence of his fraudulent intent to hinder and delay creditors. The district court affirmed. Tveten (D) appealed again, asserting that his transfers were made on the advice of counsel and merely constituted astute pre-bankruptcy planning.

ISSUE: Absent extrinsic evidence of fraud, is mere conversion of non-exempt property to exempt property fraudulent as to creditors if the motivation behind the conversion is to place those assets beyond the reach of creditors?

HOLDING AND DECISION: (Timbers, J.) No. Absent extrinsic evidence of fraud, mere conversion of non-exempt property to exempt property is not fraudulent as to creditors, even if the motivation behind the conversion is to place those assets beyond the reach of creditors. The court in *In re Ellingson*, 63 B.R. 271 (N.D. Iowa 1986), held that exemptions should further one or more social policies: (1) To provide the debtor with property necessary for his physical survival; (2) to protect the dignity and the cultural and religious identity of the debtor; (3) to enable the debtor to rehabilitate himself and financially earn income in the future; (4) to protect the debtor's family from the adverse consequences of impoverishment; and (5) to shift the burden of providing the debtor and his family with minimal financial support from society to the debtor's creditors. In this case, Tveten (D) clearly took advantage of the purpose for which the exemptions are intended and the fact that under Minnesota law the exemption was unlimited. Permitting Tveten (D), who earns over $60,000 annually as a physician, to convert all of his major non-exempt assets into sheltered property on the eve of bankruptcy with actual intent to defraud his creditors would amount to a perversion of the purposes of the Bankruptcy Code. Furthermore, Tveten's (D) reliance on his attorney's advice only protects him to the extent that the reliance was reasonable. The bankruptcy court was not clearly erroneous in inferring fraudulent intent on the part of Tveten (D). Affirmed.

DISSENT: (Arnold, J.) Although the court's result may appeal to one's general sense of righteousness, it is contrary to clearly established law. When state law creates an unlimited exception, the result may often be that wealthy debtors like Tveten (D) enjoy a windfall. Tveten (D) never made any secret about what he was attempting to do. Although such a design necessarily involves an attempt to delay or hinder creditors, in the ordinary, non-legal sense of these words, under prevailing law, such a purpose is not unlawful.

ANALYSIS

Tveten (D) does seemingly get punished for the fact that the state exemption he relied upon was unlimited. Although the court claimed that Tveten (D) was trying to take for himself a "head start," rather than the "fresh start" contemplated by bankruptcy policy, justice is not served by penalizing him for being aware of and taking advantage of his rights to the full extent permitted by law. When viewed in light of the holding in *Hanson v. First National Bank in Brookings*, 848 F.2d 866 (8th Cir. 1988), in which the same court permitted the Hansons to sell non-exempt property to family members and purchase life insurance policies

Continued on next page.

with the proceeds on the eve of bankruptcy, the outcome seems particularly unfair.

■■■

Quicknotes

EXTRINSIC EVIDENCE Evidence that is not contained within the text of a document or contract, but which is derived from the parties' statements or the circumstances under which the agreement was made.

■■■

Hanson v. First National Bank in Brookings

Debtor (P) v. Creditor (D)

848 F.2d 866 (8th Cir. 1988).

NATURE OF CASE: Appeal in action challenging a debtor's claimed exemptions.

FACT SUMMARY: First National Bank (First National) (D) attempted to prevent the Hansons (P), who converted some of their non-exempt personal property to exempt property on the eve of their bankruptcy filing, from claiming the exemptions.

🏛 RULE OF LAW
A debtor's conversion of non-exempt property to exempt property on the eve of bankruptcy for the express purpose of placing that property beyond the reach of creditors, absent extrinsic evidence of fraud, will not deprive the debtor of the exemption to which he otherwise would be entitled.

FACTS: Kenneth and Lucille Hanson (P), South Dakota farmers, defaulted on loans from First National Bank (D) after sustaining serious financial problems. In November 1983, the Hansons (P) filed a joint bankruptcy petition. The Hansons (P) had consulted with an attorney who advised them to take several steps prior to filing. On the advice of counsel, the Hansons (P) sold to their relatives particular property that would not have been exempt under South Dakota law. The Hansons (P) then used the proceeds from these sales to purchase two life insurance policies with cash values of $9,977 and $9,978, and prepaid approximately $11,000 on their homestead real estate mortgage that was held by First National (D). This property was exempt from their creditors' reach because under South Dakota law a debtor may exempt the proceeds of life insurance policies up to a total of $20,000 and his homestead property. First National (D) filed a challenge objecting to these exemptions, urging that the Hansons (D) had converted non-exempt property to exempt property on the eve of bankruptcy with the intent to defraud creditors. First National (P) asserted that none of the property allegedly sold was ever transferred to the buyers. The bankruptcy court denied First National's (D) motion objecting to the exemptions, finding that the Hansons' (P) actions were permissible under the law and did not constitute extrinsic evidence of fraud. The district court affirmed on appeal, and First National (D) appealed again.

ISSUE: Will a debtor's conversion of non-exempt property to exempt property on the eve of bankruptcy for the express purpose of placing that property beyond the reach of creditors, absent extrinsic evidence of fraud, deprive the debtor of the exemption to which he otherwise would be entitled?

HOLDING AND DECISION: (Timbers, J.) No. A debtor's conversion of non-exempt property to exempt property on the eve of bankruptcy for the express purpose of placing that property beyond the reach of creditors, absent extrinsic evidence of fraud, will not deprive the debtor of the exemption to which he otherwise would be entitled. First National (D) did not dispute the fact that the purchasers paid fair market value for the vehicles and other property, title appears to have been properly transferred, and the Hansons (P) provided reasonable explanations as to why the property they sold remained on their premises. The sale of goods to family members, standing on its own, does not establish extrinsic evidence of fraud. The decision of the bankruptcy court was not clearly erroneous in finding no fraudulent intent by the Hansons (P) and permitting them to claim their full exemptions. Affirmed.

CONCURRENCE: (Arnold, J.) The court was entirely correct in finding no extrinsic fraud. The trouble with this decision is that it cannot be reconciled with *Norwest Bank Nebraska v. Tveten*, 848 F.2d 871 (1988), also decided by this panel today. Dr. Tveten also attempted to convert property into an exempt form; however, the court apparently felt that the dollar amount was too large and found fraud. It is improper to permit distinctions to be made among debtors based on subjective considerations.

▶ ANALYSIS

The Hansons (P) were guilty of nothing more than taking full advantage of their rights under the bankruptcy laws. Nevertheless, First National (D) was clearly perturbed by the fact that the Hansons (P) had followed the advice of an attorney and successfully converted the previously non-exempt property. Although the Hansons (P) were vindicated by the decision above, sometimes when debtors are a little too savvy it can work against them, as the concurrence points out.

Quicknotes

EXTRINSIC EVIDENCE Evidence that is not contained within the text of a document or contract, but which is derived from the parties' statements or the circumstances under which the agreement was made.

Claims

Quick Reference Rules of Law

In re Piper Aircraft

[Parties not identified.]

58 F.3d 1573 (11th Cir. 1995).

NATURE OF CASE: Appeal from affirmance of bankruptcy court order disallowing a proof of claim in a Chapter 11 bankruptcy.

FACT SUMMARY: Epstein, the legal representative of future claimants (Future Claimants) in Piper Aircraft Corp.'s (Piper's) Chapter 11 bankruptcy, contended that, based on statistical assumptions about how many persons would have post-confirmation products liability claims against Piper arising from its preconfirmation manufacture of airplanes and airplane parts, the Future Claimants had a claim, as defined by § 101(5) of the Bankruptcy Code, of around $100,000,000.

RULE OF LAW

A person does not have a "claim," as defined by § 101(5) of the Bankruptcy Code, against a debtor manufacturer where the person has had no preconfirmation exposure to a specific identifiable product of the debtor or any other preconfirmation relationship with the debtor.

FACTS: Piper Aircraft Corp. (Piper), an airplane and airplane parts manufacturer, filed for voluntary Chapter 11 bankruptcy protection. Piper's plan of reorganization contemplated finding a purchaser of substantially all of its assets or obtaining investments from outside sources, with the proceeds of such transactions serving to fund distributions to creditors. Eventually, Piper and Pilatus Aircraft Ltd. (Pilatus) signed a letter of intent pursuant to which Pilatus would purchase Piper's assets. The letter of intent required Piper to seek the appointment of a legal representative to represent the interests of future claimants by arranging a set-aside of monies generated by the sale to pay off future product liability claims. Epstein was appointed as the legal representative, and the bankruptcy court defined Future Claimants as all persons who might, after the confirmation date, assert product liability claims against Piper or its successor arising out of or relating to aircraft or parts manufactured and sold, designed, distributed or supported by Piper prior to the confirmation date. Epstein then filed a $100,000,000 proof of claim on behalf of the Future Claimants, based on statistical assumptions regarding the number of persons likely to fit the definition of Future Claimants. The Official Committee of Unsecured Creditors (Official Committee) and Piper objected to the claim on the ground that the Future Claimants did not hold § 101(5) claims against Piper. Under § 101(10), only parties that hold preconfirmation claims may participate in a Chapter 11 case and share in payments pursuant to a Chapter 11 plan. Section 101(5) defines claim as either a right to payment, or a right to an equitable remedy for breach of

performance if such breach gives rise to a right to payment. The bankruptcy court ruled that the Future Claimants did not hold § 101(5) claims against Piper, and the district court affirmed. The court of appeals granted review.

ISSUE: Does a person have a "claim," as defined by § 101(5) of the Bankruptcy Code, against a debtor manufacturer where the person has had no preconfirmation exposure to a specific identifiable product of the debtor or any other preconfirmation relationship with the debtor?

HOLDING AND DECISION: (Black, J.) No. A person does not have a "claim," as defined by § 101(5) of the Bankruptcy Code, against a debtor manufacturer where the person has had no preconfirmation exposure to a specific identifiable product of the debtor or any other preconfirmation relationship with the debtor. Congress intended to define the term claim very broadly under § 101(5), so that "all legal obligations of the debtor, no matter how remote or contingent, will be able to be dealt with in the bankruptcy case." Several tests are used to determine whether certain parties hold claims pursuant to that section: the accrued state law claim test, the conduct test, and the prepetition relationship test. The bankruptcy court and district court adopted the prepetition relationship test in determining that the Future Claimants did not hold claims pursuant to § 101(5). Epstein argues that those courts should have used the conduct test because that test is more consistent with the text, history, and policies of the Code. Under the conduct test, a right to payment arises when the conduct giving rise to the alleged liability occurred. Epstein contends that any right to payment arising out of the prepetition conduct of Piper, no matter how remote, should be deemed a claim. Under this test, Piper's conduct was its prepetition manufacture, design, sale and distribution of allegedly defective aircraft. Epstein's theory is that because Piper performed these acts prepetition, the potential victims, although not yet identifiable, would hold claims as defined in § 101(5). The Official Committee and Piper assert that this is too broad a definition of claim. Because the conduct test may define claim too broadly in certain circumstances, several courts have recognized "claims" only for those individuals with some type of prepetition relationship with the debtor. The prepetition relationship test, as adopted by the bankruptcy court and district court, requires "some prepetition relationship, such as contact, exposure, impact, or privity, between the debtor's prepetition conduct and the claimant" in order for the claimant to hold a § 101(5) claim. This was the proper test in deciding that the Future Claimants did not hold a claim

Continued on next page.

under § 101(5), since even the courts applying the conduct test recognize that focusing solely on prepetition conduct would stretch the scope of § 101(5) and accordingly also presume some prepetition relationship between the debtor's conduct and the claimant. However, the district court's application of this test was too restrictive insofar as it restricted the class of claimants to those who could be identified prior to the filing of the petition. Those claimants having contact with the debtor's product post-petition but prior to confirmation also could be identified during the course of the bankruptcy proceeding as potential victims and Future Claimants. Thus, the correct test in this case, to be referred to as the "Piper test," for determining whether there is a "claim" under § 101(5) is as follows: "an individual has a § 101(5) claim against a debtor manufacturer if (i) events occurring before confirmation create a relationship, such as contact, exposure, impact, or privity, between the claimant and the debtor's product; and (ii) the basis for liability is the debtor's prepetition conduct in designing, manufacturing and selling the allegedly defective or dangerous product." Here, the Future Claimants failed the minimum requirements of the Piper test, as there was no preconfirmation exposure to a specific identifiable defective product or any other preconfirmation relationship between Piper and the broadly defined class of Future Claimants. Therefore, the Future Claimants did not have a claim. Affirmed.

▶ ANALYSIS

A contingent claim is included in the definition of claim. A claim is contingent as to liability if the debt is one which the debtor will be called upon to pay only upon the occurrence or happening of an extrinsic event that will trigger the liability of the debtor to the alleged creditor and if such triggering event or occurrence was one reasonably contemplated by the debtor and creditor at the time the event giving rise to the claim occurred. Thus, in the case of the classic contingent liability of a guarantor of a promissory note executed by a third party, both the creditor and guarantor knew there would be liability only if the principal maker defaulted. No obligation arises until such default. In the case of a tort claim for negligence, the parties at the time of the alleged negligent act would be presumed to have contemplated that the alleged tortfeasor would be liable only if it were so established by a competent tribunal. Such a tort claim is contingent as to liability until a final judgment is entered fixing the rights of the parties. On the other hand, in the ordinary debt arising from, for example, a sale of merchandise, the parties to the transaction would not at that time view the obligation as contingent. Subsequent events might lead to a dispute as to liability because of, for example, defective merchandise, but that would merely serve to render the debt a disputed one but would not make it a contingent one. A legal obligation arose at the time of the sale, although the obligation can possibly be avoided. Such a claim is disputed, but it is not contingent. A claim is contingent as to liability if the debtor's legal duty to pay does not come into existence until triggered by the occurrence of a future event and such future occurrence was within the actual or presumed contemplation of the parties at the time the original relationship of the parties was created. On the other hand, if a legal obligation to pay arose at the time of the original relationship, but that obligation is subject to being avoided by some future event or occurrence, the claim is not contingent as to liability, although it may be disputed as to liability for various reasons. Likewise, an unmatured obligation is not contingent as to liability.

■━■

Quicknotes

CHAPTER 11 BANKRUPTCY A legal proceeding whereby a debtor, who is unable to pay his debts as they become due, is relieved of his obligation to pay his creditors through reorganization and payment from future income.

■━■

United States v. Apex Oil Co.

Federal government (P) v. Polluter's successor (D)

579 F.3d 734 (7th Cir. 2009), *cert. denied*, 131 S. Ct. 67.

NATURE OF CASE: Appeal from grant of injunction for plaintiff Environmental Protection Agency requiring a polluter's successor to clean up a contaminated site.

FACT SUMMARY: Apex Oil Co. (Apex) (D) contended that the Environmental Protection Agency (P) could not require it to abate an environmental nuisance because its Chapter 11 bankruptcy had discharged all of Apex's (D) debts, including the ordered cleanup, because it would have to pay another company to perform the cleanup work.

RULE OF LAW

The cost of complying with an equitable decree is not dischargeable in bankruptcy where the claim does not give rise to a right of payment.

FACTS: Apex Oil Co.'s (Apex's) (D) debts were discharged in Chapter 11 bankruptcy. Subsequently, The Environmental Protection Agency (EPA) (P) sought, and obtained, an injunction under the Resource Conservation and Recovery Act (RCRA) requiring Apex (D) to abate an environmental nuisance that had been caused by Apex's (D) predecessor. Apex (D) estimated that it would have to pay another company around $150 million to do the cleanup work. Apex (D) contended that the EPA's (P) claim had been discharged in bankruptcy, and, therefore, could not be brought by the EPA (P) in a subsequent suit. Accordingly, it challenged the district court's grant of the injunction to the EPA (P), and the court of appeals granted review.

ISSUE: Is the cost of complying with an equitable decree dischargeable in bankruptcy where the claim does not give rise to a right of payment?

HOLDING AND DECISION: (Posner, J.) No. The cost of complying with an equitable decree is not dischargeable in bankruptcy where the claim does not give rise to a right of payment. Under the Bankruptcy Code, "debt" is defined as "liability on a claim," and a "claim" is defined as either a "right to payment," or a "right to an equitable remedy for breach of performance if such breach gives rise to a right to payment . . . ." Thus, the key issue here is the meaning of "gives rise to a right to payment." Under the plain language of the Bankruptcy Code, if a holder of an equitable claim can, in the event that the equitable remedy turns out to be unobtainable, obtain a money judgment in its place, the claim is dischargeable. So are certain equitable remedies that are orders to pay, subject to exceptions specified in the code. Here, however, RCRA does not entitle a plaintiff to demand payment in lieu of action, and, in fact, it does not authorize any form of monetary relief. All the EPA (P) can do

is require action—cleanup of a contaminated site at a defendant's expense. The cost to the defendant of complying with the equitable order is not, and should not be deemed, a money claim. The Code clearly did not intend for every equitable decree to be dischargeable—but that is what would happen if the cost of complying with an equitable decree were deemed a money claim. Almost every equitable decree imposes a cost on a defendant, whether the decree requires the defendant to do something or to refrain from doing something. Thus, cost incurred is not equivalent to "right to payment," and discharge of debt must be limited to cases in which the claim gives rise to a right of payment because the equitable decree cannot be executed, rather than merely imposing a cost on the defendant. Even if, as Apex (D) argues, denying discharge in cases such as this one might lead companies to liquidate, rather than reorganize in bankruptcy, the EPA (P) here has determined that, on balance, the Government (P) is better off if the cost of cleanup is not dischargeable. Affirmed.

▶ **ANALYSIS**

One situation where an equitable decree ordering environmental cleanup was permitted to be discharged was where a debtor had been ordered to clean up a contaminated site it owned; an injunction ordering the cleanup had been issued before the bankruptcy; the debtor had failed to comply with the injunction; and a receiver had been appointed to take possession of the debtor's assets and obtain from the debtor the money needed to pay for the cleanup. See *Ohio v. Kovacs,* 469 U.S. 274 (1985). That case, however, is distinguishable from the *Apex* case because in *Kovacs,* the receiver was seeking money rather than an order that the debtor clean up the contaminated site. i.e., the claim was a claim to a "right to payment."

Quicknotes

CHAPTER 11 BANKRUPTCY A legal proceeding whereby a debtor, who is unable to pay his debts as they become due, is relieved of his obligation to pay his creditors through reorganization and payment from future income.

EQUITABLE REMEDY A remedy that is based upon principles of fairness as opposed to rules of law; a remedy involving specific performance rather than money damages.

INJUNCTION A court order requiring a person to do, or prohibiting that person from doing, a specific act.

Associates Commercial Corporation v. Rash

Secured creditor (P) v. Debtor (D)

520 U.S. 953 (1997).

NATURE OF CASE: Review of judgment approving bankruptcy plan and limiting secured claim to net foreclosure value of collateral.

FACT SUMMARY: Associates Commercial Corporation (P) filed an objection to the Rashes' (D) Chapter 13 reorganization plan, seeking repossession of their tractor truck and alleging a secured interest of $47,171 constituting the replacement value of the truck.

> ### 🏛 RULE OF LAW
> Where a debtor exercises the cramdown option of Bankruptcy Code § 1325(a)(5)(B), seeking to retain and utilize a secured creditor's collateral pursuant to a Chapter 13 plan, the value of that collateral is to be determined in accordance with a replacement-value standard.

FACTS: Rash (D) purchased a tractor truck for use in his freight-hauling business for $73,700. He made a down payment on the truck and agreed to pay the seller the balance in sixty monthly installments. The seller assigned the loan and lien to Associates Commercial Corporation (ACC) (P). The Rashes (D) subsequently filed a petition in bankruptcy under Chapter 13. ACC (P) was listed as a secured creditor. Under Bankruptcy Code § 506(a), ACC's (P) claim was only secured to the extent of the value of the collateral, and any amount of the claim above the value of the truck was unsecured. In order for the Rashes' (D) plan to be confirmed, it had to satisfy the requirements of § 1324(a). Pursuant to this section, the plan may be confirmed if the secured creditor accepts the plan, the debtor surrenders the secured property to the creditor, or the debtor selects the cramdown option. Under the cramdown option, the debtor retains the secured property in which the creditor still has a lien, and the debtor tenders payments to the creditor in conformity with the plan amounting to the value of the secured interest in the collateral, equal to its present value. The Rashes (D) selected the cramdown option. Their plan proposed their continued use of the truck for business purposes and payment to ACC (P) of the present value of the truck in fifty-eight monthly installments totaling $28,500. ACC (P) filed an objection seeking to remove the application of the automatic stay to the truck, alleging a secured interest of $47,171. The bankruptcy court held that the proper valuation of the claim was the net amount ACC (P) would obtain from a foreclosure sale of the property, determined to equal $31,875. The bankruptcy court approved the plan, and the district court affirmed. The court of appeals reversed, then affirmed upon a rehearing en banc. The United States Supreme Court granted review.

ISSUE: Where a debtor exercises the cramdown option of Bankruptcy Code § 1325(a)(5)(B), seeking to retain and utilize a creditor's collateral pursuant to a Chapter 13 plan, is the value of that collateral to be determined in accordance with a replacement-value standard?

HOLDING AND DECISION: (Ginsburg, J.) Yes. Where a debtor exercises the cramdown option of Bankruptcy Code § 1325(a)(5)(B), seeking to retain and utilize a creditor's collateral pursuant to a Chapter 13 plan, the value of that collateral is to be determined in accordance with a replacement-value standard. Bankruptcy Code § 506(a) provides that a creditor's claim is secured to the extent of the bankruptcy estate's interest in the property. Therefore, in a cramdown context, the value of the collateral is to be ascertained in accordance with the price a buyer in the debtor's business would pay to obtain similar property for a comparable use. The creditor's secured claim is limited by this section to the value of the collateral. In order to determine this amount, the court must compare the creditor's claim with the value of the collateral. The section requires such value to be determined in accordance with the proposed use of the property and the purposes of the valuation. Where, as in the present case, the debtor retains the property and uses it for business purposes, the proper valuation method is in accordance with the cost the debtor would incur in obtaining similar property for a comparable use. Reversed and remanded.

▶ ANALYSIS

Note that the determinative issue in evaluating the amount of the creditor's secured claim is the proposed use or disposition of the collateral. Where a secured creditor rejects a debtor's Chapter 13 reorganization plan, the debtor has two options regarding the proposed use of the collateral. First the debtor can relinquish possession of the collateral to the creditor. Alternatively, the debtor can retain possession of the collateral and tender payments equaling the collateral's present value. The conflict among the circuits was in reference to the determination of the present value of the collateral for cramdown purposes. Where the debtor chooses to surrender the collateral, the creditor obtains immediate possession and may sell the property at a foreclosure sale. However, where the debtor elects to retain the property and make continued business use of the collateral, the Court determines that a foreclosure sale valuation is inappropriate and the replacement-value standard is more in conformity with the

Continued on next page.

requirement that such valuation be made consistent with the proposed use of the property.

■━■

Quicknotes

CHAPTER 13 BANKRUPTCY Debtor may modify plan at any time before the completion of the payments under such plan.

COLLATERAL Property that secures the payment of a debt.

CRAMDOWN Refers to a court's confirmation of a reorganization plan in a bankruptcy proceeding despite the opposition of creditors.

SECURED CLAIM A claim, the repayment of which is secured by collateral sufficient to repay the debt owed.

■━■

In re Jartran

Creditors (D) v. Debtor (P)

732 F.2d 584 (7th Cir. 1984).

NATURE OF CASE: Appeal from order in bankruptcy proceeding categorizing a claim upon the estate.

FACT SUMMARY: Creditors (D) of Jartran, Inc. (P) contended that monies due them for Yellow Pages ads they had provided pursuant to a prepetition contract were administrative expenses.

🏛 RULE OF LAW
Monies due on account of postpetition services provided to a bankrupt pursuant to a prepetition contract are not administrative expenses.

FACTS: Jartran, Inc. (P) contracted with Reuben H. Donnelley Corp. (D) and Sandra C. Tinsley, Inc. (D) for the latter to provide certain advertising services. Jartran (P) subsequently filed for bankruptcy. The ads were not published until after the commencement of the bankruptcy proceedings. Donnelley (D) and Tinsley (D) filed claims against the estate, seeking to have the debts owed them classified as administrative expenses to the estate. As such, they would be afforded priority over claims of other creditors. The bankruptcy court denied the claim, and the district court affirmed. Donnelley (D) and Tinsley (D) appealed.

ISSUE: Are monies due on account of postpetition services provided to a bankrupt pursuant to a prepetition contract administrative expenses?

HOLDING AND DECISION: (Cudahy, J.) No. Monies due on account of postpetition services provided to a bankrupt pursuant to a prepetition contract are not administrative expenses. Section 503(b) of the Bankruptcy Code classifies as administrative expenses, among other things, "the actual, necessary costs and expenses of preserving the estate." Thus, expenses incurred after filing that arise from a transaction with the debtor and are beneficial to the operation of the debtor's business will be afforded administrative expense status. However, this rule should not apply to expenses incurred due to obligations that arose before the filing. The purpose of the section is to induce potential future creditors to do business with the bankrupt, as they would have little motivation to do so were they not assured a preferred creditor status. When the creditor assumes such a role prior to filing, the purposes behind § 503(b) are not advanced by giving the creditor preferred status. Here, since Donnelley (D) and Tinsley (D) incurred their obligations before the petition's filing, they are not protected by § 503(b). Affirmed.

► ANALYSIS

Administrative expenses are given priority in a bankruptcy proceeding. Absent status as an administrative expense, Donnelley (D) and Tinsley (D) faced the prospect of being general unsecured creditors. Generally speaking, a general unsecured creditor takes considerably less than 100 cents on the dollar, so a creditor will do whatever it can to reclassify itself. Here, the effort failed.

Quicknotes

ADMINISTRATIVE EXPENSES In determining priority of claims in a Chapter 7 liquidation, refers to expenses of preserving the estate, including payment for services rendered after filing of the bankruptcy petition.

Discharge

Quick Reference Rules of Law

In re Madaj

Creditors (D) v. Debtors (P)

149 F.3d 467 (6th Cir. 1998).

NATURE OF CASE: Appeal from denial of motion to reopen case and judgment finding a debt dischargeable.

FACT SUMMARY: A loan that foster parents (D) gave to their son and his wife (P) was discharged after the couple's (P) Chapter 7 bankruptcy proceeding had been closed. The foster parents (D) allege that the debt should not have been discharged because the debt was not listed in the petition.

RULE OF LAW

A no-asset Chapter 7 case in which the debtor received a discharge does not have to be reopened in order to schedule a previously omitted debt so that the debt will be discharged because that debt has already been discharged if it otherwise would be dischargeable and the creditor received notice of the bankruptcy so that he could file a proof of claim.

FACTS: A foster child and his wife (Debtors) (P) borrowed money from his foster parents (Creditors) (D) and did not pay it back. The Debtors (P) did not list their foster parent Creditors (D) in their no-asset Chapter 7 bankruptcy petition and their debt to them was not discharged. Had the debt been timely scheduled, it would have been discharged. Moreover, if it had been listed and a proof of claim filed, there would have been no payment on the debt because this was a no-asset case. The foster parent Creditors (D) filed suit in state court and obtained a judgment against the Debtors (P) for the unpaid balance of the loan. The Debtors (P) moved to reopen their Chapter 7 action so that they could list the debt. The bankruptcy court denied their motion. The court nonetheless held that the debt to the foster parent Creditors (D) was discharged. The district court affirmed and the Creditors (D) appealed.

ISSUE: Does a no-asset Chapter 7 case in which the debtor received a discharge have to be reopened in order to schedule a previously omitted debt so that that debt will be discharged?

HOLDING AND DECISION: (Batchelder, J.) No. It is not necessary to reopen a Chapter 7 no-asset case in which the debtor received a discharge in order to schedule a prepetition debt that was not listed in the petition so that the debt will be discharged. That nonscheduled debt has already been discharged if it otherwise would be dischargeable and the creditor received notice of the bankruptcy so that he could file a proof of claim. According to the Bankruptcy Code, a discharge discharges every prepetition debt, whether or not a proof of claim has been filed, unless that debt is specifically exempted from discharge under § 523 because it was incurred by fraud, false pretenses, or malicious conduct. The only other debts excepted from discharge are those the debtor did not list in his petition in time for the creditor to file a timely claim. If the creditor had notice of the bankruptcy in time to file a claim, however, that unscheduled debt is still discharged. In a Chapter 7 no-asset case, a creditor may file a proof of claim at any time because there is nothing to recover, and therefore there is no concern for the creditor's opportunity to participate in the distribution of the assets of the estate by having their debts scheduled. In the present case, had the debt been timely filed it would not have been classified as a debt excepted from discharge. Furthermore, had the Creditors (D) known about the bankruptcy prior to the discharge, the debt would not have been excepted from discharge because the Creditors (D) had actual knowledge in time to file a proof of claim. That the Creditors (D) learned of the bankruptcy after the discharge order does not change the debt into one that is excepted from discharge. The reopening or not of the case to amend the schedule to include this debt does not alter the fact that the debt has been discharged because there is no deadline as to when proof of claims need to be filed and because the Creditors (D) have notice of the bankruptcy. Affirmed.

ANALYSIS

Notwithstanding the holding in this case, a bankruptcy judge may reopen a case so that a creditor can be added in order for the debtor to have a complete list of all discharged debts.

Quicknotes

CHAPTER 7 BANKRUPTCY A legal proceeding whereby a debtor, who is unable to pay his debts as they become due, is relieved of his obligation to pay his creditors by liquidation and distribution of his remaining assets.

DISCHARGEABLE DEBTS Debts subject to discharge in a bankruptcy proceeding.

DISCHARGE OF DEBTS In bankruptcy, the relief of a debtor who is unable to pay his debts as they become due from an obligation to pay his creditors.

In re Werthen

[Parties not identified.]

329 F.3d 269 (1st Cir. 2003).

NATURE OF CASE: Appeal from affirmance of order determining that debtor's obligations were non-dischargeable.

FACT SUMMARY: Werthen argued that bonuses and stock awarded to his ex-wife in divorce proceedings constituted property division rather than alimony or support—because the divorce court had labeled them as property division—and, therefore, were dischargeable in his Chapter 7 bankruptcy proceeding.

> ## RULE OF LAW
> The intent of, rather than the label used by, a court in a divorce proceeding is determinative of whether an award in divorce constitutes alimony or support, and, therefore, whether such an award is dischargeable in Chapter 7 bankruptcy proceedings.

FACTS: Werthen and his ex-wife divorced. During the marriage, Werthen was the primary income earner, and the ex-wife was the primary caretaker of the home and of the couple's four relatively young children. The final divorce decree awarded the ex-wife, under the rubric "Child Support and Alimony," one-third of Werthen's future bonuses and $450 per week in child support. Under the rubric "Property Division," the state court awarded the ex-wife (1) $222,000, representing 60% of the gross bonuses received by Werthen in the years 1996–1999, reduced to $124,485.84 by amounts in savings accounts already awarded the ex-wife (the "past bonus award"); and (2) $611,163.20, representing the ex-wife's 40% marital share of Werthen's 22% equity interest in a family-owned business (the "stock award"). With respect to these two awards, the court structured Werthen's payment schedule as yearly installments of $50,000 for nine years beginning in 2000, with the remaining balance due in two separate payments in the tenth and the eleventh years. Werthen then filed for Chapter 7 bankruptcy protection. In that proceeding, the ex-wife sought a ruling that the past bonus and stock awards—largely unpaid at that point—were not dischargeable because, under § 523(a)(5), they were alimony or support. The bankruptcy court, looking to the intent of the divorce court, ruled that both awards were alimony or support, and, therefore, nondischargeable under § 523(a)(5). A Bankruptcy Appellate Panel (BAP) affirmed, and the court of appeals granted review.

ISSUE: Is the intent of, rather than the label used by, a court in a divorce proceeding determinative of whether an award in divorce constitutes alimony or support, and, therefore, whether such an award is dischargeable in Chapter 7 bankruptcy proceedings?

HOLDING AND DECISION: (Boudin, C.J.) Yes. The intent of, rather than the label used by, a court in a divorce proceeding is determinative of whether an award in divorce constitutes alimony or support, and, therefore, whether such an award is dischargeable in Chapter 7 bankruptcy proceedings. Section 523(a)(5) turns upon a supposed distinction between "support" payments for spouse and children and other kinds of divorce awards, such as property division. The problem is that these two supposedly separate categories overlap because the need for ongoing support will often depend on how much property the less well-off spouse is given outright. The federal courts have been unwilling to treat the label applied by the divorce court as controlling for Bankruptcy Code purposes. Nominally, the critical issue is whether the divorce court judge "intended" a particular award to be for support or for something else. To determine such intent, courts look to various factors, including the language the divorce court used and whether the award seems designed to assuage need. Although the facts here do not line up neatly on either side, they weigh in favor of the ex-wife. First, the $450 per week for the four children seems quite limited, and the award of future bonuses is evanescent. Thus, it is no great leap to suppose that $50,000 per year for the next decade, representing the structured pay-out of the past bonus and stock awards, was intended in some measure to close the gap. Moreover, under the state statute, an award of property may be made in lieu of alimony. Favoring Werthen, however, is that the payment period did not end with anyone's death or exact majority, and that the payments in the catch-up period in years 10–11 appear to total over $200,000, which does not sound like annual alimony or support (except in the world of the very wealthy). Finally, without the awards, the ex-wife would be underfunded relative to her expenses. Accordingly, there is no basis for disturbing the decision below. Affirmed.

ANALYSIS

The court in this case indicated that its decision was a close one and called for a revision of § 523(a)(5), noting that the 1970 Commission on the Bankruptcy Laws of the United States recommended that the line-drawing approach between alimony and property division be abandoned. The court also observed that had the case been remanded—which Werthen did not request—the outcome could have been different if he had argued that the disputed awards were partly intended as support and

Continued on next page.

partly as an equitable division of joint property over and above the amount needed for adequate support. Some allocation of the awards between the two categories might reflect the "right" answer; some courts have so analyzed such problems. Nonetheless, such division would be difficult and expensive to calculate.

■━■

Quicknotes

DISCHARGE OF DEBTS In bankruptcy, the release of a debtor who is unable to pay his debts as they become due from the obligation to pay his creditors.

■━■

Kawaauhau v. Geiger

Malpractice judgment holder (P) v. Doctor (D)

523 U.S. 57 (1998).

NATURE OF CASE: Review of judgment discharging a malpractice award.

FACT SUMMARY: Kawaauhau (P) sought to enforce a judgment against Dr. Geiger (D) for malpractice on the basis that it constituted a nondischargeable debt for willful and malicious injury under Bankruptcy Code § 523(a)(6).

🏛 **RULE OF LAW**
The bankruptcy discharge exception of § 523(a)(b) encompasses acts done with the actual intent to cause injury rather than acts, done intentionally, that cause injury.

FACTS: Dr. Geiger (D), in treating Kawaauhau (P) for a foot injury, admitted her to a hospital. In order to prevent an infection, he prescribed oral penicillin, although he knew that intravenous penicillin would be more effective, in an attempt to minimize Kawaauhau's (P) expenses. Geiger (D) then departed on a business trip. In his absence, other physicians determined that Kawaauhau (P) should be transferred to an infectious disease specialist. When Geiger (D) returned, he canceled the transfer and ceased all medication. Kawaauhau's (P) condition deteriorated, resulting in the amputation of her lower right leg. Kawaauhau (P) sued Geiger (D) for malpractice. A jury awarded Kawaauhau (P) $335,000 in damages. Geiger (D), who did not have malpractice insurance, moved to Missouri, where his (D) wages were garnished by the Kawaauhaus (P). Geiger (D) subsequently petitioned for bankruptcy. The Kawaauhaus (P) sought to have the judgment held nondischargeable under the § 523(a)(6) exception on the grounds that it constituted a debt for willful and malicious injury. The bankruptcy court held the debt nondischargeable, and the district court affirmed. The court of appeals reversed. The Kawaauhaus (P) appealed.

ISSUE: Does the bankruptcy discharge exception of § 523(a)(6) encompass acts done with the actual intent to cause injury rather than acts, done intentionally, that cause injury?

HOLDING AND DECISION: (Ginsburg, J.) Yes. The bankruptcy discharge exception of § 523(a)(6) encompasses acts done with the actual intent to cause injury rather than acts, done intentionally, that cause injury. Bankruptcy Code § 523(a)(6) provides that a debt for willful and malicious injury by the debtor to another is not dischargeable. A debt arising from a recklessly or negligently inflicted injury does not fall within this exception. The Court distinguishes between intentional acts that cause an injury, as opposed to actions taken with an intention to cause the particular harm. The plain language of the statute requires the finding of such an intent. Furthermore, courts have ruled that exceptions to discharge under the Bankruptcy Code should be narrowly construed. Thus, a medical malpractice judgment for negligent or reckless conduct is dischargeable and does not fall within the exception provided by Bankruptcy Code § 523(a)(6). Affirmed.

▎ *ANALYSIS*

The Court's holding in this case is consistent with its previous interpretations of § 523(a)(6). The Court has held that the intentional disposition of another's property by a broker constitutes an intentional injury to another party's property and thus the debt arising from that conduct is nondischargeable. However, the Court has also held that not all judgments arising from claims of conversion are nondischargeable. Negligent or reckless acts alone are insufficient to trigger the § 523(a)(6) exclusion.

■═■

Quicknotes

CONVERSION The act of depriving an owner of his property without permission or justification.

NEGLIGENCE Conduct falling below the standard of care that a reasonable person would demonstrate under similar conditions.

RECKLESSNESS The conscious disregard of substantial and justifiable risk.

■═■

American Express Travel Related Services Co. v. Hashemi

Credit card company (P) v. Credit card holder (D)

104 F.3d 1122 (9th Cir. 1996).

NATURE OF CASE: Appeal from district court judgment affirming the nondischargeability of a debt in a bankruptcy court proceeding.

FACT SUMMARY: American Express (P) sought to have expenses charged by Hashemi (D) on a family vacation declared nondischargeable under Bankruptcy Code § 523(a)(2)(A) on the basis that the debt was obtained through actual fraud.

RULE OF LAW
A debt obtained by false pretenses, a false representation, or actual fraud is nondischargeable under Bankruptcy Code § 523(a)(2)(A) where the creditor demonstrates the debtor knowingly and purposefully made the representation with the intent of deceiving the creditor and the creditor's reliance on the representation was the proximate cause of his injury.

FACTS: Hashemi (D) charged over $60,000 to his American Express (P) account during a six-week family vacation to Europe. He subsequently filed for bankruptcy. American Express (P) sought to have the debt declared nondischargeable under Bankruptcy Code § 523(a)(2)(A), which prohibits the discharge of debts incurred through actual fraud. The bankruptcy court held the debt was nondischargeable and ordered Hashemi (D) to pay American Express (P) $69,793.67 with interest. The district court affirmed. Hashemi (D) appealed.

ISSUE: Is a debt obtained by false pretenses, a false representation, or actual fraud nondischargeable under Bankruptcy Code § 523(a)(2)(A)?

HOLDING AND DECISION: (Kozinski, J.) Yes. A debt obtained by false pretenses, a false representation, or actual fraud is nondischargeable under Bankruptcy Code § 523(a)(2)(A) where the creditor demonstrates the debtor knowingly and purposefully made the representation with the intent of deceiving the creditor, and the creditor's reliance on the representation was the proximate cause of his injury. The burden is on the creditor to prove the existence of these elements by a preponderance of the evidence. First of all, fraudulent intent may be implied where the totality of the circumstances indicate deceptive conduct on the part of the debtor. This element is satisfied where the court determines that the record weighs in favor of a finding of fraudulent intent. Here the evidence supports the conclusion that Hashemi (D) intended to defraud American Express (P). Hashemi (D) incurred $60,000 in charges in addition to more than $300,000 in unsecured credit card debt, which he owed prior to the trip. His one

major asset, a one-half ownership in a real estate venture, was in the process of foreclosure. Thus, Hashemi (D) could not have believed in good faith that he would be able to pay the charges. Secondly, when a card holder utilizes his card, he impliedly represents that he will repay the debt incurred as a result. If he has no such intent to repay the debt, this action constitutes a fraudulent representation. Since the total amount of expenses charged exceeded Hashemi's (D) annual income, and foreclosure proceedings had already been commenced against his one major asset, he could not have intended to repay the debt. Finally, the credit card issuer may justifiably rely on the representations as long as the card holder is not in default on any payments and there is no indication of such default after preliminary investigations. Hashemi (D) was not in default at the time the charges were incurred. Moreover, he had a credit history of repaying such balances in the past. Based on the foregoing, American Express (P) has succeeded in asserting a claim pursuant to § 523(a)(2)(A), and thus the debt was properly held nondischargeable. Affirmed and remanded.

▎ANALYSIS

In determining whether a debtor's intent was in fact fraudulent, the Ninth Circuit Bankruptcy Appellate Panel had delineated twelve factors for a court's consideration. While the court in *Hashemi* adopted this list as the law, it did not hold it to be exclusive. The list included such factors as: (1) the length of time between the charges and the bankruptcy filing; (2) the number of charges made; (3) the amount of the charges; (4) whether the debtor was employed; and (5) whether the purchases made were luxuries or necessities.

Quicknotes

FALSE PRETENSES The unlawful obtaining of money or property from another with an intent to defraud and with the utilization of false representations.

MATERIAL FALSE REPRESENTATIONS A statement or conduct by one party to another that constitutes a false representation of a material fact.

PREPONDERANCE OF THE EVIDENCE A standard of proof requiring the trier of fact to determine whether the fact sought to be established is more probable than not.

PROXIMATE CAUSE The natural sequence of events without which an injury would not have been sustained.

In re Majewski

[Parties not identified.]

310 F.3d 653 (9th Cir. 2002).

NATURE OF CASE: Appeal from affirmance of dismissal of action for violation of the Bankruptcy Code's anti-discrimination provisions.

FACT SUMMARY: The trustee for Majewski's bankruptcy estate contended that Majewski's employer violated Bankruptcy Code § 525(b), the anti-discrimination provision, when it terminated Majewski's employment for the sole reason that he owed the employer money and informed the employer that he planned to file for bankruptcy.

🏛 RULE OF LAW
Bankruptcy Code § 525(b) does not protect from termination an employee who informs his employer that he plans to file for bankruptcy protection but has not as yet done so.

FACTS: Majewski was hospitalized and incurred large medical expenses. He went to work for the hospital, but could not pay off his debt. After repayment negotiations failed, he told the hospital he intended to file for bankruptcy, and the hospital summarily fired him before he did so. The trustee in Majewski's bankruptcy brought a proceeding contending that the firing violated Bankruptcy Code § 525(b), the anti-discrimination provision, which bars termination of an individual who "is or has been" a bankruptcy debtor "solely because" the individual is or has been a debtor in bankruptcy. The bankruptcy court dismissed the claim, holding that the statute did not protect persons who had not yet filed for bankruptcy, and the district court affirmed. The court of appeals granted review.

ISSUE: Does Bankruptcy Code § 525(b) protect from termination an employee who informs his employer that he plans to file for bankruptcy protection but has not as yet done so?

HOLDING AND DECISION: (Schroeder, C.J.) No. Bankruptcy Code § 525(b) does not protect from termination an employee who informs his employer that he plans to file for bankruptcy protection but has not as yet done so. A liberal reading of the statute, as requested by the trustee, is not warranted by the language or purpose of the statute. Majewski was not, and had not been, a debtor in bankruptcy at the time his employer fired him. Therefore, he cannot obtain the statute's protection. Bankruptcy's fresh start comes at the cost of actually filing a bankruptcy petition, turning one's assets over to the court and repaying debts that can be paid. One is not entitled to the law's protections, including employment security and the automatic stay of litigation, before being bound by its other consequences. Affirmed.

DISSENT: (Reinhardt, J.) The case at bar presents exactly the kind of retaliation Congress intended to ban. The majority's decision, however, gives free reign to employers to engage in such discrimination against debtors who make a good faith effort to become protected debtors. Congress has determined that employees have the right to seek bankruptcy protection without fear of reprisal from their employers. Section 525(b) was enacted precisely to give individuals like Majewski a "fresh start." The majority's reading of the statute is unduly narrow and rigid, and unjustly undoes an important part of the protections that Congress intended to offer working people. Majewski should not have been stripped of those protections merely because his employer succeeded in firing him before he could get his papers on file in bankruptcy court.

▶ ANALYSIS

The statute involved in this case was § 525(b) of the code, which deals with discrimination of private employers. Section 525(a) addresses discrimination by the government, and prohibits a governmental unit from denying, revoking, suspending, or refusing to renew a license, permit, charter, franchise, or other similar grant to, from conditioning such a grant to, from discrimination with respect to such a grant against, deny employment to, terminate the employment of, or discriminate with respect to employment against, a person that is or has been a debtor or that is or has been associated with a debtor. The prohibition extends only to discrimination or other action based solely on the basis of the bankruptcy, on the basis of insolvency before or during bankruptcy prior to a determination of discharge, or on the basis of nonpayment of a debt discharged in the bankruptcy case. It does not prohibit consideration of other factors, such as future financial responsibility or ability, and does not prohibit imposition of requirements such as net capital rules, if applied nondiscriminatorily.

■━■

Quicknotes

BANKRUPTCY A legal proceeding whereby a debtor, who is unable to pay his debts as they become due, is relieved of his obligation to pay his creditors either by liquidation and distribution of his remaining assets or through reorganization and payment from future income.

GOOD FAITH An honest intention to abstain from taking advantage of another.

■━■

Toth v. Michigan State Housing Development Authority

Loan applicant (P) v. Governmental lending agency (D)

136 F.3d 477 (6th Cir. 1998).

NATURE OF CASE: Appeal from summary judgment dismissing action alleging discrimination in violation of § 525(a) of the Bankruptcy Code.

FACT SUMMARY: Toth (P) claimed that the Michigan State Housing Development Authority (D) wrongfully discriminated against her in refusing her application for a low income home improvement loan.

🏛 RULE OF LAW
A governmental entity may not deny a "license, permit, charter, franchise, or other similar grant," or discriminate "with respect to such a grant," solely on the basis that the person seeking such a boon has been bankrupt.

FACTS: Toth (P) received a discharge in bankruptcy and several months later applied to the Michigan State Housing Development Authority (MSHDA) (D) for a home improvement loan. When the application was denied due to MSHDA's (D) policy of requiring at least three years to lapse after the date of a bankruptcy discharge before a loan application would be processed, Toth (P) sued. Toth (P) claimed that MSHDA (D) had discriminated against her in violation of Bankruptcy Code § 525(a). The district court granted MSHDA's (D) motion for summary judgment. Toth (P) appealed.

ISSUE: May a governmental entity deny a "license, permit, charter, franchise, or other similar grant" or discriminate "with respect to such a grant" solely on the basis that the person seeking such a boon has been bankrupt?

HOLDING AND DECISION: (Norris, J.) No. A governmental entity may not deny a "license, permit, charter, franchise, or other similar grant" or discriminate "with respect to such a grant" solely on the basis that the person seeking such a boon has been bankrupt. The items enumerated in § 525(a)—licenses, permits, charters, and franchises—are benefits conferred by government that are unrelated to the extension of credit. Section 525(a) is directed against governmental entities that might deny former bankruptcy debtors permission to pursue certain occupations or professions. However, the plain language of the statute cannot be expanded to insulate a debtor from all adverse consequences of a bankruptcy filing or discharge. A reckoning of the applicant's financial responsibility is an essential part of any lender's evaluation of a post-discharge application for a loan. Affirmed.

▶ ANALYSIS

The courts have consistently read § 525(a) narrowly. In 1994, § 525(a) was added to the Bankruptcy Code to avoid an "unduly narrow" interpretation of the statute. A grant of credit is not considered included under the terms of the statute.

■=■

Quicknotes

DISCHARGE OF DEBTS In bankruptcy, the relief of a debtor, who is unable to pay his debts as they become due, from the obligation to pay his creditors.

■=■

CHAPTER 5

Stays and Injunctions

Quick Reference Rules of Law

In re Soares

Debtor (D) v. Creditor (P)

107 F.3d 969 (1st Cir. 1997).

NATURE OF CASE: Appeal from denial of a motion to reconsider an order lifting the automatic bankruptcy stay retroactively.

FACT SUMMARY: Soares (D), a debtor who filed a bankruptcy petition two days after the lender bank (P) sought a default order in foreclosure proceedings against him, alleged that the foreclosure judgment was issued in contravention of the stay.

RULE OF LAW
Ministerial acts, even if undertaken in a state judicial proceeding subsequent to a bankruptcy filing, do not fall within the proscription of the automatic stay, but acts undertaken in the course of carrying out the core judicial function are not ministerial.

FACTS: The debtor, Soares (D), became disabled following a motorcycle accident and lagged in his monthly mortgage payments on his home. The lender (P) commenced foreclosure proceedings and, when Soares (D) did not file an answer, petitioned the court for a default order. Soares (D) then filed for bankruptcy, triggering the automatic stay. Since no one notified the state court regarding the bankruptcy petition, a default foreclosure judgment was entered on the property. The lender (P) then successfully filed a motion seeking relief from the automatic stay, without apprising the bankruptcy court of the orders previously obtained in the state court proceedings. At the foreclosure sale, the lender itself bid on the mortgaged premises and paid the overdue taxes to clear the title. Soares (D) then sought relief in the state court on the ground that the foreclosure judgment had been issued in contravention of the automatic stay. The state court denied the motion, saying that its post-petition actions had been "ministerial" and that any error was harmless. The bankruptcy court then vacated the automatic stay retroactively "such that the state judgment and movant's foreclosure shall not be deemed to have violated the automatic stay." Soares (D) then unsuccessfully filed a motion to reconsider the grant of relief from the automatic stay. Soares (D) appealed, and the district court determined that the retroactive lifting of the automatic stay did not constitute an abuse of discretion. Soares (D) again appealed.

ISSUE: Do ministerial acts, even if undertaken in a state judicial proceeding subsequent to a bankruptcy filing, fall within the proscription of the automatic stay and are acts undertaken in the course of carrying out the core judicial function ministerial?

HOLDING AND DECISION: (Selya, J.) No. Ministerial acts, even if undertaken in a state judicial proceeding subsequent to a bankruptcy filing, do not fall within the proscription of the automatic stay, but acts undertaken in the course of carrying out the core judicial function are not ministerial. The state court's actions in ordering a default and directing the entry of a judgment possess a distinctly judicial, rather than a ministerial, character. Because the decision that animated the entry of the order and judgment occurred after the stay was in force, those actions continued the state judicial proceeding within the meaning of § 362(a)(1) of the Bankruptcy Code. Consequently, the actions violated the automatic stay. Although courts possess a limited discretion to grant retroactive relief, this case involved no sufficiently unusual circumstances and the bankruptcy court therefore abused its discretion in granting retroactive relief from the automatic stay. Reversed and remanded.

ANALYSIS

Some courts have held that acts in violation of the automatic stay are void. Other courts have held that such acts are merely voidable. A 1993 decision did away with this distinction and held that "invalid" is a more appropriate term to use because something that is invalid is not incurable, in contrast to a void action which is incapable of being ratified. See *Easley v. Pettibone Michigan Corp.*, 990 F.2d 905 (6th Cir. 1993).

Quicknotes

AUTOMATIC STAY Upon the filing of a voluntary bankruptcy petition, creditors are prohibited from attempting to recover payment from the debtor or his property.

MINISTERIAL An action performed by a public official at the direction of a superior officer or pursuant to statute.

Johnson v. First National Bank

Mortgagor (P) v. Mortgagee (D)

719 F.2d 270 (8th Cir. 1983).

NATURE OF CASE: Appeal from order tolling the running of a statutory redemption period.

FACT SUMMARY: A bankruptcy court ordered that a statutory redemption period for foreclosed-upon real estate be tolled during the pendency of the bankruptcy.

🏛 RULE OF LAW
A bankruptcy court cannot extend the statutory redemption period for real estate.

FACTS: First National Bank (Bank) (D) had a mortgage on property owned by Johnson (P). When Johnson (P) went into default, the Bank (D) foreclosed on the property. Johnson (P) later went into bankruptcy. On motion of Johnson (P), the bankruptcy court issued an order tolling the state redemption period, which was one year. The Bank (D) appealed.

ISSUE: Can a bankruptcy court extend the statutory redemption period for real estate?

HOLDING AND DECISION: (Roberts, J.) No. A bankruptcy court cannot extend the statutory redemption period for real estate. Property interests are created by state law, and federal courts should not disturb state control over this subject absent clear congressional mandate that they do so. A redemption period represents a legislative balancing of the rights of a secured creditor and a mortgagor, and constitutes a property interest on the part of both the mortgagor and the mortgagee: the mortgagor in that he has the right to redeem, and the mortgagee in that the period only lasts a specific time. It is appropriate for the state to make this balance. Here, the bankruptcy court disturbed that balance, relying partly on the automatic stay of § 362 and the general powers of bankruptcy courts to issue orders that prevent waste of bankrupt estate assets. This court is of the opinion that had Congress wanted to vest in bankruptcy courts this power, it would have done so specifically. This has not been done. A court's general equitable power does not include the right to create a property right in the face of contrary state law, and therefore the order tolling the redemption period was invalid. Reversed and remanded.

▶ ANALYSIS

Generally speaking, federal bankruptcy law does not create or define property interests; this is a matter of state law. Bankruptcy law exists to regulate creditor priority to a debtor's property, but should not say what that property is. This case is an example of that premise.

Quicknotes

REDEMPTION PERIOD The period during which a mortgagor has the right to reclaim forfeited property, following a default on mortgage payments, by the payment of the mortgage debt and any other interest, fees, and costs.

SECURED CLAIM A claim, the repayment of which is secured by collateral sufficient to repay the debt owed.

A.H. Robins Co. v. Piccinin

Bankruptcy filer (P) v. Plaintiff in civil action (D)

788 F.2d 994 (4th Cir. 1986).

NATURE OF CASE: Appeal from order enjoining prosecution of a civil action against co-defendants of a bankrupt.

FACT SUMMARY: A district court enjoined the prosecution of a civil suit against co-defendants of bankrupt entity A.H. Robins Co. (P).

🏛 RULE OF LAW
A court may enjoin a suit against a bankrupt's co-defendant if circumstances exist such that prosecution could endanger the bankrupt estate.

FACTS: In the face of numerous product liability lawsuits based on the allegedly defective intrauterine contraceptive device, the Dalkon Shield, A.H. Robins Co. (Robins) (P) filed under Chapter 11. Robins (P) filed an adversary proceeding wherein it attempted to obtain an injunction against prosecution of the actions against its co-defendants. The district court found that an identity of interest existed between Robins (P) and the other defendants in that the pool of assets available for settlement or payment was shared by all. The court concluded that prosecution of the actions endangered the estate, and ordered the actions stayed as to Robins's (P) co-defendants. Piccinin (D), a plaintiff in one of the civil actions, appealed.

ISSUE: May a court enjoin a suit against a bankrupt's co-defendant if circumstances exist such that prosecution could endanger the bankrupt estate?

HOLDING AND DECISION: (Russell, J.) Yes. A court may enjoin a suit against a bankrupt's co-defendant if circumstances exist such that prosecution could endanger the bankrupt estate. The automatic stay of Bankruptcy Code § 362 stays all pending actions against a bankrupt; it does not automatically stay an action against a bankrupt's co-defendants. Normally, these actions can go forward. Something more than the mere fact that one of the parties to the lawsuit has filed a Chapter 11 bankruptcy must be shown in order that proceedings be stayed against non-bankrupt defendants. That something generally is a showing that there is such an identity or alignment between the bankrupt and its co-defendant(s) that a judgment against the co-defendant would be tantamount to a judgment against the bankrupt. Here, the court found that the non-bankrupt defendants were so closely aligned with Robins (P) that any settlement or other payment would have to come out of the same funds. Since depleting these funds would adversely affect the bankrupt estate of Robins (P), the district court properly enjoined prosecution of the actions as to the co-defendants. Affirmed.

▶ ANALYSIS

There will usually be two situations where there is a common settlement pool for co-defendants in an action. One example is where the individual defendants are all employees or officers of a bankrupt corporation. The other is when two or more defendants share a common insurer.

■■■

Quicknotes

ENJOIN The ordering of a party to cease the conduct of a specific activity.

■■■

Credit Alliance Corp. v. Williams

Lender (P) v. Loan guarantor (D)

851 F.2d 119 (4th Cir. 1988).

NATURE OF CASE: Appeal from order holding garnishment proceeding valid.

FACT SUMMARY: Creditor Credit Alliance Corp. (P) sought to enforce a judgment against the guarantor (D) of a bankrupt debtor.

🏛 RULE OF LAW
A guarantor of a bankrupt's loan is not protected against recourse by a creditor on the basis of the bankrupt's automatic stay.

FACTS: Credit Alliance Corp. (P) loaned certain monies to Penn Hook Coal Co. (D). Williams (D) guaranteed the loan. Penn Hook (D) later defaulted, and Credit Alliance (P) sued both Penn Hook (D) and Williams (D), who both defaulted. After obtaining a default judgment, Credit Alliance (P) sought to execute. Prior to execution, Penn Hook (D) filed for bankruptcy. Credit Alliance (P) effected the execution anyway. A bankruptcy court held that the execution had violated the automatic stay, and voided the transaction. The district court reversed as to Williams (D), holding that the automatic stay did not benefit him. Williams (D) appealed.

ISSUE: Is a guarantor of a bankrupt's loan protected against recourse by a creditor on the basis of the bankrupt's automatic stay?

HOLDING AND DECISION: (Wilkinson, J.) No. A guarantor of a bankrupt's loan is not protected against recourse by a creditor on the basis of the bankrupt's automatic stay. The plain language of Bankruptcy Code § 362 provides only for the automatic stay of judicial proceedings and enforcement of judgments "against the debtor or the property of the estate." Nothing in § 362 suggests that Congress intended that provision to strip from the creditors the protection they sought and received when they required that a third party guarantee the debt. Congress knew how to do so if it wished; indeed, there is something of a limited protection for guarantors in Chapter 13 proceedings. There is none in Chapter 11, so the plain language of § 362 in only protecting the bankrupt shall be applied. Affirmed.

▶ ANALYSIS

The usual guaranty situation occurs when a creditor of a corporation requires one or more principals of that corporation to guarantee the debt in case the corporation defaults. This appears to have been the case here. To hold that the bankruptcy of the corporation would also insulate the guarantors from liability would be a major change in debtor-creditor law, not to be undertaken in a cavalier fashion.

■ ▬ ■

Quicknotes

CHAPTER 11 BANKRUPTCY A legal proceeding whereby a debtor, who is unable to pay his debts as they become due, is relieved of his obligation to pay his creditors through reorganization and payment from future income.

CHAPTER 13 BANKRUPTCY Debtor may modify plan at any time before the completion of the payments under such plan.

GUARANTOR A party who agrees to be liable for the debt or default of another.

■ ▬ ■

In re Holtkamp

Unsecured personal injury judgment holder (P) v. Tortfeasor (D)

669 F.2d 505 (7th Cir. 1982).

NATURE OF CASE: Appeal from judgment denying automatic stay of a personal injury action.

FACT SUMMARY: Holtkamp (D) contended that the automatic stay could be lifted pursuant to § 362(d) of the Bankruptcy Code only as to secured creditors.

RULE OF LAW
A bankruptcy court may grant relief from the automatic stay as to unsecured creditors.

FACTS: Littlefield (P) filed a personal injury action against Holtkamp (D), who later filed for bankruptcy. Littlefield (P) filed a petition in the bankruptcy action seeking to have the stay lifted. The bankruptcy court lifted the stay as to prosecution of the suit, but not as to collection of any judgment Littlefield (P) might receive. Defense was being handled by Holtkamp's (D) insurer. Littlefield (P) obtained a judgment of over $5,000,000. Holtkamp (D) appealed, contending that the bankruptcy court erred in allowing the lawsuit to be prosecuted, in that the stay could be lifted pursuant to § 362(d) only with respect to secured creditors.

ISSUE: May a bankruptcy court grant relief from the automatic stay as to unsecured creditors?

HOLDING AND DECISION: (Bauer, J.) Yes. A bankruptcy court may grant relief from the automatic stay as to unsecured creditors. Section 362(d) of the Code allows lifting of the stay for cause, including lack of adequate protection of an interest in property of the applying party. The bankruptcy court is given wide discretion in deciding whether to lift the stay, and there is nothing in the language of the section to suggest that it applies only to secured creditors. Moreover, there are numerous reported cases where lifting has been upheld as to unsecured creditors, and no argument has been made that the courts did not have the power to lift the stay as to unsecured creditors. Here, it was shown that trial on the merits of the action would be beneficial to the bankruptcy as the verdict therein would remove a major area of uncertainty as to the obligations of the estate. The assets of the estate were not put at risk, as enforcement of any judgment was stayed. It appears to this court that the bankruptcy court acted well within its discretion when it allowed the litigation to proceed. Affirmed.

▌ANALYSIS

One of the more common scenarios in lifting the automatic stay involves insurance proceeds. If a potential judgment is covered by insurance, it is usually unlikely that a judgment will endanger estate assets. By stipulating to seek recourse against the policy only, a plaintiff will almost always be able to get the stay lifted.

Quicknotes

AUTOMATIC STAY Upon the filing of a voluntary bankruptcy petition, creditors are prohibited from attempting to recover payment from the debtor or his property.

SECURED CREDITOR A creditor, the repayment of whose loan is secured by collateral sufficient to repay the debt owed.

Executory Contracts and Leases

Quick Reference Rules of Law

Lubrizol Enterprises v. Richmond Metal Finishers

Patent-holder (P) v. Licensee (D)

756 F.2d 1043 (4th Cir. 1985).

NATURE OF CASE: Appeal from order denying rejection of a contract in a bankruptcy proceeding.

FACT SUMMARY: Richmond Metal Finishers (D) sought to reject a technology licensing agreement with Lubrizol Enterprises (P) as an executory contract.

🏛 RULE OF LAW
A technology licensing agreement may be rejected by a bankrupt as an executory contract.

FACTS: Richmond Metal Finishers (Richmond) (D) held a patent on a certain metal coating process. It licensed this process to Lubrizol Enterprises (Lubrizol) (P). Under the agreement, Richmond (D) was obligated to defend any patent infringement suit, and to notify Lubrizol (P) of any other licensing of the process. Lubrizol (P) owed Richmond (D) the duty of accounting for its profits and paying royalties. Richmond (D) filed under Chapter 11 in 1983. As a debtor in possession, it sought to reject the licensing agreement as an executory contract. The bankruptcy court approved the rejection, but the district court held the agreement to no longer be executory. Richmond (D) appealed.

ISSUE: May a technology licensing agreement be rejected by a bankrupt as an executory contract?

HOLDING AND DECISION: (Phillips, J.) Yes. A technology licensing agreement may be rejected as an executory contract. A contract may be rejected by a bankrupt as executory if core obligations imposed under the contract remain unperformed by both sides. Here, the district court concluded that the contract was no longer executory because the only obligation owed by Lubrizol (P) to Richmond (D) was to make royalty payments. It is true that when the only obligation a party to a contract has is to make payment to the other party, the contract will no longer be considered executory. However, in this instance, Lubrizol (P) was not only obligated to make payments, but it was also obligated to render an accounting of earnings on a periodic basis. This was a continuing obligation, and rendered Lubrizol's (P) obligations under the contract to be not fully performed, meaning that the contract was executory. [The court went on to agree with the bankruptcy court that rejection of the contract would be advantageous to the estate, and therefore reinstated the bankruptcy court order.] Reversed and remanded.

▶ *ANALYSIS*

Rejection of a contract in a bankruptcy is a two-step process. First, a court must determine whether or not a contract remains executory as of the date of the filing. If it answers this question in the positive, then the court must determine that rejection would be advantageous to the estate. Successful challenges to rejection usually relate to the first step of the analysis; courts will generally defer to the conclusions of the debtor in possession or trustee as to the advantageousness of rejection, under an analysis similar to the business judgment rule.

━■━

Quicknotes

EXECUTORY CONTRACT A contract in which performance of an obligation has yet to be rendered.

INTELLECTUAL PROPERTY A body of law pertaining to the ownership of rights in intangible products of the human intellect.

━■━

In re Catapult Entertainment

Patent licensor (P) v. Licensee (D)

165 F.3d 747 (9th Cir. 1999).

NATURE OF CASE: Appeal of allowed assumption of licenses under a reorganization plan.

FACT SUMMARY: Catapult Entertainment, Inc. (D) was allowed in its Chapter 11 bankruptcy proceeding to assume, as part of its reorganization, licensed patents it had from Perlman (P), over Perlman's (P) objection.

🏛 RULE OF LAW
A debtor-in-possession can assume executory contracts and leases it has, irrespective of any contrary provisions appearing in such contracts, unless applicable law excuses a party to such contract from accepting performance from an entity other than a debtor-in-possession and that party does not consent to such an assumption.

FACTS: Catapult Entertainment, Inc. (Catapult) (D) was formed to create an online gaming network for console videogames. Perlman (P) licensed patents to Catapult (D). Catapult (D) filed for reorganization under Chapter 11. The reorganization plan involved a reverse triangular merger and left Catapult (D) as the surviving entity. The end result would leave Catapult's (D) creditors and equity holders with $14 million in cash, notes and securities, and Catapult (D) would be the wholly owned subsidiary of Mpath Interactive, Inc., a party to the merger. Catapult (D) filed a motion to assume 140 executory contracts and leases, including Perlman's (P) licenses, as part of its reorganization plan. The bankruptcy court approved the assumption of the licenses and confirmed the reorganization plan. The district court affirmed and Perlman (P) appealed.

ISSUE: Can a Chapter 11 debtor-in-possession assume nonexclusive patent licenses over a licensor's objection?

HOLDING AND DECISION: (Fletcher, J.) No. A Chapter 11 debtor-in-possession cannot assume nonexclusive patent licenses over a licensor's objection. Section 365 of the Bankruptcy Code allows a debtor-in-possession, such as Catapult (D), to assume the executory contracts and leases it has, irrespective of any contrary provisions appearing in such contracts, unless applicable law excuses a party to such contract, such as Perlman (P), from accepting performance from an entity other than a debtor-in-possession and that party does not consent to such an assumption. The plain language of the statute establishes a hypothetical test which in this case is that Catapult (D) may not assume the licenses over Perlman's (P) objection if patent law would bar assignment to a hypothetical third party, even if Catapult (D) has no intention of assigning

the contract to any such third party. Federal patent law makes nonexclusive patent licenses personal and nondelegable. The plain language of the statute, therefore, makes it clear that since Perlman (P) has withheld his consent, Catapult (D) is barred from assuming the Perlman (P) licenses. Catapult (D) argues, however, that Congress did not intend to bar debtors-in-possession from assuming their own contracts where no assignment is contemplated. Despite Catapult's (D) contention, the plain language of the statute should not be abandoned because such a literal reading does not create inconsistency within the Code, it is not incompatible with the legislative history, and it is not contrary to sound bankruptcy policy. There would not be inconsistency between § 365(c)(1) and § 365(f)(1) because each subsection recognizes an applicable law of different scope. Section 365(f)(1) states that a law which prohibits assignment is trumped by § 365(f)(1). Section 365(c)(1), on the other hand, is more narrow and states that the applicable law, which excuses a party from accepting performance from a party different from the one it originally contracted with, prevails over § 365(c)(1). In addition, the literal approach to the statute does not render the phrase "or the debtor-in-possession" superfluous because it addresses both assumption and assignment. If a nondebtor consents to the assumption, the statute will have to be applied a second time if the debtor-in-possession wants to assign the contract. It would be on that second application that the relevant law in regard to performance, would be considered in relation to the debtor-in-possession. A literal reading of § 365(c)(1) would also not impact § 365(c)(2) because it is the national uniformity of applicable state law that renders § 365(c)(2) superfluous, not § 365(c)(1). Moreover, § 365(c)(2), unlike (c)(1), bans assumption and assignment, notwithstanding the consent of the nondebtor. In addition to there not being inconsistencies within the Code if the statute is read strictly, legislative history also does not require the statute not to be read strictly. There is no ambiguity in the statutory language, and therefore the legislative history need not be considered. In addition, the legislative history does not indicate that Congress meant something other than what it said. A report by one committee in the House, relating to a different proposed bill and which predates the enactment of § 365(c)(1), is not a clear indication of contrary intent sufficient to overcome the unambiguous language of the statute. Lastly, policy arguments may favor a different analysis, but they cannot displace the plain language of the statute. Reversed.

Continued on next page.

▶ *ANALYSIS*

The court in this case takes a strict constructionist approach to its analysis in that it reasons that there is no need to look beyond the plain language of the statute.

■▬■

Quicknotes

DEBTOR-IN-POSSESSION In a Chapter 11 proceeding, refers to a debtor who retains control of assets or property pursuant to a plan of reorganization.

EXECUTORY CONTRACT A contract in which performance of an obligation has yet to be rendered.

■▬■

In re Pioneer Ford Sales

Secured creditor (P) v. Franchisor (D)

729 F.2d 27 (1st Cir. 1984).

NATURE OF CASE: Appeal from order allowing a bankrupt franchisee to assign the franchise contract without the franchisor's consent.

FACT SUMMARY: Bankrupt Ford dealership Pioneer Ford Sales, Inc. (Pioneer), sought to assign its franchise agreement to another dealership, despite the objections of franchisor Ford Motor Co.

🏛 RULE OF LAW
A bankrupt franchisee may not assign a franchise contract if the franchisor reasonably withholds consent.

FACTS: Pioneer held a Ford dealership franchise. Pioneer filed for bankruptcy. Subsequently, Pioneer's principal secured creditor (P) sought to assign the franchise agreement to another dealer, Toyota Village, Inc. Ford Motor Co. (Ford) (D), the franchisor, refused to consent to this assignment. Ford (D) required its dealers to have at least $172,000 working capital; Toyota Village had $37,610. Also, it had been losing money for years. The trustee filed a motion for an order allowing the assignment. The bankruptcy court granted the motion and the district court affirmed. Ford (D) appealed.

ISSUE: May a bankrupt franchisee assign a franchise contract if the franchisor reasonably withholds consent?

HOLDING AND DECISION: (Breyer, J.) No. A bankrupt franchisee may not assign a franchise contract if the franchisor reasonably withholds consent. Bankruptcy Code § 365(f)(1) allows a trustee to assign many sorts of contracts even if the contract itself forbids such assignments. Section 365(c)(1)(A) forms an exception to this rule, in that assignment is prohibited regardless of the terms of the contract if applicable law would otherwise prohibit assignment. "Applicable law" has been interpreted to mean nonbankruptcy law. In this instance, Rhode Island state contract law would be the applicable law. Under state law, a dealer can veto a dealership assignment, but only if it does so reasonably. Here, Ford (D) had, for good reason, imposed certain capitalization requirements on its franchisees, which Toyota Village was unable to meet. Also, Toyota Village had a history of losing money. In light of this, Ford's (D) decision to withhold consent appears to have been quite reasonable. Reversed.

▶ ANALYSIS

Section 365(f)(1) is a generally applicable bankruptcy law rule; § 365(c)(1)(A) is a specific exception to this rule. The purpose of the latter section exists so that the former

section will not be used to make assignable contracts which, outside a bankruptcy context, would not be assignable. It has been argued that § 365(c)(1)(A) should be applied only to personal services contracts, but this argument has for the most part been rejected.

Quicknotes

ASSIGNMENT A transaction in which a party conveys his or her entire interest in property to another.

FRANCHISE An agreement whereby one party (the franchisor) grants another (the franchisee) the right to market its product or service.

SECURED CREDITOR A creditor, the repayment of whose loan is secured by collateral sufficient to repay the debt owed.

Matter of Whitcomb & Keller Mortgage Co.

Unsecured contractor (P) v. Debtor (D)

715 F.2d 375 (7th Cir. 1983).

NATURE OF CASE: Appeal from order allowing a bankrupt to reject an executory contract.

FACT SUMMARY: Data-Link Systems, Inc. (P), an unsecured contractor of bankrupt Whitcomb & Keller Mortgage Co., Inc. (Whitcomb) (D), contended that it should not have been compelled to perform an executory contract that was later rejected by Whitcomb (D).

🏛 RULE OF LAW
A contractor of a bankrupt may be compelled to continue performance of an executory contract while the debtor is making its decisions whether to assume or reject the contract.

FACTS: Whitcomb & Keller Mortgage Co., Inc. (Whitcomb) (D) contracted with Data-Link Systems, Inc. (Data-Link) (P) for the latter to provide computer services to maintain Whitcomb's (D) customer service accounts. At the time Whitcomb (D) filed for bankruptcy, it owed Data-Link (P) $12,954.63 in arrearages under the contract. Upon learning that it was to be considered a general unsecured creditor, Data-Link (P) discontinued its services. As the services were vital to Whitcomb's (D) operations, this discontinuation paralyzed Whitcomb's (D) operations. The trustee obtained an order mandating Data-Link (P) to continue its services. This it did, until Whitcomb (D) decided to reject the contract. A trial was held on the issue. The bankruptcy court concluded that Whitcomb (D) was entitled to reject the executory contract and that Data-Link's (P) debt under the contract was an unsecured claim. The district court affirmed, and Data-Link (P) appealed.

ISSUE: May a contractor of a bankrupt be compelled to continue performance of the contract even if the contract is later rejected?

HOLDING AND DECISION: (Jameson, J.) Yes. A contractor of a bankrupt may be compelled to continue performance of an executory contract while the debtor is making its decision whether to assume or reject the contract. Under § 365 of the Bankruptcy Code, a trustee or debtor in possession has the power to affirm or reject any executory contract up to the time of confirmation of the reorganization plan. Until the moment of rejection, the contract is to be continued in full force. A bankruptcy court has the power to protect the bankrupt estate by preserving the status quo until this decision is made, which it did here. This is fully in keeping with the goal of bankruptcy law, which is to promote preservation of the bankrupt estate. The order issued by the bankruptcy court in this instance was a legitimate use of its powers. Affirmed.

▶ ANALYSIS

Under bankruptcy law, Data-Link (P) was entitled to priority status as to the work performed after the filing of the petition. Consequently, it was most likely not too worried about being paid for this work. It probably took the position it did to try to obtain some leverage with respect to its position as to the arrearages. Unfortunately for it, bankruptcy courts are quite sensitive to attempts like this by general creditors, and do not hesitate to oppose them.

Quicknotes

EXECUTORY CONTRACT A contract in which performance of an obligation has yet to be rendered.

UNSECURED CREDITOR A creditor, the repayment of whose loan is not backed by specified collateral or a security agreement.

Precision Industries, Inc. v. Qualitech Steel SBQ, LLC

Lessee (P) v. Lessor (D)

327 F.3d 537 (7th Cir. 2003).

NATURE OF CASE: Appeal from reversal of decision extinguishing a lessee's possessory interests in a leasehold in a Chapter 11 proceeding.

FACT SUMMARY: Qualitech Steel SBQ, LLC (New Qualitech) (D) contended that a sale order under § 363(f) extinguished Precision Industries, Inc.'s (Precision's) (P) interests in a leasehold that New Qualitech (D) obtained in a Chapter 11 sale; Precision (P) contended that its lease interests were protected by § 365(h).

RULE OF LAW

A sale order pursuant to § 363(f) of the Bankruptcy Code extinguishes a lessee's possessory interest where the lease has been rejected.

FACTS: Qualitech entered into agreements with Precision (P) whereby Precision (P) would build a warehouse on land Precision (P) would lease from Qualitech for ten years. The lease, which was never recorded, granted Precision (P) exclusive possession of the warehouse and any improvements or fixtures it installed on the land for the term of the lease, for nominal ($1) rent. At the end of the lease term, Qualitech had the right to purchase the warehouse, fixtures and improvements for $1. The parties also had a supply agreement. Precision (P) built the warehouse. A month after the parties entered into the lease agreement, Qualitech filed for Chapter 11 bankruptcy protection, and a few months later all of Qualitech's assets were sold at auction to a group of pre-petition lenders. The bankruptcy court entered an order approving the sale (Sale Order), to which Precision (P) did not object. That order directed Qualitech to convey its assets "free and clear of all liens, claims, encumbrances, and interests," except for specifically enumerated liens, pursuant to § 363(f). The purchasers subsequently transferred their interest in the purchased assets to Qualitech Steel SBQ, LLC (New Qualitech) (D). Precision's (P) lease and supply agreements were ultimately de facto rejected (because they were not assumed), and New Qualitech (D), without Precision's (P) knowledge or consent, changed the locks on the warehouse. New Qualitech's (D) takeover of the warehouse led to a dispute over whether Precision's (P) possessory interest in the leased property, pursuant to § 365(h), survived the bankruptcy sale. Finding itself locked out of the warehouse, Precision (P) filed a diversity suit in the district court contending that New Qualitech (D) was guilty of trespass, conversion, wrongful eviction, breach of an implied contract, and estoppel. New Qualitech (D) in turn asked the district court to refer Precision's (P) complaint—which was premised on the notion that Precision (P) retained a possessory interest

in the warehouse under the lease—to the bankruptcy court, and New Qualitech (D) also filed a request with the bankruptcy court asking it to clarify that the Sale Order had extinguished Precision's (P) possessory interest. The district court, agreeing with New Qualitech (D), referred Precision's (P) complaint to the bankruptcy court, and that court ruled that Precision (P) no longer retained a possessory interest in the warehouse. The district court reversed, finding that §§ 363(f) and 365(h) conflict, and the court of appeals granted review.

ISSUE: Does a sale order pursuant to § 363(f) of the Bankruptcy Code extinguish a lessee's possessory interest where the lease has been rejected?

HOLDING AND DECISION: (Rovner, J.) Yes. A sale order pursuant to § 363(f) of the Bankruptcy Code extinguishes a lessee's possessory interest where the lease has been rejected. Section 363(f) purports to authorize the transfer of a debtor's property "free and clear of all liens, claims, encumbrances, and interests." On the other hand, § 365(h) protects the rights of a lessee when the debtor rejects a lease of the property at issue. Here, Precision's (P) right to possess the property as a lessee qualifies as an interest for purposes of § 363(f), and, therefore, the statute on its face authorized the sale of Qualitech's property free and clear of that interest. Moreover, both parties agree that § 363(f) standing alone permits the sale of estate property free and clear of a lessee's possessory interest. However, under § 365(h), which grants the right to reject executory contracts but limits the power of rejection so as to preclude eviction of the lessee, Precision (P) would be allowed to remain in possession of the warehouse. The district court, following the lead of other lower courts, concluded that the limitations imposed by § 365(h) relating to rejection of leases necessarily conflict with and override the debtor-in-possession's ability to sell estate property free and clear of a lessee's possessory interest. The district court's ruling was incorrect. First, the statutory provisions themselves do not suggest that one supersedes or limits the other. Unlike other provisions of each section, they do not cross-reference to each other, suggesting that Congress did not intend for § 365(h) to limit § 363(f). Second, the plain language of § 365(h) suggests that it has the limited scope of applying where there is an express rejection of a lease. There is nothing in the section that suggests it applies to all events that threaten the lessee's possessory rights. It says nothing at all about sales of estate property, which are the province of § 363. The two statutory provisions thus apply to

Continued on next page.

distinct sets of circumstances. Third, § 363 itself provides a mechanism to protect the rights of parties whose interests may be adversely affected by the sale of estate property. It provides that the lessee has the right to insist that its interests be protected. Although such protection does not necessarily mean continued possession, it does mean that the lessee can insist that it be compensated for the value of its leasehold—usually from the proceeds of the sale. Lessees like Precision (P) are, therefore, not without recourse in the event of a sale free and clear of their interests. Thus, the two sections can be read together whereby § 365 does not disable § 363, and where neither conflicts with the other. That is, where there is a sale, § 363 applies, and where there is a rejection of the lease, § 365 applies. Such an interpretation is consistent with the process of marshaling the estate's assets for the twin purposes of maximizing creditor recovery and rehabilitating the debtor, which are central to the Bankruptcy Code. Accordingly, Qualitech's sale terminated Precision's (P) possessory interest in the property as a lessee. Reversed.

▶ ANALYSIS

This decision has been criticized, and rejected, on the grounds that under the sale-rejection distinction, the provisions of § 365(h) would be eviscerated. This is in part because the option to sell or reject lies with the debtor-lessor, and a sale of the leased premises free and clear of the lessee's interests, as Precision (P) argued, is a de facto rejection of the lease. This is an especially significant concern where the term of the lease is exceptionally long, e.g., 100 years.

■━■

Quicknotes

POSSESSORY INTEREST The right to possess particular real property to the exclusion of others.

■━■

In re Klein Sleep Products

Landlord (D) v. Lessee (P)

78 F.3d 18 (2d Cir. 1996).

NATURE OF CASE: Appeal from a judgment affirming the bankruptcy court's order assigning administrative priority to a landlord's claim.

FACT SUMMARY: When Klein Sleep Products (P) filed for bankruptcy, it assumed an unexpired lease from the landlord (Nostas Associates) (D) which the trustee later rejected, and the bankruptcy court held that the landlord (D) could recover as an administrative expense only the rent that had come due before the trustee rejected the lease.

🏛 RULE OF LAW
Damages arising from future rent under an assumed lease must be treated as an administrative expense.

FACTS: After entering bankruptcy, the debtor, Klein Sleep Products (Klein Sleep) (P), assumed, with court approval, the unexpired lease it had with Nostas Associates (its landlord (D)). When it later became clear that the reorganization had failed so completely that liquidating Klein Sleep's (P) assets would not cover even the administrative expenses of the estate, the Chapter 11 trustee rejected the lease and surrendered possession of the store to Nostas (D). The bankruptcy court held, and the district court agreed, that Nostas (D) was entitled to recover as an administrative expense only the rent that had come due before the trustee rejected the lease. Nostas (D) claimed that Klein Sleep's (P) court-approved lease assumption converted all liability under the lease into administrative expenses that warranted a first priority under Bankruptcy Code § 507(a)(1), and appealed.

ISSUE: Must damages arising from future rent under an assumed lease be treated as an administrative expense?

HOLDING AND DECISION: (Calabresi, J.) Yes. Damages arising from future rent under an assumed lease must be treated as an administrative expense. Special priority is accorded to expenses incurred by post-bankruptcy creditors and under pre-existing contracts that the debtor "assumes." This bankruptcy policy granting priority to creditors who continue to do business with an insolvent debtor may conflict with the pro rata rule that similarly situated creditors be treated alike. Administrative expense status is granted to post-petition claims only if consideration was both supplied to and beneficial to the debtor-in-possession in the operation of the business. Klein Sleep (P) did benefit by assuming its lease, despite the fact that it was no longer profitable at the time it stopped displaying mattresses on the premises. When Klein Sleep (P) as the debtor-in-possession assumed the lease, it retained the right to occupy the leased premises immediately and in the future. Its ability to assign this immediate right of possession, as well as its ability to assign the future right of possession under the lease, had a present value at the time of possession. Claims for future rent arising out of assumed leases are administrative expenses of the debtor's estate, regardless of whether they are subsequently rejected, and they are not capped at a year's worth of unpaid rent. Reversed to the extent that the court disallowed Nostas's (D) claim for future rent as an administrative expense and remanded.

▌ ANALYSIS

If a lease is assumed in Chapter 11 proceedings, the liabilities flowing from the rejection of that lease will ever after be regarded as a Chapter 11 administrative expense. Expenses arising out of a transaction between the debtor and the creditor fall into this category only to the extent that consideration supporting the claimant's right to payment was both supplied to and beneficial to the debtor-in-possession. Once future rent is treated merely as an unsecured claim, it is capped by § 502(b)(6) at one year's worth of unpaid rent.

Quicknotes

PRIORITY The relative preference of different claims to specific property.

In re Trak Auto Corporation

Lessee (P) v. Lessor (D)

367 F.3d 237 (4th Cir. 2004).

NATURE OF CASE: Appeal from affirmance of order permitting assignment of a shopping center lease in a Chapter 11 proceeding.

FACT SUMMARY: West Town Center, LLC (D), lessor, contended that under § 365(b)(3)(C), debtor-tenant Trak Auto Corporation's (P) shopping center lease could not be assigned in contravention of lease provisions that restricted the use of the premises to the sale of auto parts.

> ## RULE OF LAW
> Section 365(b)(3)(C) of the Bankruptcy Code does not permit assignment of a shopping center lease by a Chapter 11 debtor-tenant in contravention of lease provisions restricting the use of the premises.

FACTS: Trak Auto Corporation (P), a retailer of auto parts and accessories, leased premises from West Town Center, LLC (West Town) (D) in West Town's (D) shopping center. The lease restricted use of the premises to the retail sale of auto parts and accessories. Trak Auto (P) filed for Chapter 11 bankruptcy protection and sought to assign the lease to A & E Stores, Inc. (A & E), which planned to use the premises for apparel sales. West Town (D) objected, arguing that the lease restriction on premises use was enforceable under § 365(b)(3)(C). This section of the Bankruptcy Code specifically requires a debtor-tenant at a shopping center to assign its store lease subject to any provision restricting the use of the premises. The bankruptcy court granted Trak Auto's (P) request, concluding that the lease's use restrictions amounted to anti-assignment provisions that were prohibited by § 365(f)(1). This provision generally permits a debtor to assign its lease notwithstanding a provision restricting assignment. The district court affirmed, and the court of appeals granted review.

ISSUE: Does section 365(b)(3)(C) of the Bankruptcy Code permit assignment of a shopping center lease by a Chapter 11 debtor-tenant in contravention of lease provisions restricting the use of the premises?

HOLDING AND DECISION: (Michael, J.) No. Section 365(b)(3)(C) of the Bankruptcy Code does not permit assignment of a shopping center lease by a Chapter 11 debtor-tenant in contravention of lease provisions restricting the use of the premises. The two provisions at issue in this case, both in § 365, are conflicting, and it is the court's task to resolve this conflict. Section 365(a) permits a Chapter 11 debtor to assume an unexpired lease, and § 365(f)(2)(B) permits assignment of the lease if there is adequate assurance of future performance by the assignee. Section 365(b)(3)(C) provides that such adequate assurance must include assurance that the assignment of a shopping center lease is subject to all the provisions there-of. On the other hand, § 365(f)(1) contains a general provision that prohibits the enforcement in bankruptcy of anti-assignment clauses in leases. The issue, therefore, is whether Congress intended, notwithstanding § 365(f)(1), for a debtor's assignee to provide adequate assurance that it will comply with use restrictions in a shopping center lease, such as the restriction here that limits the use of the space to the sale of auto parts and accessories. The legislative history shows that Congress in 1984 amended the Bankruptcy Code to provide shopping center landlords with sufficient protection against debtor-tenant lease assignments made in breach of use (and other) restrictions. It did so, inter alia, by amending § 365(b)(3)(C) so that instead of having to show that an assignment would not breach "substantially" any lease provision, adequate assurance would entail a showing that the lease would be subject to "all" lease provisions. Under the canons of statutory construction, the more specific provision (here, § 365(b)(3)(C)) controls a more general provision when the two conflict. This construction is consistent with Congress's intent, which was to preserve the landlord's bargained-for protections with respect to premises use. Because A & E does not propose to use the premises for the sale of auto parts and accessories, Trak Auto (P) may not assign the lease to it. Reversed and remanded.

▶ ANALYSIS

As the court notes, some shopping center lease provisions may still be subject to § 365(f)(1), notwithstanding the court's decision. An example of such a provision would be a prohibition on any assignment whatsoever. Another situation covered by § 365(f)(1) would be where a provision sought to require operations under a specified trade name.

Quicknotes

ASSIGNMENT A transaction in which a party conveys his or her entire interest in property to another.

LEASE An agreement or contract that creates a relationship between a landlord and tenant (real property) or lessor and lessee (real or personal property).

Matter of U.L. Radio Corp.

Lessee (P) v. Landlord (D)

19 B.R. 537 (Bankr. S.D.N.Y. 1982).

NATURE OF CASE: Motion by debtor to assume and assign a lease.

FACT SUMMARY: U.L. Radio (P), a debtor in bankruptcy, sought to assign its lease in an outdoor shopping center.

🏛 RULE OF LAW
Debtor lessees may assign their leases as long as there are adeqate assurances of future performance by the assignee and the lessor is unable to demonstrate any actual and substantial detriment.

FACTS: U.L. Radio (P), a repair shop, leased a store in New York City from Jemrock Realty (Jemrock) (D). In the same building were a grocery store, a Chinese restaurant, and a liquor store. A use clause in the lease allowed only the type of business engaged in by U.L. Radio. When U.L. Radio (P) went into bankruptcy, it sought to assign its lease to Just Heaven, a restaurant. Jemrock (D) opposed the assignment, and U.L. Radio (P) moved for an order allowing the assignment.

ISSUE: May debtor lessees assign their leases as long as there are adequate assurances of future performance by the assignee and the lessor is unable to demonstrate any actual and substantial detriment?

HOLDING AND DECISION: (Galgay, J.) Yes. Debtor lessees may assign their leases as long as there are adequate assurances of future performance by the assignee and the lessor is unable to demonstrate any actual and substantial detriment. Section 365 of the Bankruptcy Code governs the assumption and assignment of leases and provides broad authority to a trustee or debtor in possession to assign unexpired leases. Subsection (f)(1) expressly restricts third parties from imposing limits on assignments. Assignment is allowed as long as adequate assurances of future performance are provided to the other contracting party. Adequate assurance is to be determined on the factual conditions, taking into account the broad authorization to allow assignment. The primary focus is the ability to satisfy financial obligations. The ability to satisfy a use clause in a lease is not a factor that prevents assignment unless the landlord can show that actual and substantial detriment would be incurred if the deviation is permitted. In the present case, there is evidence that Just Heaven could meet the financial obligations under the U.L. Radio (P) lease. Furthermore, Jemrock (D) has not demonstrated that it would suffer by allowing another restaurant in the building. Accordingly, U.L. Radio (P) must be allowed to assign its lease.

▌ ANALYSIS

Congress has established different rules for shopping centers and malls. These leases often involve complex designs for the right tenant mix. Thus, assignment is not allowed on the broad basis seen in this case.

■■■

Quicknotes

ASSIGNEE A party to whom another party assigns his interest or rights.

LEASE An agreement or contract that creates a relationship between a landlord and tenant (real property) or lessor and lessee (real or personal property).

LESSEE One who leases property from a landlord, receiving the right to immediate possession of the property but not legal title.

■■■

In re Standor Jewelers West

Lessee (P) v. Lessor (D)

129 B.R. 200 (B.A.P. 9th Cir. 1991).

NATURE OF CASE: Motion to assume and assign a lease by a debtor.

FACT SUMMARY: Standor Jewelers West, Inc. (P), a debtor in bankruptcy, operated a jewelry store in the South Coast Plaza (D) mall and sought to assign its lease.

🏛 RULE OF LAW
A provision that conditions or restricts the ability of a debtor to fully realize the economic value of its lease upon assignment is invalid under Bankruptcy Code § 365(f).

FACTS: Standor Jewelers West, Inc. (Standor) (P) operated a store in the South Coast Plaza (South Coast) (D) mall. When Standor (P) went into bankruptcy, it sought to sell its assets and assign its lease in the mall to Sterling. South Coast (D) sought to prevent the assignment because a provision in the lease required the lessee to remit 75% of the appreciation in value of the lease to South Coast (D) in return for consent to assignment. The bankruptcy court held that this provision was invalid under § 365(f) of the Bankruptcy Code.

ISSUE: Is a provision that conditions or restricts the ability of a debtor to fully realize the economic value of its lease upon assignment invalid under Bankruptcy Code § 365(f)?

HOLDING AND DECISION: (Jones, J.) Yes. A provision that conditions or restricts the ability of a debtor to fully realize the economic value of its lease upon assignment is invalid under Bankruptcy Code § 365(f). In order to facilitate the assignment of unexpired leases by debtors, § 365(f)(1) renders unenforceable any provisions in a lease that tend to restrict assignment. Under California law, lessors in commercial leases may condition assignment upon payment of some or all of the amounts received in excess of the rent by the lessee. However, this type of provision adversely affects the ability of the debtor in its rehabilitation efforts. Accordingly, § 365 invalidates this type of provision. Therefore, the conditional assignment clause in South Coast's (D) lease is not effective, and Standor (P) may freely assign the lease. Affirmed.

▶ ANALYSIS

This case is in accord with other decisions reaching this issue. In *In re Howe*, Bankr., 78 B.R. 226 (S.D. 1987), the court struck down a provision in an executory contract mandating a 4% assumption fee. The different rules for shopping centers and malls based on tenant mix did not come into play here because Standor (P) assigned its lease to another jewelry store operator.

Quicknotes

ASSIGNMENT A transaction in which a party conveys his or her entire interest in property to another.

LEASE An agreement or contract that creates a relationship between a landlord and tenant (real property) or lessor and lessee (real or personal property).

The Avoiding Powers of the Trustee

Quick Reference Rules of Law

Union Bank v. Wolas

Bank (D) v. Bankruptcy trustee (P)

502 U.S. 151 (1991).

NATURE OF CASE: Appeal from decision allowing trustee to recover payments.

FACT SUMMARY: A trustee (P) claimed that payments by ZZZZ Best, the debtor, on a long-term debt should be avoided as a preference.

🏛 RULE OF LAW
Payments on long-term debts may qualify as a preference exception for transfers made in the ordinary course of business.

FACTS: ZZZZ Best borrowed $7 million from Union Bank (Union) (D) in 1986. Six months later, ZZZZ Best filed for Chapter 7 bankruptcy. During the 90 days prior to the filing, ZZZZ Best made two interest payments to Union (D) totaling $100,000. The trustee (P) filed a complaint to recover those payments as a preference under Bankruptcy Code § 547(b). The bankruptcy court found that the payments to Union (D) were made in the ordinary course of business and thus qualified as an exception to the usual preference rules. However, the court of appeals reversed, holding that the exception was not available to long-term creditors. Union (D) appealed.

ISSUE: May payments on long-term debts qualify as a preference exception for transfers made in the ordinary course of business?

HOLDING AND DECISION: (Stevens, J.) Yes. Payments on long-term debts may qualify as a preference exception for transfers made in the ordinary course of business. The plain text of § 547 authorizes trustees to avoid any property transfer to satisfy antecedent debt that occurs within ninety days of the bankruptcy filing if the creditor is able to receive a larger share of the estate through the transfer. This is because the debtor is presumed to be insolvent ninety days prior to the filing. An exception is made for transfers that happen in the ordinary course of business. There is no suggestion in the text that different rules apply to long- and short-term debts. The legislative history of § 547 also does not provide any support for the view that long-term debts should be treated differently. Furthermore, the policies behind § 547 also fail to support a distinction. Section 547 is designed to prevent creditors from racing to dismember the debtor during the slide into bankruptcy and it also facilitates the equality of distribution among creditors. The ordinary-course-of-business exception tends to favor the payee, but also can benefit all creditors because it enables the struggling debtor to continue operating the business. Accordingly, the court of appeals is reversed and the case is remanded.

CONCURRENCE: (Scalia, J.) The plain text of the statute should have made this litigation unnecessary. It is unbelievable that the court of appeals accepted the trustee's (P) argument.

▶ ANALYSIS

The only real argument that the trustee (P) had in this case is that the exception was created to address the problems of short-term creditors. It is certainly true that the provision of short-term credit to a struggling operation is more important in avoiding bankruptcy. However, the Court correctly pointed out that the text of the statute contains no suggestion whatsoever that it should be limited to those creditors.

Quicknotes

ORDINARY COURSE OF BUSINESS The conducting of business in accordance with the standard customs and practices.

PREFERENCE A transfer made by the insolvent debtor to a creditor prior to filing the bankruptcy petition, giving priority to one creditor over others, in respect to the debtor's assets.

In re National Gas Distributors

[Parties not identified.]

346 B.R. 394 (Bankr. E.D.N.C. 2006)

NATURE OF CASE: Motion for summary judgment in bankruptcy proceeding seeking to avoid preferential transfers.

FACT SUMMARY: The trustee (P) of chapter 11 debtor National Gas Distributors, LLC (NGD) sought to avoid and recover preferential transfers made by NGD to Branch Banking and Trust Company (D), contending that they were not made pursuant to "ordinary business terms" as used in § 547(c)(2)(B) of the Bankruptcy Abuse Prevention and Consumer Protection Act of 2005.

RULE OF LAW

Repayment of corporate loans, which is made pursuant to a corporation's owner's end-of-year personal financial planning, and which represents repayment of debt guaranteed by the owner that is collateralized by his assets, is not made pursuant to "ordinary business terms" under § 547(c)(2)(B) of the Bankruptcy Abuse Prevention and Consumer Protection Act of 2005.

FACTS: National Gas Distributors, LLC (NGD) was owned by Lawing. NGD had several credit transactions with Branch Banking and Trust Company (BB&T) (D), including a line of credit, a working capital loan, and letters of credit. None of NGD's obligations to BB&T (D) were secured by NGD's assets, but all of the obligations were subject to the guaranties of Lawing and his wife, and all of the obligations were secured by assets owned by Mrs. Lawing. Prior to seeking chapter 11 bankruptcy, NGD repaid BB&T's (D) outstanding debt on the revolving line of credit and the working capital loan, the maturity dates of which had been extended several times, with one repayment of $755,329.80, and another of $2,508,186.35, for a total of $3,263,516.15. The repayments were made shortly before the extended due dates for each loan. The chapter 11 trustee (P) sought to avoid these repayments as preferential transfers. BB&T (D) asserted the "ordinary business terms" defense under § 547(c)(2)(B) of the Bankruptcy Abuse Prevention and Consumer Protection Act of 2005 (BAPCPA), contending that the repayments had been made pursuant to the ordinary business terms of the banking industry. BB&T (D) asserted that the terms of the line of credit and working capital loan were typical of those in loans extended to similar businesses; it was customary within the banking industry for a lender to extend maturity dates of promissory notes for borrowers; it was typical for borrowers to pay a note in full on the maturity date or within several weeks before the maturity date; and the payments, in general, were well within the standard terms

and practice at BB&T (D), as well as a standard practice in the banking industry in general. The trustee (P) moved for summary judgment.

ISSUE: Is repayment of corporate loans, which is made pursuant to a corporation's owner's end-of-year personal financial planning, and which represents repayment of debt guaranteed by the owner that is collateralized by his assets, made pursuant to "ordinary business terms" under § 547(c)(2)(B) of BAPCPA?

HOLDING AND DECISION: (Small, J.) No. Repayment of corporate loans, which is made pursuant to a corporation's owner's end-of-year personal financial planning, and which represents repayment of debt guaranteed by the owner that is collateralized by his assets, is not made pursuant to "ordinary business terms" under § 547(c)(2)(B) of BAPCPA.. It is undisputed that the repayments qualify as preferential transfers that may be avoided unless BB&T (D) can prevail on its "ordinary business terms" defense. The trustee (P) also conceded that the transfers were in payment of debts that were incurred by NGD in the ordinary course of business of NGD and BB&T (D). Here, BB&T (D) bears the burden of proof on its defense. The preliminary determination that must be made is the meaning of "ordinary business terms" as used in § 547. The phrase "ordinary business terms" is so inclusive that a plain meaning analysis is not helpful. Neither is the legislative history. Under the amendments to BAPCPA, § 547(c)(2)(B) became a stand-alone defense, whereas before the amendments, "ordinary business terms" was part of the "ordinary course of business" defense. Thus, "ordinary business terms" had been interpreted by courts, but not as a stand-alone defense. Under the prior case law, the inquiry focused on the relationship between the debtor and creditor, and whether the payment practice at issue comported with industry standards. Reviewing industry standards provides an objective standard by which to measure the practices between the debtor and creditor. In some case, the debtor and creditor are in entirely different industries, such as here, where the creditor is a commercial lender and the debtor is a distributor of natural gas commodities. To identify the relevant standard, the relevant industry or industries must also be determined. Under BAPCPA, the standards of both the creditor's and debtor's respective industries must be considered. In addition, there are general business standards that are common to all business transactions in all industries that must be met. Based on the evidence presented, BB&T (D) cannot meet those

Continued on next page.

standards. First, BB&T's (D) characterization of the banking industry's standards was at too high a level of generality, rather than being applied to the factual circumstances of the transfer at issue. It is not standard in the banking industry for a borrower with a multi-million dollar enterprise to pay all of its corporate loans based upon the owner's end-of-the-year personal financial planning, especially where the corporation has not arranged for financing to continue the business. Even if such conduct is standard within the banking industry, it is certainly not ordinary from the debtor's perspective and is not consistent with sound business practice in general. Notwithstanding that BB&T (D) did nothing out of the ordinary, had no knowledge that NGD was having financial difficulties, did not pursue any collection activity against NGD, and merely received payment on its loans when those loans became due, BB&T (D) may not prevail on its "ordinary business terms" defense because the debtor's industry standards must also be considered. Here, the evidence makes clear that NGD's conduct in paying the loans was not in accordance with such standards. What was going on was that NGD was going out of business and was paying off those debts which the Lawings had guaranteed and for which Mrs. Lawing's assets stood as collateral. Accordingly, these payments were not made "according to ordinary business terms" and are not the type of transfers that the "ordinary business terms" defense is designed to protect. Judgment for the trustee (P).

▌ ANALYSIS

The change made by the BAPCPA amendments, by severing the yoke between the "ordinary course of business" defense, now on its own in § 547(c)(2)(A), and the "ordinary business terms" defense, now on its own in § 547(c)(2)(B), substantially lightens the creditor's burden of proof, by allowing the creditor protection from preference recovery if the transfer meets industry standards, regardless of whether it was in the ordinary course of business of the debtor and the creditor. As this case illustrates, however, despite this lightened burden and the broadened protection for creditors, the "ordinary business terms" defense will not let a creditor prevail in every preference avoidance situation.

Quicknotes

BANKRUPTCY A legal proceeding whereby a debtor, who is unable to pay his debts as they become due, is relieved of his obligation to pay his creditors either by liquidation and distribution of his remaining assets or through reorganization and payment from future income.

BURDEN OF PROOF The duty of a party to introduce evidence to support a fact that is in dispute in an action.

COLLATERAL Property that secures the payment of a debt.

MOTION FOR SUMMARY JUDGMENT Judgment rendered by a court in response to a motion by one of the parties, claiming that the lack of a question of material fact in respect to an issue warrants disposition of the issue without consideration by the jury.

PREFERENTIAL TRANSFER A transfer made by the insolvent debtor to a creditor prior to filing the bankruptcy petition, giving a priority to one creditor over others with respect to the debtor's assets.

PROMISSORY NOTE A written promise to tender a stated amount of money at a designated time and to a designated person.

In re Powerine Oil Co.

Committee of unsecured creditors (P) v. Company in bankruptcy (D)

59 F.3d 969 (9th Cir. 1995).

NATURE OF CASE: Appeal from summary judgment protecting a transfer in a bankruptcy case.

FACT SUMMARY: Koch Oil (D) contended that payment it had received from Powerine Oil Company was not a preference because it could have recovered the money owed it by drawing on a third-party letter of credit.

> ## 🏛 RULE OF LAW
> The key factor in determining whether a payment is a preference is the percentage creditors' claims are entitled to draw out of the estate of the bankrupt.

FACTS: Using its personal property as collateral, Powerine Oil Company (Powerine) obtained a $250.6 million line of credit from First National and other lenders. Koch Oil (Koch) (D) agreed to sell crude oil to Powerine. To secure the obligation, Powerine designated Koch (D) as beneficiary of two irrevocable standby letters of credit issued by First National. Powerine paid Koch (D) $3.2 million for the oil but then filed for bankruptcy less than 90 days later. The Committee of Creditors Holding Unsecured Claims (Committee) (P) brought an action to recover the payment, claiming it was a preference. The bankruptcy court granted Koch's (D) motion for summary judgment and the Bankruptcy Appellate Panel affirmed, holding that the payment was not a preference because it did not enable Koch (D) to recover more than it would in a Chapter 7 liquidation. This is because Koch (D) could have drawn on the letters of credit as a last resort. The Committee (P) appealed.

ISSUE: Is the key factor in determining whether a payment is a preference the percentage creditors' claims are entitled to draw out of the estate of the bankrupt?

HOLDING AND DECISION: (Kozinski, J.) Yes. The key factor in determining whether a payment is a preference is the percentage creditors' claims are entitled to draw out of the estate of the bankrupt. In other words, the fact that Koch (D) had recourse against a third party if Powerine defaulted has no bearing on this issue. However, the payment Koch (D) received may be protected by the "contemporaneous exchange for new value" exception. When Powerine paid Koch (D), First National's exposure under the letters of credit was reduced by a corresponding amount, and its contingent claim against Powerine's assets was thereby released. Thus, Powerine received new value equal to the amount of the secured portion of First National's reimbursement claim, but not to the unsecured portion. It is not clear from the record how much of First National's contingent reimbursement claim against Powerine was secured. This amount must be determined by the bankruptcy court. Reversed and remanded.

DISSENT: (Farris, J.) The plain language of the Bankruptcy Code states that a trustee may avoid any transfer that enables the creditor to receive more than it would receive under a Chapter 7 liquidation. Contrary to the majority's decision, it does not limit consideration to funds from Powerine's estate only.

▶ ANALYSIS

Note that vis-à-vis Powerine, Koch (D) was an unsecured creditor since it held no security interest in Powerine's property. Because most of Powerine's assets on the date it filed for bankruptcy were subject to the lien held by the secured creditors, Powerine's unsecured creditors could expect to receive much less than one hundred cents on the dollar in a Chapter 7 liquidation. Consequently, Powerine's $3.2 million pre-petition payment enabled Koch (D) to recover more than it would have in a Chapter 7 liquidation. Therefore, the payment met the definition of a preference pursuant to § 547(b). Had Koch (D) been a fully secured creditor, the payment would not have been preferential because Koch (D) would not have received more than in a Chapter 7 liquidation.

Quicknotes

LETTER OF CREDIT An agreement by a bank or other party that it will honor a customer's demand for payment upon the satisfaction of specified conditions.

PREFERENCE A transfer made by the insolvent debtor to a creditor prior to filing the bankruptcy petition, giving priority to one creditor over others, in respect to the debtor's assets.

Citizens Bank of Maryland v. Strumpf

Bank (D) v. Depositor/borrower (P)

516 U.S. 16 (1995).

NATURE OF CASE: Appeal from sanctions imposed for violating the automatic stay.

FACT SUMMARY: Citizens Bank (D) refused to pay withdrawals from Strumpf's (P) checking account in order to offset the sum that it claimed was due on Strumpf's (P) loan.

RULE OF LAW
A creditor may, in order to protect its setoff rights, temporarily refuse to pay a debt that it owes to the debtor in bankruptcy without violating the automatic stay imposed by § 362(a) of the Bankruptcy Code.

FACTS: Strumpf (P) had a checking account with Citizens Bank (D) and also owed $5,068 on a loan from Citizens Bank (D). He filed for relief under Chapter 13, giving rise under § 362(a) of the Code to an automatic stay of creditor activity, including the setoff of any debt owing the debtor that arose before the bankruptcy against any claim against the debtor. Eight months later, Citizens Bank (D) placed an "administrative hold" on so much of Strumpf's (P) checking account as it claimed it was due on the loan. Citizens Bank (D) then petitioned the bankruptcy court for relief from automatic stay and for setoff. The bankruptcy court ultimately granted the motion, but not before sanctioning Citizens Bank (D) for violating the automatic stay. The district court reversed, but the court of appeals reinstated the sanctions, concluding that Citizens Bank's (D) hold constituted a setoff within the meaning of § 362(a)(7). The United States Supreme Court granted certiorari.

ISSUE: May a creditor, in order to protect its setoff rights, and without violating the automatic stay imposed by § 362(a) of the Bankruptcy Code, temporarily refuse to pay a debt that it owes to the debtor in bankruptcy?

HOLDING AND DECISION: (Scalia, J.) Yes. A creditor may, in order to protect its setoff rights, temporarily refuse to pay a debt that it owes to the debtor in bankruptcy without violating the automatic stay imposed by § 362(a) of the Bankruptcy Code. A setoff has not occurred until three steps have been taken: (1) a decision to effectuate a setoff; (2) some action accomplishing the setoff; and (3) a recording of the setoff. In this case, Citizens Bank (D) refused to pay its debt, but not permanently or absolutely, so its action was technically not a setoff. Furthermore, § 542(b) of the Code specifically excuses a creditor from paying a claim to which a defense of setoff applies. Finally, Citizens Bank's (D) administrative hold neither took possession of Strumpf's (P) property nor exercised control over it; instead Citizens Bank (D) merely refused, temporarily, to perform its promise to pay a depositor, which it is permitted to do. Reversed.

▶ ANALYSIS

The right of setoff allows entities that owe each other money to apply their mutual debts against each other. This right avoids the absurdity of making A pay B when B owes A. Although no federal right of setoff is created by the Bankruptcy Code, § 553(a) provides that, with certain exceptions, whatever right of setoff otherwise exists is preserved in bankruptcy.

■■■

Quicknotes

AUTOMATIC STAY Upon the filing of a voluntary bankruptcy petition, creditors are prohibited from attempting to recover payment from the debtor or his property.

SETOFF RIGHTS A claim made pursuant to a counterclaim, arising from a cause of action unrelated to the underlying suit, in which the defendant seeks to have the plaintiff's claim of damages reduced.

■■■

BFP v. Resolution Trust Co.

Debtor-in-possession (P) v. Receiver (D)

511 U.S. 531 (1994).

NATURE OF CASE: Appeal from affirmance of summary judgment dismissal of action to set aside a transfer as fraudulent.

FACT SUMMARY: BFP (P), a Chapter 11 debtor-in-possession, contended that consideration received in a noncollusive real estate mortgage foreclosure sale conducted in conformance with applicable state law did not constitute reasonably equivalent value, as required by Bankruptcy Code § 548(a)(2)—because the real estate was worth considerably more than was received at the sale—and sought to set aside the conveyance as fraudulent.

🏛 RULE OF LAW
The consideration received from a noncollusive, real estate mortgage foreclosure sale conducted in conformance with applicable state law conclusively satisfies the Bankruptcy Code's requirement that transfers of property by insolvent debtors within one year prior to the filing of a bankruptcy petition be in exchange for "a reasonably equivalent value."

FACTS: BFP (P), a partnership formed for the acquisition of real estate, took title to a home subject to, inter alia, a deed of trust in favor of Imperial Savings Association (Imperial) (D). (The Resolution Trust Corporation (RTC) became Imperial's (D) receiver.) After Imperial (D) entered a notice of default because its loan was not being serviced, the home was purchased by Osborne for $433,000 at a properly noticed foreclosure sale. BFP (P) then petitioned for Chapter 11 bankruptcy protection, and, acting as a debtor-in-possession, filed suit to set aside the sale to Osborne as a constructively fraudulent transfer, claiming that the home's fair market value was over $725,000 when sold and, thus, was not exchanged for a "reasonably equivalent value" under § 548(a)(2) of the Bankruptcy Code. The bankruptcy court granted summary judgment to Imperial (D). The district court affirmed the dismissal, and a Bankruptcy Appellate Panel (BAP) affirmed the judgment, holding that consideration received in a noncollusive and regularly conducted nonjudicial foreclosure sale establishes "reasonably equivalent value" as a matter of law. The court of appeals affirmed and the United States Supreme court granted certiorari.

ISSUE: Does the consideration received from a noncollusive, real estate mortgage foreclosure sale conducted in conformance with applicable state law conclusively satisfy the Bankruptcy Code's requirement that transfers of property by insolvent debtors within one year prior to the filing of a bankruptcy petition be in exchange for "a reasonably equivalent value"?

HOLDING AND DECISION: (Scalia, J.) Yes. The consideration received from a noncollusive, real estate mortgage foreclosure sale conducted in conformance with applicable state law conclusively satisfies the Bankruptcy Code's requirement that transfers of property by insolvent debtors within one year prior to the filing of a bankruptcy petition be in exchange for "a reasonably equivalent value." Section 548 of the Bankruptcy Code sets forth the powers of a trustee in bankruptcy (or, in a Chapter 11 case, a debtor-in-possession) to avoid fraudulent transfers. It permits to be set aside not only transfers infected by actual fraud but certain other transfers as well—so-called constructively fraudulent transfers. One of the situations where a transfer may be set aside as constructively fraudulent is where the debtor received "less than a reasonably equivalent value in exchange for such transfer." Contrary to the positions taken by some courts of appeals, fair market value is not necessarily the benchmark against which determination of reasonably equivalent value is to be measured. It may be presumed that Congress acted intentionally when it used the term "fair market value" elsewhere in the Bankruptcy Code but not in § 548, particularly when the omission entails replacing standard legal terminology with a neologism. Moreover, fair market value presumes market conditions that, by definition, do not obtain in the forced-sale context, since property sold within the time and manner strictures of state-prescribed foreclosure is simply worth less than property sold without such restrictions. "Reasonably equivalent value" also cannot be read to mean a "reasonable" or "fair" forced-sale price, such as a percentage of fair market value. To specify a federal minimum sale price beyond what state foreclosure law requires would extend bankruptcy law well beyond the traditional field of fraudulent transfers and upset the coexistence that fraudulent transfer law and foreclosure law have enjoyed for over 400 years. While, under fraudulent transfer law, a "grossly inadequate price" raises a rebuttable presumption of actual fraudulent intent, it is black letter foreclosure law that, when a state's procedures are followed, the mere inadequacy of a foreclosure sale price is no basis for setting the sale aside. Absent clearer textual guidance than the phrase "reasonably equivalent value"—a phrase entirely compatible with preexisting practice—the Court will not presume that Congress intended to displace traditional state regulation with an interpretation that would profoundly affect the important state interest in the security and stability of title to real property. This conclusion does not render § 548(a)(2) superfluous. The

Continued on next page.

"reasonably equivalent value" criterion will continue to have independent meaning outside the foreclosure context, and § 548(a)(2) will continue to be an exclusive means of invalidating foreclosure sales that, while not intentionally fraudulent, nevertheless fail to comply with all governing state laws. Affirmed.

▶ ANALYSIS

In his dissent, Justice Souter pointed out that Justice Scalia, who habitually invokes the plain meaning rule, had in the majority opinion taken liberties with the meaning of a statute clear to any "ordinary speaker of English." Souter also noted that under the majority's ruling, absurdly low consideration could constitute "reasonably equivalent value." The example he used was "a peppercorn paid at a non-collusive and procedurally regular foreclosure sale to be treated as the 'reasonable equivalent' of the value of a California beachfront estate." Obviously, the majority's decision could result—and in fact has resulted—in grossly inequitable outcomes.

■■■

Quicknotes

DEBTOR-IN-POSSESSION In a Chapter 11 proceeding, refers to a debtor who retains control of assets or property pursuant to a plan of reorganization.

SUMMARY JUDGMENT Judgment rendered by a court in response to a motion made by one of the parties, claiming that the lack of a question of material fact in respect to an issue warrants disposition of the issue without consideration by the jury.

■■■

Robinson v. Wangemann

Creditor (D) v. Holder of bankrupt company's note (P)

75 F.2d 756 (5th Cir. 1935).

NATURE OF CASE: Appeal from judgment allowing a claim against an estate.

FACT SUMMARY: Arthur Wangemann, the president of Wangemann-Reichert Company (W-R), sold his shares back to the corporation just prior to its insolvency. W-R issued him notes for the exchanged stock, which were never repaid; and Wangemann (P), the executrix of this estate, sought to have the notes paid.

🏛 RULE OF LAW
Stockholders are not entitled to sell their stock to an insolvent corporation unless the creditors are fully paid.

FACTS: Arthur Wangemann, the president of Wangemann-Reichart Company (W-R), sold 500 shares of stock to the corporation at $110 per share. The purchase was authorized by the stockholders and the corporation delivered a note to Mr. Wangemann. At the time, W-R was solvent, but the corporation did not pay off the note and the renewal notes were issued periodically. W-R was later adjudicated bankrupt and its assets were not sufficient to pay creditors in full. Wangemann (P), the executrix of Arthur Wangemann's estate and the holder of the notes, made a claim based on the unpaid notes. The referee held that since the stock purchase was in good faith and could have been paid without prejudice to creditors at the time, Wangemann (P) was entitled to prove her claim and participate equally with other creditors in the distribution of the assets.

ISSUE: Are stockholders entitled to sell their stock to an insolvent corporation if the creditors are not fully paid?

HOLDING AND DECISION: (Foster, J.) No. Stockholders are not entitled to sell their stock to an insolvent corporation unless the creditors are fully paid. A transaction by which a corporation acquires its own stock from a stockholder for money is not really a sale. The corporation does not acquire anything of value equivalent to the depletion of its assets. It is simply a method of distributing assets to the stockholders. In the present case, the stock sale was executory until the stock was paid for in cash. The company's solvency at the time of the agreement is not relevant. The corporation must be solvent at the time of the payment. Since W-R was not solvent, there was no surplus to pay Wangemann (P) as a holder of the note, and her (P) claims are therefore subordinate to the other creditors. Reversed and remanded.

▌ *ANALYSIS*

This decision is in accord with other jurisdictions. It should be considered a general policy that stock redemption debt must be subordinate because creditors enjoy priority over stockholders. The decision correctly noted that redemption is not actually different from dividend payments.

Quicknotes

EXECUTORY That which has not been fully completed or performed.

INSOLVENT One's liabilities exceed one's assets; inability to pay one's debts.

In re Northern Merchandise

Bankruptcy trustee (P) v. Lender (D)

371 F.3d 1056 (9th Cir. 2004).

NATURE OF CASE: Appeal from affirmance of partial summary judgment to debtor's trustee in Chapter 7 proceeding.

FACT SUMMARY: Frontier Bank (Frontier) (D) contended that debtor Northern Merchandise, Inc. (Debtor) had received reasonably equivalent value under § 548(a)(1) when Frontier (D) deposited $150,000 into Debtor's account on a loan Frontier (D) made with Debtor's shareholders, but for which Debtor gave Frontier (D) a security interest in its inventory and other assets.

🏛 RULE OF LAW
A debtor receives reasonably equivalent value under § 548(a)(1)(B) of the Bankruptcy Code when it receives the proceeds of a loan made with a third party for debtor's benefit so that the net effect of the transfer is to not deplete the bankruptcy estate or to prejudice debtor's creditors.

FACTS: Frontier Bank (Frontier) (D) loaned $150,000 to the shareholders (collectively, Shareholders) of Northern Merchandise, Inc. (Debtor) with the understanding that the money would be used to provide Debtor with working capital. Frontier (D) deposited the funds in Debtor's checking account. However, while the funds themselves were transferred directly from Frontier (D) to Debtor, the transaction was documented as a loan to Shareholders, who then turned the funds over to Debtor. The loan was evidenced by a promissory note in favor of Frontier (D) executed by Shareholders. However, on the same day that Shareholders entered into the loan with Frontier (D), Debtor executed a commercial security agreement granting Frontier (D) a security interest in its inventory, chattel paper, accounts, equipment, and general intangibles. A few months later, Debtor ceased doing business and transferred $400,000 worth of inventory to a company owned by one of the Shareholders for $125,000. This $125,000 was paid to Frontier (D) and credited to the loan. The remaining $25,000 was paid to Frontier (D) by another company from the proceeds of prior sales of inventory. About two weeks later, creditors filed an involuntary Chapter 7 petition against Debtor, and a trustee (P) was appointed. Approximately two years later, the trustee (P) filed suit against Frontier (D) and a motion for partial summary judgment, asserting that the grant of the security interest and the $125,000 transfer were fraudulent conveyances under § 548(a). The bankruptcy court agreed and granted the summary judgment motion. A Bankruptcy Appellate Panel (BAP) affirmed, and the court of appeals granted review.

ISSUE: Does a debtor receive reasonably equivalent value under § 548(a)(1)(B) of the Bankruptcy Code when it receives the proceeds of a loan made with a third party for debtor's benefit so that the net effect of the transfer is to not deplete the bankruptcy estate or to prejudice debtor's creditors?

HOLDING AND DECISION: (Wardlaw, J.) Yes. A debtor receives reasonably equivalent value under § 548(a)(1)(B) of the Bankruptcy Code when it receives the proceeds of a loan made with a third party for debtor's benefit so that the net effect of the transfer is to not deplete the bankruptcy estate or to prejudice debtor's creditors. It is well settled that "reasonably equivalent value can come from one other than the recipient of the payments, a rule which has become known as the indirect benefit rule." Thus, a debtor may receive fair value even though the consideration given for his property or obligation initially goes to a third party. The proper focus is on the net effect of the transfers on the debtor's estate and the funds available to the unsecured creditors. As long as unsecured creditors are no worse off because the debtor, and consequently the estate, has received an amount reasonably equivalent to what it paid, no fraudulent transfer has occurred. Here, the trustee (P) reasons that because the transfer from Shareholders to Debtor was technically a capital contribution, rather than a loan, Debtor was under no legal obligation to grant a security interest to Frontier (D). Such a formalistic view must be rejected, since Debtor clearly received a benefit from the loan—the proceeds of which went directly into its bank account. Its grant of the security interest, therefore, resulted in no net loss to Debtor's estate nor the funds available to unsecured creditors. To hold otherwise would result in an unintended $150,000 windfall to Debtor's estate. Reversed.

▌ANALYSIS

Under the indirect benefit rule, a transfer solely for the benefit of the third party does not furnish reasonably equivalent value. In addition, the benefit received by the debtor must approximate the value of the property or obligation the debtor has given up; otherwise it is not "reasonably equivalent."

▬▬▮

Quicknotes

PARTIAL SUMMARY JUDGMENT Judgment rendered by a court in response to a motion by one of the parties,

Continued on next page.

claiming that the lack of a question of marital fact in respect to one of the issues warrants disposition of that issue without going to the jury.

■━■

Bay Plastics v. BT Commercial Corp.

Bankrupt company (P) v. Selling shareholders (D)

187 B.R. 315 (Bankr. C.D. Cal. 1995).

NATURE OF CASE: Plaintiff's motion for summary judgment in adversary proceeding in bankruptcy.

FACT SUMMARY: The trustee (P) of an insolvent corporation claimed that the selling shareholders (D) in a leveraged buyout had engaged in a fraudulent transfer.

🏛 RULE OF LAW
The selling shareholders of a constructive fraudulent transfer rendering the debtor insolvent are accountable to creditors.

FACTS: The shareholders (D) of Bay Plastics, Inc. (P) sold their stock in a leveraged buyout (LBO). As a result, Bay Plastics (P) filed for bankruptcy. The bankruptcy trustee (P), standing in the shoes of a creditor, claimed that the shareholders (D) had violated the California version of the Uniform Fraudulent Transfer Act. The shareholders (D) claimed that the debtor was not a qualifying pre-transaction creditor.

ISSUE: Are the selling shareholders of a constructive fraudulent transfer rendering the debtor insolvent accountable to creditors?

HOLDING AND DECISION: (Bufford, J.) Yes. The selling shareholders of a constructive fraudulent transfer rendering the debtor insolvent are accountable to creditors. Here, the shareholders (D) acted in bad faith. The various pieces of this transaction were collapsed into one integral transaction, in which the funds went to the selling shareholders (D), not to Bay Plastics (P) or its new parent BPI Acquisition Corp. (BPI). The loan obligation, in contrast, was undertaken by Bay Plastics (P), which also provided the security for the loan. Bay Plastics (P) received no reasonably equivalent value for the security interest it gave. It was appropriate to apply fraudulent transfer law to an LBO. The debtor had a massive requirements contract with Bay Plastics (P) and was a present creditor for purposes of fraudulent transfer law. Motion granted to the trustee (P).

▶ ANALYSIS

Leveraged buyouts are frequently used in corporate takeovers. Old equity holders may finance the takeover, leading to what is known as seller financing. Many of these transactions were found to be fraudulent transfers in the 1980s and 1990s.

Quicknotes

BANKRUPTCY TRUSTEE Individual charged with the administration of the bankruptcy estate.

LEVERAGED BUYOUT A transaction whereby corporate outsiders purchase the outstanding shares of a publicly held corporation mostly with borrowed funds.

SECURITY INTEREST An interest in property that may be sold upon a default in payment of the debt.

McCannon v. Marston

Condominium purchaser (P) v. Bankruptcy trustee (D)

679 F.2d 13 (3d Cir. 1982).

NATURE OF CASE: Appeal from dismissal in action requesting specific performance.

FACT SUMMARY: McCannon (P) sought to enforce a real property purchase with a debtor, but the bankruptcy trustee (D) sought to avoid her interest.

▥ RULE OF LAW
Transferees of real property need only give constructive notice of their interest to protect against claims from subsequent purchasers.

FACTS: McCannon (P) purchased a condominium from the Drake Hotel partnership. McCannon (P) never registered her agreement for sale. Six years later, the partnership filed for bankruptcy. McCannon (P) filed a complaint seeking relief from the automatic stay and requesting specific performance of the purchase agreement. The bankruptcy court ruled that the trustee (D), as a bona fide purchaser for value without regard to knowledge of McCannon's (P) interest, could avoid that interest. The district court affirmed, and McCannon (P) appealed.

ISSUE: Do transferees of real property need only give constructive notice of their interest to protect against claims from subsequent purchasers?

HOLDING AND DECISION: (Gibbons, J.) Yes. Transferees of real property need only give constructive notice of their interest to protect against claims from subsequent purchasers. Under Pennsylvania Law, the purchaser of real property by written contract is the equitable owner of that property. Subsequent purchasers of real property are given priority over the rights of prior purchasers if they are bona fide purchasers for value without notice of the prior property interest. Record interest would defeat the claim of the subsequent purchaser, but in this case McCannon (P) failed to record her interest. However, in Pennsylvania, clear and open possession of real property provides constructive notice to subsequent purchasers. In § 544 of the Bankruptcy Code, there is a phrase "without regard to any knowledge of the trustee." But Congress did not intend to equate knowledge with notice. Congress did not intend to nullify state law protections for those with equitable interests. The phrase in § 544 was used to clear up Article 9 problems with the trustee acting as lien creditor. Accordingly, McCannon's (P) constructive notice applies against the trustee (D).

▶ ANALYSIS

The court also rejected the trustee's (D) contention that there was no constructive notice. The trustee (D) claimed that since McCannon (P) lived in a condominium, the normal rules did not apply. However, the court found no reason that condos should be treated differently from single-family homes.

■■■

Quicknotes

CONSTRUCTIVE NOTICE Knowledge of a fact that is imputed to an individual who was under a duty to inquire and who could have learned of the fact through the exercise of reasonable prudence.

REAL PROPERTY Land, an interest in land, or anything attached to the land that is incapable of being removed.

TRUSTEE A person who is entrusted to keep or administer something.

■■■

CHAPTER 8

Equitable Subordination and Substantive Consolidation

Quick Reference Rules of Law

Matter of SI Restructuring

Trustee (P) v. Insider creditors (D)

532 F.3d 355 (2008).

NATURE OF CASE: Appeal from affirmance of order in adversary proceeding equitably subordinating secured claims.

FACT SUMMARY: The Wooleys (D), former officers and directors, and the largest shareholders, of Schlotzsky's, Inc. (Schlotzsky's), contended that their secured claims should not be equitably subordinated and converted to unsecured claims because their conduct with respect to loans they made to Schlotzsky's was either not inequitable or did not injure Schlotzsky's or its general creditors.

🏛 RULE OF LAW

A secured claim belonging to a corporate debtor's insider creditors will not be equitably subordinated where there is no showing either that the creditors' conduct was inequitable, or that there was injury to the debtor or its other creditors.

FACTS: The Wooleys (D), officers and directors, and the largest shareholders, of Schlotzsky's, Inc. (Schlotzsky's), to relieve a critical cash crunch faced by Schlotzsky's, made two loans to the corporation: one in April for $1 million and another in November for $2.5 million. Both loans were secured with Schlotzsky's royalty streams from franchisees, intellectual property rights, and other intangible property. Schlotzsky's and the Wooleys (D) were represented by separate legal counsel for the April loan negotiations, the loan terms were approved by the audit committee and Schlotzsky's board of directors as a related-party transaction, and the transaction was disclosed in the company's filings with the Securities and Exchange Commission (SEC). Despite the April loan, the company still desperately needed capital, and efforts to obtain outside funding continued and were known to the board, and were addressed at an October board meeting. A bank finally agreed to permit the Wooleys (D) to personally borrow capital, which they in turn would be permitted to lend to Schlotzsky's. The bank formally approved the loan to the Wooleys (D) on November 10, and the board was notified on November 11 of a special meeting to be held on November 13 to approve the Wooleys' (D) loan to the company. Before the special meeting, the board members were provided with copies of the proposed promissory note and the security agreement along with e-mails from the company's counsel. When the loan was made, the Wooleys (D) had in place personal guarantees that guaranteed pre-existing Schlotzsky's debt. As part of the November loan package, the Wooleys (D) also secured this potential liability under the guarantees with the same collateral that secured the April and November loans. (The Wooleys' (D) potential obligation on the guaranty agreements was never triggered, however, because the company never defaulted on its principal obligation covered by the guarantees.)

At the November 13 board meeting, conducted via telephone conference call, the board was told that without the infusion of additional funds, payroll could not be met and that the company would default on a payment to a secured creditor. All of the non-interested directors in attendance approved the loan without objection, an independent audit committee also approved the loan, and the transaction was publicly disclosed in SEC filings. The proceeds of the loan were used to pay the unsecured creditors and keep the company in operation. Several months later, the Wooleys (D) were terminated as officers and resigned as directors. Shortly afterward, the company filed for Chapter 11 bankruptcy protection, and the Wooleys (D) filed secured claims relating to the April and November loans. The committee of unsecured creditors brought an adversary proceeding against the Wooleys (D), seeking to have their secured claims equitably subordinated and treated as unsecured claims. The bankruptcy court found that the Wooleys (D) had breached their fiduciary duties with respect to the November loan for several reasons: first, because they had presented the loan to the board as the only option to prevent the company from collapsing; second, because the loans were putatively meant to be temporary, until permanent financing could be obtained, so there was no reason to secure the loans; third, because the collateral was the company's "crown jewels," so the Wooleys (D) took as much as they could for themselves; and fourth, because by securing their pre-existing contingent liability on their personal guarantees with the revenue stream of the franchise company, the Wooleys' (D) effectively released themselves as guarantors on the debt at the expense of the corporation and its unsecured creditors. Notwithstanding these conclusions, the bankruptcy court failed to make specific findings that the Wooleys' (D) conduct regarding the loans or their pre-existing contingent liability on the guarantees resulted in harm to the corporation or to the unsecured creditors. It nevertheless ordered the Wooleys' (D) secured claims equitably subordinated and, thus, converted to unsecured status. The district court affirmed, and the court of appeals granted review.

ISSUE: Will a secured claim belonging to a corporate debtor's insider creditors be equitably subordinated where there is no showing either that the creditors' conduct was inequitable, or that there was injury to the debtor or its other creditors?

HOLDING AND DECISION: (Davis, J.) No. A secured claim belonging to a corporate debtor's insider creditors will not be equitably subordinated where there is no showing either that the creditors' conduct was inequitable, or that there was injury to the debtor or its other

Continued on next page.

creditors. The law regarding when equitable subordination should be applied is not found in the Code, but in case law, which provides that the claimant must have engaged in inequitable conduct; the misconduct must have resulted in injury to the creditors of the debtor or conferred an unfair advantage on the claimant; equitable subordination of the claim must not be inconsistent with the provisions of the Code; and a claim should be subordinated only to the extent necessary to offset the harm that the debtor or its creditors have suffered as a result of the inequitable conduct. Here, the bankruptcy court made no findings of inequitable conduct by the Wooleys (D) with respect to the April loan, and with regard to the November transactions, even assuming that there was inequitable conduct and unfair advantage, the bankruptcy court made no finding of harm, and the record does not support a finding that either the debtor or the unsecured creditors were harmed by the November transaction. Given that the proceeds of the loan were used to pay unsecured creditors, it cannot be said that unsecured creditors as a class were harmed by the November transaction, even if some unsecured creditors benefited at the expense of other unsecured creditors. Therefore, the argument by the Trustee (P) that when the company secured the Wooleys' (D) loan with franchise assets, the assets available to the unsecured creditors were reduced, thus injuring them, must fail. As to the Wooleys' (D) securing their existing personal guarantees with the same collateral used for the loans, there was never any harm to the company because the Wooleys' (D) potential obligation on the guaranty agreements was never triggered because the company never defaulted on its principal obligation covered by the guarantees. Thus, they also did not gain any unfair advantage as to this transaction. Finally, although the Trustee (P) denies it, it seems that he also is claiming damages under a "deepening insolvency theory," defined as prolonging an insolvent corporation's life through bad debt, causing the dissipation of corporate assets. The Trustee's (P) expert used this theory in determining that the company lost $3.5 million as a result of the loans. However, the bankruptcy court rejected this expert's testimony because it recognized that the Wooleys (D) were "highly committed" to keeping the company going. Moreover, the deepening insolvency theory has been rejected by many courts as a measure of damages, and, even if it were an accepted theory, it would not be supported by the record here, since there was no evidence that the company was undercapitalized or insolvent. For all these reasons, neither of the Wooleys' (D) claims should have been subordinated. Judgment for the Wooleys (D). Reversed.

▌ANALYSIS

Many courts, e.g., the Delaware Court of Chancery—the nation's preeminent court for corporate law matters—reject the doctrine of deepening insolvency as an independent cause of action or as a theory of damages. These courts reason that even when a company is insolvent, its directors may, in the appropriate exercise of their business judgment, take action that might, if it does not pan out, result in the company losing value or going into insolvency. The fact that the residual claimants of the company at that time are creditors does not mean that the directors cannot choose to continue the firm's operations in the hope that they can improve the company's financial health so that the company's creditors get a greater recovery. By doing so, however, the directors do not guaranty success—and do not breach their fiduciary duties.

Quicknotes

CHAPTER 11 REORGANIZATION A plan formulated pursuant to Chapter 11 of the Bankruptcy Code whereby a debtor, who is unable to pay his debts as they become due, is relieved of his obligation to pay his creditors through reorganization and payment from future income.

POST-PETITION After bankruptcy petition has been filed.

Matter of Clark Pipe & Supply Co.

Lender (D) v. Bankruptcy trustee (P)

893 F.2d 693 (5th Cir. 1990).

NATURE OF CASE: Petition for rehearing in action to equitably subordinate claims.

FACT SUMMARY: Associates Commercial Corp. (Associates) (D), a lender, had a loan agreement with Clark Pipe & Supply Co. (Clark) whereby Associates (D) exercised significant control over Clark's business.

RULE OF LAW
Loan agreements giving significant control to a creditor do not make the borrower an instrumentality for purposes of equitable subordination.

FACTS: Clark Pipe & Supply Co. (Clark) bought and sold steel pipe for offshore drilling platforms. In 1980, Associates Commercial Corp. (Associates) (D) agreed to make Clark revolving loans secured by an assignment of accounts receivable and an inventory mortgage. Under the agreement, the amount Associates (D) would lend was determined by a formula based on the accounts receivable. Associates (D) had discretion to reduce the advance rate at any time. When Clark's business slumped in 1981, Associates (D) began reducing the advances so that Clark would have just enough cash to pay direct operating expenses. However, Associates (D) did not direct Clark to pay certain vendors or threaten a credit cutoff if it paid vendors. Eventually, Clark was forced into bankruptcy. The Trustee (P) sought equitable subordination of Associates' (D) claims. The bankruptcy court agreed, and the district court affirmed. Associates (D) appealed, and the appellate court initially affirmed, but then agreed to a rehearing.

ISSUE: Do loan agreements giving significant control to a creditor make the borrower an instrumentality for purposes of equitable subordination?

HOLDING AND DECISION: (Jolly, J.) No. Loan agreements giving significant control to a creditor do not make the borrower an instrumentality for purposes of equitable subordination. A three-pronged test is used to determine equitable subordination. The claimant must have engaged in inequitable conduct, the misconduct must have resulted in injury or conferred an unfair advantage, and subordination must be consistent with the Bankruptcy Code. The Trustee (P) here alleged that Associates (D) used and controlled Clark as an instrumentality to liquidate Associates' (D) unpaid loans to the detriment of the other creditors. The loan agreement was made at a time when Clark was solvent and was negotiated at arm's length. While Associates (D) did exercise a great deal of control over Clark, it had every right to do so under the agreement. The evidence shows that the amounts of the advances were consistent with the funding formulas of the loan agreement. There is a distinction between the existence of control and the exercise of that control to direct the activities of the debtor. Associates (D) did not own any stock in Clark, nor did it interfere with management decisions. Associates (D) did not expressly dictate to Clark which bills should be paid and did not mislead creditors to continue supplying Clark. Accordingly, Associates (D) did not engage in inequitable conduct, despite the fact that it had a great deal of control over Clark. Reversed.

ANALYSIS

This case seems to require a substantial and significant amount of controlled conduct to rise to the level of inequitable conduct. The court seemed swayed by the fact that Associates' (D) control was more implicit than explicit. It attained its desired result through effective use of the loan agreement rather than by direct orders.

Quicknotes

EQUITABLE SUBORDINATION DOCTRINE The placement of a party's rights or claims in lower priority to the rights and claims of others.

FIDUICARY DUTY A legal obligation to act for the benefit of another, including subordinating one's personal interests to that of the other person.

FRAUDULENT CONVEYANCE Conveyances made within one year of filing the bankruptcy petition with intent to defraud creditors and which may be voidable.

UNSECURED CREDITOR A creditor, the repayment of whose loan is not backed by specified collateral or a security agreement.

In re Owens Corning

[Parties not identified.]

419 F.3d 195 (3d Cir. 2005).

NATURE OF CASE: Appeal from grant of motion of substantive consolidation.

FACT SUMMARY: Banks that had extended a $2 billion unsecured loan to Owens Corning, a Delaware corporation (OCD), and some of its subsidiaries argued that it would not be appropriate to substantively consolidate OCD's and its subsidiaries' assets and liabilities since doing so would result in the elimination of guarantees made to the Banks by some OCD subsidiaries and result in a windfall to other OCD creditors.

> ## 🏛 RULE OF LAW
> A debtor is not entitled to deemed nonconsensual substantive consolidation where the debtor can show neither pre-petition disregard of separateness permitting the inference that the entities are one legal entity nor post-petition entanglement of such magnitude that disentanglement is prohibitive and hurts all creditors.

FACTS: Owens Corning, a Delaware corporation (OCD), and its subsidiaries constituted a multinational corporate group, with different entities within the group having different purposes, e.g., tax, regulatory, liability limitation, etc. A syndicate of banks (the Banks) agreed to extend a $2 billion loan to OCD and some of its subsidiaries. As a part of the loan transaction, the banks required certain OCD subsidiaries to guarantee the loan. The guarantees of these subsidiaries gave the Banks direct claims against the guarantors for payment defaults. Moreover, the loan agreement expressly limited the ways in which OCD could deal with its subsidiaries: it could not enter into transactions with a subsidiary that would result in losses to that subsidiary, and the separateness of OCD and its subsidiaries was protected and preserved. Three years later, OCD and 17 subsidiaries (collectively the Debtors) filed for reorganization under Chapter 11. Subsequently, the reorganization plan put forth was predicated on obtaining a "deemed" substantive consolidation of the Debtors along with three non-Debtor subsidiaries. Pursuant to a deemed consolidation, the consolidation is deemed to exist for purposes of valuing and satisfying creditor claims, voting for or against the plan, and making distributions for allowed claims under the plan. Under such a deemed consolidation, all the Debtors' guarantees would be deemed eliminated, so that any claim against any Debtor and any guarantee thereof would be deemed to be one obligation of the Debtors. The district court granted the proposed consolidation on the grounds that there was "substantial identity between . . . OCD and its wholly-owned subsidiar-

ies." The court also found there was no basis for finding that the Banks had relied on the separate credit of any of the subsidiary guarantors in extending the loan.

ISSUE: Is a debtor entitled to deemed nonconsensual substantive consolidation where the debtor can show neither pre-petition disregard of separateness permitting the inference that the entities are one legal entity nor post-petition entanglement of such magnitude that disentanglement is prohibitive and hurts all creditors?

HOLDING AND DECISION: (Ambro, J.) No. A debtor is not entitled to deemed nonconsensual substantive consolidation where the debtor can show neither pre-petition disregard of separateness permitting the inference that the entities are one legal entity nor post-petition entanglement of such magnitude that disentanglement is prohibitive and hurts all creditors. Substantive consolidation, a construct of federal common law, emanates from equity. It treats separate legal entities as if they were merged into a single survivor left with all the cumulative assets and liabilities (except inter-entity liabilities, which are erased). Under such consolidation, certain creditors, instead of looking to assets of the subsidiary with whom they dealt, must share those assets with all creditors of all consolidated entities, raising the specter for some creditors of a significant distribution diminution. Thus, this equitable remedy must be used sparingly as a last resort. What must be proven (absent consent) concerning the entities for whom substantive consolidation is sought is that (i) pre-petition they disregarded separateness so significantly that their creditors relied on the breakdown of entity borders and treated them as one legal entity, or (ii) post-petition their assets and liabilities are so scrambled that separating them is prohibitive and hurts all creditors. Moreover, it may be used only defensively to remedy identifiable harms caused by entangled affairs, but may not be used offensively to disadvantage certain creditors or to alter creditor rights. Applying these principles to this case, a "deemed" consolidation fails to meet any of the principles. In the loan transaction, the Banks bargained for "structural seniority" whereby they obtained a direct claim against the guarantors (and thus against their assets levied on once a judgment is obtained) that other creditors of OCD did not have. To undo this bargain is a demanding task. As to pre-petition disregard of corporate separateness, there was no evidence supporting such disregard. To the contrary, the loan transaction was premised on such separateness. Accordingly, the district court was incorrect in finding "substantial identity"

Continued on next page.

of OCD and its subsidiaries. Even though the Banks did not receive separate financial statements for each subsidiary, they nonetheless obtained detailed information about each subsidiary guarantor from OCD, including information about that subsidiary's assets and debts. Moreover, there is no justification for a rule that a creditor must obtain financial statements from a debtor in order to rely reasonably on the separateness of that debtor. Creditors are free to employ whatever metrics they believe appropriate in deciding whether to extend credit free of court oversight. As to post-petition "hopeless commingling," there also is no meaningful evidence that Debtors' assets and liabilities were commingled hopelessly. There is no issue as to which entity owns which assets and has which material liabilities. Thus, the district court erred in concluding that the commingling of assets would justify consolidation when "the affairs of the two companies are so entangled that consolidation will be beneficial." Commingling justifies consolidation only when separately accounting for the assets and liabilities of the distinct entities will reduce the recovery of every creditor—that is, when every creditor will benefit from the consolidation. Moreover, the benefit to creditors should be from cost savings that make assets available rather than from the shifting of assets to benefit one group of creditors at the expense of another. Mere benefit to some creditors, or administrative benefit to the court, falls far short of this standard. Under the district court's construct, the test for hopeless commingling will almost always be met since substantive consolidation will nearly always produce some benefit to some in the form of simplification and/or avoidance of costs. In addition, neither the impossibility of perfection in untangling the affairs of the entities nor the likelihood of some inaccuracies in efforts to do so is sufficient to justify consolidation. Here, at its core, Debtors' argument is that because intercompany accounting was not perfect, untangling the finances of the various entities is a hopeless endeavor. However, such imperfection most likely occurs in most large, complex company structures. A court could properly order and oversee an accounting process that would sufficiently account for the interest and royalty payments owed among the OCD group of companies for purposes of evaluating intercompany claims—dealing with inaccuracies and difficulties as they arise and not in hypothetical abstractions. Therefore, the Debtors have failed to carry their burden of showing that that Debtors' affairs were even tangled, let alone that the cost of untangling them would be so high relative to their assets that the Banks, among other creditors, would benefit from consolidation. Finally, the other principles governing substantive consolidation warrant reversal. For example, if the Debtors' corporate and financial structure was such a sham before the filing of the motion to consolidate, then how is it that past the plan's effective date this structure stays largely undisturbed, with the Debtors reaping all the liability-limiting, tax and regulatory benefits achieved by forming subsidiaries in the first place? In effect, the plan proponents seek to remake sub-

stantive consolidation not as a remedy, but rather as a stratagem to "deem" separate resources reallocated to OCD to strip the Banks of rights under the Bankruptcy Code, favor other creditors, and yet trump possible plan objections by the Banks. Reversed and remanded.

▶ *ANALYSIS*

Substantive consolidation is most commonly used consensually, where the parties are in agreement over its use for distribution purposes. It is arguable that after this case, at least in the Third Circuit, and any others that follow it, nonconsensual substantive consolidation will be restricted to cases in which no objecting creditor is prejudiced by the consolidation. As the court indicates, nonconsensual substantive consolidation will not be granted where certain creditors have lawfully bargained for unequal treatment by obtaining guarantees of separate entities. As the court quotes: "Equality among creditors who have lawfully bargained for different treatment is not equity but its opposite. . . ."

▬▭▬

Quicknotes

POST-PETITION After bankruptcy petition has been filed.
PRE-PETITION Before bankruptcy petition has been filed.

▬▭▬

The Consumer Debtor in Chapters 7 and 13

Quick Reference Rules of Law

Ransom v. FIA Card Services

Debtor (P) v. Creditor (D)

131 S. Ct. 716 (2011).

NATURE OF CASE: Appeal from affirmance by court of appeals of bankruptcy panel's affirmance of denial of confirmation of Chapter 13 debtor's proposed plan.

FACT SUMMARY: Ransom (P), a Chapter 13 debtor, claimed a car-ownership deduction and car-operating costs for his vehicle, which he owned outright, in calculating his monthly disposable income. One of his creditors, FIA Card Services, N.A. (D) contended that Ransom (P) was not permitted to take these deductions because he did not make loan or lease payments on his car.

RULE OF LAW

A debtor who does not make loan or lease payments for his wholly-owned vehicle may not take the car-ownership deduction in calculating disposable income under Chapter 13 of the Bankruptcy Code.

FACTS: Ransom (P) filed for Chapter 13 bankruptcy relief, listing FIA Card Services, N.A. (FIA) (D) as an unsecured creditor. Among his assets, Ransom (P) reported a car that he owned free of any debt. As part of Ransom's (P) proposed plan, he determined his monthly expenses by using the National and Local Standards (Standards) issued by the Internal Revenue Services (IRS), as provided in § 707(b)(2)(A)(ii)(I) of the Bankruptcy Code (Code). The Standards include an allowance for transportation expenses, divided into vehicle "Ownership Costs" and vehicle "Operating Costs." Ransom (P) claimed a car-ownership deduction of $471, the full amount specified in the "Ownership Costs" table, as well as a separate $388 deduction for car-operating costs. Based on his means-test calculations, which Ransom (P) used to determine his disposable income under § 1325(b)(2) of the Code, Ransom's (P) proposed plan would result in repayment of approximately 25% of his unsecured debt. FIA (D) objected on the ground that the plan did not direct all of Ransom's (P) disposable income to unsecured creditors. FIA (D) contended that Ransom (P) should not have claimed the car-ownership allowance because he did not make loan or lease payments on his car. Agreeing, the bankruptcy court denied confirmation of the plan. The court of appeals bankruptcy appellate panel affirmed, as did the court of appeals. The United States Supreme Court granted certiorari to resolve a split among the circuits as to the case's key issue.

ISSUE: May a debtor who does not make loan or lease payments for his wholly-owned vehicle take the car-ownership deduction in calculating disposable income under Chapter 13 of the Bankruptcy Code?

HOLDING AND DECISION: (Kagan, J.) No. A debtor who does not make loan or lease payments for his wholly-owned vehicle may not take the car-ownership deduction in calculating disposable income under Chapter 13 of the Bankruptcy Code. The resolution of the issue presented begins with the language of the Bankruptcy Code, which provides that a debtor may claim only "applicable" expense amounts listed in the Standards. Because the Code does not define the key word "applicable," the term carries its ordinary meaning of appropriate, relevant, suitable, or fit. What makes an expense amount "applicable" in this sense is most naturally understood to be its correspondence to an individual debtor's financial circumstances. Congress established a filter, permitting a debtor to claim a deduction from a National or Local Standard table only if that deduction is appropriate for him, and a deduction is appropriate for the debtor only if the debtor will incur the kind of expense covered by the table during the life of the bankruptcy plan. Had Congress not wanted to separate debtors who qualify for an allowance from those who do not, it could have omitted the term "applicable" altogether. Without that word, all debtors would be eligible to claim a deduction for each category listed in the Standards. Interpreting the statute to require a threshold eligibility determination thus ensures that "applicable" carries meaning, as each word in a statute should. This reading draws support from the statute's context and purpose. The Code in § 1325(b)(2) initially defines a debtor's disposable income as his "current monthly income . . . less amounts reasonably necessary to be expended." It then instructs in § 1325(b)(3) that such reasonably necessary amounts "shall be determined in accordance with" the means test. Because Congress intended the means test to approximate the debtor's reasonable expenditures on essential items, a debtor should be required to qualify for a deduction by actually incurring an expense in the relevant category. Further, the statute's purpose—to ensure that debtors pay creditors the maximum they can afford—is best achieved by interpreting the means test, consistent with the statutory text, to reflect a debtor's ability to afford repayment. Thus, the vehicle-ownership category encompasses the costs of a car loan or lease and nothing more. The expense amount listed ($471) is the average monthly payment for loans and leases nationwide; it is not intended to estimate other conceivable expenses associated with maintaining a car. Maintenance expenses are the province of the separate "Operating Costs" deduction. A person who owns a car free and clear is entitled to the "Operating Costs" deduction for all

Continued on next page.

driving-related expenses. But such a person may not claim the "Ownership Costs" deduction, because that allowance is for the separate costs of a car loan or lease. The IRS' Collection Financial Standards reinforce this conclusion by making clear that individuals who have a car but make no loan or lease payments may take only the operating-costs deduction. Because Ransom (P) owned his vehicle outright, he incurred no expense in the "Ownership Costs" category, and that expense amount was therefore not "applicable" to him. Further, Ransom's (P) argument that his reading of the key word "applicable" is necessary to account for the means test's distinction between "applicable" and "actual" expenses is unpersuasive. Ransom (P) argues that "applicable" cannot mean the same thing as "actual," and from this premise he concludes that an "applicable" expense can be claimed under the means test even if no "actual" expense was incurred. However, the Court's interpretation does not conflate "applicable" with "actual" costs. Although the expense amounts in the Standards apply only if the debtor incurs the relevant expense, the debtor's out-of-pocket cost may well not control the amount of the deduction. If a debtor's actual expenses exceed the amounts listed in the tables, for example, the debtor may claim an allowance only for the specified sum, rather than for his real expenditures. For the Other Necessary Expense categories, by contrast, the debtor may deduct his actual expenses, no matter how high they are. Thus, the Court's reading of the means test gives full effect to "the distinction between "applicable" and "actual" without taking a further step to conclude that "applicable" means "nonexistent." Ransom's (P) policy arguments are equally unpersuasive. First, he correctly observes that debtors who have even just one car payment left would be eligible to claim a monthly ownership deduction, thus encouraging debtors not to pay off their entire debt. This anomalous result is the inevitable result of standardized formula such as the means test that, by its nature, is over- and under-inclusive. Even so, creditors can cure this outlier problem by moving to modify the plan once the debtor's car payments cease during the life of the plan. Ransom (P) is also unpersuasive in arguing that the Court's position sends the wrong message, namely, that it is advantageous to be deeply in debt on car loans, rather than to pay them off. This argument fails to acknowledge that money is fungible; the money Ransom (P) spent on owning his car was money he did not use to pay down his credit card debt, and Congress did not express a preference for one use of these funds over the other. Finally, the ownership cost deduction was not intended to provide either car-owning debtors or debtors with no cars an emergency cushion in the event they would need to purchase a car. Instead, the appropriate way to account for unanticipated expenses like a new vehicle purchase is not to distort the scope of a deduction, but to use the method that the Code provides for all debtors and their creditors: modification of the plan in light of changed circumstances. Affirmed.

ANALYSIS

The deductions in the means test, rather than effecting any broad federal policy as to saving or borrowing, are intended merely to ensure that debtors in bankruptcy can afford essential items. The car-ownership allowance thus safeguards a debtor's ability to retain a car throughout the plan period. If the debtor already owns a car outright, he has no need for this protection, and this decision reflects the narrower purpose behind the deductions.

Quicknotes

BANKRUPTCY A legal proceeding whereby a debtor, who is unable to pay his debts as they become due, is relieved of his obligation to pay his creditors either by liquidation and distribution of his remaining assets or through reorganization and payment from future income.

CHAPTER 13 BANKRUPTCY Debtor may modify plan at any time before the completion of the payments under such plan.

FUNGIBLE GOODS Interchangeable or substitutable goods.

Hamilton v. Lanning

Trustee (P) v. Debtor (D)

130 S. Ct. 2464 (2010).

NATURE OF CASE: Appeal from affirmance of confirmation of modified bankruptcy plan in Chapter 13 bankruptcy.

FACT SUMMARY: Hamilton (Trustee) (P), a private Chapter 13 bankruptcy trustee, contended that under a mechanical approach to calculating Lanning's (Debtor's) (D) monthly projected disposable income, she was committing less than all of such income to the repayment of creditors. Debtor (D) contended that a "forward-looking approach," which accounted for her actual income, should be used to determine her projected disposable income.

RULE OF LAW

When a bankruptcy court calculates a debtor's projected disposable income, the court should apply the "forward-looking approach" and account for changes in the debtor's income or expenses that are known or virtually certain at the time of confirmation.

FACTS: A one-time buyout from Lanning's (Debtor's) (D) former employer caused her current monthly income for the six months preceding her Chapter 13 petition to exceed her state's median income. However, based on the income from her new job, which was below the state median, and her expenses, she reported a monthly disposable income of $149.03. She thus filed a plan that would have required her to pay $144 per month for 36 months. Hamilton (Trustee) (P), a private Chapter 13 bankruptcy trustee, objected to confirmation of the plan because the proposed payment amount was less than the full amount of the claims against Debtor (D), and because, he argued, she had not committed all of her "projected disposable income" to repaying creditors. Trustee (P) claimed that the mechanical approach was the proper way to calculate projected disposable income, and that using that approach, Debtor (D) should pay $756 per month for 60 months, even though her actual income was insufficient to make such payments. The bankruptcy court endorsed Debtor's (D) proposed monthly payment of $144, but required a 60-month plan period. In arriving at its decision, the court adopted the majority view that the word "projected" in § 1325(b)(1)(B) of the Bankruptcy Code requires courts to consider a debtor's actual income. The court of appeals affirmed, concluding that while the result obtained by application of the mechanical approach is presumptively correct, it may be rebutted by evidence of a substantial change in the debtor's circumstances. The United States Supreme Court granted certiorari.

ISSUE: When a bankruptcy court calculates a debtor's projected disposable income, should the court apply the "forward-looking approach" and account for changes in the debtor's income or expenses that are known or virtually certain at the time of confirmation?

HOLDING AND DECISION: (Alito, J.) Yes. When a bankruptcy court calculates a debtor's projected disposable income, the court should apply the "forward-looking approach" and account for changes in the debtor's income or expenses that are known or virtually certain at the time of confirmation. Upon objection to confirmation by an unsecured creditor, and before a court can confirm the plan, § 1325(b)(1) requires a Chapter 13 debtor to pay unsecured creditors in full or to pay all "projected disposable income" to be received by the debtor over the life of the plan. The Bankruptcy Abuse Prevention and Consumer Protection Act of 2005 (BAPCPA), did not define the term "projected disposable income," but it did specify in detail how to calculate "disposable income." Disposable income is arrived at by determining "current monthly income received by the debtor" less "amounts reasonably necessary to be expended" for, e.g., the debtor's maintenance and support. "Current monthly income," in turn, is calculated by averaging the debtor's monthly income during a 6-month look-back period preceding the petition's filing. If a debtor's income is below the median for his or her state, "amounts reasonably necessary" include the full amount needed for "maintenance or support," but if the debtor's income exceeds the state median, only certain specified expenses are included. Because she had to include her one-time buyout amount from her former employer in calculating her income for 6-month look-back period, she showed average income that exceeded the state's median income for a family of one. Thus, on Form 22C, she showed a monthly "disposable income" of $1,114.98, after deducting monthly expenses. However, given that the income from her new job was below the state median, she reported monthly disposable income of only $149.03. Applying the mechanical approach, as advocated by the Trustee (P), projected disposable income would be past average monthly disposable income multiplied by the number of months in the Debtor's (D) plan. While Debtor (D) did not contest that the mechanical approach should be determinative in most cases, she argued that in exceptional cases, where significant changes in a debtor's financial circumstances are known or virtually certain, a bankruptcy court has discretion to make an appropriate adjustment. Debtor (D) has the better argument. First, such a forward-looking approach is supported by the ordinary meaning of "projected." In ordinary usage, future occurrences are not "projected" based on the assumption that the past will

Continued on next page.

necessarily repeat itself. While a projection takes past events into account, adjustments are often made based on other factors that may affect the outcome. Second, "projected" appears in many federal statutes, yet Congress rarely uses it to mean simple multiplication. By contrast, as the Bankruptcy Code shows, Congress can make its mandate of simple multiplication unambiguous, commonly by using the term "multiplied." Third, under pre-BAPCPA case law, the general rule was that courts would multiply a debtor's current monthly income by the number of months in the commitment period as the first step in determining projected disposable income, but would also have discretion to account for known or virtually certain changes in the debtor's income. This is significant, since the Bankruptcy Code must not be interpreted to erode past bankruptcy practice absent a clear indication that Congress intended such a departure," and Congress did not amend the term "projected disposable income" in 2005, and pre-BAPCPA practice reflected a widely adhered to view that the court could take into account known or virtually certain changes to a debtor's income or expenses when projecting disposable income. Had Congress wanted to change this historical practice, it would have said so. Further, the mechanical approach clashes repeatedly with the terms of § 1325. First, § 1325(b)(1)(B)'s reference to projected disposable income "to be received in the applicable commitment period" strongly favors the forward-looking approach. Because Debtor (D) would have far less than $756 per month in disposable income during the plan period, Trustee's (P) projection does not accurately reflect disposable income "to be received." In such circumstances, the mechanical approach effectively reads that phrase out of the statute. Second, § 1325(b)(1)'s direction to courts to determine projected disposable income "as of the effective date of the plan," i.e., the confirmation date, is more consistent with the view that they are to consider post-filing information about a debtor's financial situation. Had Congress intended for projected disposable income to be no more than a multiple of disposable income, it could have specified the plan's filing date as the effective date. Third, § 1325(b)(1)(B)'s requirement that projected disposable income "will be applied to make payments" is rendered a hollow command if, as of the plan's effective date, the debtor lacks the means to pay creditors in the calculated monthly amounts. Further, the arguments supporting the mechanical approach are unpersuasive. The claim that the Code's detailed and precise "disposable income" definition would have no purpose without the mechanical approach overlooks the important role that this statutory formula plays under the forward-looking approach, which begins with a disposable income calculation. The court of appeals' reference to a rebuttable "presumption" analysis was not erroneous, as it simply heeded the ordinary meaning of "projected," i.e., a person makes a projection by using past occurrences as a starting point. Also rejected is the Trustee's (P) argument that only the mechanical approach is consistent with § 1129(a)(15)(B), which refers to "projected disposable income of the debtor (as defined in section 1325(b)(2))." This

cross-reference offers no insight into the meaning of the word "projected." Also rejected is the Trustee's (P) inference from the fact that § 1325(b)(3) incorporates § 707—which allows courts to consider "special circumstances," but only with respect to calculating expenses—that Congress intended to eliminate, *sub silentio*, the discretion that courts previously exercised to account for known or virtually certain changes. Finally, in cases in which debtor's disposable income during the 6-month look-back period is either substantially lower or higher than the debtor's disposable income during the plan period, the mechanical approach would produce senseless, unintended results. In cases in which the debtor's disposable income is higher during the plan period, the mechanical approach would deny creditors payments that the debtor could easily make. In cases where the debtor's disposable income during the plan period is substantially lower, the mechanical approach would deny the protection of Chapter 13 to debtors who meet the Chapter's main eligibility requirements. The Trustee's (P) other arguments are flawed or unpersuasive. Affirmed.

▶ ANALYSIS

This decision resolved the split among the circuit courts over the correct interpretation of "projected disposable income," favoring a pragmatic and flexible approach over a rigid, mechanical approach. As the Court indicates, such an approach is likely to benefit both debtors and creditors. As here, the forward-looking approach can help debtors obtain Chapter 13 relief by permitting the courts to confirm their plan when circumstances warrant it. Creditors could also be helped by having a means to counter a debtor's strategic manipulation of the BAPCPA computation of disposable income.

Quicknotes

BANKRUPTCY A legal proceeding whereby a debtor, who is unable to pay his debts as they become due, is relieved of his obligation to pay his creditors either by liquidation and distribution of his remaining assets or through reorganization and payment from future income.

CERTIORARI A discretionary writ issued by a superior court to an inferior court in order to review the lower court's decisions; the Supreme Court's writ ordering such review.

CHAPTER 13 BANKRUPTCY Debtor may modify plan at any time before the completion of the payments under such plan.

SUB SILENTIO Under silence; without mention.

In re Crawford

[Parties not identified.]

324 F.3d 539 (7th Cir. 2003).

NATURE OF CASE: Appeal from affirmance of denial of confirmation of Chapter 13 plan.

FACT SUMMARY: Crawford contended that his Chapter 13 plan, whereby two-thirds of his non-dischargeable child support debt would be shifted to nonsecured creditors and leave them with nothing, should have been confirmed under § 1322(b) because it was not "unfair."

🏛 RULE OF LAW
It is unfair discrimination under a Chapter 13 plan to classify nondischargeable debt so that two-thirds of such debt is shifted to other nonsecured creditors, leaving them with nothing.

FACTS: Crawford filed for Chapter 13 protection. His nonpriority unsecured debts consisted of about $19,000 owed the Internal Revenue Service, $18,000 owed the county for child support, and $500 owed to trade creditors. The debt Crawford owed the county was nondischargeable. His Chapter 13 plan proposed to divide his debts into two classes: the county debt and all other debts. Under the plan, he would pay two-thirds of the county debt first and the other unsecured creditors would receive nothing. The bankruptcy court refused to confirm this plan under § 1322(b), the district court affirmed, and the court of appeals granted review.

ISSUE: Is it unfair discrimination under a Chapter 13 plan to classify nondischargeable debt so that two-thirds of such debt is shifted to other nonsecured creditors, leaving them with nothing?

HOLDING AND DECISION: (Posner, J.) Yes. It is unfair discrimination under a Chapter 13 plan to classify nondischargeable debt so that two-thirds of such debt is shifted to other nonsecured creditors, leaving them with nothing. Section 1322(b)(1) provides that a Chapter 13 plan may "designate a class or class of unsecured claim . . . but may not discriminate unfairly against any class so designated." This section does not explain what "unfairly" means in this context. Various tests are used. One is a four-factor test: (1) "whether the discrimination has a reasonable basis; (2) whether the debtor can carry out a plan without the discrimination; (3) whether the discrimination is proposed in good faith; and (4) whether the degree of discrimination is directly related to the basis or rationale for the discrimination." A second test is whether the debtor has a "legitimate" basis for the classification. A third test insists that the classification presumptively give the disfavored creditors at least 80% of what they would get

without the classification. And, a fourth test adds the third test to the first test (the four-part test, which becomes a five-part test). All of these are flawed, either unduly favoring the debtor or the creditor, or just being arbitrary. The better approach is to let the bankruptcy judge seek a result that is reasonable in light of the purposes of the relevant law. One of these purposes is to protect both the debtor and creditors. This implies that if without classification the debtor is unlikely to be able to fulfill a Chapter 13 plan and the result will be to make his creditors as a whole worse off than they would be with classification, then classification will be a win-win outcome. Here, nonpayment of child support is a serious matter, which is why it is non-dischargeable. No good reason has been shown to permit Crawford to shift two-thirds of this debt to his other unsecured creditors, leaving them with nothing. Thus, the bankruptcy court did not abuse its discretion in rejecting, as unfair discrimination against his other creditors, the plan Crawford proposed. Affirmed.

▎ *ANALYSIS*

The court emphasized that its decision was case-specific. It noted that not all child-support debts may not be classified, nor did it hold that Crawford could not formulate an acceptable plan that would involve an element of classification. As an example of a permissible plan, the court indicated that had Crawford proposed to carve down his nondischargeable debt to the principal owed on it (roughly $12,000), and had he shown that without such a carve-down he would be staggering under such a crushing load of undischarged debt as to make it inevitable or nearly so that he would soon be back in bankruptcy court, this time under Chapter 7, the bankruptcy court might deem such a plan reasonable and the court of appeals presumably would affirm—especially if the unsecured creditors would do worse in Chapter 7 than they would do under Crawford's revised Chapter 13 plan.

━━

Quicknotes

UNSECURED CLAIM A claim, the repayment of which is not secured by collateral sufficient to repay the debt owed.

UNSECURED CREDITOR A creditor whose loan is not backed by specified collateral or a security agreement.

━━

In re Jones

[Parties not identified.]

591 F.3d 308 (4th Cir. 2010).

NATURE OF CASE: Appeal from reversal of order in Chapter 7 adversary proceeding holding that a secured creditor did not have the right to repossess a vehicle.

FACT SUMMARY: The Joneses (D), who had purchased a car from DaimlerChrysler Financial Services Americas, LLC (DaimlerChrysler) (P), and granted DaimlerChrysler (P) a security interest in the vehicle, contended that even though Mr. Jones (D) in his Chapter 7 bankruptcy had failed to state whether he intended to redeem the vehicle or reaffirm the debt as required by §§ 362(h) and 521(a)(2) of the Bankruptcy Code (Code), and had failed to either timely redeem the vehicle or enter a reaffirmation agreement with DaimlerChrysler (P), DaimlerChrysler (P) did not have the right to repossess the vehicle because a "ride-through" option permitted Chapter 7 debtors who were current on their installment payments to continue making payments and retain collateral after discharge without redeeming the collateral or reaffirming the debt. The Joneses (D) also contended that under state law, DaimlerChrysler (P) was required to give them prior notice of a right to cure before repossessing the vehicle.

> ## 🏛 RULE OF LAW
> (1) The Bankruptcy Abuse Prevention and Consumer Protection Act of 2005 (BAPCPA) eliminates the "ride-through option" permitting Chapter 7 debtors who are current on their installment payments to continue making payments and retain collateral after discharge without redeeming the collateral or reaffirming the debt, so that failure to timely redeem or reaffirm the debt terminates the automatic stay, thus taking the collateral out of the bankruptcy estate and subjecting it to repossession.
> (2) Pursuant to § 521(d) of the Bankruptcy Code, a secured creditor may enforce an ipso facto clause in an installment loan contract if a debtor who files for bankruptcy fails to comply with the provisions of §§ 362(h) and 521(a)(6).

FACTS: The Joneses (D) purchased a vehicle from DaimlerChrysler Financial Services Americas, LLC (DaimlerChrysler) (P) under a retail installment contract that granted DaimlerChrysler (P) a security interest in the vehicle, and the security interest was perfected. The contract provided that the Joneses (D) would be in default if they filed a bankruptcy petition or one was filed against them. This default-upon-bankruptcy clause is also known as an "ipso facto" clause. Subsequently, Mr. Jones (D) filed for Chapter 7 bankruptcy protection, and, in filing for

bankruptcy, he filed a statement of intention with respect to the vehicle contract that indicated that he would "continue payments" on the vehicle. The statement, however, did not state whether he intended to redeem the vehicle or reaffirm the debt as required by §§ 362(h) and 521(a)(2) of the Bankruptcy Code (Code). He also failed to timely redeem the vehicle or enter into a reaffirmation agreement with DaimlerChrysler (P) as required by § 521(a)(6). DaimlerChrysler (P) then moved to confirm termination of the automatic stay so it could repossess the vehicle, and the bankruptcy court entered an order confirming that the automatic stay had been terminated with respect to the vehicle. Thereafter, without providing written notice of default and the right to cure, DaimlerChrysler (P) repossessed the vehicle pursuant to the ipso facto clause. The Joneses (D) then initiated an adversary proceeding. The bankruptcy court enjoined the vehicle's sale and ordered its return, holding that DaimlerChrysler (P) did not have the right under the Code to repossess the Joneses' (D) vehicle even though Mr. Jones (D) failed to indicate either his intent to redeem the vehicle or reaffirm the debt on his statement of intention. The bankruptcy court relied on the "ride-through" option, recognized in the circuit's precedent, which permits Chapter 7 debtors who are current on their installment payments to continue making payments and retain collateral after discharge without redeeming the collateral or reaffirming the debt. The bankruptcy court also held that state law required DaimlerChrysler (P) to first give the Joneses (D) notice of the right to cure default before repossessing the vehicle. The district court reversed, finding that the ride-through option had been eliminated by the Bankruptcy Abuse Prevention and Consumer Protection Act of 2005 (BAPCPA), and the court of appeals granted review.

ISSUE:
(1) Does BAPCPA eliminate the "ride-through option" permitting Chapter 7 debtors who are current on their installment payments to continue making payments and retain collateral after discharge without redeeming the collateral or reaffirming the debt, so that failure to timely redeem or reaffirm the debt terminates the automatic stay, thus taking the collateral out of the bankruptcy estate and subjecting it to repossession?
(2) Pursuant to § 521(d) of the Bankruptcy Code, may a secured creditor enforce an ipso facto clause in an installment loan contract if a debtor who files for bankruptcy fails to comply with the provisions of §§ 362(h) and 521(a)(6)?

Continued on next page.

HOLDING AND DECISION: (Shedd, J.)

(1) Yes. BAPCPA eliminates the "ride-through option" permitting Chapter 7 debtors who are current on their installment payments to continue making payments and retain collateral after discharge without redeeming the collateral or reaffirming the debt, so that failure to timely redeem or reaffirm the debt terminates the automatic stay, thus taking the collateral out of the bankruptcy estate and subjecting it to repossession. Prior to BAPCPA, the ride-through option was consistent with the Code. BAPCPA, however, significantly amended § 521(a)(2)(C) by permitting alteration of the debtor's rights as provided in § 362(h). These sections alter the pre-BAPCPA analysis by explicitly requiring a debtor to indicate on the statement of intention an intent to either (1) redeem the property or (2) reaffirm the debt, in order to retain the property. If the debtor fails to so indicate, the stay terminates with respect to the property, which will no longer be part of the bankruptcy estate. BAPCPA also added § 521(a)(6), which provides that a debtor may not retain possession of personal property that is subject to a secured claim unless the debtor either reaffirms the debt or redeems the property, according to the statement of intention required by §§ 362(h) and 521(a)(2), within 45 days of the first meeting of creditors. Failure to reaffirm or redeem also lifts the stay and removes the property from the estate. Thus, § 521(a)(6) also evidences that the ride-through option is no longer available under BAPCPA. Therefore, here, when Mr. Jones failed to timely redeem or reaffirm, the stay was terminated, the vehicle was no longer part of the estate, and DaimlerChrysler (D) was entitled to take any action permitted by state law. Affirmed as to this issue.

(2) Yes. Pursuant to § 521(d) of the Bankruptcy Code, a secured creditor may enforce an ipso facto clause in an installment loan contract if a debtor who files for bankruptcy fails to comply with the provisions of §§ 362(h) and 521(a)(6). The general rule is that an ipso facto clause in an installment loan contract is unenforceable as a matter of law. However, BAPCPA created an exception to this rule by adding § 521(d), which expressly permits creditors to enforce ipso facto clauses in consumer loan agreements secured by personal property if the debtor fails to comply with the provisions of §§ 521(a)(6) or 362(h). Thus, here, Mr. Joneses' (D) filing the bankruptcy petition constituted default under the contract, and his failure to timely redeem the vehicle or reaffirm the debt permitted DaimlerChrysler (P) to enforce its ipso facto clause and the contract pursuant to state law. [The court held that state law did not require prior notice of default and a right to cure.] Affirmed as to this issue.

ANALYSIS

This opinion overruled one of the leading decisions permitting the ride-through option, *Home Owners Funding Corp. of Am. v. Belanger (In re Belanger)*, 962 F.2d 345 (4th Cir. 1992). Prior to BAPCPA, the courts were sharply divided as to whether to permit ride-through, and BAPCPA's amendments in this area were intended to resolve the split in favor of those courts that did not permit ride-through. As this opinion demonstrates, BAPCPA succeeded in this regard.

Quicknotes

CHAPTER 7 BANKRUPTCY A legal proceeding whereby a debtor, who is unable to pay his debts as they become due, is relieved of his obligation to pay his creditors by liquidation and distribution of his remaining assets.

IPSO FACTO By the fact itself.

PERFECTED SECURITY INTEREST A security interest that is safeguarded against other claims to the collateral; perfection is generally accomplished by legal steps necessary to give other creditors notice of the interest.

SECURITY INTEREST An interest in property that may be sold upon a default in payment of the debt.

In re Wright

[Parties not identified.]

492 F.3d 829 (7th Cir. 2007).

NATURE OF CASE: Appeal from denial of approval of Chapter 13 plan.

FACT SUMMARY: The Wrights, debtors in a Chapter 13 bankruptcy, contended that under § 1325(a) of the Bankruptcy Code their proposed plan should have been approved. Under their plan, they would surrender to their creditor their car—which served as collateral for a loan but was worth less than the value of the loan—and pay nothing on account of the difference between the loan's balance and the collateral's market value.

🏛 RULE OF LAW

Where § 1325(a) of the Bankruptcy Code operates to render § 506 inoperable, the creditor is entitled to an unsecured deficiency where the surrendered collateral is worth less than the value of the debt.

FACTS: The Wrights filed for Chapter 13 bankruptcy protection. They owed more on their purchase-money automobile loan than their car was worth. Also, they had purchased the car within 910 days of the bankruptcy's commencement. The contract between the Wrights and their lender explicitly indicated that if the debt was not paid, the car could be seized and sold. The creditor was required to account to the Wrights for any surplus, and the Wrights would be liable for any deficiency. Thus, the contract created an ordinary secured loan with recourse against the borrower. The contract also provided that the parties enjoyed all of their rights under the Uniform Commercial Code (UCC). Under Section 9-615(d)(2) of the UCC, an obligor must satisfy any deficiency if the collateral's value is insufficient to cover the amount due. The Wrights proposed a plan that would surrender the car to the creditor and pay nothing on account of the difference between the loan's balance and the collateral's market value. They argued that, as a result of § 1325(a) of the Bankruptcy Code, the lender could not separate the loan into secured and unsecured components, and that surrender of the vehicle would fully satisfy the Wrights' obligation. The bankruptcy court declined to approve the Chapter 13 plan, on the ground that the Wrights did not propose to pay any portion of the shortfall. The Wrights appealed directly to the court of appeals under 28 U.S.C. § 158, which permits bypassing the district court under certain circumstances. The court of appeals granted review under this statute to resolve a split among the bankruptcy courts and because no other federal appellate court (either a Circuit Court or the United States Supreme Court) had ruled on the issue presented.

ISSUE: Where § 1325(a) of the Bankruptcy Code operates to render § 506 inoperable, is the creditor entitled to an unsecured deficiency where the surrendered collateral is worth less than the value of the debt?

HOLDING AND DECISION: (Easterbrook, C.J.) Yes. Where § 1325(a) of the Bankruptcy Code operates to render § 506 inoperable, the creditor is entitled to an unsecured deficiency where the surrendered collateral is worth less than the value of the debt. Section 1325 of the Bankruptcy Code specifies the circumstances under which a consumer's plan of repayment can be confirmed. In the Bankruptcy Abuse Prevention and Consumer Protection Act of 2005, Congress added an unnumbered "hanging" paragraph to § 1325(a), which provides that, for the purpose of a Chapter 13 plan, § 506 does not apply, inter alia, to certain secured loans where the collateral is a car purchased for personal use 910 days before bankruptcy is commenced. Thus, this hanging paragraph applies in this case, since all of its requirements are met, and § 506 is inapplicable. Section 506 divides loans into secured and unsecured portions, where the unsecured portion is the amount by which the debt exceeds the current value of the collateral. The issue is what is the result of making § 506 inapplicable. The majority view is that with § 506 gone, creditors cannot divide their loans into secured and unsecured components. Because § 1325(a)(5)(C) allows a debtor to surrender the collateral to the lender, the majority view is that surrender fully satisfies the borrower's obligations—thus rendering a secured loan non-recourse, regardless of what the contract provides. The minority view is that UCC Article 9 plus the law of contracts entitle the creditor to an unsecured deficiency judgment after surrender of the collateral, unless the contract itself provides that the loan is without recourse against the borrower. Under this view, the unsecured balance must be treated equally with other unsecured debts under the Chapter 13 plan. The bankruptcy court adopted the minority view—which is the better view. Section 506 is not the only source of authority for a deficiency judgment when the collateral is insufficient, since state law determines rights and obligations when the Code does not supply a federal rule. Thus, by knocking out § 506, the hanging paragraph leaves the parties to their contractual entitlements. If the Wrights had surrendered their car the day before filing for bankruptcy, the creditor would have been entitled to treat any shortfall in the collateral's value as an unsecured debt. There is no reason the result should be different if the debtors surrender the collateral the day after filing for bankruptcy when, given the hanging paragraph, no operative section of the Bankruptcy Code contains any contrary rule. The purpose of the

Continued on next page.

hanging paragraph was to "Restor[e] the Foundation for Secured Credit." It is hard to imagine that Congress intended to restore the foundation for secured credit by indirectly making non-recourse lending compulsory, which would be the result if the majority view is adopted. Instead, giving effect to the agreements negotiated between the debtor and creditor promote this purpose. The even bolder argument, made by the National Association of Consumer Bankruptcy Attorneys as amicus, that loans covered by the hanging paragraph cannot be treated as secured in any respect must be rejected. That argument also rests on the faulty premise that contracts and state law are irrelevant unless specifically implemented by the Bankruptcy Code. But Supreme Court precedent holds that the presumption must go the other way: rights under state law count in bankruptcy unless the Code says otherwise. Section 502, which determines whether a claim should be allowed, neither disfavors nor curtails secured claims. Any limitations depend on § 506—which is rendered inapplicable in cases such as the one at bar. The fallback, when § 506 is knocked out of the picture, is the parties' contract—provided it is enforceable under state law. Thus, here, by surrendering their car, the Wrights gave their creditor the full market value of the collateral, and any shortfall must be treated as unsecured debt. That unsecured debt must be treated just like all of the Wrights' other unsecured debt. Affirmed.

▶ ANALYSIS

In a Chapter 13 bankruptcy, when § 506 is applicable, consumers may retain the collateral (despite contractual provisions entitling creditors to repossess) by making monthly payments that the judge deems equal to the market value of the asset, with a rate of interest that the judge will set (rather than the contractual rate). This "cramdown" procedure is usually opposed by creditors because the court may underestimate the collateral's market value and the appropriate interest rate, and the debtor may fail to make all promised payments, so that the payment stream falls short of the collateral's full value. The effect is asymmetric: if a judge overestimates the collateral's value or the interest rate, the debtor will surrender the asset and the creditor will realize no more than the market price. When the judge errs in the debtor's favor, however, the debtor keeps the asset and pays at the reduced rate. Thus, creditors lose from this asymmetry. Under the decision in this case, with § 506 out of the picture, the creditor gets the benefit of the bargain made with the debtor.

Quicknotes

CHAPTER 13 BANKRUPTCY Debtor may modify plan at any time before the completion of the payments under such plan.

INTER ALIA Among other things.

Nobelman v. American Savings Bank

Mortgagor (D) v. Mortgagee (P)

508 U.S. 324 (1993).

NATURE OF CASE: Appeal from denial of confirmation of Chapter 13 plan.

FACT SUMMARY: American Savings Bank (the Bank) (P) argued that the Nobelmans' (D) Chapter 13 proposal to bifurcate the Bank's (P) mortgage on the Nobelmans' (D) condominium—into (1) a secured claim for the $23,500 value of the condominium and (2) an essentially worthless unsecured claim—modified the Bank's (P) rights as a homestead mortgagee.

RULE OF LAW
Section 1322(b)(2) of the Bankruptcy Code prohibits a modification of the rights of the holder of a security interest when the lender's claim is secured only by a lien on the debtor's principal residence.

FACTS: American Savings Bank (the Bank) (P) loaned Mr. and Mrs. Nobelman (D) $68,250 to buy a condominium in exchange for an adjustable rate note. After falling behind on their mortgage payments, the Nobelmans (D) sought relief under Chapter 13. The Bank (P) filed a proof of claim for $71,335. The Nobelmans' (D) Chapter 13 plan valued the residence at a mere $23,500 and proposed to make payments only up to that amount. Relying on § 506(a) of the Bankruptcy Code, they proposed to treat the remainder of the Bank's (P) claim as unsecured. Under the plan, unsecured creditors would receive nothing. The Bank (P) argued that the proposed bifurcation of its claim was a violation of § 1322(b)(2), which prohibits debtors from modifying any debt secured by a mortgage on the debtor's principal residence. The bankruptcy court agreed and denied confirmation of the plan. The district and appellate courts affirmed, and the Nobelmans (D) petitioned the United States Supreme Court for review.

ISSUE: Does § 1322(b)(2) of the Bankruptcy Code prohibit a modification of the rights of the holder of a security interest when the lender's claim is secured only by a lien on the debtor's principal residence?

HOLDING AND DECISION: (Thomas, J.) Yes. Section 1322(b)(2) of the Bankruptcy Code prohibits a modification of the rights of the holder of a security interest when the lender's claim is secured only by a lien on the debtor's principal residence. The Nobelmans (D) argued that the protection against modification contained in § 1322(b)(2) applied only to the extent that the Bank (P) held a "secured claim" in their residence and that the court should look first to § 506(a) to determine the value of the Bank's (P) "secured claim." Section 506(a) provides that a claim secured by a lien on the debtor's property is a secured claim to the extent of the value of the property; to the extent the claim exceeds the value of the property, it is an unsecured claim. Under this view, the Bank (P) is the holder of a "secured claim" only in the amount of $23,500—the value of the condominium. But § 1322(b)(2) could not be administered under this interpretation without impermissibly modifying the Bank's (P) rights as to interest rate, payment amounts, and other contract terms. The Nobelmans (D) cannot possibly modify the payment and interest terms for the unsecured component of the Bank's (P) overall claim without also modifying the terms of the secured component. Affirmed.

CONCURRENCE: (Stevens, J.) Justice Thomas's literal reading of the text of the Bankruptcy Code is faithful to the intent of Congress to treat residential mortgagees favorably in order to encourage the flow of capital into the home lending market.

ANALYSIS

Under Chapter 13 of the Bankruptcy Code, individual debtors may obtain adjustment of their indebtedness through a flexible repayment plan approved by a bankruptcy court. The real estate finance industry lobbied heavily to prevent mortgages from being rewritten by way of these plans. Congress addressed those concerns by amending § 1322 of the Bankruptcy Reform Act of 1978, which sets forth the elements of a confirmable Chapter 13 plan. The new language provided that the capacity of a debtor's plan to modify the rights of holders of secured claims was limited to claims "other than a claim secured only by a security interest in real property that is the debtor's principal residence." However, Congress's purpose was thwarted when four circuits held that § 1322(b)(2) allowed bifurcation of undersecured homestead mortgages, resulting ultimately in the Supreme Court's decision above.

Quicknotes

SECURED CLAIM A claim, the repayment of which is secured by collateral sufficient to repay the debt owed.

SECURITY INTEREST An interest in property that may be sold upon a default in payment of the debt.

Reorganization in Chapter 11: Operating the Debtor, Selling Assets & Proposing a Plan

Quick Reference Rules of Law

United Savings Assoc. of Texas v. Timbers of Inwood Forest Assoc.

Undersecured creditor (P) v. Chapter 11 debtor (D)

484 U.S. 365 (1988).

NATURE OF CASE: Appeal from reversal of judgment ordering post-petition interest payments to creditor.

FACT SUMMARY: Creditor United Savings Assoc. of Texas (P) argued that it was entitled to receive interest on the amount it would have received had it not been prevented, by the automatic stay, from foreclosing on the apartment project owned by debtor Timbers of Inwood Forest Assoc., Ltd. (D).

RULE OF LAW

An undersecured creditor is not entitled to receive special compensation for the delay caused by the automatic stay in foreclosing on its collateral.

FACTS: Timbers of Inwood Forest Assoc., Ltd. (Timbers) (D), a Chapter 11 debtor, owned an apartment project that was encumbered by a security interest held by United Savings Assoc. of Texas (United Savings) (P). The value of the apartment project, which was appreciating only slightly, was less than the amount of the debt. United Savings (P) was, therefore, an undersecured creditor. United Savings (P) moved for relief from the automatic stay that was preventing it from foreclosing on the project, on the ground that there was lack of "adequate protection" of its interest within the meaning of § 362(d)(1) of the Bankruptcy Code. Timbers (D) had agreed to pay United Savings (P) the post-petition rents from the apartment project, but United Savings (P) wanted more. It argued that it was entitled to receive compensation for its right (suspended by the stay) to take immediate possession of the apartment project and apply it in payment of the debt. It argued that this right was protected pursuant to § 362(d)(1) as an "interest in property" that had not been adequately protected. The bankruptcy and district courts agreed, and conditioned continuance of the stay on monthly payments by Timbers (D) equal to 12% per annum on the estimated amount realizable on foreclosure, $4,250,000. The Fifth Circuit, however, concluded that United Savings (P) was not entitled to interest on its collateral during the stay. The United States Supreme Court granted United Savings's (P) petition for certiorari.

ISSUE: Is an undersecured creditor entitled to receive special compensation for the delay caused by the automatic stay in foreclosing on its collateral?

HOLDING AND DECISION: (Scalia, J.) No. An undersecured creditor is not entitled to receive special compensation for the delay caused by the automatic stay in foreclosing on its collateral. Section 362(d) permits the bankruptcy court to grant relief from the stay "for cause, including the lack of adequate protection of an interest in property." However, an examination of other provisions of the Code that deal with secured creditors reveals that the term "interest in property" means a creditor's security interest, but does not include his right to immediate possession of the collateral on default. Under § 1129(b), which sets forth the standards for confirming a reorganization plan, a secured claimant has a right to receive, under a plan, the present value, or "indubitable equivalent" of his collateral. However, the claimant is not assured of receiving that amount immediately, but only upon completion of the reorganization. In any event, "indubitable equivalent" does not connote reimbursement for the use value of the collateral. Moreover, the legislative history of §§ 361 and 362(d)(1) contain no hint that § 362(d)(1) entitles an undersecured creditor to post-petition interest. Affirmed.

ANALYSIS

Circuits continue to disagree on what exactly a debtor must show in order to establish that collateral is "necessary to an effective reorganization" and thereby retain use of the collateral while a reorganization plan is being formulated. A minority of courts merely require a showing that the property is necessary for rehabilitation or liquidation. But a majority of the circuits require the debtor to also prove that there is a reasonable likelihood of a successful reorganization within a reasonable time. This view is supported by dictum setting forth that requirement in *Timbers*, which Justice Scalia included to refute United Savings's (P) argument that it would be subject to inordinate and extortionate delay if it were denied compensation.

Quicknotes

AUTOMATIC STAY Upon the filing of a voluntary bankruptcy petition, creditors are prohibited from attempting to recover payment from the debtor or his property.

Matter of Kmart Corporation

[Parties not identified.]

359 F.3d 866 (7th Cir. 2004).

NATURE OF CASE: Appeal from reversal of order authorizing payment of critical vendors in Chapter 11 reorganization.

FACT SUMMARY: Kmart Corporation argued that it should be allowed to pay all of its critical vendors because doing so would provide a residual benefit to the remaining, unfavored creditors.

🏛 RULE OF LAW
A critical-vendors order may not be issued, providing preferential payments to one class of creditors, where there is no evidence in the record that there is a possibility that the class of disfavored creditors will benefit.

FACTS: Kmart Corporation, in Chapter 11 bankruptcy, sought permission to pay immediately, and in full, the pre-petition claims of all "critical vendors." The bankruptcy court granted this request, without notifying any disfavored creditors, without receiving any pertinent evidence, and without making any finding of fact that disfavored creditors would gain or come out even. The bankruptcy court's order declared that the relief Kmart requested—open-ended permission to pay any debt to any vendor it deemed "critical" in the exercise of unilateral discretion, provided that the vendor agreed to furnish goods on "customary trade terms" for the next two years—was in the best interests of Kmart, its estate, and its creditors. The order did not explain why, nor did it contain any legal analysis, though it did cite § 105(a). Kmart used its authority to pay in full the pre-petition debts to 2,330 suppliers, which collectively received about $300 million. This came from the $2 billion in new credit (debtor-in-possession or DIP financing) that the bankruptcy judge authorized, granting the lenders super-priority in post-petition assets and revenues. Another 2,000 or so vendors were not deemed "critical" and were not paid. They and 43,000 additional unsecured creditors eventually received about 10 cents on the dollar, mostly in stock of the reorganized Kmart. The district court reversed the order authorizing payment, and the court of appeals granted review.

ISSUE: May a critical-vendors order be issued, providing preferential payments to one class of creditors, where there is no evidence in the record that there is a possibility that the class of disfavored creditors will benefit?

HOLDING AND DECISION: (Easterbrook, J.) No. A critical-vendors order may not be issued, providing preferential payments to one class of creditors, where there is no evidence in the record that there is a possibility that

the class of disfavored creditors will benefit. The theory behind a critical-vendors request is that that some suppliers may be unwilling to do business with a customer that is behind in payment, and, if it cannot obtain the merchandise that its own customers have come to expect, a firm such as Kmart may be unable to carry on, injuring all of its creditors. Full payment to critical vendors thus could in principle make even the disfavored creditors better off: they may not be paid in full, but they will receive a greater portion of their claims than they would if the critical vendors cut off supplies and the business shut down. Putting the proposition in this way implies, however, that the debtor must prove, and not just allege, two things: that, but for immediate full payment, vendors would cease dealing; and that the business will gain enough from continued transactions with the favored vendors to provide some residual benefit to the remaining, disfavored creditors, or at least leave them no worse off. Here, neither of these things was proven, so the issue becomes whether the bankruptcy court had authority under the Code to prefer some vendors over others. While § 105(a) permits a bankruptcy court to "issue any order, process, or judgment that is necessary or appropriate to carry out the provisions of" the Code, this does not create discretion to set aside the Code's rules about priority and distribution. Therefore, the bankruptcy court may not authorize full payment of any unsecured debt unless all unsecured creditors in the class are paid in full. Also, a "doctrine of necessity," which permits departure from the Code, does not authorize overriding the Code's provisions. Arguably § 363(b)(1), when read broadly, may provide such authority. That provision permits the trustee, or debtor-in-possession, to use property of the estate other than in the ordinary course of administering the estate. Satisfaction of a pre-petition debt to keep "critical" supplies flowing is a use of property other than in the ordinary course of administering an estate in bankruptcy. Nonetheless, it is prudent to read, and use, § 363(b)(1) to do the least damage possible to priorities established by contract and by other parts of the Code. The court here, however, need not decide whether § 363(b)(1) could support payment of some pre-petition debts, because this particular order was unsound no matter how one reads § 363(b)(1). Again, as stated earlier, that is because there was no evidence that the disfavored creditor would be better off with reorganization than liquidation, for example, or that the purportedly critical vendors would in fact have ceased deliveries if the old debts were left unpaid during the bankruptcy proceedings. If vendors will deliver

Continued on next page.

against a promise of current payment, then a reorganization can be achieved, and all unsecured creditors will obtain its benefit, without preferring any of the unsecured creditors. Some supposedly critical vendors will continue to do business with the debtor because they must. Also, Kmart could have paid cash or its equivalent. Some of the $2 billion line of credit could have been used to assure vendors that payment would be forthcoming for all post-petition transactions. The easiest way to do that would have been to put some of the $2 billion behind a standby letter of credit on which the bankruptcy judge could authorize unpaid vendors to draw. That would not have changed the terms on which Kmart and any of its vendors did business; it just would have demonstrated the certainty of payment. Yet the bankruptcy court did not explore the possibility of using a letter of credit to assure vendors of payment. The court did not find that any firm would have ceased doing business with Kmart if not paid for pre-petition deliveries, and the scant record would not have supported such a finding had one been made. The court did not find that discrimination among unsecured creditors was the only way to facilitate a reorganization. It did not find that the disfavored creditors were at least as well off as they would have been had the critical-vendors order not been entered. Even if § 362(b)(1) allows critical-vendors orders in principle, preferential payments to a class of creditors are proper only if the record shows the prospect of benefit to the other creditors. This record does not, so the critical-vendors order cannot stand. Affirmed.

▶ *ANALYSIS*

The 2005 Bankruptcy Act has significantly improved the position of trade vendors, regardless of whether they qualify for "critical vendor" status, by creating an administrative priority in favor of vendors for the value of all goods shipped to a debtor within 20 days of bankruptcy filing, § 503(b)(9). In addition, state reclamation rights under the Uniform Commercial Code are preserved for goods shipped within 45 days of filing. Such an expansion of reclamation rights could significantly curtail any limitations on critical-vendor orders such as those imposed in this case.

■━■

Quicknotes

CHAPTER 11 BANKRUPTCY A legal proceeding whereby a debtor, who is unable to pay his debts as they become due, is relieved of his obligation to pay his creditors through reorganization and payment from future income.

DEBTOR-IN-POSSESSION In a Chapter 11 proceeding, refers to a debtor who retains control of assets or property pursuant to a plan of reorganization.

LETTER OF CREDIT An agreement by a bank or other party that it will honor a customer's demand for payment upon the satisfaction of specified conditions.

POST-PETITION After bankruptcy petition has been filed.

PRE-PETITION Before bankruptcy petition has been filed.

UNILATERAL One-sided; involving only one person.

UNSECURED CREDITOR A creditor whose loan is not backed by specified collateral or a security agreement.

■━■

General Electric Credit Corp. v. Levin & Weintraub

Secured creditor (P) v. Bankruptcy attorneys (D)

739 F.2d 73 (2d Cir. 1984).

NATURE OF CASE: Appeal from order awarding interim compensation for professional services.

FACT SUMMARY: The law firm of Levin & Weintraub (D) contended that the legal fees that debtor Flagstaff Foodservice and its related companies (Flagstaff) had incurred during its Chapter 11 reorganization should be paid from assets of Flagstaff in which General Electric Credit Corp. (P) had a security interest.

RULE OF LAW
If expenses for the preservation or disposition of property are incurred primarily for the benefit of a creditor holding a security interest in the property, such expenses may be charged against the secured creditor.

FACTS: Flagstaff Foodservice and its related companies (Flagstaff) filed for reorganization under Chapter 11 of the Bankruptcy Code. They continued to operate as debtors-in-possession. General Electric Credit Corp. (GECC) (P) had been financing Flagstaff's operations for more than ten years. In order to provide short-term support to Flagstaff, the bankruptcy court authorized Flagstaff to borrow additional money from GECC (P) pursuant to a financing order. These loans were to be secured by a super-priority interest in all present and future property of Flagstaff's estate. Nevertheless, the Flagstaff reorganization ultimately failed. Accordingly, the value of the collateral that remained was insufficient to satisfy the unpaid balance of GECC's (P) claim. Levin & Weintraub (D), bankruptcy attorneys, requested the court award them $250,000 in legal fees, to be paid from the encumbered collateral. The bankruptcy court complied, and the district court affirmed the award. GECC (P) appealed.

ISSUE: If expenses for the preservation or disposition of property are incurred primarily for the benefit of a creditor holding a security interest in the property, may such expenses be charged against the secured creditor?

HOLDING AND DECISION: (Van Graafeiland, J.) Yes. If expenses for the preservation or disposition of property are incurred primarily for the benefit of a creditor holding a security interest in the property, such expenses may be charged against the secured creditor. Thus, Levin & Weintraub (D) had the burden in this case of proving that their fees were for services performed for GECC's (P) benefit. They failed to sustain that burden. Nor did GECC (P) consent to bearing the costs of Levin & Weintraub's (D) services by employing the Chapter 11 procedure to reduce its secured claims. Although a secured creditor may consent to bearing the costs of professional fees incurred by a debtor in possession, such consent is not to be lightly inferred. There is no evidence of it here. The financing order granting GECC (P) a super-priority position was intended to give GECC (P) protection against the very award made herein. Reversed and remanded.

▶ ANALYSIS

Payment of administration expenses such as interim fees for professional services has traditionally been the responsibility of the debtor's estate, not its secured creditors. Saddling unconsenting secured creditors with professional fees would discourage those creditors from financing reorganization efforts by Chapter 11 debtors. Bankruptcy attorneys, on the other hand, must be aware that the priority ordinarily given to administration expenses may prove elusive in light of the various provisions in the Code for competing or super-priorities. They would do well to secure a portion of their fee in advance.

■━■

Quicknotes

CHAPTER 11 REORGANIZATION A plan formulated pursuant to Chapter 11 of the Bankruptcy Code whereby a debtor, who is unable to pay his debts as they become due, is relieved of his obligation to pay his creditors through reorganization and payment from future income.

SECURED CREDITOR A creditor, the repayment of whose loan is secured by collateral sufficient to repay the debt owed.

SECURITY INTEREST An interest in property that may be sold upon a default in payment of the debt.

■━■

Hartford Underwriters Ins. Co. v. Union Planters Bank, N.A.

Insurance carrier (P) v. Secured creditor (D)

530 U.S. 1 (2000).

NATURE OF CASE: Appeal of non-allowance of an administrative claimant to independently receive payment of its claim.

FACT SUMMARY: Hartford Underwriters Ins. Co. (Hartford) (P) covered Hen House's workers' compensation premiums during Hen House's attempt to reorganize under Chapter 11. Hartford (P) subsequently sought to recover those funds from property secured by Union Planters Bank, N.A. (D) once Hen House's Chapter 11 proceeding was converted into Chapter 7.

RULE OF LAW

An administrative claimant of a bankruptcy estate cannot independently receive payment of its claim from property encumbered by a secured creditor's lien.

FACTS: Hen House Interstate, Inc. (Hen House), filed for Chapter 11, and as a debtor-in-possession it retained possession of its assets and continued to operate its business. Union Planters Bank, N.A. (Union) (D) had a security interest in essentially all of Hen House's property, which secured an indebtedness of over $4 million. Union (D) loaned Hen House an additional $300,000 to help finance its reorganization. Hen House used the loan to pay expenses, including a workers' compensation policy it obtained from Hartford Underwriters Ins. Co. (Hartford) (P), which was unaware of the bankruptcy proceedings. Although Hen House did not make monthly premium payments, Hartford (P) continued to provide the insurance. The reorganization attempt failed, and the case was converted to a Chapter 7 case. It was not until after the conversion that Hartford (P) learned of the bankruptcy filing by Hen House, and by then Hen House owed $50,000 in premiums. Hartford (P) subsequently charged the premiums to Union (D) by filing an application for allowance of administrative expenses and charge against collateral. The bankruptcy court allowed the application and the district court affirmed. The Eighth Circuit Court of Appeals reversed, and Hartford (P) appealed.

ISSUE: Can an administrative claimant of a bankruptcy estate independently receive payment of its claim from property encumbered by a secured creditor's lien?

HOLDING AND DECISION: (Scalia, J.) No. An administrative claimant of a bankruptcy estate cannot independently receive payment of its claim from property encumbered by a secured creditor's lien. Only the trustee can pursue such recovery. Hartford's (P) arguments based on pre-Code practice and policy considerations are not sufficient to meet its burden of having to prove that § 506(c) extends not only to the trustee, but to others as well. Although not stated directly in the Bankruptcy Act of 1898, it has been the norm since then that trustees be permitted to recover costs of administrating and preserving the property from a secured creditor. Lower court cases and early decisions from this Court regarding people other than the trustee having been allowed to do the same, however, do not establish a bankruptcy practice sufficiently widespread to say that the Code has implicitly adopted it. Moreover, it is not evident that Congress was aware of this practice when it adopted the Code. Furthermore, when the language of the Code is clear, there is no need to rely on pre-Code practice. In this case it is clear that § 506(c) allows the charge of costs to secured assets *by the trustee.* The Code does not say "to the trustee and other parties in interest." In addition, the trustee can seek recovery under § 506(c) whenever his fiduciary duties require him to do so. Other than relying on the trustee, those who provide goods and services that benefit secured interests could protect themselves by insisting on cash payment, contracting directly with the secured creditor, attempting to obtain super-priority or a security interest, or by being conscientious about to whom they are loaning money. Lastly, allowing recovery to be sought by those other than the trustee would impair the ability of the bankruptcy court to coordinate proceedings and the ability of the trustee to manage the estate. Also, secured creditors would be less willing to provide post-petition financing if such financing might be targeted by various administrative claimants whose claims might be weak. Affirmed.

▶ ANALYSIS

This case makes sense in that it is one of the main purposes of bankruptcy law for the trustee in bankruptcy to fairly pay creditors of the estate and not for creditors to individually go after the money they are owed.

■━■

Quicknotes

CHAPTER 7 BANKRUPTCY A legal proceeding whereby a debtor, who is unable to pay his debts as they become due, is relieved of his obligation to pay his creditors by liquidation and distribution of his remaining assets.

CHAPTER 11 BANKRUPTCY A legal proceeding whereby a debtor, who is unable to pay his debts as they become

Continued on next page.

due, is relieved of his obligation to pay his creditors through reorganization and payment from future income.

DEBTOR-IN-POSSESSION In a Chapter 11 proceeding, refers to a debtor who retains control of assets or property pursuant to a plan of reorganization.

SECURED CREDITOR A creditor, the repayment of whose loan is secured by collateral sufficient to repay the debt owed.

■≡■

Matter of Saybrook Manufacturing Co.

Pre-petition unsecured creditors (P) v. Post-petition lender (D)

963 F.2d 1490 (11th Cir. 1992).

NATURE OF CASE: Appeal of order denying a stay of a cross-colleralization financing agreement.

FACT SUMMARY: The Shapiros (P) objected to an order granting a post-petition lender's unsecured pre-petition claims priority over all other unsecured pre-petition claims.

🏛 RULE OF LAW
Cross-collateralization is an impermissible means of obtaining post-petition financing.

FACTS: After initiating bankruptcy proceedings, Saybrook Manufacturing Co. Inc. (D) and related companies filed a motion for the use of cash collateral and to obtain secured debt. The bankruptcy court entered an emergency financing order. Pursuant to the order, Manufacturers Hanover (D), a pre-petition creditor, received a security interest in all of the debtors' property in exchange for lending an additional $3 million. As a result, Manufacturers Hanover's (D) pre-petition debt, previously unsecured by approximately $24 million dollars, became fully secured. The Shapiros (P), pre-petition unsecured creditors, objected to this arrangement. The bankruptcy court overruled their objection and refused to grant a stay pending appeal. The district court dismissed the claim as moot under § 364(e) of the Bankruptcy Code because the Shapiros (P) failed to obtain a stay. The court of appeals granted review.

ISSUE: Is cross-collateralization an impermissible means of obtaining post-petition financing?

HOLDING AND DECISION: (Cox, J.) Yes. Cross-collateralization is an impermissible means of obtaining post-petition financing. Cross-collateralization occurs when, as a part of a post-petition financing agreement, pre-petition debt is secured by pre- and post-petition collateral. This process is inconsistent with the bankruptcy law for two reasons. First, cross-collateralization is not expressly authorized under the Bankruptcy Code. Section 364 permits Chapter 11 debtors to incur secured credit and debt upon reorganization. The section does not authorize liens to secure pre-petition loans. Second, cross-collateralization is beyond the bankruptcy court's inherent equitable power because it directly conflicts with the fundamental priority scheme of the Bankruptcy Code. Section 507 fixes the priority order of claims and expenses so that creditors in a given class are treated equally. The bankruptcy court may not create its own rules of superiority within a single class. Cross-collateralization does exactly that, and is therefore inconsistent with the Bankruptcy Code. As a result,

cross-collateralization is not authorized by § 364, and the Shapiros' (P) appeal is not moot. Reversed and remanded.

▶ ANALYSIS

Cross-collateralization, although controversial, has been approved by several bankruptcy courts. See, e.g., *In re Vanguard Diversified, Inc.*, 31 B.R. 364 (Bankr. E.D.N.Y. 1983). The *Vanguard* court noted that cross-collateralization is disfavored and should only be used as a last resort. The court then proceeded to outline a four-part test that debtors must satisfy before cross-collateralization will be approved: (1) business operations would fail absent the proposed financing, (2) alternative financing on acceptable terms is unobtainable, (3) the lender will not accept less preferential terms, and (4) the proposed financing is in the general creditor body's best interest. Other courts have since adopted this test.

Quicknotes

CROSS-COLLATERAL AGREEMENT Agreement under which both parties provide security that performance will be rendered or that payment will be made.

POST-PETITION After bankruptcy petition has been filed.

PRE-PETITION Before bankruptcy petition has been filed.

UNSECURED CREDITOR A creditor, the repayment of whose loan is not backed by specified collateral or a security agreement.

In re Chrysler LLC

[Parties not identified.]

576 F.3d 108, *vacated as moot*, 592 F.3d 370 (2009).

NATURE OF CASE: Appeal from an order authorizing the sale of substantially all of a Chapter 11 debtor's assets.

FACT SUMMARY: Various institutional investors, tort claimants, and others (collectively, "objectors") contended that the sale of substantially all of Chrysler LLC's (debtor's) assets pursuant to § 363(b) of the Bankruptcy Code so closely approximated a final plan of reorganization that it constituted an impermissible "sub rosa plan," so that reversal of the bankruptcy court's approval of the sale was required.

> ## ⚖ RULE OF LAW
> A sale of substantially all of a Chapter 11 debtor's assets under § 363(b) of the Bankruptcy Code does not constitute an impermissible, sub rosa plan of reorganization where there are good business reasons for the sale, including the fact that the only alternative to the sale would be the immediate liquidation of the debtor, which would yield far less for the estate than the sale.

FACTS: Chrysler LLC (debtor), one of the nation's largest automobile manufacturers, filed for Chapter 11 protection following months of deepening losses, the receipt of billions of dollars of government funds. Chrysler had unsuccessfully sought a merger partner and was unable to receive additional government funds for a stand-alone restructuring. Ultimately, it settled on an asset-sale transaction under § 363(b) of the Bankruptcy Code (Code), whereby substantially all of the debtor's assets would be sold to New CarCo Acquisition LLC (New Chrysler) in exchange for New Chrysler's assumption of certain liabilities and $2 billion in cash. Fiat S.p.A (Fiat) agreed to provide New Chrysler with certain fuel-efficient vehicle platforms, access to its worldwide distribution system, and new management experienced in turning around a failing auto company. Fiat's offer, however, was open for just a short period. Financing would come from the government and from Export Development Canada. Fiat, for its contributions, would immediately own 20% of the equity with rights to acquire more (up to 51%), contingent on payment in full of the debts owed to the government and Export Development Canada. The bankruptcy court, after approving the bidding process—no additional bids were made—and after making extensive findings of fact and conclusions of law, approved the sale. After several interim stays, involving court of appeals and United States Supreme Court review, the sale was consummated. Various institutional investors, tort claimants, and others

(collectively, "objectors") contended that the sale of substantially all of the debtor's assets, including its auto-manufacturing assets, intellectual property and selected dealership contractual rights, so closely approximated a final plan of reorganization that the sale constituted an impermissible "sub rosa plan," so that reversal of the bankruptcy court's approval of the sale was required. The court of appeals granted review.

ISSUE: Does a sale of substantially all of a Chapter 11 debtor's assets under § 363(b) of the Bankruptcy Code constitute an impermissible, sub rosa plan of reorganization where there are good business reasons for the sale, including the fact that the only alternative to the sale would be the immediate liquidation of the debtor, which would yield far less for the estate than the sale?

HOLDING AND DECISION: (Jacobs, C.J.) No. A sale of substantially all of a Chapter 11 debtor's assets under § 363(b) of the Bankruptcy Code does not constitute an impermissible, sub rosa plan of reorganization where there are good business reasons for the sale, including the fact that the only alternative to the sale would be the immediate liquidation of the debtor, which would yield far less for the estate than the sale. There is a conflict between the expediency of a § 363(b) sale and the otherwise applicable features and safeguards of Chapter 11. Case law has recognized, according to a "melting ice cube theory," that no emergency is needed to justify approval of a § 363(b) sale where it is more advantageous for the debtor to begin to sell as many assets as quickly as possible to assure that the assets do not lose value. Thus, where, as here, a good business opportunity is presently available, which might soon disappear, quick action may be justified to increase or maintain the value of the estate's assets by means of a sale. Such expediency, however, must be balanced against circumventing Chapter 11's safeguards for debtors, creditors, and equity holders. To balance these competing concerns, there must be a good business reason for the transaction, and the court must consider all salient factors. The transaction cannot be the result of strong-arming by a large creditor to bypass the requirements of Chapter 11 to cash out quickly at the expense of other stakeholders, in a proceeding that amounts to a reorganization in all but name, achieved by stealth and momentum. The size of the transaction is only one factor to be considered, so that a sale of all assets may not necessarily require rejection of the sale. Here, the objectors argue that the sale is improper mainly because it gives value to unsecured

Continued on next page.

creditors without paying off secured debt in full, and without complying with the procedural requirements of Chapter 11. However, the bankruptcy judge demonstrated proper solicitude for the priority between creditors and deemed it essential that the sale in no way upset that priority. The lien holders' security interests would attach to all proceeds of the sale, and all equity stakes in the new company would be entirely attributable to new value. Most importantly, the bankruptcy court, after making extensive findings of fact, concluded that there were good business reasons for the sale. A key factor was that the only possible alternative to the sale was an immediate liquidation that would yield far less for the estate—and for the objectors—than the sale. No other buyers were forthcoming, and the Fiat transaction was the only currently available, viable option. Whereas the sale would yield around $2 billion, a liquidation would likely yield around $800 million. Fiat's offer, moreover, was open for only a short time, and Chrysler was losing going concern value of nearly $100 million each day. For these reasons, the bankruptcy court did not abuse its discretion. Finally, contrary to the objectors' assertions, New Chrysler will not be a twin of the old company: it will make new models of cars, it will have a new CEO experienced in turning around failing automobile companies, it will be working under new contracts, and it will be selling its cars in new markets. Such transformative use of old and new assets is precisely what one would expect from the § 363(b) sale of a going concern. Affirmed.

▶ ANALYSIS

As this case illustrates, to balance the competing concerns of efficiency against the safeguards of the Chapter 11 process, a bankruptcy judge should consider all salient factors pertaining to the proceeding and, accordingly, act to further the diverse interests of the debtor, creditors, and equity holders, alike. A bankruptcy judge might, for example, look to such relevant factors as the proportionate value of the asset to the estate as a whole, the amount of elapsed time since the filing, the likelihood that a plan of reorganization will be proposed and confirmed in the near future, the effect of the proposed disposition on future plans of reorganization, the proceeds to be obtained from the disposition vis-à-vis any appraisals of the property, which of the alternatives of use, sale or lease the proposal envisions and, most importantly perhaps, whether the asset is increasing or decreasing in value. This list is not exclusive, but merely provides guidance as to the types of factors to be considered. The trend, especially after the economic crisis of 2008-2009, has been an increased use in § 363(b) sales, and this "side-door" route may well replace the main route of Chapter 11 reorganization plans, especially since the speed of the process can maximize asset value and yield the highest price for the assets sold.

In re PW

Junior lienholder (P) v. Secured creditor (D)

391 B.R. 25 (B.A.P. 9th Cir. 2008).

NATURE OF CASE: Appeal from sale order and confirmation order in Chapter 11 bankruptcy.

FACT SUMMARY: Clear Channel Outdoor, Inc. (Clear Channel) (P), a junior lienholder in PW, LLC's (PW's) property, asserted that DB Burbank, LLC (DB) (D), PW's secured creditor, was not permitted under Bankruptcy Code § 363(f) to credit bid its debt and purchase PW's property, taking title free and clear of Clear Channel's (P) junior liens. DB (D) and the bankruptcy estate trustee (Trustee) (D) asserted that Clear Channel's (P) appeal from the bankruptcy court's sale order was moot.

🏛 **RULE OF LAW**

(1) **Bankruptcy Code § 363(m) does not render moot a sale order under § 363(f)(5) to the extent that it approves lien-stripping.**

(2) **Outside a plan of reorganization, 11 U.S.C.S. § 363(f) does not permit a secured creditor to credit bid its debt and purchase estate property, taking title free and clear of valid, nonconsenting junior liens.**

FACTS: PW, LLC owned prime real estate. DB Burbank, LLC (DB) (D), held a first-priority lien of more than $40 million secured by PW's property. Ultimately, because of numerous problems with its development plan, and the unfulfilled need to consolidate various real estate parcels, PW filed for Chapter 11 bankruptcy, and a trustee (Trustee) (D) was appointed. DB (D), which had previously instituted foreclosure proceedings and had secured the appointment of a receiver, worked with the Trustee (D) to obtain all the necessary parcels, consolidate all of PW's property and development rights, and sell this package, free and clear of all claims and encumbrances, at a sale supervised by the bankruptcy court. The Trustee (D) and DB (D) entered into an agreement called a "Binding Term Sheet," which established detailed sale procedures for an auction and sale of PW's assets. This agreement provided that DB (D) would serve as a stalking horse bidder for a sale of PW's property. If there were no qualified overbidders, DB (D) would buy PW's property for $41,434,465, which the parties called the "Strike Price." In addition, DB (D) agreed to pay the Trustee (D) a "Carve-Out Amount" of up to $800,000 for certain administrative fees and other expenses. DB (D) also agreed not to seek relief from the automatic stay. The bankruptcy court entered an order establishing a procedure for the sale of PW's property, and the Trustee (D) moved to approve the sale free and clear of liens under §§ 363(f)(3) and (f)(5) of the

Bankruptcy Code. However, Clear Channel Outdoor, Inc. (Clear Channel) (P), which had a $2.5 million junior lien in PW's property, opposed the motion, asserting that § 363(f) was inapplicable. Over Clear Channel's (P) objection, the bankruptcy court entered a separate order authorizing the sale free and clear of Clear Channel's (P) lien under § 363(f)(5) (Sale Order). At the sale, there were no qualified overbidders, so the terms of the Binding Term Sheet kicked in, and DB (D) was the highest bidder, paying its consideration by credit-bidding the entire amount of its debt. The bankruptcy court then confirmed the sale to DB (D), finding that DB (D) was a purchaser in good faith and entering an order to this effect (Confirmation Order). When Clear Channel (P) sought a stay of that order pending appeal, the bankruptcy court denied the requested stay, as did a motions panel of the court of appeals. Clear Channel (P) appealed both the Sale Order and the Confirmation Order, and the Court of Appeals Bankruptcy Panel granted review.

ISSUE:

(1) Does Bankruptcy Code § 363(m) render moot a sale order under § 363(f)(5) to the extent that it approves lien-stripping?

(2) Outside a plan of reorganization, does 11 U.S.C.S. § 363(f) permit a secured creditor to credit bid its debt and purchase estate property, taking title free and clear of valid, nonconsenting junior liens?

HOLDING AND DECISION: (Markell, J.)

(1) No. Bankruptcy Code § 363(m) does not render moot a sale order under § 363(f)(5) to the extent that it approves lien-stripping. Under § 363(m), sales of property of the estate under § 363(b) and (c) are protected where the purchaser has acted in good faith, unless the sale is stayed pending appeal. This provision is a codification of some aspects of equitable mootness with respect to sales, but provides for specific procedures and findings in order to provide certainty for sales. Because these procedures and findings were satisfied here, the transfer of title to DB (D) is unaffected, and Clear Channel's (P) claim as to such transfer of title is moot. Nevertheless, the Confirmation Order authorized both a sale of PW's property and lien-stripping, which raises the issue of whether § 363(m) applies to lien-stripping authorizations under § 363(f). The short answer is that it does not. First, § 363(m) applies to subsections (b) and (c), not (f), and here, Clear Channel's (P) remaining challenge is to the authorization

Continued on next page.

under subsection (f) to sell the property free of its lien. Second, § 363(m) limits only the ability to affect the validity of a sale or lease. Thus, by its plain language, § 363(m) does not protect an out-of-the-ordinary-course use approved by a bankruptcy court. Congress intended that § 363(m) address only changes of title or other essential attributes of a sale, so that the "free and clear" terms of a sale are not protected by it. Other sections of the Bankruptcy Code show that Congress knew how to, and could have, broadened the protection of § 363(m) to include lien-stripping. DB (D) argues that the lien-stripping language of the order cannot be separated from the language authorizing the sale, but it is clear that Congress did not intend the two types of actions to receive the same level of protection, i.e., transferring title is not the same as stripping a lien. Moreover, DB (D), as a sophisticated lender, knew that relying solely on § 363(f)(5) to strip Clear Channel's (P) lien was risky, and was an indirect effort to achieve what it could not achieve directly. In other words, DB (D) cannot mask an improper condition of the transfer—avoiding appellate review—by cloaking it as an essential and inseparable part of a sale, especially since it is doubtful under the circumstances, where a bond staying the consummation of the deal would have been far in excess of the lien that Clear Channel (P) was trying to protect, that seeking a stay pending the appeal was Clear Channel's (P) exclusive remedy. Under such circumstances, lien-stripping under § 363(f)(5) is not protected under § 363(m), and Clear Channel's (P) claim as to the lien-stripping is not moot.

(2) No. Outside a plan of reorganization, 11 U.S.C.S. § 363(f) does not permit a secured creditor to credit bid its debt and purchase estate property, taking title free and clear of valid, nonconsenting junior liens. Section 363(f) authorizes sales free and clear of interests under five circumstances, three of which are inapplicable here (paragraphs (1), (2), and (4)). Thus, it must be determined whether paragraphs (3) or (5) authorize stripping Clear Channel's (P) lien. Paragraph (3) provides for a sale free and clear if the interest involved is a lien and the price at which the property is to be sold is greater than the aggregate value of all liens on such property. Paragraph (5) provides for a sale free and clear if the interest holder can be compelled, in a legal or equitable proceeding, to accept a money satisfaction of the interest. These two paragraphs pose statutory construction challenges, and principles of statutory construction must be applied thereto. First, the presumption is that the accepted and plain meaning of the words used reflects the sense in which Congress used them. Second, the legislative history must inform the language of the statute, which must be read in the context of bankruptcy law. Third, even undefined words and phrases in the Bankruptcy Code should presumptively receive the same construction, even if found in different parts of the code. When these principles are

applied, it becomes clear that § 363(f)(3) is inapplicable where the property sells for less than the amount of claims secured by the property. The Trustee (D) asserts that the "aggregate value of all liens" in § 363(f)(3) means the economic value of such liens, rather than their face value, so that the paragraph applies to the lien-stripping at issue. This argument is supported by some case law that holds that the paragraph may be used to sell free and clear of the property rights of junior lienholders whose nonbankruptcy liens are not supported by the collateral's value—where the liens are "out of the money." Such an interpretation, however, expands the paragraph too far, since it would allow a trustee to sell estate property free and clear of any lien, regardless of whether the lienholder held an allowed secured claim. Based on the context of § 363(f)(3), and its language, which requires that "the price at which such property is to be sold is greater than the aggregate value of all liens . . . ," lien-stripping cannot occur under this paragraph where the price of the property is equal to or less than the aggregate amount of all claims by creditors who hold a lien or security interest in the property being sold. Otherwise, if "aggregate value of all liens" is taken to mean the aggregate amount of all allowed secured claims as used in § 506(a), then the paragraph could never be used to authorize a sale free and clear in circumstances where, as here, the claims exceed the value of the collateral that secures them. As for the proper construction of § 363(f)(5), it should be noted that courts are split over the interpretation of each of its elements. The last element of this paragraph is "interest," the meaning of which must be determined. Clear Channel's (P) assertion that "interest" must be read narrowly to exclude interests such as its junior lien must be rejected, since Congress intended "interest" to have an expansive scope. Some courts have supported such an expansive reading, and the entire section's plain language, which broadly refers to "any interest," also supports such an interpretation. Further, the definition of "lien" in the Code precludes a narrow reading, since lien is defined, in part, as an "interest" in property. Accordingly, "interest" includes the type of lien at issue in this case. The next element of § 363(f)(5) that must be interpreted is whether the nondebtor [here Clear Channel (P)] can be compelled to accept a money satisfaction. Given that a lien is an interest, the issue becomes whether Clear Channel (P) could be compelled to accept a money satisfaction of its lien. The bankruptcy court found the paragraph applicable whenever a claim or interest can be paid with money—a plausible interpretation if the paragraph is read in isolation. However, while it is axiomatic that liens securing payment obligations can

Continued on next page.

be satisfied by paying the money owed, it does not necessarily follow that such liens can be satisfied by paying any sum, regardless of how large or small. Therefore, it is assumed that the paragraph refers to those proceedings in which the interest holder can be compelled to take less than the value of the claim secured by the interest. Otherwise, if full payment were required, the paragraph would be superfluous, since it would merely mirror § 363(f)(3). Thus, there must be a showing of a basis that could be used to compel acceptance of less than full monetary satisfaction. Such an interpretation, albeit a narrow one, complements the remaining four paragraphs without overlapping with them. If, however, the interest is such that it may be vindicated only by compelling or restraining some action, it does not qualify under this element. The narrow reading of this element of § 363(f)(5) is also supported by the statutory context. Not only would a broad reading render § 363(f)(3) superfluous, it would also be inconsistent with § 1206, which supplemented a trustee's rights under § 363(f) in Chapter 12 where the sale involved farmland or farm equipment. Because § 1206 provides an absolute right, which is not contained in § 363(f)(5), a narrow interpretation of the latter is required. Section 1206 expressly applies to liens, so it would have been unnecessary with respect to liens if § 363(f)(5) already permitted a sale. Therefore, the bankruptcy court must make a finding of the existence of such a mechanism and the trustee must demonstrate how satisfaction of the lien "could be compelled." As to the final element of § 363(f)(5), a proceeding at law or equity that exists or could be brought, the issue is whether there is such a nonbankruptcy proceeding in which Clear Channel (P) could be compelled to release its lien for payment of an amount that is less than full value of its claim. The bankruptcy court, finding that all liens can be satisfied by money, reasoned that it did not need to prove the existence or possibility of a qualifying legal or equitable proceeding. However, no such proceeding has been identified. The reasoning of courts that have found that cramdown under § 1129(b)(2) is a qualifying legal or equitable proceeding is unpersuasive, since use of the cramdown mechanism to allow a sale free and clear under § 363(f)(5) uses circular reasoning by sanctioning the effect of cramdown without requiring any of § 1129(b)'s substantive and procedural protections. Moreover, § 1129(b)(2) permits cramdown of a lien only in the context of plan confirmation. Using § 363(b) instead would gut plan confirmation or render it superfluous. Accordingly, Congress did not intend under § 363(f)(5) that nonconsensual confirmation be a type of legal or equitable proceeding to which that paragraph refers. As a result, the availability of cramdown under § 1129(b)(2) is not a legal or equitable proceeding to which § 363(f)(5) is applicable. For the foregoing reasons, the bankruptcy court applied the wrong legal standard under § 363(f)(5). On remand, the parties should attempt to identify a qualifying proceeding under nonbankruptcy law that would permit stripping Clear Channel (P) of its lien. Reversed and remanded.

▶ *ANALYSIS*

Under the court's narrow reading of § 363(f)(5), there will be few instances where it can be shown that there is a basis for compelling monetary satisfaction for less than full payment of the debt related to the interest to be extinguished. Nonetheless, there are some circumstances where a narrowly construed § 363(f)(5) might be applicable. One might be a buy-out arrangement among partners, in which the controlling partnership agreement provides for a valuation procedure that yields something less than market value of the interest being bought out. Another might be a case in which specific performance might normally be granted, but the presence of a liquidated-damages clause allows a court to satisfy the claim of a nonbreaching party in cash instead of a forced transfer of property. Finally, another might be satisfaction of obligations related to a conveyance of real estate that normally would be specifically performed but for which the parties have agreed to a damage remedy. In all these instances, a court could arguably compel the holders of the interest to take less than what their interest was worth.

■▬■

Quicknotes

CHAPTER 11 BANKRUPTCY A legal proceeding whereby a debtor, who is unable to pay his debts as they become due, is relieved of his obligation to pay his creditors through reorganization and payment from future income.

LIEN A claim against the property of another in order to secure the payment of a debt.

SECURITY INTEREST An interest in property that may be sold upon a default in payment of the debt.

■▬■

Century Glove v. First American Bank of New York

Debtor (P) v. Creditor (D)

860 F.2d 94 (3d Cir. 1988).

NATURE OF CASE: Appeal of order dismissing sanctions.

FACT SUMMARY: Century Glove, Inc. (P) claimed that First American Bank (D) solicited the votes of other creditors, in violation of Bankruptcy Code § 1125.

🏛 RULE OF LAW
Section 1125 of the Bankruptcy Code does not require that all communications between creditors be approved by the court, nor does § 1125 bar discussion or negotiations over a plan leading up to its presentation.

FACTS: Century Glove, Inc. (Century) (P) filed a petition seeking reorganization and, thereafter, filed a reorganization plan, along with a drafted disclosure statement. First American Bank (FAB) (D) questioned whether the unsecured creditors' committee should endorse the Century (P) plan, arguing that lawsuits, claimed as assets by Century (P), were too speculative. Ultimately, the committee chose to follow the Century (P) plan, and the bankruptcy court approved Century's (P) disclosure statement. FAB (D) then sought to find out what other creditors thought of the Century (P) plan and to convince them to vote against it. During the course of telephone conversations with the other creditors, FAB's (D) counsel stated that no other plan was approved for presentation, but FAB (D) had drafted a plan and tried to file it. The other attorneys asked for and received copies of the plan. The copies were marked drafts, and accompanying cover letters stated that they were submitted to the creditors for comments. After receiving several rejections, Century (P) petitioned the bankruptcy court to designate or invalidate the votes of FAB (D) and two other creditors. The bankruptcy court held that a solicitee may not be given materials outside of the plan, the disclosure statement, and other court-approved material. FAB (D) violated § 1125(b) by providing additional materials such as copies of its draft plan. In addition, the court concluded that FAB (D) had violated the spirit of exclusivity periods under § 1121 since FAB (D) apparently sought approval of its unfiled plan. Upon these findings, the court imposed sanctions against FAB (D) and invalidated the vote of another creditor who rejected Century's (P) plan. On appeal, the district court reversed. Century (P) appealed.

ISSUE: Does § 1125 require that all communications between creditors be approved by the court or bar discussion or negotiations over a plan leading up to its presentation?

HOLDING AND DECISION: (Hunter, III, J.) No. Section 1125 does not require that all communications between creditors be approved by the court, nor does § 1125 bar discussion or negotiations over a plan leading up to its presentation. In this case, the bankruptcy court assumed that only approved statements may be communicated to creditors and that sending a drafted, unfiled plan equaled solicitation in violation of § 1121(b) exclusivity periods. However, the Code never limits the facts that a creditor may receive. Instead it guarantees a minimum amount of information and defines when a creditor may be solicited. Hence, a creditor may receive information from sources other than the disclosure statement. As such, FAB (D) did not violate bankruptcy rules, when it disclosed the additional material in seeking rejection of Century's (P) plan. Although § 1125 did not limit FAB (D) in solicitation of rejections, §§ 1125 and 1121 prevented FAB (D) from soliciting official votes for the acceptances of its own plan during the exclusivity period. However, FAB (D) was not barred from negotiating with other creditors regarding its unfiled plan. Here, FAB (D) never asked for votes, and as such it did not solicit acceptances within the meaning of § 1125. The order reversing imposition of costs against FAB (D) is affirmed.

▶ ANALYSIS

A reorganization plan must be submitted to the various classes of impaired claims or interests for their acceptance or rejection. Hence, a reorganization plan is usually the product of negotiation between the debtor and its creditors. However, regardless of how a plan is reached, soliciting acceptance or rejection of the plan is impermissible unless a disclosure statement has been approved by the court and issued to the holders of claims and interests.

◼▭◼

In re Figter Limited

Secured creditor (D) v. Debtor (P)

118 F.3d 635 (9th Cir 1997).

NATURE OF CASE: Appeal from decision that the holder of a first deed of trust bought twenty-one unsecured claims in good faith and that it could vote each one separately.

FACT SUMMARY: Figter Limited (P), a debtor in Chapter 11 bankruptcy, alleged that Teachers Insurance and Annuity Association of America (D), a secured creditor that bought out other unsecured claims, acted in bad faith and should be limited to a single vote.

> ## 🏛 RULE OF LAW
> On request of a party in interest, and after notice and a hearing, the court may designate (disqualify from voting) any entity whose acceptance or rejection of a plan was not in good faith.

FACTS: Figter Limited (Figter) (P), a Chapter 11 debtor and owner of an apartment complex, proposed a reorganization plan that contemplated full payment of a promissory note, but at a disputed rate of interest. Under the plan, the claim of Teachers Insurance and Annuity Association of America (Teachers) (D), a secured creditor, was not impaired and unsecured claims were impaired at only 80% of their face value. Teachers (D) then purchased 21 of the 34 unsecured claims and filed the proper notices of transfer of claims. As a result, Figter's (P) plan was unconfirmable because it was unable to meet the requirement that there would not be an impaired, consenting class of claims. That would preclude a cramdown of the secured claim. Figter (P) appealed in an attempt to avoid that result. Figter (P) asserted that Teachers (D) should be precluded from voting its purchased claims because it did not buy them in good faith. Alternatively, Figter (P) claimed that, even if they were purchased in good faith, Teachers (D) could not vote them separately, but was limited to one total vote as a Class 3 creditor. The bankruptcy court decided that, in this case, Teachers (D) was a creditor that acted in a good faith attempt to protect its interests and not with some ulterior motive, and that there was no reason to hold that the separate claims should suddenly become only one vote. The district court affirmed. Figter (P) appealed.

ISSUE: On request of a party in interest, and after notice and a hearing, may the court designate (disqualify from voting) any entity whose acceptance or rejection of a plan was not in good faith?

HOLDING AND DECISION: (Fernandez, J.) Yes. On request of a party in interest, and after notice and a hearing, the court may designate (disqualify from voting) any entity whose acceptance or rejection of a plan was not in good faith. This provision of the Bankruptcy Code was intended to apply to those who were not attempting to protect their own proper interests, but who were, instead, attempting to obtain some benefit to which they were not entitled. Figter (P) cites no authority for holding that in a single asset bankruptcy, claim purchasing activities like those of Teachers (D) are in bad faith. It cannot be said that the bankruptcy court erred in deciding that Teachers (D) acted in good faith and that it could vote each of its 21 claims separately. Affirmed.

▶ ANALYSIS

Teachers (D) ultimately was able to purchase enough of the unsecured claims in this case to block Figter's (P) plan. Only impaired classes vote since the unimpaired classes are deemed to have accepted the plan. The definition of "impairment" is set forth in § 1124 of the Bankruptcy Code.

Quicknotes

CHAPTER 11 REORGANIZATION A plan formulated pursuant to Chapter 11 of the Bankruptcy Code whereby a debtor, who is unable to pay his debts as they become due, is relieved of his obligation to pay his creditors through reorganization and payment from future income.

CRAMDOWN Refers to a court's confirmation of a reorganization plan in a bankruptcy proceeding despite the opposition of creditors.

SECURED CREDITOR A creditor, the repayment of whose loan is secured by collateral sufficient to repay the debt owed.

In re U.S. Truck Co.

Debtor (P) v. Creditor (D)

800 F.2d 581 (6th Cir. 1986).

NATURE OF CASE: Appeal from order confirming reorganization plan.

FACT SUMMARY: The Teamsters National Freight Industry Negotiating Committee (Teamsters Committee) (D) argued that debtor U.S. Truck Co. (P) impermissibly segregated its claim from other substantially similar claims in order to assure acceptance of its reorganization plan.

> **RULE OF LAW**
> There must be some limit on a debtor's power to classify creditors in such a way as to segregate those creditors who assent to the reorganization plan from those who do not.

FACTS: Following the filing of its petition for bankruptcy, U.S. Truck Co. (P) sought to reject a collective bargaining agreement it had previously entered into with the Teamsters National Freight Industry Negotiating Committee (Teamsters Committee) (D). The bankruptcy court approved such rejection, and held that it was essential to effect the reorganization plan. U.S. Truck (P) entered into new agreements with each of the local unions reducing wages and requiring the employees to purchase their own equipment, which they subsequently leased to U.S. Truck (P). The reorganization plan contained twelve classes of claims. Only the Teamsters Committee (D) opposed the plan. The district court confirmed the plan. The Teamsters Committee (D) appealed, arguing that U.S. Truck (P) impermissibly gerrymandered the classes in order to neutralize the Teamster Committee's (D) dissenting vote.

ISSUE: Must there be some limit on a debtor's power to classify creditors in such a way as to segregate those who assent from those who dissent?

HOLDING AND DECISION: (Kennedy, J.) Yes. There must be some limit on a debtor's power to classify creditors in such a way as to segregate those creditors who assent to the reorganization plan from those who do not. The requirements for confirmation of a reorganization plan are delineated in § 1129. Under § 1129(a), the plan must satisfy eleven requirements, including the requirement that all impaired classes approve the plan. Alternatively, § 1129(b) sets forth the same requirements, excluding the approval by the impaired classes, and sets forth two added requisites. Approval under this provision is called a "cramdown" since reorganization may be effected without unanimous consent by the impaired classes. The Bankruptcy Code is silent on the issue of whether similar impaired claims against the same property may be classified separately.

Courts have interpreted the omission to intend that while similar claims are not required to be classified jointly, a class of claims must be substantially similar. Traditionally, lower courts have been accorded wide latitude in reviewing the proposed classification of impaired claims. Here, the district court distinguished the claims of the Teamsters Committee (D) from those of the other impaired classes in that its employees would benefit from the plan's rejection, and the committee had alternative methods of safeguarding its interests. Thus, U.S. Truck (P) was justified in segregating the committee's claim from those of other impaired creditors due to the dissimilarity of the Teamsters Committee's (D) interests. Affirmed.

ANALYSIS

A common issue in reorganization under Chapter 11 is the amount of discretion afforded by the Bankruptcy Code to the proponent of a reorganization plan in composing the membership of its classes of claims. The § 1129 requirement that all impaired classes or interests accept the plan provides an inducement to the proponent of the plan to structure it so that dissenting claims are placed in a class where their disapproval may be diluted. Note that the holding in this case did not resolve the issue of whether the Bankruptcy Code mandates the classification of similar impaired claims collectively; rather, the Teamsters Committee's (D) separate classification was permissible in that its interest in the reorganization was determined to be substantially dissimilar.

Quicknotes

CHAPTER 11 REORGANIZATION A plan formulated pursuant to Chapter 11 of the Bankruptcy Code whereby a debtor, who is unable to pay his debts as they become due, is relieved of his obligation to pay his creditors through reorganization and payment from future income.

CRAMDOWN Refers to a court's confirmation of a reorganization plan in a bankruptcy proceeding despite the opposition of creditors.

Matter of Greystone III Joint Venture

Debtor (P) v. Deficiency creditor (D)

995 F.2d 1274 (5th Cir. 1991).

NATURE OF CASE: Appeal from district court order affirming confirmation of reorganization plan.

FACT SUMMARY: Phoenix Mutual Life Insurance Corporation (Phoenix) (D) challenged the confirmation of Greystone's (P) reorganization plan on the basis that Greystone (P) impermissibly classified Phoenix's (D) claim in a manner so as to procure approval of its plan.

⚖ RULE OF LAW
Section 1122(a) of the Bankruptcy Code mandates that claims that are substantially similar in respect to their rights and interests in the debtor's estate must be grouped in the same class.

FACTS: Phoenix Mutual Life Insurance Corporation (Phoenix) (D) loaned Greystone (P) $8.8 million for the purchase of an office building. Greystone (P) defaulted, and Phoenix (D) initiated foreclosure proceedings. Greystone (P) filed for reorganization under Chapter 11 of the Bankruptcy Code. The bankruptcy court bifurcated Phoenix's (D) claim into a secured portion of $5,825,000, constituting the market value of the property, and an unsecured portion of $3,500,000. Greystone's (P) second reorganization plan segregated the unsecured claims of Phoenix (D) from those of the other unsecured creditors. Greystone (P) also contended that its office-building tenants constituted an impaired class whose votes for the plan should be considered to satisfy cramdown. The bankruptcy court confirmed a slightly modified version of the plan, and the district court affirmed. Phoenix (D) appealed.

ISSUE: Does the Bankruptcy Code mandate that substantially similar claims must be grouped in the same class?

HOLDING AND DECISION: (Jones, J.) Yes. Section 1122(a) of the Bankruptcy Code mandates that claims that are substantially similar in respect to their rights and interests in the debtor's estate must be grouped in the same class. Such classification allows the equal treatment of creditors with similar interests in the estate and ensures that the debtor cannot manipulate the approval of the plan by discretionarily tailoring the classes of claims. While the statutory language of § 1122(a) does not prohibit the separate classification of similar claims, courts agree that such distinctions may not be made for the sole purpose of procuring the approval of a reorganization plan. Thus, if the proponent of the plan can demonstrate sufficient reasons for the classification other than manipulation of the voting process, then the classification must be upheld. Here no rationale was proffered for distinguishing the

claim of Phoenix (D) from those of other unsecured creditors. Thus, the lower courts erred in permitting the separate classification. Moreover, a party to a lease agreement is entitled to vote in respect to a reorganization plan only where the debtor rejects the lease, thereby giving rise to a claim in the bankruptcy estate. Here the record demonstrates that Greystone (P) did not reject its leases with the tenant security deposit holders. Thus, the tenants did not meet the definition of creditors entitled to vote on the reorganization plan. Reversed and remanded.

▶ ANALYSIS

The issue of classification results from the requirements of § 1129(a) regarding the approval of a reorganization plan. This section requires that each class of claims vote individually on the approval of the proffered reorganization plan. In order to be confirmed, a reorganization plan must be approved by two-thirds of the impaired classes, or in the situation of a cramdown, by at least one impaired class of creditors. Thus, the unfettered discretion on the part of the debtor to classify claims would result in a disproportionate advantage to the debtor to tailor his plan accordingly.

Quicknotes

BANKRUPTCY ESTATE   Created by the filing of a petition in bankruptcy and includes all legal and equitable interests of the debtor in property as of that time.

CHAPTER 11 REORGANIZATION   A plan formulated pursuant to Chapter 11 of the Bankruptcy Code whereby a debtor, who is unable to pay his debts as they become due, is relieved of his obligation to pay his creditors through reorganization and payment from future income.

CRAMDOWN   Refers to a court's confirmation of a reorganization plan in a bankruptcy proceeding despite the opposition of creditors.

UNSECURED CREDITOR   A creditor, the repayment of whose loan is not backed by specified collateral or a security agreement.

CHAPTER 1

Reorganization in Chapter 11: Confirming a Plan

Quick Reference Rules of Law

In re Orfa Corp. of Philadelphia

[Parties not identified.]

129 B.R. 404 (Bankr. E.D. Pa. 1991).

NATURE OF CASE: Review of reorganization plan.

FACT SUMMARY: SPNB, BEC, and Licensors challenged the confirmation of a reorganization plan on the basis that the plan was not feasible under § 1129(a)(11) of the Bankruptcy Code.

RULE OF LAW
A reorganization plan based upon funding from new investments may be deemed feasible under § 1129(a)(11) of the Bankruptcy Code.

FACTS: Orfa Corp. and two other related corporations (Debtors) were licensed to recycle solid waste. After they each declared bankruptcy, two creditors (Proponents) filed a reorganization plan. Two other creditors, SPNB and BEC, and Licensors challenged the reorganization plan on the basis that it was not feasible under § 1129(a)(11) of the Bankruptcy Code. The plan treated all the creditors as if the Debtors had been consolidated into a single case. SPNB's secured and unsecured claims were combined, and SPNB was to receive full payment on the condition that the Proponents of the plan obtained financing. In the event the condition was not satisfied, the Proponents would seek a private placement of the Debtors' preferred classes of shares. BEC's claim was placed into a pool comprising all the Debtors' unsecured claims, to be paid 20% on the effective date, and the remaining 80% quarterly thereafter. Licensors' licenses were to be assumed and their claims to be paid in full on the effective date. The bankruptcy judge ordered the plan to be amended, but addressed the feasibility issue separately.

ISSUE: May a reorganization plan based upon funding from new investments be deemed feasible under § 1129(a)(11) of the Bankruptcy Code?

HOLDING AND DECISION: (Scholl, J.) Yes. A reorganization plan based upon funding from new investments may be deemed feasible under § 1129(a)(11) of the Bankruptcy Code. In determining the feasibility of a reorganization plan, the court must consider certain factors. These include the corporation's sufficiency of capital, earning capabilities, management's skill, continuity of management, the prevailing economic atmosphere, and any other relevant factors contributing to the successful enactment of the plan. Here the discontinuation of the Debtors' management weighs heavily in favor of confirmation, due to incumbent management's lack of capable performance. Moreover, Orfa's prognosis of earning capabilities is strong due to recent technological advancements and the necessity of waste disposal and recycling in society. The plan proposing to sell SPNB's stock is a potentially successful means of generating revenue amidst contemporary economic conditions. While the Debtors lack adequate capital, the primary goal of the plan is to generate revenue. Thus, the court holds the plan to be feasible in accord with § 1129(a)(11).

ANALYSIS

In Chapter 11, in order for a reorganization plan to be confirmed by the bankruptcy court, it must be "feasible" under § 1129(a)(11). "Feasibility" refers to the determination that implementation of the plan will most probably not result in a liquidation of the bankruptcy estate or in further reorganization by the debtor. The nature of the reorganization process requires that such feasibility be determined according to the circumstances of each individual case.

Quicknotes

CHAPTER 11 REORGANIZATION A plan formulated pursuant to Chapter 11 of the Bankruptcy Code whereby a debtor, who is unable to pay his debts as they become due, is relieved of his obligation to pay his creditors through reorganization and payment from future income.

SECURED CLAIM A claim, the repayment of which is secured by collateral sufficient to repay the debt owed.

Till v. SCS Credit Corporation

Debtors (P) v. Subprime lender (D)

541 U.S. 465 (2004).

NATURE OF CASE: Challenge to rate of interest in proposed plan.

FACT SUMMARY: Congress did not specify a particular method to determine an appropriate interest rate under the Bankruptcy Code's cramdown provision. Four judicial opinions offered four separate methods.

RULE OF LAW

The formula approach is the proper method to calculate the appropriate discount interest rate under Chapter 13 reorganization.

FACTS: Lee and Amy Till (P) financed a used truck through Instant Auto, which assigned the loan to SCS Credit Corporation (SCS) (D), a subprime lender. The loan's interest rate was 21% and the Tills (P) were to make 68 payments. The Tills (P) defaulted and filed for Chapter 13 reorganization. Their proposed plan used the "formula approach" to offer to pay the secured auto loan at 9.5% interest—the prime rate of 8% plus an adjustment to account for the risk of their default. The bankruptcy court approved the cramdown interest rate and confirmed the plan. SCS (D) appealed, arguing that 21% interest was the standard in the subprime lending market. The district court reversed based on the "coerced loan" approach, which applies the interest rate at the foreclosure and similar re-investment level. Based on SCS's (D) unrebutted testimony, 21% was that rate. On appeal, the Seventh Circuit applied the "presumptive contract rate" approach, which set the 21% interest rate as a rebuttable presumption. The Seventh Circuit remanded to allow the Tills (P) the opportunity to rebut the presumptive 21%. The dissenting judge on the Seventh Circuit opinion would have applied the "cost of funds" approach, which seeks to avoid overcompensating secured creditors by discounting rates for costs associated with issuing a new loan. The United States Supreme Court granted certiorari review to determine the appropriate method from among the four proffered in this case.

ISSUE: Is the formula approach the proper method to calculate the appropriate discount interest rate under Chapter 13 reorganization?

HOLDING AND DECISION: (Stevens, J.) Yes. The formula approach is the proper method to calculate the appropriate discount interest rate under Chapter 13 reorganization. Creditors must be adequately compensated for a debtor's promise of future payment because the money is not immediately available to the creditor, inflation may occur, and the debtor could default. The interest rate is used to compensate for these factors. The approach to determine that interest rate should be a familiar financial approach, ensuring the creditor receives present-day value of its claim, and the inquiry into the terms of the cramdown loan should be an objective one. The bankruptcy court unambiguously has the right to modify the terms of the original loan to secure the most appropriate outcome for both debtor and secured creditors. Keeping these considerations in mind, the formula approach is straightforward, minimizes the need for expensive evidentiary proceedings, and ensures present value to the creditors. The formula approach simply takes the national prime rate and adjusts it to account for a risk of nonpayment. This approach differs from the dissent's approach in determining where the burden should lie, on the debtor or the creditor, to rebut the presumptive rate, whether prime or contract. Bankruptcy courts may determine the adjustment rate for risk to ensure compensation to the creditor without dooming the debtor to failure. Reversed and remanded.

DISSENT: (Scalia, J.) The prime rate is objectively known to be too low to sufficiently compensate creditors, so the contract rate is more appropriate as a presumptive rate rebuttable by either party by motion. The contract rate approach is supported by the assumptions that the subprime lending market is competitive and efficient and that the costs of default under Chapter 13 equal the costs of default under the original loan. Both assumptions are reasonable and supported by data. Justice Thomas proposes only the risk-free interest rate but the property right secured by confirmation of the plan requires accounting for risk of nonpayment. Compensation for risk is required by most jurisdictions to adequately protect creditors.

ANALYSIS

The difference among the plurality, concurrence, and dissent hinged less on the approaches to determine the appropriate interest rate and more on the appropriate level of compensation to the creditors. Justice Thomas did not believe that the risk of default should enter into the analysis, while the other two opinions strongly believed that it should but differed on the starting point (i.e., high contract rate or low prime rate). The likely result from this opinion is that creditors will now face the burden of proving the low prime rate is too low.

Continued on next page.

Quicknotes

CHAPTER 13 BANKRUPTCY Debtor may modify plan at any time before the completion of the payments under such plan.

CRAMDOWN Refers to a court's confirmation of a reorganization plan in a bankruptcy proceeding despite the opposition of creditors.

■▬■

In re Arnold & Baker Farms

Debtor (P) v. Creditor (D)

85 F.3d 1415 (9th Cir. 1996).

NATURE OF CASE: Appeal from Bankruptcy Appellate Panel's (BAP) reversal of the bankruptcy court's order confirming a reorganization plan.

FACT SUMMARY: Debtor Arnold & Baker Farms (P) proposed to satisfy the claims of its creditors by transferring real property to them, but its largest creditor, the Farmers Home Administration (D), objected.

🏛 RULE OF LAW
In order for a partial distribution to constitute the most "indubitable equivalence," the partial distribution must ensure the safety of or prevent jeopardy to the principal.

FACTS: The debtor Arnold and Baker Farms (Arnold and Baker) (P) was an Arizona partnership formed for the purpose of farming. Arnold and Baker (P) borrowed money from the Farmers Home Administration (FmHA) (D) in order to make payments on a deed of trust on the property. When a judicial foreclosure proceeding was instituted against it, Arnold and Baker (P) filed a voluntary petition for relief under Chapter 11 of the Bankruptcy Code. Arnold and Baker (P) proposed a "dirt for debt" plan and, when the FmHA (D) opposed it, invoked the "cramdown" provision of Bankruptcy Code § 1129(b). The FmHA (D) then claimed that the plan would not provide the "indubitable equivalent" of its secured claim, as required by the "cramdown" provision, and appealed to the BAP. The BAP reversed the bankruptcy court's order confirming the plan, and Arnold and Baker (P) appealed.

ISSUE: In order for a partial distribution to constitute the most "indubitable equivalence," must the partial distribution ensure the safety of or prevent jeopardy to the principal?

HOLDING AND DECISION: (Norris, J.) Yes. In order for a partial distribution to constitute the most "indubitable equivalence," the partial distribution must ensure the safety of or prevent jeopardy to the principal. The bankruptcy court's valuation in this case was not clearly erroneous, but its finding regarding the value of the real property did not provide the indubitable equivalent of the particular secured claim in question. Partial distribution will not ensure the safety of or prevent jeopardy to the principal. If FmHA (D) subsequently sells the property for less than the value calculated by the bankruptcy court, FmHA (D) has no recourse to the remaining collateral to satisfy the deficiency. As a result, the distribution to FmHA (D) may not be "completely compensatory." The principal is protected to the extent of the entire 1,320 acres held as security. Because each parcel of real property is unique, the precise value of real property is difficult, if not impossible to determine until it is actually sold. Affirmed.

▶ ANALYSIS

The court also noted that a plan cannot unfairly shift risk of plan failure to the creditor. Substitute collateral may not increase the creditor's risk exposure. In this case, the amount of collateral deemed to be the indubitable equivalent of the FmHA's (D) secured claim depended entirely on the court's valuation of the collateral.

Quicknotes

CHAPTER 11 REORGANIZATION A plan formulated pursuant to Chapter 11 of the Bankruptcy Code whereby a debtor, who is unable to pay his debts as they become due, is relieved of his obligation to pay his creditors through reorganization and payment from future income.

CRAMDOWN Refers to a court's confirmation of a reorganization plan in a bankruptcy proceeding despite the opposition of creditors.

REAL PROPERTY Land, an interest in land, or anything attached to the land that is incapable of being removed.

Great Western Bank v. Sierra Woods Group

Debtor (P) v. Creditor (D)

953 F.2d 1174 (9th Cir. 1992).

NATURE OF CASE: Appeal from the district court's decision that a proposed reorganization plan was not fair and equitable under Bankruptcy Code § 1129(b).

FACT SUMMARY: Sierra Woods Group (P) proposed a Chapter 11 reorganization plan which was challenged because it involved negative amortization.

RULE OF LAW

The bankruptcy court can confirm a plan of reorganization without creditor approval if the plan does not discriminate unfairly, and is fair and equitable.

FACTS: Sierra Woods Group's (P) only asset was an apartment complex financed by deeds of trust held by two banks. Sierra Woods (P) proposed a Chapter 11 reorganization plan that included negative amortization of the note held by Great Western Bank (GWB) (D). The bankruptcy court adopted a per se rule against negative amortization and confirmed a reorganization plan that required Sierra Woods (P) to make timely payments at the market rate of interest. Sierra Woods (P) appealed the bankruptcy court's ruling against deferral of interest to the district court. The district court ruled that the bankruptcy court properly determined that the deferral proposed in the plan did not under the circumstances provide GWB (D) with the equivalent of the present value of its claim. Sierra Woods (P) appealed.

ISSUE: Can the bankruptcy court confirm a plan of reorganization without creditor approval if the plan does not discriminate unfairly, and is fair and equitable?

HOLDING AND DECISION: (Fernandez, J.) Yes. The bankruptcy court can confirm a plan of reorganization without creditor approval if the plan does not discriminate unfairly, and is fair and equitable. Fairness of a reorganization plan that includes the deferral of interest must be determined on a case-by-case basis. Because the bankruptcy court did not make factual findings on this issue, the district court erred when it independently determined that Sierra Woods' (P) proposed plan was not fair and equitable. Reversed and remanded.

CONCURRENCE AND DISSENT: (Poole, J.) Based on the findings of fact made by the bankruptcy court, the district court was correct in concluding that the original plan calling for negative amortization would not have been fair and equitable. As a result, the failure of the bankruptcy court to conduct a hearing on the plan constituted harmless error. Reversing and remanding now would unnecessarily prolong the bankruptcy proceedings to the prejudice of the creditor.

▶ ANALYSIS

The majority also listed ten factors to be considered when making the determination of fairness. Other courts have held the market rate of interest to be a necessary, but not sufficient, factor to be considered. The district court may not make its own factual findings when reviewing a decision of the bankruptcy court.

Quicknotes

AMORTIZATION The satisfaction of a debt by the tendering of regular, equal payments over a period of time.

CHAPTER 11 REORGANIZATION A plan formulated pursuant to Chapter 11 of the Bankruptcy Code whereby a debtor, who is unable to pay his debts as they become due, is relieved of his obligation to pay his creditors through reorganization and payment from future income.

HARMLESS ERROR An error taking place during trial that does not require the reviewing court to overturn or modify judgment in that it did not affect the appellant's substantial rights or the disposition of the action.

NEGATIVE AMORTIZATION Refers to when monthly payments are insufficient to pay the interest of an adjustable rate mortgage and the uncovered portion is instead added to the loan's principal.

In re DBSD North America

[Parties not identified.]

634 F.3d 79 (2d Cir. 2011).

NATURE OF CASE: Appeal from affirmance of confirmation of Chapter 11 reorganization plan.

FACT SUMMARY: Sprint Nextel Corp., an unsecured creditor, objected to the confirmation of the reorganization plan of DBSD North America, Inc. and its subsidiaries (together, "DBSD"), contending that the plan violated the "absolute priority rule" where, under the plan, DBSD's parent company, ICO Global Communications, would receive shares and warrants in the reorganized company as a gift from secured creditors who were themselves not receiving the full value of their claims.

🏛 RULE OF LAW

A Chapter 11 reorganization plan violates the "absolute priority rule" where an equity holder, whose interest is junior to that of unsecured creditors, is to receive shares and warrants in the reorganized company as a gift from secured creditors who themselves are not receiving the full value of their claims, so that the plan should not be confirmed.

FACTS: DBSD North America, Inc. and its subsidiaries (together, "DBSD") filed for Chapter 11 bankruptcy. Among the claims against it were (1) a $40 million revolving credit facility (First Lien Debt); (2) $650 million in convertible senior secured notes, which held a second-priority security interest in substantially all of DBSD's assets (Second Lien Debt); and (3) an unliquidated, unsecured claim held by Sprint Nextel Corp. (Sprint) based on a lawsuit against a DBSD subsidiary seeking $211 million. Under DBSD's proposed plan, inter alia, the holders of the Second Lien Debt would receive the bulk of the shares of the reorganized entity, which the bankruptcy court estimated would be worth between 51% and 73% of their original claims. The holders of unsecured claims, such as Sprint, would receive shares estimated as worth between 4% and 46% of their original claims, and DBSD's parent and shareholder, ICO Global Communications (ICO Global), would receive shares and warrants in the reorganized entity. Sprint objected to the plan, arguing that, inter alia, the plan violated the "absolute priority rule" of § 1129(b)(2)(B) of the Bankruptcy Code (Code). That rule requires that, if a class of senior claim-holders will not receive the full value of their claims under the plan and the class does not accept the plan, no junior claim- or interest-holder may receive "any property" "under the plan on account of such junior claim or interest." Sprint noted that the plan provided for ICO Global, whose interest was junior to Sprint's class of general unsecured claims, to receive substantial quantities of shares and warrants in an amount that greatly exceeded that being received by all the unsecured creditors together. Sprint argued that because ICO Global was receiving property on account of its junior interest, Sprint's class of general unsecured creditors had a right to receive full satisfaction of their claims or at least an amount sufficient to obtain approval from the class. Because the plan provided for neither, Sprint contended that confirmation would be erroneous. The bankruptcy court rejected Sprint's objecting, characterizing ICO Global's receipt of shares and warrants as a "gift" from the holders of the Second Lien Debt, who were senior to Sprint in priority yet who were themselves not receiving the full value of their claims, and who could, therefore, "voluntarily offer a portion of their recovered property to junior stakeholders" without violating the absolute priority rule. The bankruptcy court held that it would permit such gifting "at least where, as here, the gift comes from secured creditors, there is no doubt as to their secured creditor status, where there are understandable reasons for the gift, where there are no ulterior, improper ends . . . and where the complaining creditor would get no more if the gift had not been made." Accordingly, the bankruptcy court confirmed the plan. The district court affirmed, and the court of appeals granted review.

ISSUE: Does a Chapter 11 reorganization plan violate the "absolute priority rule" where an equity holder, whose interest is junior to that of unsecured creditors, is to receive shares and warrants in the reorganized company as a gift from secured creditors who themselves are not receiving the full value of their claims, so that the plan should not be confirmed?

HOLDING AND DECISION: (Lynch, J.) Yes. A Chapter 11 reorganization plan violates the "absolute priority rule" where an equity holder, whose interest is junior to that of unsecured creditors, is to receive shares and warrants in the reorganized company as a gift from secured creditors who themselves are not receiving the full value of their claims, so that the plan should not be confirmed. It is well settled that stockholders are entitled neither to any share of the capital stock nor to any dividends of the profits until all the debts of the corporation are paid. The absolute priority rule arose judicially to prevent circumvention of this rule by cooperating senior creditors and shareholders to the detriment of junior creditors. The Code incorporates that absolute priority rule by providing that a plan be "fair and equitable" with respect to each class of claims that is

Continued on next page.

impaired under, and has not accepted, the plan, and by further providing that a plan is not "fair and equitable" unless either the dissenting class receives the full value of its claim or no classes junior to that class receive any property under the plan on account of their junior claims or interests. Here, under the plan, Sprint will not receive the full value of its claim. Therefore, the plan may be confirmed only if ICO Global does not receive or retain any property under the plan on account of its interest. However, ICO Global does receive "property" in the form of shares and warrants in the reorganized entity under the plan and on account of its junior interest. "On account of" can be interpreted to mean "in exchange for," and here, ICO Global is receiving new shares and warrants at least partially in exchange for its old ones. A less restrictive test interprets "on account of" to mean "because of," and here that test is also satisfied, because ICO Global is receiving property because of its prior interest. Whether ICO Global merits receiving the property is beside the point, and a transfer partly on account of factors other than the prior interest is still partly "on account of" that interest. This is made clear by the fact that ICO Global did not contribute new capital to the reorganized entity. Instead, the "gift" from the senior creditors was aimed at ensuring its continued cooperation and assistance in the reorganization—which would be useful only because of ICO Global's position as equity holder and the rights emanating from that position. The United States Supreme Court has indicated that the absolute priority rule must be read strictly, and has never suggested any exception that would cover the plan at issue. Even though DBSD was not worth enough to cover even the secured lenders' claims, let alone those of the unsecured creditors such as Sprint, the "gifting doctrine" does not defeat the requirements of the absolute priority rule. Under the gifting doctrine, senior secured creditors voluntarily offer a portion of their recovered property to junior stakeholders. The bankruptcy court erred, however, in concluding that until the debts of the secured creditors were paid in full, the Code's distributional priority scheme, as embodied in the absolute priority rule, was not implicated, so that the senior secured creditors could share their shares and warrants with ICO Global as they saw fit. Such a conclusion does not square with the Code's text, which extends the absolute priority rule to "any property," not "any property not covered by a senior creditor's lien." Here, whatever the secured creditors did not take for themselves remains in the estate for the benefit of other claim-holders, and the United States Supreme Court precedent has been clear that the absolute priority rule is aimed at stopping transactions such as the one at bar. Notwithstanding policy arguments against the absolute priority rule and in favor of the gifting doctrine, there are substantial policy arguments in favor of the rule. Shareholders retain substantial control over the Chapter 11 process, and with that control comes significant opportunity for self-enrichment at the expense of creditors. Thus, in the face of unscrupulous parties, or a less vigilant bankruptcy court, a weakened absolute priority rule could allow for serious mischief between senior creditors and existing shareholders. Regardless of the policy merits of the absolute priority rule, Congress was well aware of both its benefits and disadvantages when it codified the rule in the Code, and Congress did not make any exception for "gifts" like the one at issue here. Therefore, the bankruptcy court erred in confirming the plan. Reversed as to the order of confirmation on absolute-priority grounds.

▶ *ANALYSIS*

One policy argument against the absolute priority rule is that gifting may be used to promote an efficient and non-adversarial Chapter 11 proceeding, and no doubt the parties intended the gift to have such an effect here. For example, where the equity sponsor is out of the money, a tip may ensure a consensual bankruptcy rather than a contested one. Enforcing the absolute priority rule, by contrast, may encourage hold-out behavior by objecting creditors even though the transfer has no direct effect on the value to be received by the objecting creditors. In the Chapter 7 context, however, where the debtor is liquidated rather than reorganized, there is not the same need for a rigid absolute priority rule, and, unlike in Chapter 11 cases such as the one involved here, there is a lack of statutory support for the argument against gifting.

■≡■

Quicknotes

CHAPTER 11 REORGANIZATION A plan formulated pursuant to Chapter 11 of the Bankruptcy Code whereby a debtor, who is unable to pay his debts as they become due, is relieved of his obligation to pay his creditors through reorganization and payment from future income.

INTER ALIA Among other things.

UNSECURED CREDITOR A creditor whose loan is not backed by specified collateral or a security agreement.

■≡■

Bank of America v. 203 North LaSalle Street Partnership

Senior creditor (D) v. Debtor (P)

526 U.S. 434 (1999).

NATURE OF CASE: Review of approval of bankruptcy reorganization plan.

FACT SUMMARY: When the old equity holders in 203 North LaSalle Street Partnership (P) contributed new equity in exchange for ownership interests in the reorganized entity, Bank of America (D), the major senior creditor, objected.

RULE OF LAW
Plans providing junior interest holders with exclusive opportunities free from competition and without benefit of market valuation are prohibited under the Bankruptcy Code.

FACTS: 203 North LaSalle Street Partnership (203 North LaSalle) (P), an Illinois real estate limited partnership, was in Chapter 11 bankruptcy. Bank of America (D), the major senior creditor, objected to its reorganization plan because a group of old equity holders were to receive ownership interests in the reorganized entity and that opportunity had been given exclusively to the old equity holders without consideration of alternatives. Confirmation of the plan on a consensual basis was effectively blocked. 203 North LaSalle (P) proceeded to have the plan approved under the judicial cramdown process. To succeed under § 1129(b), the plan must be found to be fair and equitable, that is, the holder of any junior claim or interest should not receive or retain under the plan on account of such junior claim or interest any property. The plan was approved, and the appeals court affirmed. Bank of America (D) appealed, claiming that the plan was unfair, because the exclusive opportunity offered the old equity holders was property of some value that was obtained at no cost. The United States Supreme Court granted certiorari.

ISSUE: Are plans providing junior interest holders with exclusive opportunities free from competition and without benefit of market valuation prohibited under the Bankruptcy Code?

HOLDING AND DECISION: (Souter, J.) Yes. Plans providing junior interest holders with exclusive opportunities free from competition and without benefit of market valuation are prohibited under the Bankruptcy Code. The plan is unfair in that it vests equity in the reorganized business in 203 North LaSalle's (P) partners, without offering the opportunity to anyone else to compete for that equity. This opportunity should be treated as an item of property in its own right. Some form of market valuation should be applied to test the adequacy of the old equity holders' proposed contribution. Reversed and remanded.

ANALYSIS

There is a split on the application of the absolute priority rule. The Seventh and Ninth Circuits have supported confirmation of such plans. The Second and Fourth Circuits have disapproved of similar plans. The Supreme Court did not resolve the issue in this case since it found that the statute would not be satisfied by either reading.

Quicknotes

CHAPTER 11 REORGANIZATION A plan formulated pursuant to Chapter 11 of the Bankruptcy Code whereby a debtor, who is unable to pay his debts as they become due, is relieved of his obligation to pay his creditors through reorganization and payment from future income.

CRAMDOWN Refers to a court's confirmation of a reorganization plan in a bankruptcy proceeding despite the opposition of creditors.

EQUITY Fairness; justice; the determination of a matter consistent with principles of fairness and not in strict compliance with rules of law.

SECURED CREDITOR A creditor, the repayment of whose loan is secured by collateral sufficient to repay the debt owed.

CHAPTER 12

The Bankruptcy Courts

Quick Reference Rules of Law

Stern v. Marshall

Executor of decedent's wife's estate (D) v. Executor of decedent's son's estate (P)

131 S. Ct. 2594 (2011).

NATURE OF CASE: Appeal from court of appeals decision holding that the district court should have given preclusive effect to a state court's prior decision instead of treating as proposed rather than final a bankruptcy court's judgment in favor of a debtor on the debtor's compulsory counterclaim of tortious interference with a gift expectancy.

FACT SUMMARY: Vickie (D), a debtor in bankruptcy and the wife of decedent J. Howard Marshall II (J. Marshall), contended that the bankruptcy court had constitutional as well as statutory authority to render judgment on her compulsory counterclaim against Pierce (P), J. Marshall's son, for tortious interference with a gift she expected from J. Marshall of half his property.

RULE OF LAW
A bankruptcy court does not have constitutional authority to enter judgment on a state common-law compulsory counterclaim, notwithstanding that it has statutory authority to do so.

FACTS: Vickie (D), also known to the public as Anna Nicole Smith, was the wife of J. Howard Marshall II (J. Marshall), one of the wealthiest men in Texas. J. Marshall did not include Vickie (D) in his will. Before J. Howard died, Vickie (D) filed suit in Texas probate court, asserting that Pierce (P), J. Howard's son, fraudulently induced J. Howard to sign a living trust that did not include her, even though J. Howard intended to give her half of his property. After J. Howard died, Vickie (D) filed for bankruptcy in federal bankruptcy court in California. Pierce (P) filed a complaint in that bankruptcy proceeding, contending that Vickie (D) had defamed him by inducing her lawyers to tell members of the press that he had engaged in fraud to gain control of his father's assets, and seeking a declaration that the defamation claim was not dischargeable. Pierce (P) subsequently filed a proof of claim for the defamation action, seeking to recover damages for his suit from Vickie's (D) bankruptcy estate. Vickie (D) defended by asserting truth, and she also filed a counterclaim for tortious interference with the gift she expected from J. Howard. The bankruptcy court granted Vickie (D) summary judgment on Pierce's (P) defamation claim, and then, after trial, the court issued a judgment on Vickie's (D) counterclaim in her favor, awarding her over $400 million in compensatory damages and $25 million in punitive damages. Pierce (P) argued that the bankruptcy court lacked jurisdiction over Vickie's (D) counterclaim, on the grounds that the counterclaim was not a "core proceeding" under § 157(b)(2)(C) of the Bankruptcy Code (Code). The bankruptcy court determined that Vickie's (D) claim was a core proceeding and that, therefore, it had

the power to enter judgment on the counterclaim under § 157(b)(1). The district court concluded that Vickie's (D) claim was not "core" and that it would be unconstitutional to hold that any and all counterclaims are core. However, the district court determined that it was required to treat the bankruptcy court's judgment as proposed, rather than final. Accordingly, after conducting independent review of the record, the court concluded that that Vickie's (D) counterclaim was meritorious, and it awarded her around $44 million for each type of damages, notwithstanding that by this time the Texas probate court, after a jury trial, had entered judgment in favor of Pierce (P). The court of appeals reversed on the ground that Vickie's (D) counterclaim did not meet the requirements for being a core proceeding, so that the district court should have afforded preclusive effect to the Texas probate court's factual and legal determinations, as that court's judgment was the earliest final judgment entered on the matters relevant to the counterclaim. The United States Supreme Court granted certiorari.

ISSUE: Does a bankruptcy court have constitutional authority to enter judgment on a state common-law compulsory counterclaim, notwithstanding that it has statutory authority to do so?

HOLDING AND DECISION: (Roberts, C.J.) No. A bankruptcy court does not have constitutional authority to enter judgment on a state common-law compulsory counterclaim, notwithstanding that it has statutory authority to do so. Congress in § 157(a) of the Code has divided bankruptcy proceedings into three categories: those that arise under title 11; those that arise in a title 11 case; and those that are related to a case under title 11. District courts may refer any or all such proceedings to the bankruptcy judges of their district, which is how the bankruptcy court in this case came to preside over Vickie's (D) bankruptcy proceedings. District courts also may withdraw a case or proceeding referred to the bankruptcy court "for cause shown." The manner in which a bankruptcy judge may act on a referred matter depends on the type of proceeding involved. As § 157(b)(1) indicates, bankruptcy judges may hear and enter final judgments in "all core proceedings arising under title 11, or arising in a case under title 11. Core proceedings include, but are not limited to, counterclaims by a debtor's estate against persons filing claims against the estate. If a proceeding is not core, the bankruptcy court must refer the case to the district court for a final entry of judgment after de novo review of any matter to which a party objects. Designating all counterclaims as core

Continued on next page.

proceedings raises serious constitutional concerns. Here, the canon of construction that requires that federal statutes be construed so as to avoid serious doubt of their constitutionality, i.e., the canon of avoidance, cannot be used to bypass the constitutional issue presented by § 157(b)(2)(C). However, that provision authorizes the bankruptcy court to enter a final judgment on her tortious interference counterclaim. In the alternative, Pierce (P) argues that the bankruptcy court lacked jurisdiction to resolve Vickie's (D) counterclaim because his defamation claim is a "personal injury tort" that the bankruptcy court lacked jurisdiction to hear under § 157(b)(5). The issue of what constitutes a "personal injury tort" need not be reached because Vickie (D) is correct that § 157(b)(5) is not jurisdictional, and Pierce (P) consented to the bankruptcy court's resolution of the defamation claim.

Thus, although § 157 allowed the bankruptcy court to enter final judgment on Vickie's (D) counterclaim, Article III of the Constitution does not. Article III is "an inseparable element of the constitutional system of checks and balances" that "both defines the power and protects the independence of the Judicial Branch." Article III protects liberty not only through its role in implementing the separation of powers, but also by specifying the defining characteristics of Article III judges to protect the integrity of judicial decisionmaking. Article III could neither serve its purpose in the system of checks and balances nor preserve the integrity of judicial decisionmaking if the other branches could confer the government's judicial power on entities outside Article III. In *Northern Pipeline Constr. Co. v. Marathon Pipe Line Co.*, 458 U.S. 50 (1982), there was also an Article III challenge to a bankruptcy court's resolution of a debtor's suit. In that case, the Court considered whether bankruptcy judges serving under the Bankruptcy Act of 1978 (1978 Act)—who also lacked the tenure and salary guarantees of Article III—could "constitutionally be vested with jurisdiction to decide [a] state-law contract claim" against an entity that was not otherwise part of the bankruptcy proceedings. The plurality in *Northern Pipeline* recognized that there was a category of cases involving "public rights" that Congress could constitutionally assign to "legislative" courts for resolution. A full majority of the Court, while not agreeing on the scope of that exception, concluded that the doctrine did not encompass adjudication of the state law claim at issue in that case, and rejected the debtor's argument that the bankruptcy court's exercise of jurisdiction was constitutional because the bankruptcy judge was acting merely as an adjunct of the district court or court of appeals. After the decision in *Northern Pipeline*, Congress revised the statutes governing bankruptcy jurisdiction and bankruptcy judges in amendments it enacted in 1984. With respect to the "core" proceedings listed in § 157(b)(2), however, the bankruptcy courts under the 1984 Act exercise the same powers they wielded under the 1978 Act. The authority exercised by the newly constituted courts over a counterclaim such as Vickie's (D) exceeds the bounds of Article III.

It is clear that here the bankruptcy court exercised the "judicial power" of the United States in purporting to resolve and enter final judgment on a state common-law claim, just as the court did in *Northern Pipeline*. There is no "public right" that excuses the failure to comply with Article III in doing so. Vickie's (D) counterclaim does not fall within the public rights exception, however defined. The Court has long recognized that, in general, Congress may not "withdraw from judicial cognizance any matter which, from its nature, is the subject of a suit at the common law, or in equity, or admiralty." *Murray's Lessee v. Hoboken Land & Improvement Co.*, 59 U.S. 272 (1856). The Court has also recognized that "[a]t the same time there are matters, involving public rights, . . . which are susceptible of judicial determination, but which congress may or may not bring within the cognizance of the courts of the United States, as it may deem proper." Several previous decisions have contrasted cases within the reach of the public rights exception—those arising "between the Government and persons subject to its authority in connection with the performance of the constitutional functions of the executive or legislative departments"—and those that are instead matters "of private right, that is, of the liability of one individual to another under the law as defined." Shortly after *Northern Pipeline*, the Court rejected the limitation of the public rights exception to actions involving the government as a party. The Court has continued, however, to limit the exception to cases in which the claim at issue derives from a federal regulatory scheme, or in which resolution of the claim by an expert government agency is deemed essential to a limited regulatory objective within the agency's authority. In other words, it is still the case that what makes a right "public" rather than private is that the right is integrally related to particular action of the federal government. In *Granfinanciera, S.A. v. Nordberg*, 492 U.S. 33 (1989), the most recent case considering the public rights exception, the Court rejected a bankruptcy trustee's argument that a fraudulent conveyance action filed on behalf of a bankruptcy estate against a noncreditor in a bankruptcy proceeding fell within the exception. Vickie's (D) counterclaim is similar to the fraudulent conveyance claim at issue in *Granfinanciera*. It is not a matter that can be pursued only by grace of the other branches; it does not flow from a federal statutory scheme; and it is not "completely dependent upon" adjudication of a claim created by federal law. Instead, it is a claim made under state common law between two private parties; it involves the most prototypical exercise of judicial power: the entry of a final, binding judgment by a court with broad substantive jurisdiction, on a common-law cause of action, when the action neither derives from nor depends upon any agency regulatory regime. If such an exercise of judicial power may nonetheless be taken from the Article III Judiciary simply by deeming it part of some amorphous

Continued on next page.

"public right," then Article III would be transformed from the guardian of individual liberty and separation of powers "into mere wishful thinking." The fact that Pierce (P) filed a proof of claim in the bankruptcy proceedings does not change this analysis. Such filing did not give the bankruptcy court the constitutional authority to adjudicate Vickie's (D) counterclaim. Initially, Pierce's (P) defamation claim does not affect the nature of Vickie's (D) tortious interference counterclaim as one at common law that simply attempts to augment the bankruptcy estate—the type of claim that, under *Northern Pipeline* and *Granfinanciera*, must be decided by an Article III court. The cases on which Vickie (D) relies, *Katchen v. Landy*, 382 U.S. 323 (1966) and *Langenkamp v. Culp*, 498 U.S. 42 (1990), are inapposite. *Katchen* permitted a bankruptcy referee to exercise jurisdiction over a trustee's voidable preference claim against a creditor only where there was no question that the referee was required to decide whether there had been a voidable preference in determining whether and to what extent to allow the creditor's claim. The *Katchen* Court expressly noted that it did not intimate any opinion concerning whether the bankruptcy referee would have had "summary jurisdiction to adjudicate a demand by the bankruptcy trustee for affirmative relief, all of the substantial factual and legal bases for which had not been disposed of in passing on objections to the creditor's proof of claim." *Langenkamp* is to the same effect. In that case, the Court explained that a preferential transfer claim can be heard in bankruptcy when the allegedly favored creditor has filed a claim, because then the ensuing preference action by the trustee becomes integral to the restructuring of the debtor-creditor relationship. If, in contrast, the creditor has not filed a proof of claim, the trustee's preference action does not become part of the claims-allowance process subject to resolution by the bankruptcy court. In this case, by contrast, the bankruptcy court—in order to resolve Vickie's (D) counterclaim—was required to and did make several factual and legal determinations that were not "disposed of in passing on objections" to Pierce's (P) proof of claim. There was never any reason to believe that the process of adjudicating Pierce's (P) proof of claim would necessarily resolve Vickie's (D) counterclaim, notwithstanding some slight overlap between the two claims. The bankruptcy court could not rule in Vickie's (D) favor without ruling on questions of state law and the elements of her cause of action. In both *Katchen* and *Langenkamp*, moreover, the trustee bringing the preference action was asserting a right of recovery created by federal bankruptcy law. Vickie's (D) claim is instead a state tort action that exists without regard to any bankruptcy proceeding. In sum, Congress may not bypass Article III simply because a proceeding may have some bearing on a bankruptcy case; the question is whether the action at issue stems from the bankruptcy itself or would necessarily be resolved in the claims allowance process. Moreover, contrary to Vickie's (D) argument, the bankruptcy courts under the 1984 Act are not mere "adjuncts" of the district courts. The new bankruptcy courts, like the courts considered in *Northern Pipeline*, do not "ma[k]e only specialized, narrowly confined factual determinations regarding a particularized area of law" or engage in "statutorily channeled factfinding functions." A bankruptcy court is not like an adjunct agency that possesses only a limited power to issue compensation orders that can be enforced only by order of the district court. Instead, a bankruptcy court resolving a counterclaim under § 157(b)(2)(C) has the power to enter "appropriate orders and judgments"—including final judgments—subject to review only if a party chooses to appeal. Such a court is an adjunct of no one. Finally, Vickie (D) predicts that restrictions on a bankruptcy court's ability to hear and finally resolve compulsory counterclaims will create significant delays and impose additional costs on the bankruptcy process. It goes without saying that the fact that a given law or procedure is efficient, convenient, and useful in facilitating functions of government, standing alone, will not save it if it is contrary to the Constitution. In addition, the Court is not convinced that the practical consequences of such limitations are as significant as Vickie (D) suggests. The framework Congress adopted in the 1984 Act already contemplates that certain state law matters in bankruptcy cases will be resolved by state courts and district courts, Thus, the removal of counterclaims such as Vickie's (D) from core bankruptcy jurisdiction will not meaningfully changes the division of labor in the statute. Affirmed.

CONCURRENCE: (Scalia, J.) Simply put, a matter of public rights must at a minimum arise between the government and others, and there is no reason to have the numerous factors listed by the majority as part of Article III jurisprudence. Those factors have nothing to do with the text or tradition of Article III. For example, Article III gives no indication that state-law claims have preferential entitlement to an Article III judge, and it does not make pertinent the extent to which the area of the law is "particularized." The multiple factors relied on seem to have entered Article III jurisprudence almost randomly. The single test should be that an Article III judge is required in all federal adjudications, unless there is a firmly established historical practice to the contrary. Based on such a test, an Article III judge is not required for territorial courts, courts-martial, or true "public rights" cases. Regardless of whether historical practice permits non-Article III judges to render opinions on claims against the bankruptcy estate, Vickie (D) points to no historical practice that authorizes a non-Article III judge to adjudicate a counterclaim of the sort at issue here.

DISSENT: (Breyer, J.) The majority errs in concluding that § 157(b)(2)(C) is inconsistent with Article III. In part, the majority's error stems from the way in which it interprets, or at least emphasizes, certain precedents. The

Continued on next page.

majority overstates the current relevance of statements made *Murray's Lessee*, and it overstates the importance of an analysis that did not command a Court majority in *Northern Pipeline*, and which was later disavowed. The majority also understates a watershed opinion widely thought to demonstrate the constitutional basis for the current authority of administrative agencies to adjudicate private disputes, namely, *Crowell v. Benson*, 285 U.S. 22 (1932). Finally, the majority fails to follow the analysis recently used to evaluate claims that a congressional delegation of adjudicatory authority violates separation-of-powers principles derived from Article III. These cases are *Thomas v. Union Carbide Agricultural Products Co.*, 473 U.S. 568 (1985), and *Commodity Futures Trading Comm'n v. Schor*, 478 U.S. 833 (1986). As to *Murray's Lessee*, the majority relies on language from that case that is essentially dictum. More importantly, it is the case's distinction between "public rights" and "private rights" that has had the more lasting impact. Courts have seized on that distinction when upholding non-Article III adjudication, not when striking it down. The one exception is *Northern Pipeline*, where the Court struck down the Bankruptcy Act of 1978. In that case, however, there was no majority, and only a plurality, not a majority, read the statement roughly in the way the majority currently reads it. *Crowell* clarified the scope of the dictum in *Murray's Lessee*. In *Crowell*, Congress's delegation of primary factfinding authority to an agency was upheld. The majority's reading of *Crowell* greatly limits it. *Crowell* has been hailed as the premier case validating administrative adjudication, but the majority distinguishes *Crowell* as a case in which the Court upheld the delegation of adjudicatory authority to an administrative agency simply because the agency's power to make the "specialized, narrowly confined factual determinations" at issue arising in a "particularized area of law," made the agency a district court adjunct. If *Crowell's* holding is truly as narrow as the majority suggests, Congress's delegation to various agencies of authority to adjudicate disputes among private parties—a question long deemed settled—would have to be revisited. In addition, instead of leaning so heavily on the approach taken by the plurality in *Northern Pipeline*, a better approach would be to look to the Court's more recent Article III cases *Thomas* and *Schor*. Not only did these cases command a majority, they also took a more pragmatic, flexible approach to the constitutional question. They sought to determine whether, in the particular instance, the challenged delegation of adjudicatory authority posed a genuine and serious threat that one branch of government sought to aggrandize its own constitutionally delegated authority by encroaching upon a field of authority that the Constitution assigns exclusively to another branch. To reach a determination of that issue, the Court in those cases looked at several factors, including: (1) the nature of the claim to be adjudicated; (2) the nature of the non-Article III tribunal; (3) the extent to which Article III courts exercise control over the proceeding; (4) the presence or absence of the parties' consent; and (5) the nature

and importance of the legislative purpose served by the grant of adjudicatory authority to a tribunal with judges who lack Article III's tenure and compensation protections. The majority should have done so here, as well. Instead of applying a formalistic approach, it should have applied the bending, flexible approach taken by *Thomas* and *Schor*. Applying *Schor's* approach here leads to the conclusion that a grant of authority to a bankruptcy court to adjudicate compulsory counterclaims does not violate any constitutional separation-of-powers principle related to Article III. First, although the nature of the counterclaim—a state common-law claim—supports a finding of unconstitutionality, the significance of this factor is mitigated here by the fact that bankruptcy courts often decide claims that similarly resemble various common-law actions. Second, the nature of the tribunal here supports constitutionality, as the bankruptcy court is made up of judges who enjoy considerable protection from improper political influence—they are appointed and removed by the courts of appeals, and their salaries are paid by the Judiciary. Third, the control exercised by Article III judges over bankruptcy proceedings argues in favor of constitutionality. Article III judges control and supervise the bankruptcy court's determinations–at least to the same degree that Article III judges supervised the agency's determinations in *Crowell*, if not more so. Fourth, the fact that the parties have consented to bankruptcy court jurisdiction argues in favor of constitutionality, and strongly so. Here, Pierce (P) brought his claim voluntarily, and he likely had an alternative forum to the bankruptcy court in which to pursue his claim. This type of consent argues strongly in favor of using ordinary bankruptcy court proceedings. The Court's precedent, including *Northern Pipeline*, has recognized that even when private rights are at issue, non-Article III adjudication may be appropriate when both parties consent. Fifth, the nature and importance of the legislative purpose served by the grant of adjudicatory authority to bankruptcy courts argues strongly in favor of constitutionality. Congress's delegation of adjudicatory powers over counterclaims asserted against bankruptcy claimants constitutes an important means of securing a constitutionally authorized end, i.e., the establishment of uniform bankruptcy laws and to restructure debtor-creditor relations. To be effective, a single tribunal must have broad authority to restructure those relations, "having jurisdiction of the parties to controversies brought before them," "decid[ing] all matters in dispute," and "decree[ing] complete relief." When a creditor files a proof of claim in the bankruptcy court, he subjects himself to the court's equitable power and agrees to the court's resolution of his claim. When the bankruptcy estate has a related claim against that creditor, that counterclaim may offset the creditor's claim, or even yield additional damages that augment the estate and may be distributed to the other creditors. A bankruptcy court's resolution of such a claim

Continued on next page.

plays a critical role in Congress's constitutionally based effort to create an efficient, effective federal bankruptcy system. The Court should defer to Congress's determination in this area, as it is devoid of any legislative or executive motive, intent, purpose, or desire to encroach upon areas that Article III reserves to judges to whom it grants tenure and compensation protections. Taking all these factors together, the magnitude of any intrusion on the Judicial Branch would be minimal. Finally, contrary to the majority's prediction, its decision will have a great impact, as a typical bankruptcy case may give rise to counterclaims that would now have to be separately adjudicated. Such a "constitutionally required game of jurisdictional ping-pong between courts" would lead to inefficiency, increased cost, delay, and needless additional suffering among those faced with bankruptcy.

▶ *ANALYSIS*

It can be argued that *Stern* has altered the key function of the bankruptcy courts by not allowing the fiduciaries who are vested with maximizing recoveries from creditors to utilize the expedited processes within the bankruptcy court system. What a trustee or other fiduciary is left with is utilizing state court processes, which in many jurisdictions are backlogged for years. Moreover, very busy district courts may not readily undertake to initially adjudicate matters that prior to *Stern* would have been adjudicated by the bankruptcy courts. If the district courts wait to review bankruptcy court reports and conclusions on such matters, more delay will be engendered. Even more delay will arise if the district courts' decisions are appealed to the courts of appeals, rather than the bankruptcy appellate panels (BAPs), which have no authority to review district decisions. As the dissent observes, such changes would not facilitate an expedited resolution for debtor/creditor relations in the bankruptcy process, and, instead, likely will cause some bankruptcy cases to take considerably longer than they would have prior to the Supreme Court's decision in this case.

■≡■

Quicknotes

CERTIORARI A discretionary writ issued by a superior court to an inferior court in order to review the lower court's decisions; the Supreme Court's writ ordering such review.

COMPENSATORY DAMAGES Measure of damages necessary to compensate victim for actual injuries suffered.

COMPULSORY COUNTERCLAIM An independent cause of action brought by a defendant to a lawsuit that arises out of the same transaction or occurrence that is the subject matter of the plaintiff's claim.

COUNTERCLAIM An independent cause of action brought by a defendant to a lawsuit in order to oppose or deduct from the plaintiff's claim.

DAMAGES Monetary compensation that may be awarded by the court to a party who has sustained injury or loss to his person, property or rights due to another party's unlawful act, omission or negligence.

DEFAMATION An intentional false publication, communicated publicly in either oral or written form, subjecting a person to scorn, hatred or ridicule, or injuring him in relation to his occupation or business.

DE NOVO The review of a lower court decision by an appellate court, which is hearing the case as if it had not been previously heard and as if no judgment had been rendered.

DICTUM Statement by a judge in a legal opinion that is not necessary for the resolution of the action.

FIDUCIARY Person holding a legal obligation to act for the benefit of another.

PROOF OF CLAIM Statement by a creditor under oath, stating the amount of and basis for a claim.

PUNITIVE DAMAGES Damages exceeding the actual injury suffered for the purposes of punishment of the defendant, deterrence of the wrongful behavior or comfort to the plaintiff.

SUMMARY JUDGMENT Judgment rendered by a court in response to a motion made by one of the parties, claiming that the lack of a question of material fact in respect to an issue warrants disposition of the issue without consideration by the jury.

■≡■

Central Virginia Community College v. Katz

State agency (D) v. Trustee (P)

546 U.S. 356 (2006).

NATURE OF CASE: Appeal from affirmance by court of appeals of district court's affirmance of bankruptcy court's denial of a motion to dismiss proceedings to avoid preferential transfers to state agencies.

FACT SUMMARY: State institutions of higher learning (state agencies) (D) contended that proceedings to avoid alleged preferential transfers made to them should be dismissed on grounds of sovereign immunity.

> **RULE OF LAW**
> A bankruptcy trustee's proceeding to set aside the debtor's preferential transfers to state agencies is not barred by sovereign immunity.

FACTS: Katz (P), a bankruptcy trustee, commenced proceedings in bankruptcy court under §§ 547(b) and 550(a) of the Bankruptcy Code to avoid and recover alleged preferential transfers by the debtor to state institutions of higher learning (state agencies) (D). The agencies (D) claimed that the proceeding was barred by sovereign immunity. The bankruptcy court denied the motions to dismiss, and the district court and the court of appeals affirmed based on its prior determination that Congress has abrogated the states' sovereign immunity in bankruptcy proceedings. The United States Supreme Court granted certiorari.

ISSUE: Is a bankruptcy trustee's proceeding to set aside the debtor's preferential transfers to state agencies barred by sovereign immunity?

HOLDING AND DECISION: (Stevens, J.) No. A bankruptcy trustee's proceeding to set aside the debtor's preferential transfers to state agencies is not barred by sovereign immunity. The Bankruptcy Clause, Article I, § 8, cl. 4, empowers Congress to establish "uniform Laws on the subject of Bankruptcies throughout the United States." Although this case presents the question of whether Congress's attempt to abrogate state sovereign immunity in 11 U.S.C. § 106(a) is valid, resolution of that question is not necessary to a determination that the bankruptcy courts have jurisdiction over preference avoidance proceedings involving state agencies since the Bankruptcy Clause encompasses the entire subject of bankruptcy. At its core, bankruptcy jurisdiction is in rem and therefore does not implicate states' sovereignty to nearly the same degree as other kinds of jurisdiction. The Bankruptcy Clause's history, the reasons it was adopted, and the legislation proposed and enacted under it immediately following ratification demonstrate that it was intended not just as a grant of legislative authority to Congress, but also to authorize limited subordination of state sovereign immunity in the bankruptcy arena. States, whether or not they choose to participate, are bound by a bankruptcy court's order discharging the debtor no less than are other creditors. The state agencies (D) here have conceded as much. The history of discharges in bankruptcy proceedings demonstrates that these concessions are correct. The Framers' primary goal in adopting the Clause was to prevent competing sovereigns' interference with discharge, which referred both to a release of debts and release of the debtor from prison. The patchwork of wildly divergent and uncoordinated insolvency and bankruptcy laws that existed in the American Colonies resulted in one jurisdiction's imprisoning debtors discharged (from prison and of their debts) in and by another jurisdiction. The absence of extensive debate at the Convention over the Clause's text or its insertion into the Constitution indicates that there was general agreement on the importance of authorizing a uniform federal response to the problems and injustice that such a patchwork system created. Although the Framers considered encompassing insolvency laws within the Full Faith and Credit Clause, so that one jurisdiction would be required to give preclusive effect to the discharges of another jurisdiction, they opted for the Bankruptcy Clause instead, as that was seen as a better way to establish uniform laws relating to bankruptcies. Because bankruptcy jurisdiction, as understood today and at the framing, is principally in rem, the Framers would have understood the Bankruptcy Clause's grant of power to enact laws on the entire "subject of Bankruptcies" to include laws providing, in certain limited respects, for more than simple adjudications of rights in the res. Courts adjudicating disputes concerning bankrupts' estates historically have had the power to issue ancillary orders enforcing their in rem adjudications. The interplay between in rem adjudications and orders ancillary thereto is also evident in this case. Whether or not actions such as preference avoidance proceedings are properly characterized as in rem, those who crafted the Bankruptcy Clause would have understood it to give Congress the power to authorize courts to avoid preferential transfers and to recover the transferred property. Insofar as orders ancillary to the bankruptcy courts' in rem jurisdiction, like orders directing turnover of preferential transfers, implicate states' sovereign immunity from suit, the states agreed in the plan of the Constitutional Convention not to assert that immunity. That is evidenced not only by the Bankruptcy Clause's history, but also by legislation considered and enacted in the immediate wake of the Constitution's ratification. For example, the

Continued on next page.

Bankruptcy Act of 1800 specifically granted federal courts habeas authority to release debtors from state prisons at a time when state sovereign immunity was preeminent among the Nation's concerns, yet there appears to be no record of any objection to that grant based on an infringement of sovereign immunity. In fact, the habeas writ was not made generally available to prisoners for another 67 years, after ratification of the Fourteenth Amendment. This history demonstrates that the power to enact bankruptcy legislation was understood to carry with it the power to subordinate state sovereignty, albeit within a limited sphere. The relevant question thus is not abrogation [as related to 11 U.S.C. § 106(a)], but whether Congress's determination that States should be amenable to preferential transfer proceedings is within the scope of its power to enact "Laws on the subject of Bankruptcies." The answer is that it is. Congress's power, at its option, either to treat states in the same way as other creditors or exempt them from the operation of bankruptcy laws arises from the Clause itself; the relevant "abrogation" is the one effected in the plan of the Convention, not by statute.

▶ ANALYSIS

Justice Thomas in his dissent argued that the adoption of the Constitution merely established federal power to legislate in the area of bankruptcy law, but did not manifest an additional intention to waive the states' sovereign immunity against suit. Regardless of the extent to which the states agreed to waive their sovereign immunity in this area, the *Katz* decision has placed States in the same position that other governments—federal, foreign, and local—have been in all along, and has clarified that the States are subject to Bankruptcy Code enforcement to the same extent as those other jurisdictions.

■━━■

Quicknotes

CERTIORARI A discretionary writ issued by a superior court to an inferior court in order to review the lower court's decisions; the Supreme Court's writ ordering such review.

FOURTEENTH AMENDMENT Declares that no state shall make or enforce any law that shall abridge the privileges and immunities of citizens of the United States. No state shall deny to any person within its jurisdiction the equal protection of the laws.

IN REM An action against property.

MOTION TO DISMISS Motion to terminate an action based on the adequacy of the pleadings, improper service or venue, etc.

SOVEREIGN IMMUNITY Immunity of government from suit without its consent.

■━━■

Granfinanciera, S.A. v. Nordberg

Creditor (D) v. Trustee (P)

492 U.S. 33 (1989).

NATURE OF CASE: Review of denial of request for a jury trial in action for damages for fraudulent transfers.

FACT SUMMARY: Trustee-in-bankruptcy Nordberg (P) sued Granfinanciera (D) to recover fraudulent conveyances, and Granfinanciera (D) requested a trial by jury.

> 🏛 **RULE OF LAW**
> A person who has not submitted a claim against a bankruptcy estate has a right to a jury trial when sued by the trustee in bankruptcy to recover an allegedly fraudulent monetary transfer.

FACTS: The Chase & Sanborn Corporation filed a petition for reorganization under Chapter 11. The trustee, Nordberg (P), filed suit against Granfinanciera (D), alleging that it had received $1.7 million from Chase & Sanborn within one year of the bankruptcy without receiving reasonably equivalent value. Granfinanciera (D) requested a jury trial, but the bankruptcy judge denied the request. Granfinanciera (D) was found liable for constructive fraud. The appellate courts affirmed. The United States Supreme Court granted certiorari.

ISSUE: Does a person who has not submitted a claim against a bankruptcy estate have a right to a jury trial when sued by the trustee in bankruptcy to recover an allegedly fraudulent monetary transfer?

HOLDING AND DECISION: (Brennan, J.) Yes. A person who has not submitted a claim against a bankruptcy estate has a right to a jury trial when sued by the trustee in bankruptcy to recover an allegedly fraudulent monetary transfer. The Seventh Amendment provides for a jury trial for suits at common law, where the value in controversy exceeds twenty dollars. Actions to recover preferential or fraudulent transfers were often brought in law, as opposed to equity, courts in late Eighteenth-century England and therefore fall under the Seventh Amendment right to a jury. Furthermore, unless a legal cause of action involves "public rights," Congress may not deprive litigants of the Seventh Amendment guarantee. A bankruptcy trustee's right to recover a fraudulent conveyance is more accurately characterized as a private right. Therefore Granfinanciera (D) has a right to a jury trial. Reversed and remanded.

> ▶ **ANALYSIS**

The Court did not go on to decide whether bankruptcy judges may actually conduct jury trials. The circuits have since released conflicting decisions on this issue. Congress has also responded with 28 U.S.C. § 157(e), which states: "If the right to a jury trial applies in a proceeding that may be heard . . . by a bankruptcy judge, the bankruptcy judge may conduct the jury trial if specially designated to exercise such jurisdiction by the district court and with the express consent of all parties."

Quicknotes

BANKRUPTCY ESTATE Created by the filing of a petition in bankruptcy and includes all legal and equitable interests of the debtor in property as of that time.

FRAUDULENT CONVEYANCE Conveyances made within one year of filing the bankruptcy petition with intent to defraud creditors and which may be voidable.

Glossary

Common Latin Words and Phrases Encountered in the Law

A FORTIORI: Because one fact exists or has been proven, therefore a second fact that is related to the first fact must also exist.

A PRIORI: From the cause to the effect. A term of logic used to denote that when one generally accepted truth is shown to be a cause, another particular effect must necessarily follow.

AB INITIO: From the beginning; a condition which has existed throughout, as in a marriage which was void ab initio.

ACTUS REUS: The wrongful act; in criminal law, such action sufficient to trigger criminal liability.

AD VALOREM: According to value; an ad valorem tax is imposed upon an item located within the taxing jurisdiction calculated by the value of such item.

AMICUS CURIAE: Friend of the court. Its most common usage takes the form of an amicus curiae brief, filed by a person who is not a party to an action but is nonetheless allowed to offer an argument supporting his legal interests.

ARGUENDO: In arguing. A statement, possibly hypothetical, made for the purpose of argument, is one made arguendo.

BILL QUIA TIMET: A bill to quiet title (establish ownership) to real property.

BONA FIDE: True, honest, or genuine. May refer to a person's legal position based on good faith or lacking notice of fraud (such as a bona fide purchaser for value) or to the authenticity of a particular document (such as a bona fide last will and testament).

CAUSA MORTIS: With approaching death in mind. A gift causa mortis is a gift given by a party who feels certain that death is imminent.

CAVEAT EMPTOR: Let the buyer beware. This maxim is reflected in the rule of law that a buyer purchases at his own risk because it is his responsibility to examine, judge, test, and otherwise inspect what he is buying.

CERTIORARI: A writ of review. Petitions for review of a case by the United States Supreme Court are most often done by means of a writ of certiorari.

CONTRA: On the other hand. Opposite. Contrary to.

CORAM NOBIS: Before us; writs of error directed to the court that originally rendered the judgment.

CORAM VOBIS: Before you; writs of error directed by an appellate court to a lower court to correct a factual error.

CORPUS DELICTI: The body of the crime; the requisite elements of a crime amounting to objective proof that a crime has been committed.

CUM TESTAMENTO ANNEXO, ADMINISTRATOR (ADMINISTRATOR C.T.A.): With will annexed; an administrator c.t.a. settles an estate pursuant to a will in which he is not appointed.

DE BONIS NON, ADMINISTRATOR (ADMINISTRATOR D.B.N.): Of goods not administered; an administrator d.b.n. settles a partially settled estate.

DE FACTO: In fact; in reality; actually. Existing in fact but not officially approved or engendered.

DE JURE: By right; lawful. Describes a condition that is legitimate "as a matter of law," in contrast to the term "de facto," which connotes something existing in fact but not legally sanctioned or authorized. For example, de facto segregation refers to segregation brought about by housing patterns, etc., whereas de jure segregation refers to segregation created by law.

DE MINIMIS: Of minimal importance; insignificant; a trifle; not worth bothering about.

DE NOVO: Anew; a second time; afresh. A trial de novo is a new trial held at the appellate level as if the case originated there and the trial at a lower level had not taken place.

DICTA: Generally used as an abbreviated form of obiter dicta, a term describing those portions of a judicial opinion incidental or not necessary to resolution of the specific question before the court. Such nonessential statements and remarks are not considered to be binding precedent.

DUCES TECUM: Refers to a particular type of writ or subpoena requesting a party or organization to produce certain documents in their possession.

EN BANC: Full bench. Where a court sits with all justices present rather than the usual quorum.

EX PARTE: For one side or one party only. An ex parte proceeding is one undertaken for the benefit of only one party, without notice to, or an appearance by, an adverse party.

EX POST FACTO: After the fact. An ex post facto law is a law that retroactively changes the consequences of a prior act.

EX REL.: Abbreviated form of the term "ex relatione," meaning upon relation or information. When the state brings an action in which it has no interest against an individual at the instigation of one who has a private interest in the matter.

FORUM NON CONVENIENS: Inconvenient forum. Although a court may have jurisdiction over the case, the action should be tried in a more conveniently located court, one to which parties and witnesses may more easily travel, for example.

GUARDIAN AD LITEM: A guardian of an infant as to litigation, appointed to represent the infant and pursue his/her rights.

HABEAS CORPUS: You have the body. The modern writ of habeas corpus is a writ directing that a person (body) being detained (such as a prisoner) be brought before the court so that the legality of his detention can be judicially ascertained.

IN CAMERA: In private, in chambers. When a hearing is held before a judge in his chambers or when all spectators are excluded from the courtroom.

IN FORMA PAUPERIS: In the manner of a pauper. A party who proceeds in forma pauperis because of his poverty is one who is allowed to bring suit without liability for costs.

INFRA: Below, under. A word referring the reader to a later part of a book. (The opposite of supra.)

IN LOCO PARENTIS: In the place of a parent.

IN PARI DELICTO: Equally wrong; a court of equity will not grant requested relief to an applicant who is in pari delicto, or as much at fault in the transactions giving rise to the controversy as is the opponent of the applicant.

IN PARI MATERIA: On like subject matter or upon the same matter. Statutes relating to the same person or things are said to be in pari materia. It is a general rule of statutory construction that such statutes should be construed together, i.e., looked at as if they together constituted one law.

IN PERSONAM: Against the person. Jurisdiction over the person of an individual.

IN RE: In the matter of. Used to designate a proceeding involving an estate or other property.

IN REM: A term that signifies an action against the res, or thing. An action in rem is basically one that is taken directly against property, as distinguished from an action in personam, i.e., against the person.

INTER ALIA: Among other things. Used to show that the whole of a statement, pleading, list, statute, etc., has not been set forth in its entirety.

INTER PARTES: Between the parties. May refer to contracts, conveyances or other transactions having legal significance.

INTER VIVOS: Between the living. An inter vivos gift is a gift made by a living grantor, as distinguished from bequests contained in a will, which pass upon the death of the testator.

IPSO FACTO: By the mere fact itself.

JUS: Law or the entire body of law.

LEX LOCI: The law of the place; the notion that the rights of parties to a legal proceeding are governed by the law of the place where those rights arose.

MALUM IN SE: Evil or wrong in and of itself; inherently wrong. This term describes an act that is wrong by its very nature, as opposed to one which would not be wrong but for the fact that there is a specific legal prohibition against it (malum prohibitum).

MALUM PROHIBITUM: Wrong because prohibited, but not inherently evil. Used to describe something that is wrong because it is expressly forbidden by law but that is not in and of itself evil, e.g., speeding.

MANDAMUS: We command. A writ directing an official to take a certain action.

MENS REA: A guilty mind; a criminal intent. A term used to signify the mental state that accompanies a crime or other prohibited act. Some crimes require only a general mens rea (general intent to do the prohibited act), but others, like assault with intent to murder, require the existence of a specific mens rea.

MODUS OPERANDI: Method of operating; generally refers to the manner or style of a criminal in committing crimes, admissible in appropriate cases as evidence of the identity of a defendant.

NEXUS: A connection to.

NISI PRIUS: A court of first impression. A nisi prius court is one where issues of fact are tried before a judge or jury.

N.O.V. (NON OBSTANTE VEREDICTO): Notwithstanding the verdict. A judgment n.o.v. is a judgment given in favor of one party despite the fact that a verdict was returned in favor of the other party, the justification being that the verdict either had no reasonable support in fact or was contrary to law.

NUNC PRO TUNC: Now for then. This phrase refers to actions that may be taken and will then have full retroactive effect.

PENDENTE LITE: Pending the suit; pending litigation under way.

PER CAPITA: By head; beneficiaries of an estate, if they take in equal shares, take per capita.

PER CURIAM: By the court; signifies an opinion ostensibly written "by the whole court" and with no identified author.

PER SE: By itself, in itself; inherently.

PER STIRPES: By representation. Used primarily in the law of wills to describe the method of distribution where a person, generally because of death, is unable to take that which is left to him by the will of another, and therefore his heirs divide such property between them rather than take under the will individually.

PRIMA FACIE: On its face, at first sight. A prima facie case is one that is sufficient on its face, meaning that the evidence supporting it is adequate to establish the case until contradicted or overcome by other evidence.

PRO TANTO: For so much; as far as it goes. Often used in eminent domain cases when a property owner receives partial payment for his land without prejudice to his right to bring suit for the full amount he claims his land to be worth.

QUANTUM MERUIT: As much as he deserves. Refers to recovery based on the doctrine of unjust enrichment in those cases in which a party has rendered valuable services or furnished materials that were accepted and enjoyed by another under circumstances that would reasonably notify the recipient that the rendering party expected to be paid. In essence, the law implies a contract to pay the reasonable value of the services or materials furnished.

QUASI: Almost like; as if; nearly. This term is essentially used to signify that one subject or thing is almost analogous to another but that material differences between them do exist. For example, a quasi-criminal proceeding is one that is not strictly criminal but shares enough of the same characteristics to require some of the same safeguards (e.g., procedural due process must be followed in a parole hearing).

QUID PRO QUO: Something for something. In contract law, the consideration, something of value, passed between the parties to render the contract binding.

RES GESTAE: Things done; in evidence law, this principle justifies the admission of a statement that would otherwise be hearsay when it is made so closely to the event in question as to be said to be a part of it, or with such spontaneity as not to have the possibility of falsehood.

RES IPSA LOQUITUR: The thing speaks for itself. This doctrine gives rise to a rebuttable presumption of negligence when the instrumentality causing the injury was within the exclusive control of the defendant, and the injury was one that does not normally occur unless a person has been negligent.

RES JUDICATA: A matter adjudged. Doctrine which provides that once a court of competent jurisdiction has rendered a final judgment or decree on the merits, that judgment or decree is conclusive upon the parties to the case and prevents them from engaging in any other litigation on the points and issues determined therein.

RESPONDEAT SUPERIOR: Let the master reply. This doctrine holds the master liable for the wrongful acts of his servant (or the principal for his agent) in those cases in which the servant (or agent) was acting within the scope of his authority at the time of the injury.

STARE DECISIS: To stand by or adhere to that which has been decided. The common law doctrine of stare decisis attempts to give security and certainty to the law by following the policy that once a principle of law as applicable to a certain set of facts has been set forth in a decision, it forms a precedent which will subsequently be followed, even though a different decision might be made were it the first time the question had arisen. Of course, stare decisis is not an inviolable principle and is departed from in instances where there is good cause (e.g., considerations of public policy led the Supreme Court to disregard prior decisions sanctioning segregation).

SUPRA: Above. A word referring a reader to an earlier part of a book.

ULTRA VIRES: Beyond the power. This phrase is most commonly used to refer to actions taken by a corporation that are beyond the power or legal authority of the corporation.

Addendum of French Derivatives

IN PAIS: Not pursuant to legal proceedings.

CHATTEL: Tangible personal property.

CY PRES: Doctrine permitting courts to apply trust funds to purposes not expressed in the trust but necessary to carry out the settlor's intent.

PER AUTRE VIE: For another's life; during another's life. In property law, an estate may be granted that will terminate upon the death of someone other than the grantee.

PROFIT A PRENDRE: A license to remove minerals or other produce from land.

VOIR DIRE: Process of questioning jurors as to their predispositions about the case or parties to a proceeding in order to identify those jurors displaying bias or prejudice.

Casenote® Legal Briefs

80283711R00130

Manhattan Review

Test Prep & Admissions Consulting

Turbocharge Your GMAT:
Reading Comprehension Guide

part of the 6th Edition Series

April 20th, 2016

- ☐ *Thirteen proven Reading Comprehension strategies*
- ☐ *Complete & challenging training sets: 25 passages with over 200 questions*
- ☐ *Never-seen-before dedicated "Understanding the Passage" section*
- ☐ *Never-seen-before "Reading Through Creating Impressions" section*
- ☐ *Concept illustration through info-graphics*
- ☐ *Ample "reasoning-based" questions*
- ☐ *Comprehensive solutions*

www.manhattanreview.com

Copyright and Terms of Use

Copyright and Trademark

All materials herein (including names, terms, trademarks, designs, images, and graphics) are the property of Manhattan Review, except where otherwise noted. Except as permitted herein, no such material may be copied, reproduced, displayed or transmitted or otherwise used without the prior written permission of Manhattan Review. You are permitted to use material herein for your personal, noncommercial use, provided that you do not combine such material into a combination, collection, or compilation of material. If you have any questions regarding the use of the material, please contact Manhattan Review at info@manhattanreview.com.

This material may make reference to countries and persons. The use of such references is for hypothetical and demonstrative purposes only.

Terms of Use

By using this material, you acknowledge and agree to the terms of use contained herein.

No Warranties

This material is provided without warranty, either express or implied, including the implied warranties of merchantability, of fitness for a particular purpose and noninfringement. Manhattan Review does not warrant or make any representations regarding the use, accuracy or results of the use of this material. This material may make reference to other source materials. Manhattan Review is not responsible in any respect for the content of such other source materials, and disclaims all warranties and liabilities with respect to the other source materials.

Limitation on Liability

Manhattan Review shall not be responsible under any circumstances for any direct, indirect, special, punitive, or consequential damages ("Damages") that may arise from the use of this material. In addition, Manhattan Review does not guarantee the accuracy or completeness of its course materials, which are provided "as is" with no warranty, express or implied. Manhattan Review assumes no liability for any Damages from errors or omissions in the material, whether arising in contract, tort or otherwise.

10-Digit International Standard Book Number: (ISBN: 1-62926-069-X)
13-Digit International Standard Book Number: (ISBN: 978-1-62926-069-3)

Last updated on April 20th, 2016.

Manhattan Review, 275 Madison Avenue, Suite 1429, New York, NY 10016.
Phone: +1 (212) 316-2000. E-Mail: info@manhattanreview.com. Web: www.manhattanreview.com

About the Turbocharge your GMAT Series

The Turbocharge Your GMAT Series is carefully designed to be clear, comprehensive, and content-driven. Long regarded as the gold standard in GMAT prep worldwide, Manhattan Review's GMAT prep books offer professional GMAT instruction for dramatic score improvement. Now in its updated 6th edition, the full series is designed to provide GMAT test-takers with complete guidance for highly successful outcomes. As many students have discovered, Manhattan Review's GMAT books break down the different test sections in a coherent, concise, and accessible manner. We delve deeply into the content of every single testing area and zero in on exactly what you need to know to raise your score. The full series is comprised of 16 guides that cover concepts in mathematics and grammar from the most basic through the most advanced levels, making them a great study resource for all stages of GMAT preparation. Students who work through all of our books benefit from a substantial boost to their GMAT knowledge and develop a thorough and strategic approach to taking the GMAT.

- ☐ **GMAT Math Essentials** (ISBN: 978-1-62926-057-0)
- ☐ **GMAT Number Properties Guide** (ISBN: 978-1-62926-058-7)
- ☐ **GMAT Arithmetics Guide** (ISBN: 978-1-62926-059-4)
- ☐ **GMAT Algebra Guide** (ISBN: 978-1-62926-060-0)
- ☐ **GMAT Geometry Guide** (ISBN: 978-1-62926-061-7)
- ☐ **GMAT Word Problems Guide** (ISBN: 978-1-62926-062-4)
- ☐ **GMAT Sets & Statistics Guide** (ISBN: 978-1-62926-063-1)
- ☐ **GMAT Combinatorics & Probability Guide** (ISBN: 978-1-62926-064-8)
- ☐ **GMAT Data Sufficiency Guide** (ISBN: 978-1-62926-065-5)
- ☐ **GMAT Quantitative Question Bank** (ISBN: 978-1-62926-066-2)
- ☐ **GMAT Sentence Correction Guide** (ISBN: 978-1-62926-067-9)
- ☐ **GMAT Critical Reasoning Guide** (ISBN: 978-1-62926-068-6)
- ■ **GMAT Reading Comprehension Guide** (ISBN: 978-1-62926-069-3)
- ☐ **GMAT Integrated Reasoning Guide** (ISBN: 978-1-62926-070-9)
- ☐ **GMAT Analytical Writing Guide** (ISBN: 978-1-62926-071-6)
- ☐ **GMAT Vocabulary Builder** (ISBN: 978-1-62926-072-3)

About the Company

Manhattan Review's origin can be traced directly back to an Ivy League MBA classroom in 1999. While teaching advanced quantitative subjects to MBAs at Columbia Business School in New York City, Professor Dr. Joern Meissner developed a reputation for explaining complicated concepts in an understandable way. Remembering their own less-than-optimal experiences preparing for the GMAT, Prof. Meissner's students challenged him to assist their friends, who were frustrated with conventional GMAT preparation options. In response, Prof. Meissner created original lectures that focused on presenting GMAT content in a simplified and intelligible manner, a method vastly different from the voluminous memorization and so-called tricks commonly offered by others. The new approach immediately proved highly popular with GMAT students, inspiring the birth of Manhattan Review.

Since its founding, Manhattan Review has grown into a multi-national educational services firm, focusing on GMAT preparation, MBA admissions consulting, and application advisory services, with thousands of highly satisfied students all over the world. The original lectures have been continuously expanded and updated by the Manhattan Review team, an enthusiastic group of master GMAT professionals and senior academics. Our team ensures that Manhattan Review offers the most time-efficient and cost-effective preparation available for the GMAT. Please visit www.ManhattanReview.com for further details.

About the Founder

Professor Dr. Joern Meissner has more than 25 years of teaching experience at the graduate and undergraduate levels. He is the founder of Manhattan Review, a worldwide leader in test prep services, and he created the original lectures for its first GMAT preparation class. Prof. Meissner is a graduate of Columbia Business School in New York City, where he received a PhD in Management Science. He has since served on the faculties of prestigious business schools in the United Kingdom and Germany. He is a recognized authority in the areas of supply chain management, logistics, and pricing strategy. Prof. Meissner thoroughly enjoys his research, but he believes that grasping an idea is only half of the fun. Conveying knowledge to others is even more fulfilling. This philosophy was crucial to the establishment of Manhattan Review, and remains its most cherished principle.

The Advantages of Using Manhattan Review

▶ **Time efficiency and cost effectiveness.**

  – For most people, the most limiting factor of test preparation is time.

  – It takes significantly more teaching experience to prepare a student in less time.

  – Our test preparation approach is tailored for busy professionals. We will teach you what you need to know in the least amount of time.

▶ **Our high-quality and dedicated instructors are committed to helping every student reach her/his goals.**

International Phone Numbers and Official Manhattan Review Websites

Manhattan Headquarters	+1-212-316-2000	www.manhattanreview.com
USA & Canada	+1-800-246-4600	www.manhattanreview.com
Argentina	+1-212-316-2000	www.review.com.ar
Australia	+61-3-9001-6618	www.manhattanreview.com
Austria	+43-720-115-549	www.review.at
Belgium	+32-2-808-5163	www.manhattanreview.be
Brazil	+1-212-316-2000	www.manhattanreview.com.br
Chile	+1-212-316-2000	www.manhattanreview.cl
China	+86-20-2910-1913	www.manhattanreview.cn
Czech Republic	+1-212-316-2000	www.review.cz
France	+33-1-8488-4204	www.review.fr
Germany	+49-89-3803-8856	www.review.de
Greece	+1-212-316-2000	www.review.com.gr
Hong Kong	+852-5808-2704	www.review.hk
Hungary	+1-212-316-2000	www.review.co.hu
India	+1-212-316-2000	www.review.in
Indonesia	+1-212-316-2000	www.manhattanreview.id
Ireland	+1-212-316-2000	www.gmat.ie
Italy	+39-06-9338-7617	www.manhattanreview.it
Japan	+81-3-4589-5125	www.manhattanreview.jp
Malaysia	+1-212-316-2000	www.review.my
Mexico	+1-212-316-2000	www.manhattanreview.mx
Netherlands	+31-20-808-4399	www.manhattanreview.nl
New Zealand	+1-212-316-2000	www.review.co.nz
Philippines	+1-212-316-2000	www.review.ph
Poland	+1-212-316-2000	www.review.pl
Portugal	+1-212-316-2000	www.review.pt
Qatar	+1-212-316-2000	www.review.qa
Russia	+1-212-316-2000	www.manhattanreview.ru
Singapore	+65-3158-2571	www.gmat.sg
South Africa	+1-212-316-2000	www.manhattanreview.co.za
South Korea	+1-212-316-2000	www.manhattanreview.kr
Sweden	+1-212-316-2000	www.gmat.se
Spain	+34-911-876-504	www.review.es
Switzerland	+41-435-080-991	www.review.ch
Taiwan	+1-212-316-2000	www.gmat.tw
Thailand	+66-6-0003-5529	www.manhattanreview.com
Turkey	+1-212-316-2000	www.review.com.tr
United Arab Emirates	+1-212-316-2000	www.manhattanreview.ae
United Kingdom	+44-20-7060-9800	www.manhattanreview.co.uk
Rest of World	+1-212-316-2000	www.manhattanreview.com

Contents

Chapter 1

Welcome

Dear students,

At Manhattan Review, we constantly strive to provide the best educational content for the preparation of standardized tests, putting arduous effort into always making things better. This continuous evolution is very important for an examination such as the GMAT, which evolves constantly. Sadly, a GMAT aspirant is often confused with too many options on the market. The challenge is how to choose a book or a tutor that prepares you to reach your goal. Without saying that we are the best, we leave it for you to judge.

This book differs in many respects from standard books available on the market. Unlike any book from other prep companies, this book discusses as many as 13 strategies on how to approach GMAT comprehension passages in detail. We have discussed more than 25 GMAT-like passages and approximately 200 questions. Each passage is explained in a never-seen-before dedicated section entitled "Understanding the Passages". In addition, we use never-seen-before images to illustrate the concept of "Reading Through Creating Impressions". While discussing options, we explained each one in a way that shows you why the correct option is right and why incorrect options are wrong. You will find a number of questions on one of the rare categories – Application or Reasoning based questions.

With the use of graphics and a user-friendly layout, this book is easy to read and to grasp its concepts.

In a nut shell, Manhattan Review's GMAT-Reading Comprehension book is holistic and comprehensive in all respects; it is created so because we listen to what students need. Should you have any query, please feel free to write to us at *info@manhattanreview.com*.

Happy Learning!

Professor Dr. Joern Meissner
& The Manhattan Review Team

Chapter 2

Introduction to Reading Comprehension

 Reading Comprehension is one of three parts in the Verbal section of the GMAT. You are given a passage to read and then answer questions about the content, comprehension, and structure of the passage. Reading Comprehension questions are intermingled with Critical Reasoning and Sentence Correction questions in the Verbal section.

You must have seen reading comprehension passages from your school days on other standardized tests, but the GMAT passages are relatively dull, and are not meant for pleasure-reading. The GMAT seeks to measure your ability to sift through mostly convoluted and unfamiliar topics. The questions test your ability to understand, analyze, and apply information and concepts.

Although it may look like the easiest part of the Verbal section, the time constraints make this aspect very challenging. The topics of the passages are rather dry, coming from Natural Science (Astronomy, Physics, Biology etc.), Social Science (Philosophy, History etc.), Business (Business History, Marketing, Economic Theory etc.), and other assorted topics. The passages presented to you are written in typical GMAT style, which is to say that it may not be very enjoyable. Even a passage on a topic of business which may interest you, and which you plan to study in Business School, will not be an easy ride for you. You will need a careful approach to succeed at these questions. This book will deal with such an approach in detail.

On the GMAT, you can expect to see at least 4 RC passages. Each passage will ask you 3-5 questions, so that means 12 to 14 Reading Comprehension questions of the total 41 questions in the Verbal section. The passages come in two forms: long passages and short passages. Long passages are 300-350 words in 3-5 paragraphs, while short passages are 200-250 words in 2-3 paragraphs.

Of these passages, at least two will be short passages and at least one will be a long passage. Although the Verbal section is adaptive and RC, SC, and CR questions may appear in any order, once you see a RC passage, the particular passage itself is not adaptive. It means that if the passage has three questions, all three will appear one after another and in that order, irrespective of whether you answered the first question incorrectly. There will not be any intermingling of CR and SC questions in the passage. However, not all the RC passages will show

up one after another.

The passage and the questions will be presented through a split-screen. On the left-hand side of the screen, the passage will appear. There may be a vertical scroll bar in the middle of the screen. Be sure that you check it. If there's a scroll bar and you miss it, you will miss out on a chunk of the passage and answer questions incorrectly. The question will appear on the right-hand side of the screen. Once you submit the answer to the question, the next question will appear; however, the passage will remain on the left side of the screen. You cannot go back to the previous question. Also, you cannot move to the next question until you have submitted the answer to the current question. The current format of the GMAT does not number the lines in the passages as it does in the official guide. Whenever necessary, GMAT will use yellow highlighting in the passage to refer to a particular word or phrase.

There are four categories of questions asked in Reading Comprehension. However, a few question types may have two to three sub-divisions within them. We will discuss these in the next chapter.

(1) **General** questions – These questions may ask you to suggest a title for the passage, or state the central idea, or identify the author's primary purpose in writing a part of a sentence or a paragraph. Another variant may be to understand the tone and style of writing used by the author.

(2) **Detail** questions – These questions ask you to understand a specific detail from the passage, or cite a fact used in the passage.

(3) **Inference** questions – These questions ask you to understand the implied meaning of the information presented by the author, or identify the intended meaning of a word or a phrase used figuratively in the passage.

(4) **Reasoning** questions – This is a minor question category. These questions are similar to assumption, strengthen, and weaken question types in Critical Reasoning.

2.1 Reading Strategies

(1) Fall in love with the content of the passage

Whether you love or hate the topic of the passage, you cannot ignore it. The best approach for eating that bitter gourd is to sugar-coat it with your emotions by pretending that you care for the subject and find it very interesting to educate yourself. You can even fake that you like the topic. In fact, you will frequently observe that GMAT passages do add a lot of value to your knowledge bank.

If your mind-set is to wonder why at all you should be bothered to know about the respiratory system of sea-snakes, keep in mind that later in your career you may be asked by your boss to summarize a report on the anatomy of terrestrial animals to understand the environmental impact of some business project. This GMAT RC passage could actually serve you quite well someday.

At least one passage presented to you may be of some interest, but other passages may be on unfamiliar topics. If your background is bio-sciences, you will find the passage on the respiratory system of sea-snakes interesting; on the contrary, the passage on Freudian theory may bore you. If you feel bored, don't just go through the rest of the passage in a hurry; instead, move your eyes away from the computer-screen and look elsewhere, and after a while start again from where you left off. When confronted with a hard CR question, you may choose to give it a blind shot and move on; unfortunately, you cannot afford to give a bitter gourd passage the same treatment because there may be 3-4 questions based on it, and getting all of them wrong comes with a heavy penalty.

Read the first paragraph very cautiously; it sets the purpose and the topic of the passage. Once you understand the topic of the passage, you should gain momentum. There are two extreme approaches for reading the passage: one, read slowly and understand each word, and two, read too fast without comprehending the meaning of the passage. Both approaches have their demerits.

The Slow Approach will put a lot of pressure on you, as you are likely to blindly guess on 2-3 questions due to time constraints and possibly then panic and start committing mistakes.

The Fast Approach will not help you either, as for each question you will have to reread the passage to identify the location where the relevant details are found, and will likely end up reading the passage at least 3 times without a guarantee that the questions attempted are correct. Most GMAT RC questions are not necessarily based on a particular paragraph or a piece of information; they may require you to pool information from 2-3 places in the passage. Even the main point question, which is usually perceived as the one that can be answered with the reading of the first and the last paragraph, can go wrong. GMAT test-makers design the options in such a way that if you miss even one detail, you will get caught in their trap. So, the optimum approach is to read efficiently and effectively.

If you get a convoluted sentence, you should at least look for the main nouns and verbs, just to get a sense of the action going on. Ask yourself: who's doing what, or who's saying what about what? This will gives you the broad idea without too much detail.

At the end of the book, you will find a list of commonly-used words with their meanings to improve your understanding in the Reading Comprehension section.

An effective reader will read efficiently while paying attention to the message, but will side-line intricate details for the time being. This person will keep in mind that this specific detail is parked in this paragraph, and, if needed, will look it up there. Such a reader is basically a big picture reader who reads actively. The key is not to overanalyze the passage as you read it, but to get a general idea of the flow and main point of every paragraph, mentally making a map as you go along.

If you are not a native speaker of English or are not fond of reading, you may improve your reading comprehension by reading from the New York Times, the Wall Street Journal, American Scientist, Popular Science, The Economist, and other competent magazines that contain GMAT-like content. After this, you can even frequent sites that contain research journals to enable you to read complex and verbose data- based passages. You may also read certain novels to improve reading speed.

(2) **Keep summarizing**

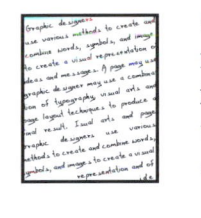 GMAT passages are deliberately drafted with the use of clever language, and made convoluted to make the gist hard to grasp. Often-times the data is hidden in the passage. Due to the sentence structure and style of writing, you will have to take some sort of notes to understand the nuances of the message because simply keeping the message in mind will not help.

Note-taking style is very subjective. Remember that these notes are only for you, and will be needed for just the space of a few minutes.

There are two distinct advantages to note-making. One, it helps you paraphrase the main point because the central message of the passage comprises all the paragraphs of the passage, and not only the first or only the first and last. Two, it helps you know exactly where to look for details when needed. There may be circumstances when specific detail for a particular question lie in two paragraphs, but notes will guide you to look at those particular paragraphs to find the necessary information for that question.

You can summarize at appropriate intervals. If you are comfortable with the content, you can summarize after each paragraph; however, if you find that the content is quite heavy, you may be better off summarizing after every 2-3 sentences.

Below we present to you a passage from medical science. Read the passage first, and then follow the techniques suggested by us. You will find that there is a marked difference in your understanding of the content.

The following passage will teach you three things; one, how to read by creating impressions; two, how to retain the information from the passage; and three, how to take notes.

Passage – Cancer of the colon

Doctors are working on a new non-invasive technique that allows them to 'fly' through the colon and pick out malignancies. Admittedly the first results have been good enough for the team behind the technique to predict that it will become a universal screening system for one of the world's biggest killers. Thus doctors say it will detect more cancers and polyps than do conventional techniques.

One of the predicaments with cancer of the colon is that it is difficult to detect it with great certainty with many of the current tests. If it can be detected at an early stage, treatment is much more effective. The options currently available to doctors include faecal blood testing, barium enema, and colonoscopy. Unfortunately none of these is optimal in terms of performance, safety, or patient acceptance, so Dr David Ahlquist, an oncologist at the Mayo Clinic in Minnesota, has been working on virtual-reality technology.

Blood testing is the most widely used at present, but it is probably the most imprecise. More than half of cancers are likely to be missed in a single test. So far, based on the results of research on 70 patients, doctors have found that despite initial programming glitches, the virtual-reality technology is far more accurate.

2.2   Reading through creating impressions

Sentence	Impression	Inference/Meaning
Doctors are working on a new non-invasive technique that allows them to 'fly' through the colon and pick out malignancies.		I understand that doctors are working on a new technique that does not involve incision. [because of the use of the word "non-invasive"] The rest I could not get—*fly*, and *colon*. **Gist**: Docs wkg. on non-invasive tech. on any disease (malignancies).
Admittedly the first results have been good enough for the team behind the technique to predict that		**Gist**: Non-invasive tech. ⇒ Decent success in predicting something.
it will become a universal screening system for one of the world's biggest killers.		I am sure that 'universal screening system' is used for non-invasive technique. [because of the use of "it" used for the "non-invasive technique"] It means that this technique will overcome the biggest disease (killers). **Gist**: Non-invasive tech. may detect the dreaded disease, and be accepted by all.

Thus doctors say it will detect more cancers and polyps than do conventional techniques.		Now I know what disease is being talked about - it's CANCER. Well, I do not know what polyps are. I guess it must be related to cancer. The statement seems to be the main point; I must keep this in mind. **Gist**: 1. # of cancer cases > conv. tech. 2. Non-invasive tech. seems better than conv. tech.

Gist of paragraph 1: It says that doctors are working on a non-invasive technique to detect cancer of the colon. It is better than the conventional technique and mostly accepted.

Paragraph 1 notes: P1: Docs wkg. on non-inv. tech.; success in predict'g; may detect disease; accepted; # of cancer > conv. tech.; better.

One of the **predicaments** with cancer of the colon is that it is difficult to detect it with great certainty with many of the current tests.	Cancer of Colon	Oh, now I get that 'colon' is a part of the body. The statement states the limitation of conventional techniques. I am becoming more sure now that the previous statement must be the MAIN POINT. I must be wary that the test maker may make a specific question on 'cancer of the colon'. **Gist**: Current tests: Detection of cancer of the colon ⇒ difficult
If it can be detected at an early stage, treatment is much more effective.	*Early detection ⇒ Effective*	They are talking about 3 tests: Hmm...Early detection is the key to treating 'cancer of the colon'.

The options currently available to doctors include faecal blood testing, barium enema, and colonoscopy.		They are talking about 3 tests: I don't know what these mean.
Unfortunately none of these is optimal in terms of performance, safety, or patient acceptance.		**Gist**: 3 tests ⇒ Not reliable
So Dr David Ahlquist, an oncologist at the Mayo Clinic in Minnesota, has been working on virtual-reality technology.		Okay, so a doctor is working on virtual-reality technology. It must be one of the non-invasive techniques. They are talking about 3 tests: A doc wkg. on virtual-reality tech. = non-invasive tech.

Gist of paragraph 2: It says that detection of colon cancer is difficult through current unreliable tests. One of the doctors is working on a virtual-reality technique, a kind of non-invasive technique.

Paragraph 2 notes: P2: Current tests: Detection of colon cancer ⇒ diff.; Early detection == key; 3 tests ⇒ unreliable; A doc wkg. on virtual-reality tech. = non-inv. tech..

Blood testing is the most widely used at present, **but** it is probably the most imprecise.	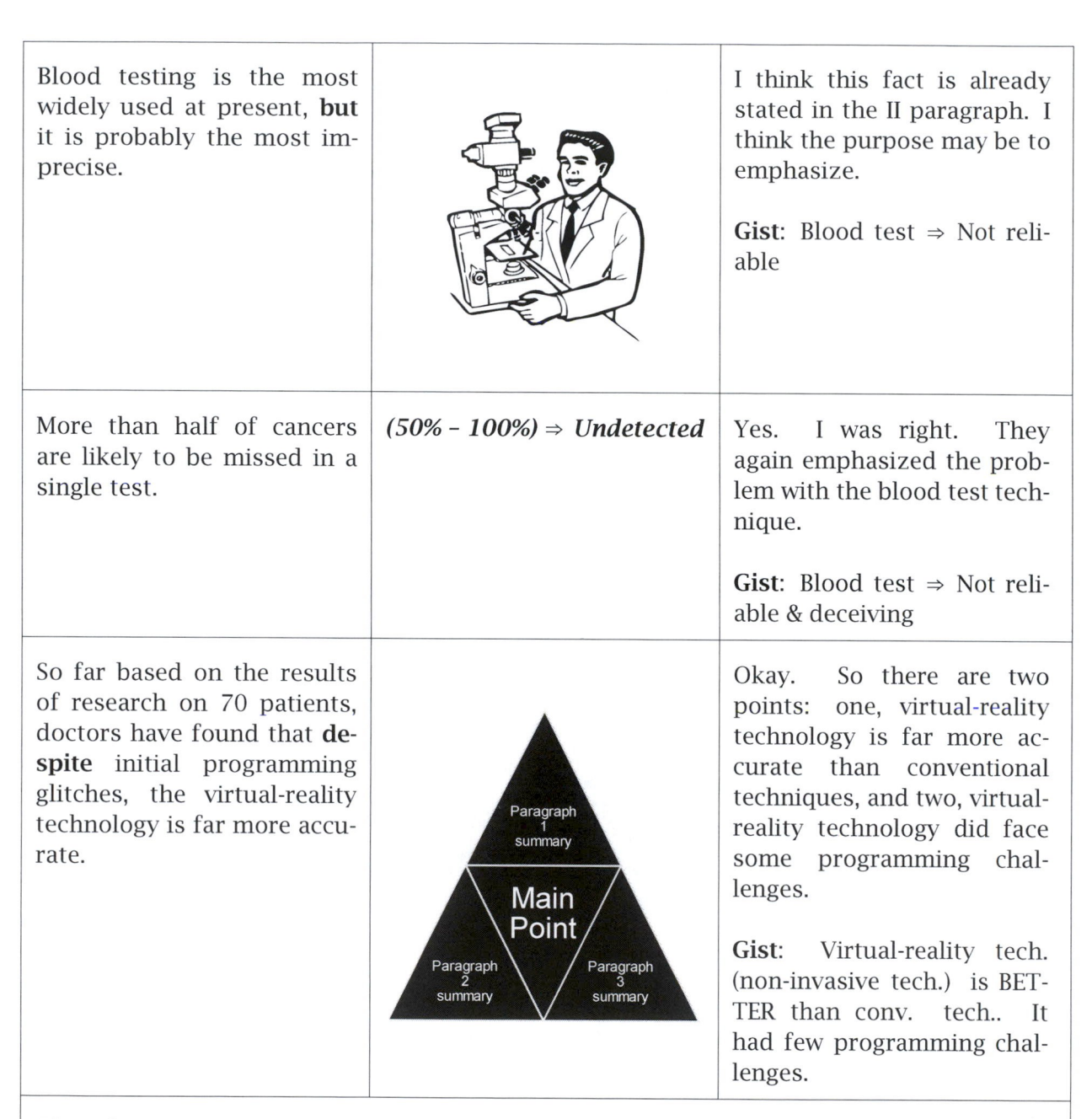	I think this fact is already stated in the II paragraph. I think the purpose may be to emphasize. **Gist:** Blood test ⇒ Not reliable
More than half of cancers are likely to be missed in a single test.	*(50% – 100%)* ⇒ *Undetected*	Yes. I was right. They again emphasized the problem with the blood test technique. **Gist:** Blood test ⇒ Not reliable & deceiving
So far based on the results of research on 70 patients, doctors have found that **despite** initial programming glitches, the virtual-reality technology is far more accurate.		Okay. So there are two points: one, virtual-reality technology is far more accurate than conventional techniques, and two, virtual-reality technology did face some programming challenges. **Gist:** Virtual-reality tech. (non-invasive tech.) is BETTER than conv. tech.. It had few programming challenges.

Gist of paragraph 3: It says that Blood test may give wrong results, and is unreliable. Virtual-reality technique gives better results than the conventional technique does.

Paragraph 3 notes: P3: Bld test ⇒ deceiving; VR tech. » conv. tech.; had challenges.

Paragraph summary

P1: Docs wkg. on non-inv. tech.; success in predict'g; may detect disease; accepted; # of cancer > conv. tech.; better.

P2: Current tests: Detection of colon cancer ⇒ diff.; Early detection = key; 3 tests ⇒ unreliable; A doc wkg. on virtual-reality tech. = non-inv. tech.

P3: Bld test ⇒ deceiving; VR tech. » conv. tech.; had challenges.

(3) **Keep a tab on transition keywords**

 Often the sentences used in the passages are long-winded, and with the use of modifiers, it becomes difficult to grasp the meaning of the sentences. However, with the use of transition words, you can keep a tab on the flow and the direction of the message communicated in the passage.

Transition words such as *however, moreover, furthermore, but, therefore,* and many others tell a lot about the next sentence in relation to the previous sentence. See the following illustration to learn more about them.

Role of furthermore/moreover

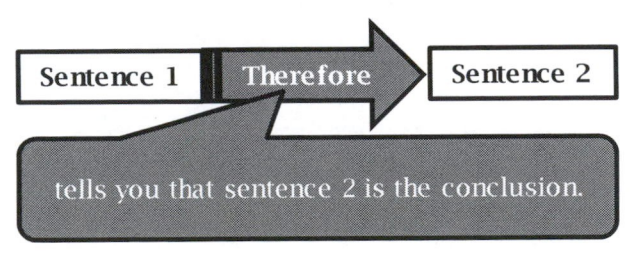

Role of however/but

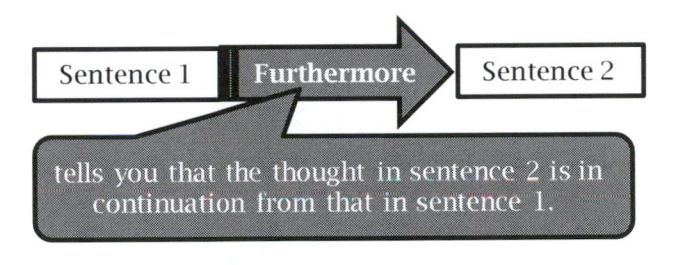

Role of therefore/hence

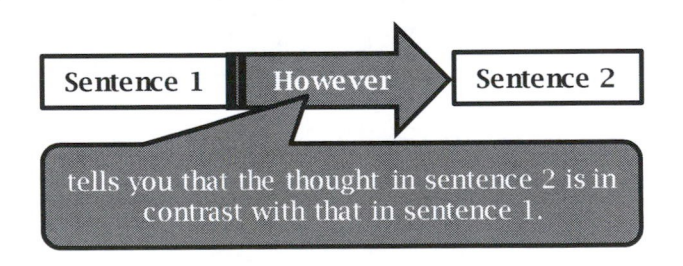

Role of If then

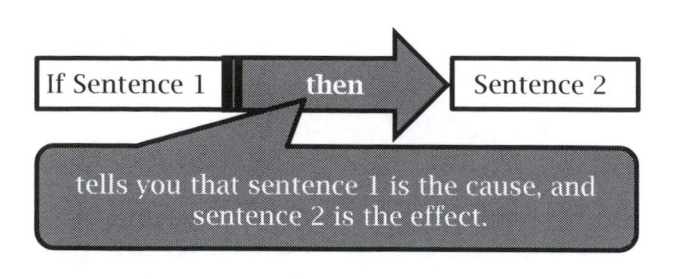

The following table of signaling, or trigger, words may help you understand the tone, style, and the meaning of the passage.

Continuation of thoughts	Opposing thought	Conclusion
Moreover	However	Therefore
Furthermore	But	Hence
In addition	Despite	So
Secondly	In spite of	Implies
Similarly	On the contrary	As a result
Also	Nevertheless	Thus
Too	Conversely	In short
For example	Instead	Inferred
Since	Yet	Consequently
Because	Rather than	In other words
Evidently	Still	
For instance	Surprisingly	
Illustrated by	While	
And	Although	
An analogy	Though	
Analogous	On the other hand	
Considering similar experiences	Even if	
	Actually	
	Notwithstanding	

Let us reexamine the passage we read before, and identify the role of the transition words.

Doctors are working on a new non-invasive technique that allows them to 'fly' through the colon and pick out malignancies. **Admittedly** th~~~~ behind the tech~~~~ screening syste~~~~

> **Admittedly** shows that the next sentence is in continuation of thought from the previous sentence.

Thus d~~~~ convention~~~~

> **Thus** shows that it is a conclusion from the doctors.

One of the predicaments with cancer of the colon is that it is difficult to detect it with great certainty with many of the current tests. **If** it can be detected at an early stage, treatment is much more effecti~~~~ l blood testing~~~~

> **If** shows the cause and effect relationship between the detection and the effectiveness of the treatment.

Unfortunately none of these is optimal in terms of performance, safety or p~~~~nt acceptance. **So** Dr David Ahlquist, an oncologist at the Mayo ~~~~ee~~~~ nnology.

> **Unfortunately** shows the opposing thought.

> **So** shows subsequent action as a result of previous thought.

Blood testing is the ~~~~ it is probably the most imprecise. Mor~~~~ be missed in a single test. **So far** b~~~~ patients, doctors has found that **despite** initial programming glitches, the virtual-reality technology is f~~~~ore accurate.

> **So far** shows the situation and circumstances up to now.

> **despite** shows the opposing thought.

(4) Skim the details and cut the crap

The passage may contain some technical terms which you may not know; however there is no need to know their exact meaning – only the purpose they serve in the passage is important. You should be able to tell what is being said about those technical terms. You should skim the details and cut the crap.

Let us refer to the second paragraph of the passage.

The options currently available to doctors include faecal blood testing, barium enema and colonoscopy. Unfortunately none of these is optimal in terms of performance, safety or patient acceptance. So Dr David Ahlquist, an oncologist at the Mayo Clinic in Minnesota has been working on virtual-reality technology.

We find that there is no need to go into the details of currently available tests–*faecal blood testing, barium enema, and colonoscopy*. At the reading stage it is sufficient to know that there are three tests, what role they play, what the opinion is about the tests, and where in the passage these tests were mentioned. You must have observed that in the paragraph summary and during the exercise of understanding the passage, we did not care much about the meanings of the words 'fly' and 'polyps'. The GMAT test makers write the passages knowing that you may not know all the material. There is no need to know it. The message is: skim the details.

Similarly, it is not important to know what the name is of the doctor researching virtual-reality technology, or what the name of his clinic is. You may refer to the doctor as Doc. The message is: cut the crap. If the need arises to get a detail for a question, you can always go back to the specified location to fetch it.

(5) Abbreviate difficult technical terms

 You may come across many difficult technical terms in the passages that give you a headache. However, there is a way not to see them again. Since you cannot avoid them, it is better that you make them look pretty. For example, if you have trouble pronouncing the name of the doctor, abbreviate the name of the doctor with Dr AH. There may be a passage in which there is a reference of two or more doctors, so it makes it important to know their names, but by abbreviating, you can retain the information without getting bogged down by heavy words.

You must have observed that we combined the three scary-looking tests–faecal blood testing, barium enema, and colonoscopy as '3 tests'. If we need to refer them, we can still make them look pleasing by abbreviating them as 3 tests–FB, BE, and colon test.

(6) Infer the meaning of unfamiliar words

 A passage may contain certain words which you do not know. We advise that you develop decent vocabulary, and that can only be developed through diversified reading of GMAT-like content. However, you can also start with non-GMAT-like content and then switch to GMAT-like content.

That said, you may still be caught off guard by unfamiliar words. The good news is that every test taker comes across such words. Keep in mind, however, that you can infer their meaning through the context in which they are used.

Let us view the first two paragraphs of the passage again.

Doctors are working on a new non-invasive technique that allows them to 'fly' through the colon and pick out **malignancies**. Admittedly the first results have been good enough for the team behind the technique to predict that it will become a universal screening system for one of the world's biggest killers. Thus doctors say it will detect more cancers and polyps than do conventional techniques.

*One of the **predicaments** with cancer of the colon is that it is difficult to detect it with great cer-*

*tainty with many of the current tests. If it can be detected at an early stage, treatment is much more effective. The options currently available to doctors include faecal blood testing, barium enema and colonoscopy. Unfortunately none of these is optimal in terms of performance, safety or patient acceptance. So Dr David Ahlquist, an **oncologist** at the Mayo Clinic in Minnesota has been working on virtual-reality technology.*

Let us infer the meaning of these three words from the context of the passage.

Malignancies: Well, it is difficult to infer the meaning of unknown words if they are used in the first sentence of the passage because we do not have any reference to bank on. With regards to the word—**malignancies**, the supporting phrase - 'fly' through the colon and pick out **malignancies** - cannot help, as 'fly' and 'colon' themselves are unfamiliar and seem to be technical terms. All we can so far infer is that doctors are able to catch **malignancies** with the use of a non-invasive technique, so **malignancies** must be something of a negative aspect if doctors fly and catch them with effort.

Let us look at the next sentence– *Admittedly the first results have been good enough for the team behind the technique to predict that **it** will become a universal screening system for one of the world's biggest killers.*

It refers to the non-invasive technique. Our inference is going in the right direction; **malignancies** must be something negative. It may even refer to **world's biggest killers**. The next sentence helps to narrow down the meaning, so we can assume that **malignancies** means **a kind of cancer (disease)**.

The dictionary meaning of **malignancies** is **menaces, enmities, a cancerous growth-tumour**. So, we were correct in inferring the meaning of the unknown word from the context.

Let us examine another word - **predicaments**

It is used in the sentence – *One of the **predicaments** with cancer of the colon is that it is difficult to detect it with great certainty with many of the current tests.* It can be inferred that **predicaments** may be an aspect or a challenge with respect to cancer of the colon because the clause – it is difficult to detect it with great certainty – hints that it is something negative.

The dictionary meaning of **predicaments** is **difficulties**. Again, we were exactly right in inferring the meaning.

Let us take a look at another word– **oncologist**.

It is used in the sentence – *So Dr David Ahlquist, an **oncologist** at the Mayo Clinic in Minnesota, has been working on virtual-reality technology.*

It is probably quite easy for you to infer the contextual meaning of **oncologist**. Even if you infer it as a **specialist**, it is fine. **oncologist** means **cancer specialist**.

2.3   Active Reading

In the above passage, we saw how we can read a passage and extract its gist by **"creating impressions"** in our minds as we read. Now, let us focus a bit on reading closely. The GMAT test makers are very clever in making scary, dense, and boring passages. They will load the passage with technical and almost indecipherable data. However, they can ask questions only on verbal data, because this is the verbal section! Hence, we must learn to read smartly to gather the right data and impressions as we read the passage. While reading the passage sentence by sentence, don't be in a hurry to understand every word. Learn to pick out the main words in a sentence (usually the nouns and the verbs). Skip technical words and read only their initials so that your flow of thought is maintained. Pay extra attention to words of contrast and comparison, because that's where data is hidden. From most of the sentences, you will end up actually reading only fifty percent of the words, but you will understand fully the intent of the author. From a cluster of words in a sentence, pick out the main words (enough to form a sensible statement) and read only those. Initially, you may find that picking the words takes time. That is okay. Take your time to pick the words, then read the sentence made by your picked words. Repeat with the next sentence. Note-making is recommended. Slowly, you will learn to pick words faster and "fly" through the passage while understanding everything.

Go over the passage again. Try to pick words and make a statement.

We will discuss all questions types in Reading Comprehension in the next chapter.

Chapter 3

Question Types

 We discussed in the introduction that there are four broad categories of questions asked in Reading Comprehension. We shall discuss these in detail now.

3.1 RC Question Types

3.1.1 General

These question types can be further divided into three sub-question types. These questions can be answered after reading the passage and referring to your notes. So, in a way, they save your time. Some test prep companies also call them the **universal** or **global** question type. You will certainly face one general question in the GMAT per passage. There may be 3-4 questions based on this question type out of all the RC questions.

3.1.1.1 Main Point

Main Point questions ask you to suggest a title for the passage, or state the main purpose of writing the passage. It is like the conclusion of the CR arguments. Some test prep companies also call it the **purpose** question type.

3.1.1.2 Function

Function questions identify the role or the function of a word, phrase, sentence, or paragraph. They can also be called main point of the paragraph. This type of question asks about the logical structure of a passage. Some test prep companies also call them **organization** or **why** question types.

3.1.1.3 Tone

Tone questions ask you to understand the tone and style of writing used by the author.

3.1.2 Detail

These questions ask you to retrieve a specific detail from the passage, or cite a fact used in the passage. You have to look up the information or data with the help of keywords in the

questions. These questions usually demand that you go back to the relevant portion of the passage and get the data or information to answer the question. Some test prep companies also call them **specific** question types. There may be 4-6 questions based on this question type out of all the RC questions.

3.1.3   Inference

These questions ask you to understand the implied meaning of the information presented by the author, or identify the intended meaning of a word or a phrase used figuratively in the passage. There may be 4-6 questions based on this question types out of all the RC questions.

3.1.3.1   Specific Inference

This type of question asks about details from the passage. The correct answer is often a paraphrase of something directly stated in the passage. It can also ask about the use of a particular word or phrase.

3.1.3.2   Application

This is a slightly more specific type of inference question where you're asked to choose an answer which mimics a process or exemplifies a situation described in the passage. It can also be called a **parallel reasoning** question type.

3.1.4   Reasoning

This is a **minor** question category. These questions are similar to assumption, strengthen, and weaken question types in Critical Reasoning on the GMAT. Like CR questions, you may be asked to pinpoint an underlying assumption, strengthen, or weaken a claim made by the author in the passage. There may be, at the most, one question based on this question type out of all the RC questions.

3.2 Strategies to solve questions

 We know that there are two types of passages in the GMAT-RC—short passages and long passages. You must understand the time allocation for each passage while attempting them.

3.2.1 Short passage

A short passage will usually come with three questions, so you have approximately 2 minutes each to answer three questions; this includes the time taken to read the passage. Ideally, you should take 2.5 - 3 minutes to read the passage and take notes, and $1 - 1\frac{1}{4}$ minutes to solve each question.

3.2.2 Long passage

A long passage will usually come with four questions, so you have approximately 2 minutes each to answer four questions, including the time taken to read the passage. Ideally, you should take 3.5 - 4 minutes to read the passage and takes notes, and $1 - 1\frac{1}{4}$ minutes to solve each question.

As soon as the passage appears, the first question also shows up. We recommend that you read the question first and then start reading the passage; however, you must not waste time in reading the options.

When you preview the first question, you know for at least one question what to look for in the passage. Mostly the first question will be a general question (main point question). Sometimes, it might be a specific or inference question focusing on a certain detail. Knowing the question beforehand can guide you to focus on the detail, thus saving some time.

> **Strategy 1:**
> *Read the first question, but do not read the options.*

Even if the first question is not a main point question, you must write down the main point of the passage immediately after finishing reading the passage. It is very likely that one of the next questions will be a main point question, and even if the passage does not ask a main point question, this exercise will help you understand the scope of the passage better.

The approach to obtain the main point is discussed in detail in the next section.

3.2.3   Strategies to solve the General question

3.2.3.1   The Main Point question

 According to the Official Guide — *each RC passage is a unified whole — that is, the individual sentences and paragraphs support and develop one main idea or central point which the student must identify.*

Let us examine the characteristics of the main point.

(1) It is a one line statement that expresses the intent of the entire passage.

(2) It is broad in scope; it covers the entire passage and is not restricted to an example or paragraph in the passage.

(3) It is precise in scope; it usually does not contain any particular detail discussed in the passage.

Typical question stems of a main point question are as follows:

- The primary purpose of the passage is...

- The main idea of the passage is...

- Which of the following best describes the organization of the passage?

- The passage as a whole can best be characterized as which of the following?

We will discuss how to derive the main point of a RC passage with the help of paragraph summaries.

We have already seen a couple of examples in the previous chapter about the paragraph summary. It is a one line statement that summarizes the paragraph. The main point of a passage is a summary of the paragraph summaries. It represents all the paragraphs.

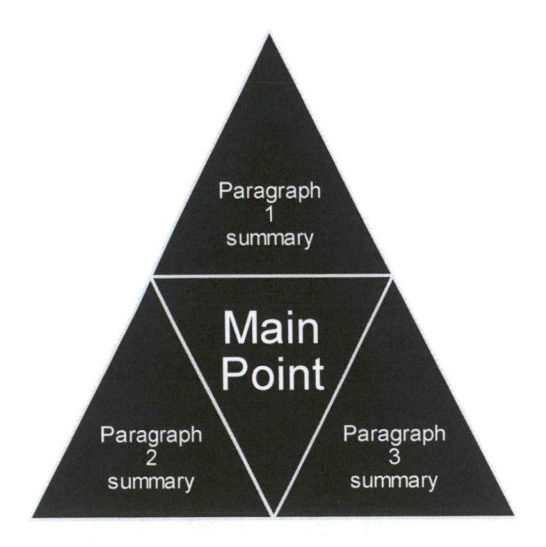

Let us view this in action. We shall present to you summaries of three paragraphs of the passage **Cancer of the Colon,** which we discussed in the first chapter.

Paragraph summary

- **P1**: Docs wkg. on non-inv. tech.; success in predict'g; may detect disease; accepted; # of cancer > conv. tech.; better.

- **P2**: Current tests: Detection of colon cancer ⇒ diff.; Early detection = key; 3 tests ⇒ unreliable; A doc wkg. on virtual-reality tech. = non-inv. tech.

- **P3**: Bld test ⇒ deceiving; VR tech. » conv. tech.; had challenges.

Gist of paragraphs

- **Paragraph 1**: It says that doctors are working on a non-invasive technique to detect cancer of the colon. It is better than the conventional technique and mostly accepted.

- **Paragraph 2**: It says that detection of colon cancer is difficult through current unreliable tests. One of the doctors is working on a virtual-reality technique, a kind of non-invasive technique.

- **Paragraph 3**: It says that a blood test may give wrong results, and is unreliable. Virtual-reality technique gives better results than the conventional technique.

The first paragraph introduces the new technique to detect colon cancer, and this technique is better than conventional ones. The second paragraph discusses the point that detecting colon cancer is difficult currently but the new technique, which is non-invasive, might turn out better. So, the second paragraph continues the first paragraph by detailing the differences between the better, new technique and unreliable conventional techniques. The third paragraph finishes this thought by providing specific details about how the most commonly used conventional method fails. It is hoped that the new technique (called the virtual-reality technique) will do better.

Main point: New hopes with a non-invasive technique that is being researched, and disillusionment with conventional techniques for detection of cancer of the colon.

> **Strategy 2:**
> *Write the main point of the passage immediately after finishing the reading of the passage.*

> **Strategy 3:**
> *Make sure that the main points of each paragraph are represented in the main point.*

> **Strategy 4:**
> *Be wary of extreme words like most, all, always, never, etc., in the options.*

Let us look at the main point question with some options from the **Cancer of the Colon** passage. You can refer to the passage given in first chapter – Introduction.

Question 1 — General, Main Point

(A)   The work involved in detecting colon cancer.

(B)   The difficulties involved in detecting cancer — the biggest killer.

(C)   Virtual reality cancer testing techniques for colon cancer.

(D)   Existing technique problems and new technique possibilities.

(E)   Colon cancer detection techniques and problems.

Solution

Based on the above deductions, we can analyze the options one by one.

(A)   This option is **incorrect** because the passage is not discussing "work" required to detect colon cancer, but rather is concerned with successful detection of colon cancer, the lack of success of conventional techniques, and the hope of success with the new, non-invasive technique.

(B)   This option is **incorrect** because this option is too general. The passage is not discussing "cancer" in general. The scope of the passage is only "colon cancer".

(C)   This option is **incorrect** because while the passage is discussing the new, non-invasive technique (virtual reality technique), it's not discussing only that. The passage also mentions the lack of success of conventional techniques.

(D)   This option is **correct** because it clearly outlines all the main issues discussed in the passage - the lack of success of conventional techniques and the hope of success with the new, non-invasive technique.

(E)   This option is **incorrect** because while this option is close, it's too general. The passage does discuss colon cancer detection techniques. However, the passage distinguishes between conventional and new, innovative techniques, but this option does not convey that. Also, this option implies that all techniques of colon cancer detection have problems, but the passage conveys that the conventional techniques are problematic but the new one is possibly going to solve the problems.

The correct answer is D.

3.2.3.2 Function questions

 Organization or Function questions ask you why the author wrote a particular paragraph, sentence, or even word. The answer to these questions depends on the context of the passage or the issue at hand. The answer to the question will lie near the word or the sentence; you will have to look at the previous sentence or the succeeding sentence to get the information. In 'Why' questions you have to think broadly and ask what role the word or the sentence used in the context plays.

These are akin to Boldfaced questions in the Critical Reasoning section of the GMAT in which you identify the role each portion plays. The same is applicable to function questions.

Typical question stems of a Function question are as follows:

- The author mentioned < something > in the third paragraph in order to...

- One of the functions of the second paragraph is to...

- The highlighted word in the first paragraph is used by the author in order to...

- The discussion of < something > is meant to...

> **Strategy 5:**
> *Apply the strategy you use in Boldfaced or Method of Reasoning question types in CR.*

Let us look at some examples by examining another question from the Cancer of the Colon passage. You can refer to the passage given in the first chapter — Introduction.

Question 2 — General, Function

What purpose does the second paragraph serve with respect to the passage as a whole?

(A) It explains why the new technique will be more successful than the conventional one.

(B) It provides the main point of the passage.

(C) It presents one of the main reasons for development of the innovative technique.

(D) It describes alternatives available for the virtual reality technique.

(E) It provides explanations for why conventional techniques are problematic.

Solution

The above question asks us to find the purpose of the second paragraph with respect to the whole passage. This is a function question from the general category. We have to figure out what function the second paragraph serves in the bigger scheme of things.

The first paragraph introduces the new technique under development.

The second paragraph contains information about conventional techniques. However, at the end of the second paragraph lies the reason behind mentioning the given information — "Unfortunately none of these is optimal in terms of performance, safety or patient acceptance. So Dr. David Ahlquist, an oncologist at the Mayo Clinic in Minnesota, has been working on virtual-reality technology." Thus the given information is serving the purpose of explaining why Dr. A has been working on a virtual-reality technique.

The third and final paragraph explains why hopes are pinned on this new technique.

The purpose of the passage is to present the hopes for the new technique and problems with conventional techniques.

Thus the second paragraph provides an excellent basis for the development of the new technique.

Let's analyze the options one by one.

(A)   This option is **incorrect** because the second paragraph does not state that the new technique will be more successful, but the third paragraph does.

(B)   This option is **incorrect** because discussing only conventional techniques is not the main point of the passage. The main point is "colon cancer detection techniques and problems". The second paragraph discusses only conventional techniques in general.

(C)   This option is **correct** because the last line (So far....accurate) of the second paragraph does provide this clue. The details of the conventional technique are given to explain why the need for a new technique exists. This is the paragraph's purpose in the passage — to explain why the new technique is under development.

(D)   This option is **incorrect** because it is factually wrong. The whole passage does not present any alternatives to virtual-reality techniques.

(E)   This option is **incorrect** because while the paragraph provides information about conventional techniques and their problematic nature, that is not the purpose of the paragraph. It does not provide explanations. The purpose of the paragraph is to explain why Dr. A is developing the virtual-reality technique. [This is substantiated by the "so" sentence]. This option is tricky because it contains an answer for "what is presented in the second paragraph?" but this option does not answer "why is the second paragraph present in the passage?"

The correct answer is C.

3.2.3.3   Tone questions

The tone of a passage is the author's emotion or feeling, associated with his content. The style is the particular way the author uses the language to articulate the content. Most style or tone questions will include the words 'attitude,'

'tone,' 'style,' 'feeling,' etc. The most important thing you should do while going through a Reading Comprehension passage is to understand the author's tone. Some information in the passage will come from the author's attitude and writing style.

The same way modulation plays an important role in speech, tone plays a role in understanding the intent of the words written by the author. Adjectives and adverbs used by the author to express his emotions form the tone and style because they are openly expressive.

GMAT passages can be categorized into three broad types of tones: **Explanatory, Analytical, and Opinionated**

- **Explanatory**: This can also be considered a **descriptive** tone. The author does not offer any opinion, recommendation, or analysis of the issue at hand.

- **Analytical**: This is the tone when the author wants to analyze a situation, topic, or problem. The tone will not necessarily be explicit, but it will contain some subjective paragraphs, sentences, or phrases with the use of suggestive adjectives and adverbs.

- **Opinionated**: A tone can be characterized as opinionated if the author clearly expresses his feelings and emotions while presenting his views or evaluating a theory.

Let us examine a paragraph written with a **neutral** tone.

> *The Morton and Jackson Company registered a 2.58% growth rate in the third and fourth quarters. During the same period, the industry clocked a 10.28% growth rate. The management and the CEO are figuring out what caused the growth rate.*

You may have observed that the paragraph is written to convey information about the performance of the Morton and Jackson Company in the third and fourth quarters. It doesn't explain or analyze the cause or offer any opinion.

Let us see the same paragraph written with an **opinionated** tone.

> *It is ironic that the Morton and Jackson Company registered a dismal growth rate in the third and fourth quarters despite the industry showing a double-digit growth rate. It is a matter of grave concern that, in spite of a much acclaimed performance in the first and second quarters, the company is going downhill.*

The passage is presented to you again highlighted with suggestive adjectives and adverbs. These will help you sense the emotions and feeling associated with them.

*It is **ironic** that the Morton and Jackson Company registered a **dismal** growth rate in the third and fourth quarters despite the industry showing a double-digit growth rate. It is a matter of **grave concern** that, in spite of a much **acclaimed** performance in the first and second quarters, the company is going **downhill**.*

Let us view the same paragraph written with an **analytical** tone.

The Morton and Jackson Company registered a 2.58% growth rate in the third and fourth quarters; however, the industry clocked a 10.28% growth rate during the same period. There are contradicting theories flying within the company to understand the dip of 7.7% points in the growth rate. On one hand, the management blames inefficient operations, alluding that the onus lies on the CEO, while on the other hand, the CEO accuses the workers' union of a 'Go-Slow' method of striking. It cannot be settled without acquiring more information about both sides of the story.

The passage is presented to you again highlighted with suggestive adjectives, adverbs, and phrases. These will help you sense the implied intent of the author.

*The Morton and Jackson Company registered a 2.58% growth rate in the third and fourth quarters; however, the industry clocked a 10.28% growth rate during the same period. There are contradicting theories flying within the company to **understand the dip of 7.7% points** in the growth rate. On one hand, the management blames **inefficient operations, alluding that the onus lies on the CEO**, while on the other hand, the **CEO accuses the workers' union of a 'Go-Slow' method of striking**. It cannot be settles without acquiring more information about both sides of the story.*

Let us read the same paragraph written with an **explanatory** tone.

The Morton and Jackson Company's 2.58% growth rate in the third and fourth quarters, despite the industry's 10.28% growth rate during the same period, is understandable. The management's wish to make the CEO accountable for the low growth rate is natural because the responsibility of efficient operations lies with the CEO. The CEO wishes to make the workers' union accountable for the low growth rate since the responsibility of efficient operations lies with the union.

The passage is presented to you again with the relevant sentences highlighted. Reading the passage, you will sense that the author's intent is to explain the causes.

The Morton and Jackson Company's 2.58% growth rate in the third and fourth quarters, despite the industry's 10.28% growth rate during the same period, is understandable. The management's wish to make the CEO accountable for the low

*growth rate is natural **because** the responsibility of efficient operations lies with the CEO. The CEO wishes to make the workers' union accountable for the low growth rate **since** the responsibility of efficient operations lies with the union.*

A typical question stem of a Tone question is as follows:

- The tone of the passage can be best described as:

- The author's attitude toward < subject > might best be described as which of the following?

- Which of the following best describes the tone of the passage?

- Based on the statements in lines < line numbers >, which of the following could be inferred about the author's attitude toward < subject >?

Strategy 6:
Write one or two words in shorthand describing the tone of the passage immediately after finishing the reading of the passage.

Strategy 7:
Don't be swayed by couple of suggestive adjectives or adverbs; judge the tone for the context as a whole.

Let us look at an example with another question from **Cancer of the Colon** passage. You can refer to the passage given in the first chapter — Introduction.

Question 3 — Tone

According to the passage, the tone of the author towards the conventional techniques mentioned in the passage can be best described as

(A) Qualified approval

(B) Cautious optimism

(C) Ruthless criticism

(D) Half-hearted acceptance

(E) Disillusionment and lack of trust

Solution

The question asks us to ascertain the tone of the author towards the conventional techniques. This is a tone question from the general category.

The author is clearly not analytical or explanatory, but is opinionated, as evidenced by use of words like "unfortunately", "admittedly", etc. The author is not neutral or positive towards the conventional techniques. He bears negative tones when discussing the conventional methods and uses the word "unfortunately" for those techniques. However, he does not criticize the techniques; he merely presents the fact that the tests are imprecise and unreliable.

Let's go over the options one by one.

(A)   This option is **incorrect** because the author does not approve but disapproves of the conventional techniques.

(B)   This option is **incorrect** because the author expresses optimism about the new technique and not about the conventional ones.

(C)   This option is **incorrect** because the author does not ruthlessly (viciously and cruelly) criticize the techniques, but points out that they're not useful and are inaccurate.

(D)   This option is **incorrect** because the author does not accept the techniques but rather disapproves of them.

(E)   This option is **correct** because the author does mention the lack of success of the conventional techniques and does not trust them because he calls them imprecise and unreliable.

The correct answer is E.

3.2.4   Strategies to solve a Detail question

 As the name suggests, Detail questions ask about the details in the passage. Your task is to locate a detail asked in the question in the relevant portion of the passage. It is likely that the words or the phrases used in the question will not match those of the passage; however, having understood the meaning from the question, look for the detail in the passage. Generally, the correct answer will be a restatement of part of the passage.

Frequently test makers make options that are true according to the passage and seem attractive, but they may not be relevant to the question asked. Your task is to find the details not only true with respect to the passage, but also relevant to the question.

Sometimes the information you need is cleverly hidden by the author. It may be possible that the correct option is a rephrasing of the specific detail, but is written in such a convoluted manner that you do not realize that it is what you want.

Typical question stems of a Detail question are as follows:

- According to the passage, the author suggests which of the following to...

- According to the passage, the reason for <detail> is due to...

- The author quotes all the following as a <danger to mankind> EXCEPT...

Strategy 8:
Test makers cleverly hide information; unearth it.

Strategy 9:
Any true detail is not necessarily the answer; the details must be true as well as relevant.

Let us look at an example with another question from the **Cancer of the Colon** passage. You can refer to the passage given in the first chapter — Introduction.

Question 4 — Detail

According to the passage, the author would most likely agree with which of the following as an advantage of virtual-reality testing over conventional methods?

(A)   It is completely reliable and yields precise results.

(B)   It has been adopted as the standard test throughout the world.

(C)   It can detect cancerous growth at an earlier stage than can conventional testing.

(D)   Results are obtained much faster than conventional tests.

(E)   Surgical invasion is not required to obtain results.

Solution

The question is to find some detail about virtual-reality testing that the author will agree with as an advantage over conventional methods.

Let's go over the options one by one.

(A) This option is **incorrect** because while the author says that the conventional methods are unreliable, he does not necessarily say that the virtual reality technique is completely reliable. In fact, he calls the technique "far more accurate" but not "completely accurate".

(B) This option is **incorrect** because the technique is still being tested and could not have been adopted all over the world.

(C) This option is **incorrect** because we cannot infer whether it can detect cancerous growth at an earlier stage than can conventional testing. All we can say is that the new technique is more accurate.

(D) This option is **incorrect** because we cannot infer whether it detects cancer faster than conventional testing. All we can say is that the new technique is more accurate.

(E) This option is **correct** because this can be inferred from the passage. The author mentions that the technique is "non-invasive".

The correct answer is E.

3.2.5   Strategies to solve Inference question

These questions are identical to the inference questions asked in Critical Reasoning on the GMAT. Inference questions ask you to draw the inference from a word, phrase, or sentence used in the context. You have to understand the implied meaning unstated by the author, but it **must be true** according to the passage.

These questions pose a challenge as the required information may be found in several places in the passage, and you have to combine them to make a must-be-true inference.

Detail questions and Inference questions are logically the same, as both ask for the must-be-true detail from the passage, but Inference questions go beyond what is written in the passage. They ask you to infer or imply what is not written, yet is true according to the passage.

The key is not to infer something that is true in real-life, but that is true as per the passage. Be confined to the boundaries of the passage.

Typical question stems of Inference question are as follows:

- The author would most likely agree with which of the following...

- It can be inferred from the passage that...

- The passage suggests that <something> may cause <something> if...

Strategy 10:
Beware of the "true in the real world" trap; be confined to the scope of the passage.

Strategy 11:
Justify all relevant information. Do not satisfy yourself with 'could be true'; strive for 'must be true'.

Strategy 12:
Beware of boundary line words (extreme words); be skeptical.

Let us look at an example from another question from the **Cancer of the Colon** passage. You can refer to the passage given in the first chapter — Introduction.

Question 5 — Specific Inference

According to the passage, which of the following can be inferred?

(A) The screening technique can be used for other types of cancers with the same precision and accuracy.

(B) This technique will make curing colon cancer a relatively simple task.

(C) More than half of cancers go undetected.

(D) There are only three alternatives to virtual reality screening.

(E) Detection is only one of the problems in treatment of colon cancer.

Solution

The question is to find the correct inference. This is a specific inference question from the Inference category.

Let's go over the options one by one.

(A) This option is **incorrect** because we cannot say that the technique will work with the same precision and accuracy for other cancers.

(B) This option is **incorrect** because the technique is meant only for detection and not for curing colon cancer. After detection, there may be other complications in the treatment.

(C) This option is **incorrect** because it is too extreme. We cannot say how many cancers go undetected. All we know is that colon cancer is one of the biggest killers and that detecting it early is one of the problems. However, we don't know all the problems or the other cancer types and their detection facts.

(D) This option is **incorrect** because the passage states that "currently" three alternatives are available, implying that there have been more alternatives in the past and might be in the future.

(E) This option is **correct** because the first line of the second paragraph (One of the predicaments ... current tests) affirms this fact. The detection of colon cancer is one of the problems. Treatment can have other complications too.

The correct answer is E.

3.2.6 Strategies to solve a Reasoning-based question

 As we have said, this is a minor type; you will seldom see more than one question based on reasoning. You may be asked to identify the underlying assumption in the conclusion by the author, or which piece of information can make the conclusion strong or weak. These questions are identical to Assumption, Strengthen, and Weaken question types in Critical Reasoning on the GMAT.

Typical question stems of Inference question are as follows.

- Which of the following, if true, would help conclude <something>?

- Which of the following, if true, would undermine the conclusion <something>?

- Which of the following was implied while concluding <something>?

> **Strategy 13:**
> *Treat it as if you were attempting a Critical Reasoning question; apply the strategies used in CR.*

Let us look at an example with another question from the **Cancer of the Colon** passage. You can refer to the passage given in the first chapter — Introduction.

Question 6 — Reasoning

Which of the following, if true, would most weaken the implications of the last sentence of the passage, keeping it in perspective of the passage?

(A) Programming glitches, if unresolved, can influence the results of the program.

(B) Patients are not always enthusiastic about virtual reality programs, especially in cases of serious illnesses.

(C) Setting up virtual-reality scanners will be quite expensive, even if it's only a one-time cost.

(D) Colon cancers are fast becoming the biggest "killers" in the USA, beaten only by diabetes.

(E) Blood testing can detect colon cancers usually when the cancer has been around for one and a half years.

Solution

The question is to weaken the last line of the passage. So, this is a Reasoning question. The last line is: "So far based on the results research on 70 patients, doctors have found that despite initial programming glitches, the virtual-reality technology is far more accurate." The last sentence states that the virtual reality technique is far more accurate, but some programming

glitches need to be worked out. This is based on results obtained from 70 patients. Any information that weakens the conclusion that this technique is more accurate will be the answer.

Let's go over the options one by one.

(A)   This option is **correct** because if this is true, then the programming glitches might have influenced the results, and the accuracy results might not necessarily be true.

(B)   This option is **incorrect** because patients' enthusiasm will not affect the technique's accuracy or results.

(C)   This option is **incorrect** because cost is not mentioned as an issue at all in the passage and, thus, this is out of scope.

(D)   This option is **incorrect** because this does not weaken or strengthen the last sentence. It is a simple fact.

(E)   This option is **incorrect** because we know that blood tests are imprecise and don't yield accurate results. From what point of time they detect cancer is irrelevant to the virtual reality technique.

The correct answer is A.

Now you should be well-versed in passage-reading, question types, and their strategies.

Let us try the same on the practice questions that follow in the next chapter.

Chapter 4

GMAT-like practice passages

4.1   Passage 1 (Sales force automation)

(From a text published in 1998)

Companies continue to miss the mark in their quest for Sales Force Automation (SFA), over-looking the most critical success factor-the user. In technology deployment, the implementation team assumes the intended users only have a baseline level of computer discipline but frequently mistake the lack of technology use as low literacy on computers. This leads them
5 to adopt unsuitable training techniques. In reality, today's sales department are mostly made up of users who have been exposed to computers but who have never had to use them consistently and struggle to grasp how much strategic value SFA will have. An SFA project's success hinges on creating a situation where both sales representatives and managers can reap the benefits of the SFA tools but all too often they haven't relied on technology as a strategic tool
10 to meet objectives.

Their compensation and job performance are very quantifiable, based on how well they do against a set of revenue targets so inevitably they tend to define SFA in terms of its usefulness handling the transactions they normally work on. The SFA market has done a good job of
15 selling the benefits of SFA tools to drive sales performance but, having convinced companies to purchase systems, there is intense pressure to achieve a strong return on investment. To ensure a successful SFA implementation, companies need to set realistic expectations and consider issues that are unique when deploying the system.

1.   The main purpose of the author in discussing the various aspects of SFA is to

   (A)   explain how difficult it is to get any return on investment from SFA

   (B)   discuss the various advantages and disadvantages of SFA

   (C)   point out how companies are missing out on getting maximum benefit from SFA

   (D)   criticize the SFA market for not having trained the users well enough in SFA

   (E)   present the idea that SFA is only useful practically in keeping transactional entries

2.   According to the passage, traditional training approaches are inappropriate for SFA projects because

   (A)   the number of SFA users is too low and the users are too inexperienced

   (B)   user management teams lack experience to properly define transactional goals

   (C)   these attempt to correct a perceived technology ignorance among SFA users

   (D)   these fail to improve computer literacy, a missing component among users

   (E)   these are not capable of helping companies accurately define transactional goals as needed

3.   The author implies which of the following regarding SFA in recommending that SFA be used optimally?

   (A)   SFA is a perfect tool to keep track of transactional goals of the sales teams.

   (B)   SFA can be used for much more than just handling transactions.

    (C)   SFA can yield a lot of quantifiable benefits to the managers of the sales force.

    (D)   SFA can be used to keep track of the revenue targets set to the sales force.

    (E)   SFA must be used only by experienced users who can maximize its benefits.

4. According to the passage, what does the effective implementation of SFA projects depend on?

    (A)   training users for more than baseline functions of SFA

    (B)   making sure managers and sales staff meet SFA goals

    (C)   ensuring staff accepts SFA into their routines

    (D)   raising the literacy level of SFA trainers

    (E)   quantifying job performance against revenue goals

5. The author would most likely agree with which of the following actions of a company as being crucial to a positive outcome for SFA projects?

    (A)   Properly training the training staff

    (B)   Defining SFA applications in terms of the nature of transactions and goals

    (C)   Factoring in organizational characteristics to accordingly set attainable goals

    (D)   Intensifying the pressure on managers to achieve a return on SFA investments

    (E)   Linking use of sales performance with SFA to ensure return on investment

4.2 Passage 2 (The WTO and sustainable development)

(From a text published in 1999)

Environmental concern and development are inextricably linked. Experience demonstrates that environmental standards and cleaner production are compatible with and supportive of economic growth. Healthy people and ecosystems are more productive. This link between economic growth and environmental improvement is enshrined, together with the commitment
5 to development, in the World Trade Organization's Preamble, which includes sustainable development as a basic objective of the trading system. In endorsing this concept, despite some reservations, WTO members unanimously recognized that trade and the economic growth WTO helps to create must be fostered in the context of sustainable development which integrates economic, social and environmental policies. Economic growth, sustainable development, and
10 opportunity for citizens are fundamental goals of every society. And the record of the past five decades clearly shows how the trading system has helped us reach some of these goals.

Since 1960, the WTO has negotiated a 90% drop in tariffs, and non-tariff barriers to trade have also been dramatically reduced. Moreover, market access for agriculture and services will be
15 further expanded upon conclusion of the next Uruguay Round. Thus, since 1960 trade has grown fifteen-fold; world economic production has quadrupled; and world per capita income has more than doubled. However, has the World Trade Organization done enough to promote sustainable development and protect the environment? The answer is yet to be presented by WTO. In reference to the concept of sustainable development, the Brundtland Commission Re-
20 port of 1987 stated "we must meet the needs of the present without compromising the ability of future generations to meet their own needs." Have any laws been made to make sustainable development mandatory? Taking into account state practice, treaty law, international case law and relevant legal literature, sustainable development is not yet a norm of international law. Currently it reflects a policy goal of the international community. This method of taking
25 a concept so important only as a precautionary guideline has brought the WTO's intentions regarding sustainable development into question.

1. Which of the following titles would be most appropriate for this passage?

   (A) The Work of the WTO
   (B) WTO Measures to Protect the Environment
   (C) Healthy trade and ecosystems
   (D) The WTO and the Environment
   (E) The Link between Trade and the sustainable development

2. According to the passage, under what conditions did the WTO endorse the link between the environment and sustainable development?

   (A) By recognizing that development is the fundamental goal of every society
   (B) By committing the WTO itself to environmental improvement
   (C) By declaring that trade must be based on sustainable development
   (D) By refuting the concept of temporary development as a basis for trade
   (E) By understanding healthy ecosystems

3. Why does the author present the question "... has the World Trade Organization done enough ... environment?" in the second paragraph (line 17)?

   (A) To question the WTO on its actions taken so far to assess them

   (B) To suggest that the WTO hasn't done enough towards sustainable development

   (C) To imply that sustainable development is an impossible goal to attain for the WTO

   (D) To create doubts in the readers' minds about the usefulness of the WTO

   (E) To introduce doubts about the WTO's actions since its inception

4. According to the information presented in the passage, with which of the following would the writer of the passage most likely disagree?

   (A) It isn't necessary to compromise on economic goals to achieve sustainable growth.

   (B) The WTO should encourage countries to care for the environment as well as economic progress.

   (C) The WTO is not more motivated by the desire for expanding trade than towards environmental concerns.

   (D) Decreasing tariffs increases world trade.

   (E) The WTO is not instrumental in protecting the global environment.

5. It can be inferred from the passage that the conclusion of the Uruguay Round will

   (A) open the way to environmental protection measures

   (B) bring new laws towards sustainable development

   (C) lead to new global trade agreements

   (D) see more reductions in tariffs and trading obstacles

   (E) lead to dramatic trade expansion and global growth

4.3   Passage 3 (Sourcing therapeutic proteins)

(From a text published in 1999)

Once a rarely used subset of medical treatments, protein therapeutics have increased dramatically in number and frequency of use since the introduction of the first recombinant protein therapeutic–human insulin–25 years ago. Protein therapeutics already have a significant role in almost every field of medicine, but this role is still only in its infancy. Human proteins, such
5   as erythropoietin, granulocyte colony–stimulating factor and alpha-L-iduronidase, are in great demand for the treatment of a variety of diseases. Whereas some can be purified from blood, this is expensive and runs the risk of contamination by AIDS or hepatitis C. Proteins can be produced in human cell culture but costs are very high and output small. Much larger quantities can be produced in bacteria or yeast but the proteins produced can be difficult to purify
10   and they lack the appropriate post-translational modifications that are needed for efficacy in vivo.

By contrast, human proteins that have appropriate post-translational modifications can be produced in the milk of transgenic sheep, goats and cattle. Currently, research groups around
15   the world are investigating whether transgenic animals such as goats, cattle, pigs, rabbits and chickens can be used to produce therapeutic proteins. The animals are used as sterile bioreactors to produce large, complex proteins or proteins that can't be made in other cell systems. Output can be as high as 40 g per liter of milk and costs are relatively low. An advantage of producing transgenic animals is it uses less than half the experimental animals than does
20   pronuclear injection. Also, it is possible to specify the sex of offspring and thereby reduce the time taken to generate a flock. The main disadvantages of making therapeutic proteins in animals are that it takes a long time to generate and validate transgenic animals, that proteins can't be harvested until lactation begins, and that the transgene may affect the animal, for example, as the transgene inserts randomly into a chromosome, it may disrupt a gene required
25   for an important function. Notwithstanding these, the number of therapeutic proteins being developed by the biomedical industry is growing rapidly, and some scientists are predicting that demand for proteins will soon exceed their ability to supply them. Transgenic animals could provide an alternative source of therapeutic proteins to help meet these demands.

1.   Which of the following would best serve as an appropriate title for the given passage?

   (A)   Transgenic animals and proteins

   (B)   Human proteins from transgenic animals

   (C)   Human protein harvesting

   (D)   Protein therapeutics

   (E)   Advantages and disadvantages of protein therapeutics

2.   According to the passage, what is one of the advantages of human proteins over proteins obtained from bacteria?

   (A)   They can be produced in much larger quantities.

   (B)   They can be produced in exceedingly pure forms.

    (C)   They can be produced at much higher costs than any other.

    (D)   They take the least amount of time to produce.

    (E)   They can be given the appropriate post-translational modifications.

3.   Which of the following questions does the passage answer?

    (A)   Why is the output of proteins from human cell cultures limited?

    (B)   Why are the proteins produced from bacteria unsuitable for use in treatments?

    (C)   How much usable protein is produced by a flock of transgenic animals?

    (D)   Why are animals better for transgenic production than sheep?

    (E)   What diseases can be cured from protein therapeutics and not by any other method?

4.   According to the passage, all of the following is unsupported about protein therapeutics, EXCEPT that they

    (A)   can be used to treat AIDS and Hepatitis C.

    (B)   cure diabetes in humans.

    (C)   cannot be produced in transgenic animals.

    (D)   are used to create human insulin.

    (E)   treat undefined conditions.

5.   According to the passage, which of the following can be said about animals produced by pronuclear injection?

    (A)   It takes twice the time to produce a pronuclear flock.

    (B)   It isn't possible to predict their sex.

    (C)   More than double the number of transgenic animals is required to produce the same quantity of tissue activators.

    (D)   They make better test animals than do transgenic animals.

    (E)   Most animals cannot be produced with pronuclear injection but sheep can.

6.   According to the passage, with which of the following statements would the author most likely agree?

    (A)   Producing human proteins in transgenic animals can be an alternative source of treatment.

    (B)   Human proteins are the best possible way for future research in medicine.

    (C)   Human proteins from transgenic animals is the only way we can meet the demands of the medical industry.

    (D)   Harvesting human proteins from bacteria or blood is absolutely unnecessary and economically unfeasible.

    (E)   Protein therapeutics is the most important discovery of the previous century in medical research.

7.   Which of the following, if true, would most weaken the author's contention against proteins produced from human cell culture?

   (A)   Proteins from human cell culture are the purest possible forms.

   (B)   The bigger the output required, the lower the cost of human cell culturing.

   (C)   Human cell culture is not opposed, as is producing transgenic animals, by animal rights activists.

   (D)   Culturing human cells in a lab is possible with a minimum amount of equipment and takes half the time of producing transgenic animals.

   (E)   Proteins produced in human cell culture are devoid of contamination and very accurate in replication.

4.4   Passage 4 (Climate change due to volcanic eruptions)

(From a text published in 1999)

Previous studies on understanding the potential of Icelandic volcanic eruptions in modifying the environment have concentrated on the degree of induced climate change but the complex interaction of the processes which control the atmospheric circulation patterns of the earth were imperfectly understood and even with advanced equipment have proved difficult
5   to model.

Documentary evidence suggests that during the Laki fissure eruption, in 1783, severe acid damage to crops occurred in northern Europe and acid pulses killed fish in Scotland. Although an induced climatic change was probably the primary mechanism responsible, the degree to
10   which atmospheric circulation responds to volcanic forcing is uncertain so it is unsatisfactory to suggest that stress in the paleo-environmental record, associated with a volcanic eruption, has inevitably occurred in response to volcanic forcing of climate. The only volcanic eruptions which possess the theoretical ability to bring about climate change are those which emit substantial volumes of volatile gases. "Climate change theories" require that these be injected into
15   the stratosphere and remain in the troposphere. They must inevitably settle and be deposited on the surrounding sea and land rather than distant ecosystems. Despite plenty of excavations, such sedimentary evidence still eludes researchers around the Laki central fissure.

1.   The author is primarily concerned with

   (A)   explaining the way volcanic eruptions work.

   (B)   discussing various theories concerning volcanoes and climate change.

   (C)   providing evidence that explains climate change in Europe with volcanic eruption.

   (D)   refuting the suggestion that climate change occurred due to volcanic eruption.

   (E)   rejecting a controversial hypothesis about the climate change phenomena in Europe.

2.   According to the passage, which of the following can be concluded about previous studies of volcanic eruptions?

   (A)   The findings were refuted by research results done eventually in Europe.

   (B)   The paleo-environmental record suggested positively that volcanoes were responsible.

   (C)   The findings were invalidated by accepted climate change theories.

   (D)   The findings are difficult to support with evidence and can't be conclusively determined.

   (E)   Volcanic eruptions are likely to have brought about environmental changes.

3. Which of the following is best supported by the passage with regard to the volcanic eruptions in 1783?

    (A) The emissions forced climate change by raising the temperature of the atmosphere.

    (B) Volcanic emissions were injected into the stratosphere and then the troposphere.

    (C) The volcanic emissions were not substantial enough to form a stratosphere layer.

    (D) It modified the climate of Northern Europe.

    (E) Attempts to link it with climate change have not been substantiated yet.

4. According to the passage, what evidence, if provided, would suggest that Icelandic volcanic activity has been a force for environmental change and prove the author incorrect?

    (A) Volcanic emissions deposited in the sea and on land around Northern Europe

    (B) Environmental stress induced by the paleo-environmental record

    (C) Written accounts of dead fish in Scotland and crop damage in Germany

    (D) Induced climatic fluctuation documented in northern and western Europe

    (E) 18th century environmental records of Europe and its changes

5. In the given passage, what is the purpose of the first paragraph with respect to the second paragraph?

    (A) To explain the various theories concerning induced climate change by volcanic eruptions.

    (B) To lay the groundwork for the implication that volcanic eruptions lack the environmental stress to induce climate change.

    (C) To explain how Laki fissure eruptions could have affected crops and fish in Northern Europe.

    (D) To prove that volcanic eruptions cannot bring about climate change because they lack environmental pressure.

    (E) To explain how volcanic eruptions can bring about climate change in specific cases.

4.5   Passage 5 (Stock options in CEO pay)

(From a text published in 1999)

Defenders of runaway CEO pay argue that market forces are at work determining executive compensation levels and CEOs are rewarded for increasing their company's stock prices. But are America's CEOs entitled to such lucrative pay deals based on their performance? In 1998, the business press exploded with stories of pay for mediocrity: When it comes to executive
5 pay, stock option grants appear to have the Midas touch. As the stock market has broken record after record, they have become an increasingly popular form of executive compensation.

According to compensation analysts, stock options make up two-thirds of a CEOs pay, up
10 from one-third in the 1960s. Instead of having to beat their competitors, CEOs with stock option-fueled compensation packages are graded on a curve: the rising stock market. As stock prices increase generally, even mediocre CEOs can realize large gains from their options. Analysts estimate that only a quarter of option grants awarded to CEOs contain any sort of link to performance, such as premium-priced or indexed stock options. But executive equity
15 incentive plans can hurt shareholders. A recent research studied the largest U.S. companies by adjusting for the value of their executive's stock options. The study found that 11 firms went from profit to loss, and 13 had their profits halved. In addition, the study found that the average potential dilution of shareholder value from stock options is 9.2 percent for S&P 500 companies.

1. The primary purpose of the passage is

    (A)   to explain CEOs stock-option-fueled compensation packages.

    (B)   to criticize the excessive wages of corporate CEOs.

    (C)   to demonstrate the lack of parity among CEO compensation packages.

    (D)   to argue against non-performance-rated bonuses and point out the repercussions.

    (E)   to prove that paying CEOs through stock-options is doing more bad than good.

2. In the given passage, the author mentions the "Midas touch" near the end of first paragraph to

    (A)   compare the current economic situation to a historical one

    (B)   add a literary tone to a rather dreary financial text

    (C)   emphasize the lucrative nature of share option compensation packages

    (D)   criticize the mediocrity of some executives

    (E)   demonstrate the absurdity of share option compensation packages

3. According to the passage, which of the following is the basis on which the author criticizes CEOs stock-option compensation plans?

    (A)   They are determined by market forces.

    (B)   They have become an increasingly awarded form of compensation package.

    (C)   Their value is directly determined by company performance.

    (D)   They undermine the value of shares.

    (E)   They feature more and more as performance-based incentives.

4.   According to the passage, keeping in view the CEOs stock option compensation packages, with which of the following would the author agree?

    (A)   Currently companies consider their stocks' performances more than their actual performances.

    (B)   The number of stock option compensation packages has risen two thirds over the last few decades.

    (C)   CEOs stock option compensation packages should consist of premium-priced or indexed stock options only.

    (D)   CEOs stock option compensation packages are unduly awarded to CEOs despite companies performing well in the market.

    (E)   CEOs stock option compensation packages enhance only stock market figures, especially in the case of the compensation packages of mediocre CEOs.

5.   Which of the following would best categorize the author's attitude towards stock-option-based CEO pay, as given in the passage?

    (A)   Restrained criticism

    (B)   Conditional approval

    (C)   Unconditional disgust

    (D)   Absolute intolerance

    (E)   Unjustified disapproval

6.   According to the passage, which of the following can be inferred?

    (A)   Potential dilution of shareholder value stemming from CEOs compensation was less in the 1960s.

    (B)   Shareholders did not get hurt by companies in the 1960s.

    (C)   CEOs and top executives were not mediocre in the 1960s.

    (D)   Companies will accrue more profits if CEOs are paid according to performance.

    (E)   A CEO's pay should be linked to the company's performance in the stock market.

4.6 Passage 6 (Rising health care costs & medical malpractice)

In 1990, a Harvard Medical Practice study came to the conclusion that 95,000 deaths a year in the United States are attributable to medical malpractice. Not surprisingly, an additional 700,000 individuals are subject to injury as a result of medical malpractice. These numbers can jar even the most dispassionate observer. A jumbo jet would have to crash every day for
5 a year to reproduce these casualties. Despite the multitudes of people who die or suffer as a result of medical malpractice, fewer than 2,100 doctors a year are disciplined in connection with a malpractice claim. Of those health care providers that do come under scrutiny and censure, the lion's share of them are subject to sanctions on the premises of substance abuse or fraud, rather than malpractice. These facts resurface at a time when federal legislators are
10 considering measures to limit the monetary amount a patient can claim as compensation for damages incurred as a result of medical malpractice.

It is the hope of lawmakers in capping jury awards to plaintiffs that it may be possible to reverse the tide of rising health care costs. Since those costs are ultimately imposed on pa-
15 tients in the form of insurance premiums, the reigning logic dictates that limits on awards will save the patient money, and bring the cost of high quality healthcare within the reach of more Americans. However, the soundness of this approach is called into question when we consider that a Congressional Budget Office report found that only one percent of national health care costs results from the expense of malpractice insurance premiums being passed on to the
20 patient. However, accidents, misdiagnosis and conflicting prescriptions cost the nation nearly sixty billion dollars a year.

Even with these losses imposed on patients and on taxpayers yearly, less than half a percent of all civil cases in state courts sought to charge doctors with medical malpractice. The 2000
25 plus doctors who are disciplined each year amount to hardly one percent of all acting health care providers. Thus the amount of money going back into the hands of victims is a relatively inconsequential contribution to the overall cost of health care in America when compared to the cost of making good the harm of malpractice. Rising health care costs may more predictably be driven back by improving the way in which the health care industry polices itself
30 and removing unreliable doctors from practice.

1. The main theme of this passage can be summarized as:

    (A) Widespread policing is the answer to cutting health care costs.

    (B) Health care costs are the result of too few of the guilty being held accountable.

    (C) The source of high health care costs is difficult to localize.

    (D) Rising health care costs have more to do with the behavior of doctors than with the behavior of patients.

    (E) Traditional government approaches to the health care issue have been disappointing.

2. The main purpose of comparing the number of malpractice victims to the number of jumbo jet accident casualties is

    (A) to exemplify how a dispassionate observer could be caught off guard

    (B)   to show that even if we do not consider the several hundred thousand injured, the number of people who die from malpractice every year is absurdly high

    (C)   to compare the gravity of airline accidents to the seriousness of medical malpractice

    (D)   to note the disparity between airline safety regulations and health care oversight

    (E)   to point out the similarity between the number of people killed in air crashes and the number killed through medical malpractice

3.   The main concern voiced over the penalties levied on rogue practitioners is

    (A)   penalties are given out for the wrong reasons

    (B)   penalties given out are not severe enough

    (C)   penalties are given out to only a few

    (D)   penalties are given out to the wrong offenders

    (E)   penalties given out are not levied with enough charges to be a threat

4.   The implication of the Congressional Budget Office report is that

    (A)   awards from malpractice claims are not a substantial source of health care costs

    (B)   placing a limit on malpractice claims will significantly reduce the cost of health care to the end user

    (C)   malpractice insurance premiums are not as high as they could be

    (D)   congressional research is polarized and thus often contradictory

    (E)   insurance companies only charge what is fair based on the size of claims and the number of claimants

5.   The author of this passage would most likely agree with the argument that

    (A)   insurance companies will try to inflate their rate of return on premiums

    (B)   the cost of health care is inflated by the availability of expensive treatments

    (C)   doctors are compelled to reduce their services in order to cover their own expenses

    (D)   patients could reduce the cost of health care by being more careful in the home, using generic drugs, and seeking a second opinion

    (E)   the cost of health care is increased by the negligence of doctors

6.   The purpose of the sentence beginning with "Despite the multitudes..." (lines: 5-7) and the sentence beginning with "These facts resurface..." (lines: 9-11) is to

    (A)   demonstrate the underlying logic for capping jury awards

    (B)   remind readers that those who do not remember history are doomed to repeat it

    (C)   note that this subject is contemporary and topical

    (D)   show that Congress is operating under a false premise

    (E)   show that things are not always as they appear

7. The conclusion that greater policing of doctors will reduce the incidence of malpractice and drive down costs assumes that

    (A) most doctors are not up to their responsibilities

    (B) many more doctors are guilty of substance abuse and fraud than the portion accused

    (C) policing will encourage doctors to improve their performance

    (D) doctors will never protect one another from investigation on the grounds that they believe they are best equipped to make decisions for the patients

    (E) there is unchecked corruption among doctors

8. The notion of reducing jury awards places the blame for high health care costs most directly on:

    (A) Patients

    (B) Medical malpractice

    (C) Controlling doctors

    (D) The inability of the justice system to work with the health care system

    (E) Lawsuits

9. Which of the following is the **MOST INAPPROPRIATE** in describing the author's tone of the passage?

    (A) Distraught

    (B) Apathetic

    (C) Infuriated

    (D) Dire

    (E) Disparaging

4.7 Passage 7 (Whistleblower laws)

Whistleblower laws, as the moniker might imply, are pieces of legislation existing at the federal and state level intended to encourage employees to bring a stop to corruption and misman-agement. On the typical assembly line, a person may physically pull or blow a whistle to halt production in order to correct a faulty production process.

5

Likewise, the federal government has passed legislation to provide incentives, as well as protec-tion, to government employees who witness co-workers, and, now more than ever, managers, who are behaving in ways that can be construed as an abuse of their position, or as an outright violation of the law.

10

Increasingly, the term whistleblower has come to be associated with somebody who informs on a group of trusting co-workers. However, it is exactly this type of connotation that whistle-blower laws seek to remove from the mind of the public. Government bureaucracy and state-financed corporations can at times appear to operate above the law, outlasting administrations,

15   evading the discipline of elective review, and oiling their machinery while largely hiding from the public eye. Therefore, it is especially important to make it possible for courageous em-ployees who find themselves entangled in a business or department with its own agenda in mind to be able to speak out on behalf of the larger interests of voters, to whom these entities are responsible. Since an employee who decides to report illegal or unreasonable behavior to

20   the authorities regularly finds himself to be the subject of intense scrutiny, or even fabricated accusations, if he continues to stay at his place of employment, it is necessary to make the act of bringing unethical performance to light appealing enough to outweigh the disincentives posed by angry co-workers, punitive bosses, and a national culture that can frown on disloy-alty, even if it is for all the right reasons. In line with this reasoning, whistleblower laws often

25   provide the employee with a percentage of the money considered 'saved' by his honesty. More-over, a settlement or court award reached as a result of the disclosure of these problematic issues is often paid to the successful whistleblower to compensate for the risk he has assumed.

From another perspective, the employee is simultaneously given protection against undue dis-

30   missal and other retaliatory measures that a corporation or department might privately take against the plaintiff after official investigations are underway. These incentives were meant to make whistleblower laws both a progressive reform and effective legislation, so much so that the lucrative prospects of being a whistleblower have not only brought many reluctant em-ployees forward, but also have encouraged some to go into the business of poaching through

35   phonebooks for dubious employers with an eye towards reporting them to government inves-tigators and collecting their prize once a decision is reached.

1. Whistleblower laws were put in place

    (A) to discourage employees from reporting corruption in the workplace

    (B) to foster the connotation that employee reporting is disloyal

    (C) to ensure that all corrupt practices are discovered

    (D) to save money

    (E) to protect employees from the negative consequences of reporting malfeasance

2. The added measures to provide whistleblowers with pecuniary incentives and protection against unfair dismissal imply that

    (A) lawmakers were concerned that legislation aimed at reforming bureaucracy would be ineffective without financial inducements

    (B) the government should offer corporations more funding in exchange for reducing internal costs through better management and quarterly reviews

    (C) many lawmakers were whistleblowers themselves at one point

    (D) co-workers will be more understanding if they realize that reporting is not the product of disloyalty but of business acumen and private incentive

    (E) government bureaucracies do not need to respond to legislative pressure

3. The need for whistleblowers to help control the behavior of bureaucracy is because

    (A) a customary independent third party review process is mendatory

    (B) lack of competition with other bureaucracies may corrupt those bureaucracies

    (C) the incompetence of bureaucracy should be well understood by lawmakers

    (D) at times bureaucracies function outside the discipline of elective review

    (E) a bureaucracy's organizational mission should be separate from the mission of the federal government

4. In the passage, the effectiveness of whistleblower laws is demonstrated by

    (A) the number of corporations with federal contracts who have adopted the cost plus system

    (B) the high prosecution rate of managers who abuse their power and embezzle money

    (C) the inclusion of practical measures to make the legislation realistic

    (D) the willingness of most people to consider whistleblowers as patriots

    (E) the eagerness of a few employees to become deliberate investigators of corrupt corporations

5. It can be inferred from the passage that lawmakers viewed a need for so many practical incentives to be part of whistleblower legislation because

    (A) there have been laws passed but they have not had the full expected reach

    (B) federal employees make decisions out of self-interest more readily than out of a sense of purpose

    (C) corrupt bureaucracies result in a culture of corruption among all employees

    (D) federal bureaucracies are large and unwieldy

    (E) the federal government may be able to change a bureaucracy's leaders but not all of its employees

6. In the line 15, the phrase 'oiling their machinery' is probably a metaphor for:

    (A) Refusing to obey federal mandates

    (B) Writing laws

    (C) Proposing laws

    (D) Pitting state governments against federal governments

    (E) Running the day to day operations of an organization

7. The attitude of the author towards whistleblower legislation can be described as:

    (A) Suspicious but relenting

    (B) Supportive and objective

    (C) Agreeable but nonplussed

    (D) Implacable but journalistic

    (E) Prohibitive and histrionic

8. In the line 31, the word 'plaintiff' most nearly means

    (A) applicant

    (B) pretender

    (C) claimant

    (D) dissenter

    (E) perpetrator

4.8   Passage 8 (Rising European Union and the U.S.)

The size of the European Union market is exponentially larger than it was in the 1950's, when European integration was first proposed. While today the European Union is the only region with the economic might to challenge the United States for meaningful influence over international trade policies, the United States is noncommittal on E.U. proposals calling for the
5   alignment of labor regulations, the opening of consumer forums and the offer of an audience to environmental groups. As the constituencies calling for these developments have been relegated to peripheral positions in the dialogue over trans-Atlantic economic unification, those with an interest in these groups see a trend towards liberalizing the rules for corporate advantage in the economic co-ordination that has sprung up between the United States and Europe.
10   Much of the current communication between the United States and the European Union is focused on establishing an agreement that codifies the rules of trans-Atlantic trade and that acknowledges the extent of trade conducted between the U.S. and Europe, greater in bulk than between any other pair of regions in the world, without disregarding the efforts European producers must make to satisfy interest groups and regulations.
15

The heated dialogue between the United States and the European Union on this issue has come hard on the heels of the joining of the U.S., Mexico and Canada in the North American Free Trade Agreement: NAFTA. This agreement seeks to standardize industrial and labor regulations between the United States and its neighbors so that tariffs can be reduced, international
20   transport encouraged, and corporate investment diversified. While bringing standards of production into alignment is a goal that ought to raise the quality of production and the level of cooperation across the continent, it also creates an opportunity to establish a standard contra to European expectations of international regulation. As a solution, the E.U. has proposed TAFTA, the Trans-Atlantic Free Trade Agreement, but the United States has repeatedly
25   hesitated at the proposal, seeking to protect its dominance in the Western Hemisphere. This dominance is secured by its ability to protect its factories and corporations from sources of comparable European production and demanding practices of review and concessions popular in Europe as a nod to social consensus.

30   These issues have resulted in the plethora of interest groups with a voice in the matter simultaneously accusing the U.S of brinkmanship, protectionism, callous deregulation, third world exploitation and anti-competitive practices. The route to economic expansion is a prominent issue in both the U.S. and the European Union, and some with a say in the matter repeat these protests as a screen for their own plans to tip the balance of economic advantage towards their
35   own region at the expense of all other involved parties in the process of exploring for parity.

1. The intent of the author in noting the size of the European Union in the first sentence of the passage is to

    (A) demonstrate the difference between the past E.U. and the present E.U.

    (B) clarify the number of parties in trans-Atlantic trade

    (C) establish the importance of one of the leading parties in world markets

    (D) show that the E.U. cannot be exploited for U.S. self-interest

    (E) demonstrate why the United States is non-committal about cooperation

2. Which of the following words best substitutes for the term 'heated dialogue' in the line 16?

    (A) impasse

    (B) dispute

    (C) shuttle diplomacy

    (D) brinkmanship

    (E) banter

3. The main concern of the European Union regarding NAFTA is that

    (A) North America will have a higher standard of living than Europe

    (B) North America will improve its standard of living at the expense of Europe

    (C) North America will adopt production standards that are incompatible with Europe's

    (D) North America will flood Europe with cheap, low quality goods

    (E) North America will promote the exploitation of labor

4. It can be inferred from the passage that less stringent production and environmental standards than those of North America are unfavorable to the European Union because

    (A) they unfairly lower the quality of life in Europe

    (B) they reduce the amount of cheap labor entering Europe from the third world

    (C) they damage the European environment

    (D) they encourage European workers to move to the United States

    (E) they make it easy for already dominant North American industries to do trade

5. In the sentence (line 31), the term "callous deregulation" is meant to imply:

    (A) A deregulation driven by an uncaring attitude

    (B) A well-reasoned desire for deregulation

    (C) An insatiable drive towards deregulation

    (D) A balanced deregulation

    (E) An inconsistent deregulation

6. It can be inferred from the passage that the author believes the range of accusations against the United States made by groups on the periphery of trade talks is

   (A) credible but lacking influence

   (B) credible but irrelevant

   (C) biased

   (D) well-balanced

   (E) incredible but accurate

7. The unwillingness of the United States to upset trade relations with the European Union is demonstrated by

   (A) the U.S.'s unwillingness to engage in any new agreements

   (B) the U.S.'s insistence on avoiding future talks

   (C) the U.S.'s back-up plan to secure relations with Mexico and Canada

   (D) the U.S.'s decision not to turn down TAFTA while avoiding any commitment to it

   (E) the U.S.'s willingness to mimic the cries of its own social groups

4.9   Passage 9 (In-fighting Indian princes and the rise of the British)

For 17th century Europeans, the history of Eastern monarchies, like everything else in Asia, was stereotyped and invariable. According to accounts of Indian events, history unfolded itself with the predictable rituals of heavy-handed folklore. Typically, the founder of a dynasty, a brave soldier, is a desperate intriguer, and expels from the throne the feeble and degenerate
5   scions of a more ancient house. His son may inherit some of the talent of the father, but in two or three generations luxury and indolence do their work, and the feeble inheritors of a great name are dethroned by some new adventurer, destined to bequeath a like misfortune to his degenerate descendants. Thus rebellion and deposition were the correctives of despotism, and therefore, a recurrence, at fixed intervals, of able and vigorous princes through the medium
10 of periodical anarchy and civil war, occurred. It was this perception of history that allowed Britain's rulers to lay claim to the governance of the subcontinent. The British claimed to be interested in avoiding these periods of bloodshed. This claim justified British policy, as well as dictated how they thought about gaining the favor of India's local monarchies.

15 British armies and British administrators were able to insinuate rule over India by setting up native princes in positions of power. Their methods took advantage of existing "doctrines of lapse", and made use of what was already the declared law in cases of heredity. By intervening on behalf of one prince or another, both of whom may have been equally suited to claim the right to the throne in cases in which the rights to leadership lapsed, they put themselves in a
20 position to support a leader they selected, and to maintain his power as long as it was in their interests. In this way the princes became practically obliged to cooperate with the British. The result was two generations of petty despots, insulated from the consequences of misrule by British bayonets. The despots spent their lives in listless debauchery, broken by paroxysms of cruelty and oppression.

1. It can be inferred from the passage that Britain could easily impose a proxy rule on the Indian subcontinent because of

   (A)   a language in common with that of the Indians

   (B)   a lack of corruption within the British administration

   (C)   the deployment of well-trained British soldiers

   (D)   superior weaponry

   (E)   the use of pre-existing laws of leadership lapses

2. The author of the passage would be likely to agree with statement:

   (A)   British intervention in India left it no worse off than when the British arrived

   (B)   British intervention in India requires closer monitoring than they were given after their arrival

   (C)   British intervention in India was a positive influence on India

   (D)   The system of rule in India before the British arrived had no faults

   (E)   India would have been better off carrying out its cycle of lapse and renewal without British influence

3. The attitude of the author towards the reported cycle of rule can best be described as:

    (A) Disparaging

    (B) Despairing

    (C) Skeptical

    (D) Matter of fact

    (E) Approving

4. The damage caused by British rule to the subcontinent was brought about by

    (A) the refusal of the people to be ruled

    (B) the inability of the people to choose their leader

    (C) the inability of the people to resist oppression

    (D) the demoralization of the Indian identity

    (E) the exploitative nature of the relationship between Britain and the princes

5. One judgment about the British offered by this passage might be that

    (A) they never pretended to undertake socially responsible activity

    (B) they were interested exclusively in exploiting India's resources

    (C) they got involved in governing colonies which they knew were beyond their powers of governance

    (D) they had a benign influence on India

    (E) they sought practical opportunity when their self-interest matched local rulers' objectives

6. The "doctrines of lapse" which positioned princes against one another for regional thrones gave Britain a foothold in India by

    (A) allowing them to exchange a little influence at a critical time for significant influence later.

    (B) offering an opportunity to take over the leadership role in these areas while no one was in charge.

    (C) letting the British act as arbitrators in discussions between the dueling princes.

    (D) positioning the British as an impartial party in Indian politics.

    (E) ensuring there were no local candidates for leadership.

7. From the passage, the attitude of Britain towards Indian politics can be described as:

    (A) Conflicted

    (B) Hypocritical

    (C) Opportunistic

    (D) Fair

    (E) Unbiased

4.10 Passage 10 (The Belgian economy: from devastation to restoration)

For 200 years until World War I, French-speaking Wallonia was a technically advanced, industrial region, while Dutch-speaking Flanders was predominantly agricultural. This disparity began to fade during the interwar period. When Belgium emerged from World War II with its industrial infrastructure relatively undamaged, the stage was set for a period of rapid de-
5 velopment, particularly in Flanders. The older, traditional industries of Wallonia, particularly steelmaking, began to lose their competitive edge during this period, but the general growth of world prosperity masked this deterioration until the 1973 and 1979 oil price shocks and resultant shifts in international demand sent the economy into a period of prolonged recession.

10 In the 1980s and 1990s, the economic center of the country continued to shift northwards to Flanders. The early 1980s saw the country facing a difficult period of structural adjustment caused by declining demand for its traditional products, deteriorating economic performance, and neglected structural reform. Consequently, the 1980-82 recession shook Belgium to its core–unemployment rose, social welfare costs increased, personal debt soared, the govern-
15 ment deficit climbed to 13% of GDP, and the national debt, although mostly held domestically, mushroomed. Against this grim backdrop, in 1982, Prime Minister Martens' center-right coalition government formulated an economic recovery program to promote export-led growth by enhancing the competitiveness of Belgium's export industries through an 8.5% devaluation. Economic growth rose from 2% in 1984 to a peak of 4% in 1989. In May 1990, the govern-
20 ment linked the franc to the German Mark, primarily through closely tracking German interest rates. Consequently, as German interest rates rose after 1990, Belgian rates increased and contributed to a decline in the economic growth rate.

Although Belgium is a wealthy country, it overspent income and under-collected taxes for
25 years. The Belgian government reacted to the 1973 and 1979 oil price hikes with poor macroeconomic policies: it transferred workers made redundant in the private sector to the public sector and subsidized ailing industries–coal, steel, textiles, glass, and shipbuilding–in order to prop up the economy. As a result, cumulative government debt reached 121% of GNP by the end of the 1980s *(versus a cumulative U.S. federal public debt/GNP ratio of 31.2% in 1990)*.
30 However, thanks to Belgium's high personal savings rate, the Belgian Government managed to finance the deficit mainly from domestic savings. This minimized the deleterious effects on the overall economy.

1. An appropriate title for this passage might be:

    (A) The rise of Flanders to domestic leadership

    (B) Managing the challenge of structural adjustment in the post-war Belgian economy

    (C) Dead weight: How Greater Belgium lost Flanders the industrial advantage

    (D) Fiscal rally: How P.M. Martens found his legs

    (E) Which way: Fickle government starves a state with too many choices

2. The information in the beginning of the passage concerning the rise of Flanders over Wallonia serves to

    (A) introduce the protagonist of the author's text early in the passage

    (B) foreshadow the counterpoint between successful and unsuccessful policy-making

    (C) introduce and demonstrate the idea of a compositional sea-change in the greater Belgian economy

    (D) show how runaway development was ready to take hold of the Belgian economy before it was mismanaged and eventually recouped

    (E) provide the reader with the factor responsible for driving away development in the greater Belgian economy

3. The oil price hikes of the 1970's can be most accurately considered

    (A) a structural problem in the Belgian economy

    (B) a pivotal turning point leading to an immediate improvement in economic policy-making

    (C) comparable to the story in which the child tells the emperor that he has no clothes

    (D) an unpredictable stroke of bad luck reversing Belgian economic momentum

    (E) a wasted opportunity to focus on pre-emptive export-driven reform

4. The phrase "Against this grim backdrop" (line 16) used by the author to

    (A) show that no matter how bad things are, a politician can make them worse.

    (B) make light of Martens' genuine but misspent efforts to turn around the economy.

    (C) show that Martens brought real change in the face of a formidable challenge.

    (D) pardon Martens by showing that even the most expert of handlers could not have changed the hand Belgium was dealt.

    (E) imply that there was no hope for Belgium.

5. The genre of the passage can be categorized as:

    (A) Apologetic

    (B) Historical

    (C) Polemical

    (D) Argumentative

    (E) Encyclopaedic

6. In the passage, the author's use of the phrase "poor macroeconomic policies" (line 25) and the word "prop" in (line 28) regarding government subsidies suggests what about his opinion of government intervention in the economy?

   (A) The government should not intervene in economic issues that can be handle privately.

   (B) The government should not support industries that are ailing.

   (C) The government can encourage sustainable progress without working with market forces.

   (D) The government must be more decisive in its decision-making.

   (E) The government cannot avoid being at the mercy of market fluctuations.

7. The author's critical portrayal of the Belgian government's reactions to the oil crises in the 1970's does not necessarily make its officials economically malfeasant because

   (A) no economist could have done better

   (B) economists are academics; politicians are pragmatists

   (C) this economic review of the Belgian economy is retrospective; the decisions made at the time were without the benefit of hindsight

   (D) there are no right or wrong answers in economics

   (E) administrators were giving the public what they wanted

8. In the end of paragraph 2 (line 19), the author notes that linking the franc with the German mark raised interest rates in the Belgian economy, setting off a decline in the rate of growth. However, in the last sentence of paragraph 3 (line 30), the passage states that abundant personal savings made it possible for Belgium to pay off its debts.

   If higher interest rates lead to higher personal savings from which debts can be paid off, what is the best way to describe the tone of the passage regarding high interest rates?

   (A) Ambivalent
   (B) Skeptical
   (C) Foreboding
   (D) Accepting
   (E) Defeatist

4.11   Passage 11 (Craving for fast food: who to blame – behavior or the brain?)

Recent evidence from scientists has shown that eating "fast food" can be addictive in much the same way as using controlled substances can be. According to researchers, "fast food" such as hamburgers, processed sugar, and a wide range of deep fried foods can trigger a dependency in the brain that perpetuates a habit of further use. It is a view that is increasingly supported by
5   scientists who see a co-dependency between people's decisions and environmental influences *(including the wide availability of "fast food")* that have structural effects on human development. The proposed conclusions contend that the brains of overeaters experience chemical changes in response to unbalanced diets with a high content of processed sugar, salt, and saturated fats.
10

In time and in some cases, if people continue a pattern of consumption containing too much unhealthy food, their intake of this food will initiate changes in the brain that elevate the minimum level of ingestion the brain needs for satiation. Moreover, since high consumption of "fast foods" stimulates opiates in the brain *(substances which act as natural pain relievers),*
15   large, recurrent doses of "fast food" can mimic the effects of opiates, albeit in a less intense form. Scientists raising rats on a diet of twenty-five percent sugar found that upon suddenly eliminating glucose from the rats' food supply, the animals experienced all the symptoms of withdrawal attributed to reducing traditional addictive opiates, including shivering and chattering teeth. Later, by treating rats with drugs that block opiate receptors, scientists were able
20   to lower the amount of dopamine in the nucleus acumen of rats' brains, an area linked with the dynamics of reward. Such neurochemistry can be seen in heroin addicts coping with withdrawal. By this reasoning, obesity, like other addictions, can be viewed as a disease beyond the control of those afflicted by it.

25   This has brought lawyers to argue that civil society has a responsibility to regulate food and educate people about the abuse of "unhealthy foods" in a way that is comparable to society's control of opiates and narcotics. Corporations that target this vulnerability in human beings can then be held liable for the sicknesses that result from the poor eating habits overwhelming their customers. Still, some scientists scoff at the lengths to which their colleagues seek to
30   separate the decision making process from people's behavior. For these researchers, the distinction between a habit and an addiction is not quantitative but qualitative. Their consensus is that individuals can still moderate their behavior to control the effects of what they eat on their systems.

1.   The passage seems to suggest that scientists who see a co-dependence between people's decisions and environmental influences would affirm that

   (A)   human decision-making has unconscious, chemical influences

   (B)   human beings have a responsibility to control their surroundings

   (C)   overeaters are not responsible for their behavior and their eating disorders

   (D)   obesity is a public health crisis

   (E)   overeaters continue to eat because they are unable to overcome the difficulties of withdrawal

2. Which among the following is the best argument for the lawyers defending corporations against the findings of researchers on the effects of "fast food"?

   (A) Obesity is a pre-existing condition in individuals.

   (B) Obese people must treat their disease with medication that blocks opiate receptors.

   (C) The distinction between a habit and an addiction is "not quantitative but qualitative".

   (D) Corporations were not aware that "fast food" caused chemical dependency because the science confirming it is so new.

   (E) It is the responsibility of consumers to stay informed about their choices.

3. By labeling obesity as a disease, the scientists in the passage seek to point out that

   (A) the obese need to obey a strict diet

   (B) the obese are more vulnerable to the health hazards of chronic consumption of "fast food" than those who are not obese

   (C) obesity is a condition that targets those with a genetic precondition to it

   (D) obesity is a result of factors that cannot be understood solely as the results of the behavior of individuals

   (E) obesity exists in an individual whether or not they overeat

4. Some scientists in the passage who dispute the conclusions of their colleagues who link obesity with chemical factors find fault with their colleagues'

   (A) findings

   (B) expertise

   (C) assumptions

   (D) methodology

   (E) comparisons between data

5. The phrasing of dissenting scientists that notes "the distinction between habit and addiction is not quantitative but qualitative" in line 30 objects to the assumption

   (A) that linking a chemical process to a behavioral pattern is sufficient to categorize someone as diseased

   (B) that there is only one factor which determines a person's behavior

   (C) that difference in behavior or choices do not contribute at all to eventual addiction and possible neurochemistry changes

   (D) that any amount of fast food is bad for people

   (E) that people should only eat foods without sugar

6. From the passage, the role of dopamine in the rats' brain seems to

    (A) reduce food intake

    (B) block opiates

    (C) replace opiates when they are blocked

    (D) punish rats when opiates are received

    (E) instruct the rat to eat more

7. As presented in the passage, lawyers who would seek to take "fast food" restaurants to court for damaging public health would agree with which of the following?

    (A) The government is not knowledgeable enough to safeguard public health.

    (B) Corporations are responsible for the consequences of their products.

    (C) The responsibility to determine what a good product is should be determined by the market.

    (D) People who suffer from obesity are victims of governmental incompetence.

    (E) People should take responsibility for their own diets.

4.12   Passage 12 (Masks & gas attacks during WW II)

The attack on Pearl Harbor by the Japanese introduced America to the world theater of World
War II. What was unique about this battle was that American citizens experienced it as the first
attack on American soil in what was then recent memory. Throughout World War I, Americans
mostly felt secure in their homes. However, the changing times and the audacity of nationalis-
5 tic world powers, raised questions as to the need for civilian defense.

The highest priority was the protection of children from possible attack. The escalation of
World War II already involved lengthy campaigns of civil terror waged by opposing powers.
No power with a soldiering part in the war was immune or blameless. Germany unleashed the
10 lengthiest bombing campaign of the war on the people of London primarily to weaken British
morale. Later, the Allied Forces would fire bomb on the German city of Dresden. Dresden had
housed an almost entirely civilian population and had incidental wartime production.

Early on, Britain and the United States enacted an emergency measure to protect their youth
15 population. A leading concern was the exposure to gas attack, an effective measure against un-
witting urban dwellers. Immediately after Pearl Harbor, thousands of military training masks
were rushed to people living on the islands. However, the available equipment was unsuitable
for protecting children. Instead, Hawaiian officials produced an expedient made up of bunny
ears and a hood. This would lead to further improvisation in the protection of the child civilian
20 population. The Sun Rubber Company designed a mask based on the universal Walt Disney
cartoon figure Mickey Mouse. The Mickey Mouse gas mask was then approved by the Chemical
Warfare Service of the U.S. Department of Defense, with the assumption that other winning
designs could follow the success of this first run. The popularity of these masks was dependent on internalizing their use in children by making their presence part of a perceived game.
25 This potentially reduced the element of fear that the masks conveyed on their recipients. If
the element of fear could be diminished, gas masks might be employed by their owners more
quickly in the event of an attack, and also worn without interruption.

All of this would increase the chances of survival of the youth population, of no small concern
30 to a nation with large numbers of its working age males facing the perils of combat overseas.

1. According to the passage, the main distinction between World War I and World War II for
    Americans was:

    (A)   The lengthy campaigns of civil terror

    (B)   The blame shared by all participating powers

    (C)   The mobilization of civilian factories for military use

    (D)   The first violation of national security in several generations

    (E)   The threat of nationalism from foreign aggressors

2. The purpose of national armies engaging in civil terror is presented by the passage as a
    way to

    (A)   destroy the civilian wartime infrastructure

    (B)   reduce the number of potential reinforcements for dwindling armies

   (C)   keep armies and pilots active during long periods without confrontation

   (D)   destroy the enemy's willingness to continue fighting

   (E)   kill key people

3.   The design of gas masks to look like a cartoon character was intended to

   (A)   make the war seem less omnipresent to children

   (B)   make children less afraid of a foreign attack

   (C)   induce children to learn how to use the mask properly

   (D)   increase sales of gas masks to families

   (E)   bring a level of normalcy back to everyday life

4.   The passage observes that the special efforts taken to protect young people were based on concerns that

   (A)   they may be needed to replenish the lines of men in the trenches

   (B)   they would be needed to repopulate the country if the men overseas did not return

   (C)   they may have been the only ones available to work jobs after the war

   (D)   they were the main concern of parents who voted

   (E)   once children get sick, they are the most difficult to bring back to health

5.   The topic of the passage can best be described as:

   (A)   The coordination of the wartime economy to meet civilian defense

   (B)   The special efforts to protect children in response to heightened civilian vulnerability

   (C)   The need for all nations to engage in civilian terror tactics

   (D)   The incorporation of popular images in the tools of war

   (E)   The resourcefulness of the American military machine in meeting wartime production

6.   In paragraph 3, in the sentence beginning with (line 18): "Instead, Hawaiian officials...", the word "expedient" most nearly means

   (A)   a dire consequence

   (B)   a cleaning agent

   (C)   a response to an urgent need

   (D)   a terror tactic

   (E)   a placebo

7. The benefit of internalizing the use of these masks in children was that

    (A) they would wear them to bed

    (B) they would take the masks to school

    (C) they would encourage friends to use them

    (D) they would lack fear upon wearing them

    (E) they would love the cartoon character Mickey Mouse

8. It can be inferred from the passage that a significant avoidable danger of a wartime terror attack is

    (A) enemy propaganda

    (B) the youth of the civilian population

    (C) poor decision making on the part of unprepared civilians

    (D) plunging civilian morale

    (E) lack of warning of an attack

4.13   Passage 13 (Lord Dalhousie's uniform rate of postage in India)

Lord Dalhousie is credited with the creation of the modern postal system in India. Dalhousie, who held many roles in the administration and internal development of the region, contributed to the Indian postal system by sweeping away the fabric of its past obstructions and levying a uniform rate of postage.

5

All letters weighing less than a prescribed amount in weight would require the same postal fee (half an Anna) regardless of their destination or origin. This idea of instituting a uniform unit of weight and of charge for the whole of the vast Indian empire seemed sheer folly to many orthodox financiers of his time. It was, they said, pushing Rowland Hill's scheme of a-penny

10 postage for England to an extreme. For these onlookers, Dalhousie's plan was not so much an extension of the English penny postage scheme, as a reductio ad absurdum of the reform that had been effected in Great Britain. What could be more extravagant or more unjust than to levy the same charge on two letters, one of which was to be delivered to the adjoining street, and the other to the opposite side of India?

15

Lord Dalhousie was not significantly deterred by the criticism. Because of the uniform rate of postage, the old wrangle over the payment for delivery of every letter, from which the rural postman invariably managed to squeeze something additional for himself at the expense of the recipient, could be replaced by a simple system of postage stamps. The system was more

20 reliable for the person mailing the letter, and encouraged increased patronage.

The proof of his success was the renewal of the postal system as a self-sustaining organization rather than its continuance as a chronic drain on British colonial finances. The social results were even more important. It has been said that the half-penny post that Lord Dalhousie put

25 in place in India was more consequential than the telegraph, the railway and even Public Instruction for reversing the isolation which predated it.

1. The objections to the uniform postal rate in India were related to

    (A) the fact that it was not fair to charge the same rate for different degrees of service

    (B) the fact that it was an unproven method

    (C) the fact that it conveyed a lack of trust in postal workers

    (D) the inability of the letter delivery service to handle a flood of cross-India mail

    (E) an attempt by critics to put their own recommendations in place

2. According to the passage, the main benefit of the half-penny post system to India was

    (A) an increase in the rate of communication throughout the subcontinent

    (B) increased rates of literacy

    (C) reduced corruption among postmen

    (D) its independence from British financial support

    (E) a trade-off between reliability and patronage

3. It can be inferred from the results of Dalhousie's revisions of India's postal system that

(A) he only way to see whether something will be successful is to put it into practice

(B) if something works on a small scale, it should work on a large scale as well

(C) disorganization and unreliability may be more costly than charging at uniform and low rates

(D) britain's financial support of the postal system gave it no incentive to improve

(E) india was a single, coherent state in a way no one had anticipated

4. One lesson that can be taken from Dalhousie's success is that

(A) personal experience can be more informed than extensive theoretical knowledge

(B) postal systems are one example of goods that are not subject to supply and demand curves

(C) there had been British mismanagement

(D) long term social gains can compensate for short term capital losses

(E) for Britain's purposes, the penny postage scheme should have preceded the telegraph, the railway, and public instruction

5. In the middle of the second paragraph (line 11), the term "reductio ad absurdum" most closely means

(A) to misunderstand the purpose of an idea

(B) to simplify an idea while losing its key elements

(C) to extend an idea to a scale beyond which it is practical

(D) to make a functional premise seem ridiculous

(E) to apply an idea to an unrelated problem

6. The passage specifies that simplifying the mail system compensated the post office for the costs of uniform postage by

(A) reducing staff

(B) increasing patronage

(C) increasing reliability

(D) creating postage stamps

(E) creating a market for written communication

7. The most decisive evidence of Dalhousie having made the right decision in instituting his postal system is:

(A) Increased reliability

(B) Reduced corruption in India

(C) Its previous success in England as Rowland Hill's postal system

(D) The attainment of a financially sound postal system

(E) The quieting of critics

8. The experience of Lord Dalhousie in the passage demonstrates that

   (A) larger markets may experience increased transaction costs
   (B) transaction costs are negligible
   (C) postal workers are always corrupt
   (D) letters are the most efficient means of communication
   (E) standardization has the ability to reduce transaction costs

4.14   Passage 14 (New global economic order)

There is a perception among many legislators in post-industrial economies that there is a worn path to economic prosperity that leads to an increase in the standard of living. This perception is embodied in the common language which compares nations competing with one another to "big corporations" competing with one another, an idea Bill Clinton used in trying to establish
5   a path towards an information services economy in America. However, this perception, that there is a specific, and even predictable, direction growth must go in, and that it must be done at the expense of manufacturing industries, as well as to the detriment of other countries, overlooks the way in which social groups, productivity, and technology interact. Moreover, it overlooks the fact that, as economist Paul Krugman favors saying, countries are not direct com-
10 petitors with one another. In fact, the term "competitive," in regards to national economies, begins to lose all useful meaning when it is applied to rival states. As such, quickly removing a manufacturing sector in order to encourage the growth of an information and service sector can unnecessarily remove jobs from an economy and destroy the balance that is necessary, even in a post-industrial economy, between the manufacturing sector and the information pro-
15 cessing sector. Seeing this sort of move as the inevitable path to technological development can be presumptuous and misdirected, especially if the goal is seen as economic growth at the expense of a perceived competitor, with whom one must continue to trade goods and purchase economic inputs.

20 Thus, innovation does not define a set path on which a national economy must embark to take full advantage of its resources. Indeed, matching the skills of the labor force and the present resources of the country with demand in the international market is not a policy that can be discounted or that is devalued in the face of technological advances. The standard of living within a country is not a function of the size of the white collar workforce, but of how well an
25 economy matches the skills of its workers to its productive activities, and how well it fulfills the demands of global markets. Institutions within a country can help improve and direct the skills of a national workforce, while accommodating quality of life considerations, without an economy having to be at a disadvantage compared to a foreign managerial or information economy. This does not assume that an information economy does not give a nation certain
30 political, military and status advantages over other nations, but the relationships among nations do not have to be limited to equalizing their information processing sectors.

1. One drawback of attempting to spur the economy of a nation through premature service sector concentration stated in the passage is that

    (A)   states are not in competition with one another

    (B)   growth is not predictable

    (C)   there is a decline in manufacturing output

    (D)   there is a loss of jobs

    (E)   there is a threat to the military from a decline in manufacturing

2. The passage views Bill Clinton's comparison between nation states and big corporations to be

    (A)   premature

    (B)   anticipatory

    (C)   inaccurate

    (D)   plausible

    (E)   hyperbole

3. One reason the passage offers for why it is inaccurate to view national economies as competitors is:

    (A)   Lack of statistical proof

    (B)   The inability of nation states to conform to the tenets of game theory

    (C)   The ineffectiveness of viewing economic actors as competitors

    (D)   The need to purchase key inputs from one another

    (E)   Cultural similarities

4. It can be inferred from the passage that one reason the economies of nations might be considered competitors is because

    (A)   as one nation's economy improves, another's deteriorates

    (B)   there are finite resources in the world

    (C)   economies seek to draw talented labor from one another

    (D)   certain types of economies facilitate military strength

    (E)   it is the only explanation that matches modern political events

5. According to the passage, which of the following would best correspond with the suggested measures a nation should take to improve its economic outlook?

    (A)   cutting luxury taxes to encourage the construction of residential high-rise buildings

    (B)   establishing a close relationship between educational institutions and businesses

    (C)   phasing out agricultural production for cheaper imported crops

    (D)   permitting a trade deficit in order to eventually increase the export of intellectual goods

    (E)   eliminating manufacturing

6. From the passage, which of the following can be concluded?

    (A)   Growth is predictable.

    (B)   Social groups are not involved in technological growth.

    (C)   Manufacturing is detrimental to the service sector.

    (D)   Manufacturing is the key sector in an economy.

    (E)   Manufacturing should be subsidized by government.

7. An appropriate title for this passage might be:

    (A) How to reinvent an economy

    (B) Corporate competition among nation states

    (C) Relevance of the service economy over the manufacturing economy

    (D) Old is gold and new is just glitter

    (E) How economies perish

8. The purpose of this passage is to

    (A) answer a question

    (B) outline a problem

    (C) provide a set of directions

    (D) dispel a myth

    (E) compare two possible solutions

4.15   Passage 15 (Randomness in modern physics)

However inventive Newton's clockwork universe seemed to his contemporaries, by the early twentieth century, it had become a sort of smugly accepted dogma. Luckily for us, this deterministic picture of the universe breaks down at the atomic level. The clearest demonstration that the laws of physics contain elements of randomness is the behavior of radioactive atoms.
5   Pick two identical atoms of a radioactive isotope, say naturally occurring uranium 238, and watch them carefully. They will begin to decay at different times, even though there was no difference in their initial behavior.

We would be in big trouble if these atoms' behavior were as predictable as expected in the
10 Newtonian world-view, because radioactivity is an important source of heat for our planet. In reality, each atom chooses a random moment at which to release its energy, resulting in a nice steady heating effect. The earth would be a much colder planet if only sunlight heated it and not radioactivity. Probably there would be no volcanoes, and the oceans would never have been liquid. The deep-sea geothermal vents in which life first evolved would never have
15 existed.

But there would be an even worse consequence if radioactivity were deterministic: after a few billion years of peace, all the uranium 238 atoms in our planet would presumably pick the same moment to decay. The huge amount of stored nuclear energy, instead of being spread out
20 over eons, would all be released simultaneously, blowing our whole planet to kingdom come. (This is under the assumption that all the uranium atoms were created at the same time.) In reality, we have only a general idea of the process that might have created the heavy elements in the gas cloud from which our solar system condensed. Some portion may have come from nuclear reactions in supernova explosions in that nebula, some from intra-galactic supernova
25 explosions and others still from exotic events like the collisions of white dwarf stars. The new version of physics, incorporating certain kinds of randomness, is called quantum physics. It represented such a dramatic break with the previous, deterministic tradition that everything that came before is considered classical, even the theory of relativity.

1.   The main theme of this passage discusses

   (A)   how Newtonian physics is irrelevant
   (B)   the difference between supernova explosions and star collisions
   (C)   the worldly benefits of uranium 238
   (D)   how randomness is a fundamental principle of modern physics
   (E)   the danger of accepting an idea without continuing to challenge it

2.   The author discusses the activity of uranium 238 atoms to show

   (A)   that no two atoms are exactly alike
   (B)   the dangers of nuclear power
   (C)   how sunlight alone could never heat the planet
   (D)   how Newtonian physics can explain all aspects of the physical world
   (E)   how randomness exists in the most basic constructs of the physical world

3. According to the passage, identical radioactive isotopes

    (A) were overlooked by Newton

    (B) can have different chemical properties

    (C) are subject to different physical events

    (D) decay at different rates

    (E) may begin to decay at different times

4. According to the passage, the Theory of Relativity is considered

    (A) the pinnacle of quantum physics

    (B) a Newtonian explanation of randomness

    (C) incorrect

    (D) deterministic

    (E) a bridge between the classical tradition and quantum physics

5. The passage demonstrates how central randomness was to the development of life on Earth by saying that if it had not existed, the most important consequence would have been that

    (A) deep sea vents could never have evolved

    (B) light would travel at different speeds depending on its point of origin

    (C) uranium 238 atoms would decay simultaneously and destroy the earth

    (D) the earth would not have a way to store the sun's heat

    (E) Ggenetic mutations would have been rampant

6. An appropriate title for this passage might be:

    (A) Randomness and supernovas: theories and events which lead to life

    (B) A review of classical physics and Newtonian tenets

    (C) Revising the model: the most basic principle of physics

    (D) Einstein's dice: the classic-quantum debate

    (E) Renaming physics: accepting the role of randomness in the principles we learned

7. The style of this piece can be best regarded as:

    (A) Journalistic

    (B) Extemporaneous

    (C) Hortatory

    (D) Encyclopedic

    (E) Explicative

8. The author presents quantum physics as:

    (A) The incorrect interpretation of physical events

    (B) A way of explaining events using Newtonian physics

    (C) An explanation of the rules of the physical world

    (D) The replacement of Newtonian physics

    (E) The missing piece of Newtonian physics

4.16 Passage 16 (Synergetics)

Synergetics is an epistemology for interpreting concepts in life through geometric relationships.

Buckminster Fuller, a multi-disciplinary scholar and inventor, coined the term synergetics to
5 describe what he considered a "coordinate system" for the physical universe, summoning the
language of the Cartesian coordinate plane with which mathematicians graph physical space.
Synergetics has come to serve as a method for describing the behavior of whole systems whose
behavior cannot be predicted from independent analyses of their parts. In Fuller's conception
of synergetics, this coordinate system seeks to map not only the physical characteristics of the
10 universe, but also the rationale structuring mankind's heuristic interpretations of the world.
The basis of Fullers' model is that all observable phenomena can be codified as interactive systems, and those systems can be principally understood as a geography of spherical networks
comprised of interrelated points of interest. Those interrelationships then equate with the
morphology of observable phenomena.

15

At its most discrete, Fuller understood a "system" as being the first division one could make
of the universe. That logic could then be applied to all things that existed. It follows that
conceptual thoughts themselves are synergistic systems. Not the least of his intentions was to
have a better way of speaking about the dynamics of the universe by understanding the struc-
20 ture of thinking, man's tool for hashing through observation, and composing it in relational
terms. This would then lead to a model that demonstrated the nature of the paradigms that
enveloped thought. If the known laws of the universe could be said to be bottled in thoughts,
then Fuller sought better carafes in which to carry and relay the derived logic of empirical
knowledge. His immediate language for contending with these ideas, and creating a fluid, in-
25 teractive metaphor for the activities of observable phenomena (in the form of physical energy,
or ideas, or knowledge) was what came to him most readily, geometry. The unit of that geometry was the tetrahedron. It became the unit of his explanations.

Ultimately, Fuller offers a science of sociological networks and the internal riggings of the
30 mind in order to construct a system of rules for otherwise unruly occurrences. His subject
matter was the pattern of all activities. Synergetics sought to create an explanatory model for
experiencing natural occurrences by pointing to the underlying order of activity that is universally in harmony with mathematic rationality.

1. Synergetics can best be described as:

    (A) A hard science
    (B) A mathematical revolution
    (C) An interpretation of knowledge
    (D) A reorganization of the laws of physics
    (E) A new lexicon for an unprecedented discussion

2. Synergetics can be best described as:

    (A) A model for inventing information

    (B) A model for better teaching of complicated relations among systems

    (C) A model for social networks

    (D) A model for both a real world and routine application of knowledge

    (E) A tautological model but not a heuristic one

3. In the last sentence of the second paragraph (line 14), "morphology" refers to

    (A) the empirical characteristics of the world

    (B) the theoretical relationships of phenomena

    (C) the changing relationships of matter

    (D) the science of categorizing matter

    (E) the nomenclature of taxonomy

4. Through Fuller's epistemology, a "system" can best be understood as:

    (A) A series of related mechanisms

    (B) A unit

    (C) A subgroup

    (D) A component

    (E) A conceptual thought

5. Fuller's most basic device for teaching synergetics as a model for thinking about empirical reality geometrically was:

    (A) The system

    (B) The morphology

    (C) The thoughts

    (D) The tetrahedron

    (E) The logic

6. Fuller would likely consider synergetics a scientific way of making sense of

    (A) unpredictable outcomes

    (B) unobservable phenomena

    (C) inexplicable relationships

    (D) unrealistic undertakings

    (E) uncharted space

7. Fuller's "carafes" refer to

   (A) transmitters of knowledge

   (B) laws of physics

   (C) uses of language

   (D) Arabian cisterns

   (E) geometrical shapes

8. Which of the following best categorizes the tone of the passage?

   (A) critical

   (B) exploratory

   (C) analytical

   (D) intriguing

   (E) principled

4.17 Passage 17 (Sustainability of homo sapiens)

The positioning of human beings as one of the species with the largest biomasses on earth, and as the leading influence on earth's ecosystems, is the result of the ecological processes which brought about their migration from the African Savannah, and geographically dispersed them throughout the world. It can be said the most rudimentary measure of the success of
5 the species is its position near the top of the aggregate biomass scale. Biomass is the total mass of all living members of a species. For human beings, it is a reflection of their claim on territory, and their consumption of resources as a species. It might be short-sighted to belittle the success of an emerging species or breed for being small in number if it is evident that the members of the species are elegant and well-adjusted. However, the ability to adapt one's
10 habitat to the largest ecosystem, while still retaining the flexibility to deal with local demands on the population may be considered high art in the annals of successful adaptation. It is here that human beings have had nearly unparalleled success (insects being larger in worldwide biomass). As a result human beings exist in huge numbers. It is the fact that human beings have remained in a generally undifferentiated form that allows them to rank highly as a single
15 successful species.

The whole world has been tenanted with life. Human beings are considered unique as they retain their form as they travel from environment to environment. Historically, human beings, like all organisms, may be driven into new areas, or a new environment may spring up around
20 them as a result of drought, competition or geological changes.

Still, human beings have been able to adjust their behavior sufficiently to avoid having nature make such extensive piecemeal adjustments to them that entirely distinct workable alternatives of the same model occupy the new space. It was through such piecemeal adjustments
25 that dinosaurs yielded to pigeons, primitive fish to amphibians and then eventually to whales, even Homo sapiens partially to Neanderthals for a time.

In all cases, these offshoots and also-rans of each species had to co-exist alongside their preceding heritage. Thus, it can be said that many species, through one of their members, were
30 able to succeed in carrying the genetic information of the group into another ecosystem. But eventually, each derivation became classified as something other than its ancestor. In this way, the transfer of genetic material circles the globe, and a species takes on scientifically unique identities at different times and in different places. Humans thus remain distinct not because they are the first to exist in so many habitats, and take advantage of so many resources, but in
35 that they have become one of the relatively few organisms to accomplish widespread population of different habitats while being able to exchange genetic material with others from their group, even if they had been largely geographically isolated over many generations.

1. According to the passage, the high ranking of human beings on a planetary biomass scale directly demonstrates which aspects of their success?

   (A) their position at the top of the food chain

   (B) their ability to eat almost anything and engineer their environment

   (C) their ability to navigate their evolution

   (D) their consumption of resources and claim on territory

   (E) their mobility

2. What makes human beings unique in their colonization of Earth is that

   (A) they have existed at the same time in several genetic forms

   (B) genetically they followed a similar path to that of dinosaurs

   (C) they withstood dispersal while becoming the only surviving species in their genus

   (D) they are the highest ranked organisms on the biomass scale

   (E) they carried their genetic code to all parts of the world

3. According to the passage, what characteristic has allowed human beings to avoid splitting into different species?

   (A) their ability to reproduce with all the members of their species

   (B) minimal exposure to geographic isolation

   (C) the death of all their competing species

   (D) their ability to adjust their behavior to fit their environment

   (E) the presence of a very diverse genetic code with many permutations in a large population

4. The passage quantifies success of any species in terms of

   (A) the length of time a species has been in its state

   (B) the population density of a species

   (C) the population size of a species

   (D) the global dispersion of its genetic code

   (E) the degree of adaptation to its environment

5. In the passage, an important factor in the success of a species is

   (A) geographic dispersion

   (B) the elimination of all but a few members of an original species

   (C) the age of the preceding species

   (D) mutation

   (E) sexual selection

6. In the first sentence of the third paragraph (line 28), "In all cases, ... preceding heritage.", the word "preceding" means

    (A) existing at the same time

    (B) receding from

    (C) diminishing with every generation

    (D) previous

    (E) migratory

7. The passage discusses genetic material in regard to which of the following

    (A) consumable resources

    (B) mutations of genes

    (C) the spiral form of genes

    (D) the migration of species

    (E) disease carriers

8. The style of the passage may be considered

    (A) biased

    (B) polemical

    (C) balanced

    (D) vague

    (E) idealistic

4.18   Passage 18 (Punctuated equilibrium updates Darwin)

Beginning with Darwin's publication of the Origin of Species, the topic of evolution and speciation of organisms has emerged as a science within biology that is subject to considerable branching and reinterpretation. Origin of Species introduced the notion of fitness within a specific environment as the determinant in the success or failure of a new species. For Dar-
5   win, fitness supplied some of the organisms of a species with a competitive advantage. Thus some members of a species were able to propagate while others slowly were outmaneuvered for food, territory, security, and the opportunity to mate. As intuitive as Darwinian logic has come to be, and as sensibly as it interprets, the empirical behavior and location of similar species, Darwinian adaptation has had to weather much reinterpretation focusing on the pre-
10   cise processes that transform competitive advantage into speciation. The notion of punctuated equilibrium is one such challenge to Darwinian 'elegance'.

Punctuated equilibrium is a theory akin to Darwinian logic, but it asks specific questions as to just how fitness turns a minority of an organism's phenotype into a separate non-impregnable
15   species altogether. Darwin's logic expects species to rise from a beneficial perforation of the line of continuity of that species. Darwin states if one organism contains all the elements of its breed of organisms, but also some uncommon advantageous trait, it will successfully reproduce, and spawn progeny who enjoy an iteration of that process as long as their permutation makes them more fit for prevailing conditions. Punctuated equilibrium takes another
20   approach to the conditions necessary to turn an organism tailored by mutation or another differentiation into an out and out species.

Punctuated equilibrium views Darwinian gene flows and causation to be overly ambitious, or simplistic. In actuality, say its proponents, any comparative advantage acquired by the
25   member of a species would, under most conditions, be re-absorbed and 'averaged out' among a sizable number of members of the species before it had time to be visible, a gradation too subtle for Darwin and his naturalists to observe outside the isolation of the tiny Galapagos Islands. Punctuated equilibrium updates Darwin by noting that the sudden emergence of a differentiation, endowing an organism with more fitness than its former species, would not
30   usually give that organism or its descendants a significant degree of independence in the absence of disastrous conditions. For the evolution reformers, this comparative advantage only leads to a speciation event if the conditions in which it occurs are cataclysmic for the species as a whole, including massive geographic reformations (such as the flooding of the Mediterranean basin) or unexpected ecological devastation. What this says is that in order
35   for a deviation to turn into a species, conditions surrounding that deviation must always be sufficiently harsh to drive the evolutionary pressure of speciation. This creates a timescale for speciation that is better represented by a pendulum swing in one swift motion, than by seeping growth and petty attrition of a Darwinian forbear fanning out over successive generations.

1. The most appropriate title for this passage might be:

    (A) Debunking Darwin: why fitness was never an issue

    (B) One better: coming closer to the makings of fitness hence species

    (C) Taking turns: how fitness became a proxy issue for second line Darwinists

    (D) Repairing history for Darwin and his apologists

    (E) Making an honest man out of Darwin

2. The primary difference between Darwinian evolution and punctuated equilibrium is

    (A) the number of supporters of each theory

    (B) the possibility of cataclysmic events as a contributing factor in extinction

    (C) the areas of the world providing support for each theory

    (D) that punctuated equilibrium simply fills in unexplained aspects of Darwinian evolution

    (E) that Darwin views mutations as the source of new traits while punctuated equilibrium considers ecological disasters to be the source of new traits

3. According to the passage, the principal objection of punctuated equilibrium's supporters to the Darwinian theory of fitness and speciation is that

    (A) it moves too slowly to account for the progress of the fossil record

    (B) Darwin does not consider that ecological disasters often drive speciation

    (C) species is a relative term for a collection of individual gene permutations

    (D) it is dependent on microclimates or controlled circumstances

    (E) it assumes the principles it sets out to prove

4. Punctuated equilibrium may be best described as:

    (A) A corollary to Origin of Species

    (B) An abbreviation of Origin of Species

    (C) A refinement of Origin of Species

    (D) A contradiction of Origin of Species

    (E) A continuation of Origin of Species

5. With reference to "The notion of punctuated equilibrium is one such challenge to Darwinian 'elegance'" (line 10), the advocates of punctuated equilibrium would likely fault the "elegance" of Origin of Species for it being

    (A) unproven

    (B) unscientific

    (C) discursive

    (D) oversimplified

    (E) deceptive

6. Punctuated equilibrium would be likely to describe the occurrence of speciation as

   (A) unpredictable

   (B) malefic

   (C) plodding

   (D) unrealistic

   (E) inevitable

7. According to the theory of punctuated equilibrium, which of the following events would be less explicable than the others?

   (A) an increase in the hardness of the beak of a certain bird in response to all the local soft fruit being lost in a fire

   (B) darkening in the color of the fur of the Belgian bilge rat upon landing in a polluted foreign country

   (C) an increase in the muscle density of a dingo allowing it to run faster than others in its pack

   (D) the thickening of the skull and general size of some members of homo sapiens at the onset of the ice age

   (E) the disappearance of a species following a tsunami

8. In the middle of the last paragraph beginning with (line 31): "For the evolution", the word "unexpected" (line 34) is used to mean

   (A) epidemic

   (B) on a large scale

   (C) immediate

   (D) unforeseen

   (E) at once

4.19   Passage 19 (Abortion law)

The question of legalized abortion in America has largely been considered in terms of moral objections resulting from competing perceptions of human rights and freedom of choice. While the representatives of these views have been influential actors for whom lawmakers must tweak any legislation pertaining to abortion, economists now offer tangible evidence that
5 the abortion issue must be evaluated with some very practical considerations as well. While the importance of the life of a fetus brought-to-term is never a forgotten aspect of the debate on abortion, the relevance of the abortion issue to the lifestyle opportunities for all of society has yet to be weighed heavily in the debate.

10 However, in their retrospective examination of many years' evidence, John Donahue and Steven Levitt, researchers from Harvard University and the University of Chicago, have pointed out that a suggested correlation between the passage of Roe vs. Wade, the integral piece of abortion empowerment legislation, and reported crime statistics twenty years later can in fact be noted. This is because the period during which most perpetrators engage in the majority of
15 any society's illegal activity is when they are in their late teens and early twenties. Adolescent and young adult males are considered to be the most likely to engage in illegal activity. Their relative inexperience in the world, the paucity of opportunities and their group relationships make them more prone to violence and defiance than women or older males. The researchers note that within a few years of the U.S. Supreme Court Roe vs. Wade decision, up to a quarter
20 of all pregnancies in the United States resulted in abortions. Also, they observe that crime rates between 1985 and 1997 declined. The researchers note that children who would have otherwise been born in the early years after the Roe vs. Wade decision would be reaching their late teen years between 1985 and 1997. However, they were not born, and crime decreased in this time frame. These researchers interpret the termination of an unwanted pregnancy as
25 the rational response of a woman who is not prepared to care for a child. Going forward with an unwanted pregnancy presumably confers on the woman too great a challenge in raising a child she is poorly prepared for, and provides the child with an upbringing that is suboptimal, making him more vulnerable to be party to illegal conduct.

30 These numbers signify less crime as a result of letting more mothers choose when to have a baby. Crime is financially costly to taxpayers as well. Lawmakers may take heed of this evaluation if they consider Donahue and Levitt's calculation that the economic benefit to society from the termination of unwanted pregnancies may be as high as $30 billion annually. As the ideological arguments over abortion refuse to abate, it may be time for hamstrung legis-
35 lators to consider new sources of information to simplify their decisions about reopening the question of abortion reform and government aid.

1. The primary difference between the original abortion debate and the present one presented by the researchers is that

   (A)   the original debate was subjective while the present debate is objective

   (B)   the previous debate was based on ethics while the present debate is based on religion

   (C)   the original debate was between completely oppositional parties while the present debate has more heterogeneous participants

   (D)   the previous debate was phrased ideologically while the present debate is concerned with practicality

   (E)   the original debate was supported scientifically while the present debate does not involve science

2. The style of the passage may be

   (A)   persuasive

   (B)   encyclopedic

   (C)   historiographic

   (D)   scientific

   (E)   journalistic

3. One fact which would strengthen the claims of the researchers would be if

   (A)   there was also a sharp decrease in white collar crime during the period of reported statistics

   (B)   there was a decline in the economy during the period of reported statistics

   (C)   states which legalized abortion first saw earlier decreases in crime during the period of reported statistics

   (D)   young males were shown to be avid watchers of violent programming

   (E)   states which legalized abortion first saw increases in crime during the period of reported statistics

4. The implication of the passage regarding unwanted pregnancies is that

   (A)   they are more common in poor families

   (B)   they are more likely to yield males

   (C)   they are more common with women likely to be criminals

   (D)   they are unwanted for a good reason

   (E)   the children resulting from unwanted pregnancies are raised by women

5. What is the assumption of the author regarding the historical abortion debate when presenting Donahue and Levitt's research as the premise for legislative decisions?

   (A) Both sides were equally wrong.

   (B) It is not the role of the state to make decisions based on the personal politics of its citizens.

   (C) The research is weighed as heavily as either of the ideological arguments in the debate.

   (D) Moral debates on economic issues like abortion cannot ever help in formulating legislation.

   (E) Legislators view the ideological abortion debate as politically irresolvable for practical purposes.

6. In the last sentence of the last paragraph (line 33) beginning "As the ideological ... government aid", the author seeks to do what to the abortion debate?

   (A) confine the debate to a small audience

   (B) emphasize its complexity

   (C) increase the influence of narrow interest groups

   (D) argue for a return to a debate on ideological grounds

   (E) simplify the dialogue

7. Which of the following, according to the researchers, depicts the practical consideration of abortion?

   (A) More abortions will result in less crime.

   (B) Crime decreases and money is saved when women have freedom of choice.

   (C) Crime is a function of population growth.

   (D) Abortions of non-violent females are an unavoidable consequence of allowing women the right to an abortion.

   (E) Crime increases when there is a right to abortion.

8. In the last sentence of the second paragraph (line 27), the word "suboptimal" could be replaced with which of the following without changing its contextual meaning

   (A) inadequate

   (B) almost perfect

   (C) inefficient

   (D) economically advantaged

   (E) second best

4.20 Passage 20 (Surveillance)

While clandestine observation has always played a part in investigation, the most important difference between modern database surveillance and traditional legwork is the proliferation of surveillance of the systems of mundane transactions and of social behavior. No less fore-boding is analysis through calculations of regression and methods of associated comparison,
5 to broaden scientifically the range of 'suspicious' behavior in order to justify the oversight of new types of actors, and an increased number of actors. These abilities are being incorporated into a policy about which the public is not aware, and one, which is outside the scope of current legislation.

10 Given that most people regard themselves as 'law abiding,' and that the avoidance of crime, drug abuse and other quality of life infractions rates highly in citizens' priorities, the development of improved surveillance systems is widely seen as a benign invasion that improves policing. This sort of perception has led the U.K., after it was able to pinpoint two young men as being the culprits in the murder of a young boy, to be the country with the most widespread
15 use of surveillance cameras. The impracticality of, and lack of interest in, prosecuting every transgression caught by the system obscures its threat to individual liberty. But while this may keep the disadvantages of surveillance from bringing people to vocal dissent, what should be raised in the public consciousness is that what surveillance changes is the amount of leverage a minority of actors (authorities, bureaucrats, or system managers) receive over the general pop-
20 ulation. In any encounter in which one individual must confront the state, the state achieves an advantage by having so many more 'leads' on the individual with which to use bullying tactics, and by engaging in non-judicial activities such as Secret Service searches, the disbanding of rallies, and the detention of political and foreign activists.

25 Compiling a file of criminal activities engaged in by a subject under surveillance is routine. But there can also be an insinuation of an activity that a government uses politically to undermine the position of a subject. That action changes the direction of prosecution, reiterating the importance of, and the reasoning behind, such safeguards as the Miranda acts, designed to protect suspects from incriminating themselves in the absence of their lawyer. The greatest
30 danger is that the rules of criminal justice can be controlled by a bureaucratic, authoritarian organization to prolong detention, and to control the flow of information under conditions of the confinement of a subject, in order to improve the ability of investigators to aid the prosecution. The monopoly which public bureaucracies have on prosecution and investigation allows them to use or disregard official rules in ways that are not transparent to a defendant.
35 It has been shown that increasing the level of surveillance in the public arena does not improve the ability to identify offenders, but improves the ability of the government to operate extra-judicially. This offers authorities the opportunity of manufacturing opportunities for themselves to control behavior in ways that are beyond redress.

1. The main concern of the passage regarding improvements in surveillance is

    (A) the ability to record the activity of everybody

    (B) the lack of knowledge many people have regarding their surveillance

    (C) the ability of the government to influence prosecution

    (D) the disbanding of rallies and detention of political prisoners

    (E) the fact that surveillance is technically illegal

2. The passage suggests that which of the following is true of most people?

    (A) They have consented to surveillance.

    (B) They consider surveillance to be no more widespread than in the past.

    (C) They do not consider themselves law abiding.

    (D) They are unaware of the details of surveillance.

    (E) They consider surveillance to be beneficial.

3. According to the passage, which of the following is the most important benefit of improved surveillance for the state?

    (A) It makes it possible to identify and punish criminals far more effectively than before.

    (B) It makes it possible to improve the case against suspects.

    (C) It makes it possible to track down many more criminals.

    (D) It increases the number of jobs available in the public sector.

    (E) It limits the power of the police.

4. The author would be most likely to agree with which of the following?

    (A) Government should be able to police itself to avoid overstepping its powers.

    (B) Government has a need to protect itself from criminals.

    (C) Government power lies partly outside the law.

    (D) Government is only as trustworthy as its people.

    (E) Government fulfills the wants of the people it represents.

5. In the passage, the biggest danger of improved surveillance to the public has to do with

    (A) falsely identifying criminals

    (B) allowing the government to act without a process of review

    (C) empowering a minority of the public

    (D) reversing democracy

    (E) increasing costs

6. It can be inferred from the passage that the author believes that the example of the boys from the U.K. collared in the murder case

    (A)   is a good example of the need for surveillance

    (B)   validates the use of surveillance

    (C)   is not sufficient evidence of the value of surveillance

    (D)   is an extreme and isolated case

    (E)   is a reproducible result

7. The passage shows that laws that are passed to protect the rights of defendants are intended to

    (A)   reduce the role of government in people's lives

    (B)   acknowledge that a defendant is innocent until proven guilty

    (C)   allow defendants the opportunity to explain their side of the story

    (D)   limit the power of government to aid the prosecution

    (E)   show that the public is more sympathetic to defendants than to prosecutors

8. One problem the passage sees with the capacity of government to contribute to the prosecution is

    (A)   the unreasonable punishment of offenders

    (B)   the inability of government to prove its case

    (C)   the monopoly of the government over prosecuting offenders

    (D)   the lack of press access to a case

    (E)   the inability of the public to regulate government

4.21   Passage 21 (Reforms in the European education system)

Universities in Europe are increasingly under the influence of the globalization movement, with examples of this trend widespread across the continent. European universities must answer the perceived needs of multinational corporations, as these firms aspire to draw on an employee base that is borderless, and highly mobile. The system of German engineering schools

5   provides a lucid example for understanding the logic behind transforming European education from a system of segmented and self-contained schools into a system with much more inter-reliance among institutions. Engineering schools are good examples of the myopia of many European institutions because of the common misreading by these schools that they are safe in exclusively focusing on the engineering content of their programs while claiming inde-

10 pendence from political transformations taking place outside their one specific discipline; in outlining the alternative view, a clear example of how closely linked educational environments are to their coursework is provided.

The attitude that professional schools only need to be concerned with the immediate issues

15 pertaining to students' core competencies raises objections from corporate onlookers and many international educators across the engineering fields. Leading concerns for critics of the German university system are that there is limited intercourse between different academies, and that too few courses are taught in English.

20 The lack of availability of English courses in German engineering schools contributes to there being a paucity of international students in German programs. In addition, German engineering students can find themselves painted into a corner midway through their studies if they seek to change the direction of their education. This is because they have limited experience in taking courses in other German universities, and taking engineering courses abroad is the

25 exception, never the rule. Moreover, if these students were to transfer to another school, it is commonplace that much of their course history would not count towards a future degree in a different program. For these reasons, engineering education has come under well-lit scrutiny by businessmen, educators and government officials.

30 In response, engineering administrators have developed a better head for global issues that pertain to their students' desire for varied post-university employment, as well as their students' access to borderless knowledge during their university years. These issues have jointly led educators to identify the need for a new Magna Carta of universities in order to transfer their awareness into solutions. The outcome of this collective attention is the Bologna Dec-

35 laration. Its recommendations are fourfold: to establish a system of comparable degrees to facilitate international competitiveness, to adopt the two cycle (undergraduate and graduate) system of schooling, to establish a standard credit system for classroom work, and to find a way to ensure the quality of programs offered Europe-wide. These improvements in European education increase the international marketability of matriculating students. However,

40 of equal importance, they also increase the mobility of students during their university years.

1. Mention of German sociology programs was probably not included in the passage because

    (A) they do not have the same difficulties as other programs

    (B) they are by nature peopled by a diverse and interactive student body

    (C) their discipline has a heightened focus on external conditions

    (D) one example is sufficient for the purposes of the passage

    (E) multinational corporations have little interest in the graduates of sociology programs, and exert no pressure on the heads of these programs

2. Critics of German university programs seem to prefer that more courses be taught in English in order to

    (A) make German students less likely to attend foreign schools

    (B) make students better qualified to accept employment positions throughout Europe

    (C) make more research available to German students

    (D) make it easier for students from abroad to get credit for German university courses

    (E) encourage more students from abroad to take courses in Germany

3. The term "well-lit scrutiny" in the last sentence of paragraph 3 (line 27) implies

    (A) criticism that is overdue

    (B) critique under the worst of conditions

    (C) critique from many sources is the most thorough

    (D) critique that is deserved

    (E) thoroughly executed critique with many perspectives

4. Which of the following best replicates the use of "paucity" in the middle of the third paragraph (line 21)?

    (A) sufficient

    (B) small number

    (C) significant number

    (D) over-abundance

    (E) diversity

5. The author would most likely agree with the principle that

    (A) the purpose of education is to raise active citizens

    (B) the purpose of education is to create well-rounded individuals

    (C) education should provide students with the flexibility they need to function effectively later in life in whatever field they choose

    (D) education ought to ease cultural tensions

    (E) education should encourage students to work outside of their national origins

6. The Bologna Declaration, mentioned in the middle of the last paragraph, declares the goal of

    (A) creating educational standards

    (B) promoting English in European schools

    (C) regulating engineering programs

    (D) allowing students to pursue a greater selection of vocational opportunities

    (E) decreasing student mobility

7. The author's primary concern about the unlikelihood of engineering students ever changing their course of study is best expressed in which statement?

    (A) Engineering degrees should not count towards a variety of credit programs.

    (B) Engineering schools should not be reformed.

    (C) Engineering schools are obligated to prove their competitiveness.

    (D) Engineering schools can no longer overlook the potential in other fields of study.

    (E) It is important to facilitate a variety of choices for students.

8. According to the passage, the importance of students being mobile during their university years is related to

    (A) the need for students to choose a city they like in which to study

    (B) the attractiveness of engineering as a career

    (C) the fact that too few cities have engineering schools

    (D) the desire for an amalgamation of engineering schools

    (E) the need for multinationals to have access to such a labor pool

4.22 Passage 22 (The U.S.'s Nuclear Energy Program)

In 1957, the United States invested in mining the atom for its stores of energy, and funneling this cache into an engineering and military revolution. Wartime uses of atomic energy went largely towards the development of more powerful weapons of mass destruction, though the Department of Defense also utilized it as a more efficient means of long-range propulsion for
5 warships and submersibles. At the same time, the United States Atomic Energy Commission (AEC) created what it would later call the "Plowshare Program". This initiative was intended to develop peaceful applications of modern nuclear power, then under feverish development by scientists primarily for Cold War armaments, and to develop domestic energy sources "too cheap to meter".
10
In August of 1958, scouts from the AEC conducted something of a reconnaissance of Point Hope, in Northwest Alaska. They had selected Ogotoruk Creek in this region as a possible site for the detonation of an atomic bomb. The logic behind the detonation was political and practical. The AEC had decided to bowdlerize the discussion of nuclear weapons by teaming
15 nuclear arms with civil engineering. If the science of Cold War defense could be a proven boon to civil engineering, the AEC felt it could dilute the intense public skepticism towards above ground nuclear testing. Romanticizing their ingenuity, the AEC identified their plan as "Operation Plowshare", alluding to the Biblical panegyric of a world after war when men may someday "beat their swords into plowshares". Atomic technology was presented as being an
20 engineering wonder, the driver of the future instead of the idle sentry needed for John Marshall's Mutual Atomic Destruction policy.

The need for something positive to add to the discussion on the nuclear weapons program came as Russia's successful launch of the Sputnik I satellite into space induced shallow breath-
25 ing in members of America's scientific and engineering elite. The immediate reaction, in the name of one-upmanship, was that "earth excavation" would be the surest demonstration of impressive and beneficial applications of America's existing nuclear capabilities. Their preferred advice was to detonate a 2.4 megaton atomic device on the northwest coast of Alaska, to create a deep water hole facilitating the shipping of coal, timber and oil, while developing
30 Alaska's coast, with obvious benefits for the 48 mainland U.S. states. This proposal would be accepted by the AEC, who designated it 'Project Chariot'. It was marketed to Alaska's financial community and lawmakers, but they remained unconvinced of the plan's commercial viability. The AEC then attempted to sell the plan to the U.S. Congress as a unique opportunity to uncover scientifically the benefits of nuclear energy. However, local unit objected and wrote to
35 President John F. Kennedy of their unease about heavy metals leaching and radiation (a plea backed by detractors in the continental United States). In turn, the AEC came to reconsider the reaction backing their proposed demonstration would realistically earn them. Project Chariot was shelved indefinitely and replaced by less visible undertakings which would be declassified decades later.

1.   According to the passage, the AEC's purpose of "Operation Plowshare" was to

     (A)   find cheaper ways to produce energy for export

     (B)   innovate in the field of mechanical engineering

     (C)   improve the reputation of the nuclear arms program

     (D)   partake in weapons development

     (E)   diversify export industries

2.   The phrase "obvious benefits for the 48 mainland states" in the mid of third paragraph (line 30) probably refers to

     (A)   a more respectable nuclear arms program

     (B)   better access to Alaska's resources

     (C)   political undermining of the arms program's opponents

     (D)   the development of a national market for nuclear arms in civil engineering

     (E)   increased knowledge of the effect of nuclear weapons on geographic landmasses

3.   The selection of Ogotoruk Creek as a site for the detonation was the result of

     (A)   resistance from surrounding populations

     (B)   executive fiat

     (C)   a scan of the area

     (D)   cartographic research and topographical comparisons of Northwest Alaska

     (E)   political decisions

4.   The passage regards American scientists as thinking of Sputnik I as

     (A)   an international political statement

     (B)   a scientific achievement

     (C)   proof of Russia's scientific superiority

     (D)   specious showmanship

     (E)   a precursor to the escalation of the arms race

5.   The attitude of American citizens regarding nuclear weapons testing can be inferred to be

     (A)   doubtful

     (B)   gung-ho

     (C)   competitive

     (D)   inventive

     (E)   complacent

6. The unwillingness of the AEC to proceed with Project Chariot as planned was the result of

    (A) disapproval from president Kennedy

    (B) its inability to achieve its original purpose

    (C) financial impracticality

    (D) better technological opportunities in undisclosed plans

    (E) the politics by detractors

7. The decision by the AEC to name their plan "Operation Plowshare" was related to which characteristic?

    (A) political shrewdness

    (B) humor

    (C) irony

    (D) anticipation

    (E) realism

8. In the context of "Operation Plowshare", what does "beat their swords into plowshares" (line 19) best mean?

    (A) making ugly look pretty

    (B) turning evil into good

    (C) molding useless to useful

    (D) transforming lethal into blunt

    (E) transforming blunt into lethal

4.23   Passage 23 (Mechanized production systems in Europe)

The 1870s were a time of drastic technological challenges to industrializing nations. These challenges resulted in stark differences in the path of development pursued by economies organizing themselves for productive capacity. Manufacturing centers reacted differently to the opportunities blooming in these challenges, each assessing the benefits of rationalization and
5 taking stock of their relevance to its production process. But while scores of industries in a variety of countries predicted some benefits from mechanization, the opportunity to increase production while reducing costs was rightly subject to pervasive debate.

German printing and textile firms showed why industrialization was not a cut and dried pro-
10 cess. German and Austrian companies appeared to acknowledge certain impetuses to move over to mechanical production of a particular category of printed cotton handkerchiefs. The production of these handkerchiefs was reliant on the handiwork of individual workmen. These handcrafted articles were the pride and joy of certain regional manufacturers who settled in this niche of the international market. Select German firms obtained the ability to double and
15 triple production while reducing their work force. But risks accompanied this methodology. While this rationalization did bring a substantial fall in the total remuneration of labor, it also significantly lowered the sale price and presented risks of overproduction. Head over heels production of items, with lowered regard for the ability of the market to absorb such production, had latent negative features.
20

The case of 'double printing' of 'Turkish bonnets' provides one example of why the adoption of fast, cheap production techniques was not a forgone conclusion for established manufacturers. In the case of these bonnets, a sudden, unpredictable drop in the demand for these items, faster than producers could react to changed preferences, concurrent with a monetary
25 crisis in eastern markets, produced friction in the industry, opening up public debate as the relationship between bosses and workers became strident.

Reaction to production innovations was regional. It seemed as if the American system of production, from the start, sidestepped some dangers. It was precisely the American system that
30 had drawn European attention to standardized production, which did offer an increase in profits while containing labor costs and unpredictability. American production was synonymous with standardization, mechanization and mass production. But in actuality, the American system was not uniquely immune to the conditions of the world market. Manufacturers of watches in Switzerland, of scarves in Germany and weavers in 19th century Glarus were reserved about
35 their approval of change. Class disparity and capital rigidity would become built-in pressure points on the American economy. These were just the things that also kept many European producers from settling around a consistent, reproducible pattern of mechanization.

1. The central theme of the passage is that

    (A) the American economy is better equipped to withstand the rigidity of standardization

    (B) negotiation is important in selecting a path of development

    (C) many businesses have failed in their attempt to industrialize

    (D) employed labor is an unavoidable contributor to the development path of companies

    (E) european companies' responses to early industrialization were mixed – some were camphor and some were wet wood

2. The author of this passage would most likely agree that

    (A) industrial plants should consider their potential contribution to a national war machine before making changes to their assembly line

    (B) the reduced cost of processed sugar makes it a better source of calories than other types of sugar

    (C) protectionism can be a valuable asset in industrial development

    (D) firms should consider the risks of overproduction

    (E) overproduction is not a problem

3. For the author, the proof of the relevance of considering the local situation is expressed by

    (A) the example of the American Great Depression

    (B) the number of watches produced in Switzerland

    (C) the type of cotton used in handkerchiefs

    (D) the design of Swiss watches

    (E) the problems in the bonnet market because of an Eastern currency crisis

4. In the passage, the threat posed by standardization involves

    (A) lack of variety in color

    (B) lack of detail

    (C) elimination of regional differences

    (D) overproduction

    (E) alienation of the workforce

5. The example of the bonnet manufacturers aims to demonstrate

    (A) that technological advancement guarantees success

    (B) the irrelevance of the debate regarding advances in industrialization

    (C) that new technologies should not be used if sales are good

    (D) that there is no need for market research

    (E) the relationship between technological advance and market adaptability

6. The passage presents the difficulties eventually faced by American industrialization as being

   (A) the quirks that needed to be ironed out of an unprecedented opportunity

   (B) unforeseen by American capitalists

   (C) issues irrelevant to a decision to standardize production

   (D) a danger of standardized industrialization anticipated by some European industrialists

   (E) unavoidable

7. One lesson the author might impart to his readers is that

   (A) innovation must overcome the resistance of many self-interested parties before it can rationalize the work process to cut expenses.

   (B) labor will always reduce the rate of progress for socialized countries.

   (C) a benefit can also be a cost down the line.

   (D) national systems of industry are compelled to industrialize by competitive pressure from industrializing nations.

   (E) social agendas should not stand in the way of progress.

8. An appropriate title for this passage might be:

   (A) American industrial pressure on the European regional economy

   (B) Examples of industrial growth and industrial decline

   (C) Discussion on the sporadic start of industrialization in Europe

   (D) Avoiding the American mistake: why industrial innovation will create unemployment and unrest

   (E) Industrial rationalization: getting more for less

4.24   Passage 24 (Gangsta rap)

Gangsta rap is a genre of rap music, with lyrics based on the violence, hedonism and misogyny inherent in the gangster lifestyle. Gangsta rap is typically identified with the American West Coast, while the broader Hip Hop music phenomenon is a potpourri of different styles. While it is unclear whether the violence in gangsta rap is actually based on real violence, the imagery
5   and "thug" iconoclasm of gangsta rap, when packaged with smooth technical production, enabled West Coast rap to distinguish itself within Hip Hop music.

Gangsta rap brought recognition to California as a legitimate music scene capable of African-American social commentary. Ultimately, Gangsta rap embraced a commercial production style, which differentiated it from the music's roots in East Coast rap. The combination of Los
10   Angeles' advanced technical production methods (Los Angeles had an extensive music post-production industry making wide use of synthesizers) and socio-economic and racial messages effectively branded Gangsta rap as a uniquely West Coast style of music. A brash and militant attitude born out of the experiences of disadvantage and racism differentiated West Coast
15   artists from their East Coast counterparts.

While initially all West Coast rap was pigeonholed as Gangsta rap, audiences' appreciation of Gangsta rap as a genre in itself made it possible for Hip Hop to solidify its foothold in American music.

20

Hip Hop had historically evolved among the economically challenged inner cities of the American East Coast. Previously, music of this style, characterized by a heavy emphasis on rhyming with a syncopated beat, had been universally labeled Hip Hop. This definition was challenged by rap group N.W.A.'s Straight Outta Compton. The album's aggressive, stripped-down sound
25   defied the traditional conventions of rap. The group's lyrical celebration of indulgence and unrelenting criticism of an American society which produced a culture of disadvantage for American blacks indicated that the old categories were not sufficient to classify its style.

Ironically, such social commentary found commercial and critical success despite the music's
30   highly commercial production style. Rap aficionados who valued conventional Hip Hop for its authenticity and "street cred" still respected the music despite its slick production techniques. Rappers were thus able to diversify, continuing to appeal to traditional rap audiences, while courting a mainstream bank of fans. Artists such as Dr. Dre, once a young Turk of West Coast rap and the most enduring of the region's vocalists, made use of funk music,
35   notwithstanding its disco lineage, to find a sound that overlaid his message with the "canned beat" post-production style popular in the region's studios. The combination allowed Hip Hop to reach a more heterogeneous audience, an audience that had already become familiar with West Coast production methods. This coupling allowed audiences to contextualize this style of Hip Hop, facilitating the listener's ability to appreciate Gangsta rap's lyricism and musical
40   production style on its own terms rather than solely against the yardstick of East Coast rap. Once West Coast rap was acknowledged as a unique style, fans were able to compare apples to apples, in evaluating the quality of East Coast and West Coast rap.

1.   The main reason why Gangsta rap became commercially successful is because it

   (A)   distinguished itself from East coast rap through rhyming

(B) appealed to rap aficionados

(C) synthesized commercial production techniques and biting social observations

(D) moved from general frameworks into highly contextualized topics for song-writing

(E) freed vocalists from the drudgery of post-production work

2. The passage suggests that images of violence associated with Gangsta rap led to what outcome?

   (A) It further confused audiences.

   (B) It earned rap commercial success but critics were nonplussed.

   (C) It made rap solely black art with a surprisingly limited range of topics.

   (D) It differentiated Gangsta rap within Hip Hop.

   (E) It coupled indulgence with social activism.

3. The militant, misogynistic and self-indulgent imagery of Gangsta rap was linked to a machined post-production process with what effect?

   (A) It made it possible to understand Gangsta rap in contrast to Hip Hop.

   (B) It alienated audiences.

   (C) It made it possible to discuss Gangsta rap as a new style.

   (D) It did not garner a wide enough audience of followers to achieve critical mass.

   (E) It maintained its street credibility.

4. The attitude of the author towards the hedonism and misogyny of rap lyrics seems to

   (A) be in favor of "Gangsta rap"

   (B) view these characteristics as a means to an end

   (C) doubt the sincerity of their use in rap songs

   (D) dispassionately acknowledge a relationship between the national rise of Gangsta rap and its hedonism and misogyny

   (E) be a non-judgmental observation of the way other people live

5. The importance of "canned beat" (line 35) to the appeal of rap to a more diverse audience implies what about rap's growing listener base?

   (A) They listen to rap's sound more carefully than its message.

   (B) They are not interested in the challenges facing inner city blacks.

   (C) They prefer to listen to a sound they are familiar with.

   (D) They are only willing to support revolutionary ideas if they are impressed by the even-tempered reviews big business can offer.

   (E) They consider the merging of hedonism and politics to be an attack on to their political sensibilities.

4.25   Passage 25 (Women's contraceptives)

In the marketing of any new product, the number of potential consumers is not the only variable that a responsible corporation needs to take into consideration in its analysis of potential profits. Even though a given product may have numerous possible uses and a willing market of consumers, the effect of that product on a corporation's image and the public's good will is
5   not guaranteed to be in direct correlation to its commercial success. While some corporations use loss-leader products to increase the profits of unrelated products through their benefits to branding, corporations are equally wary of successful products that will hamper the sales of other product lines and the ability of the corporation to function politically in its market.

10 This reality is most striking in the American contraceptive industry, where endless surveys of women reveal that more choices always seem to equate to more satisfied consumers. Still, there appears to be as many as 100 new contraceptives trapped between development and market. Consider that when we speak of research and development in the contraceptive industry, it is products for females that we concern ourselves with almost exclusively. The un-
15 willingness of corporations to supply female consumers with their products of choice makes a statement about the political inferiority of these women as consumers. Undeniably, while men have a single, relatively simple and effective measure for contraception, women are afforded a cornucopia of alternatives that suit their lifestyles, sexual appetites, and personal habits. However, for women's sake, this patchwork of options should never be viewed as too varied
20 or as colorful enough.

Since it is women who are at risk of an unwanted pregnancy, not men, women have an interest in protecting themselves from the result of their sexual relations. Being proactive about contraception is a safer course of action than relying on the benevolent consideration of their partner
25 and uncertain availability of his "wallet condom." However, while American women spend 3/4 of their reproductive lives evading unwanted pregnancies, and 60% of pregnancies remain unplanned, evidence suggests that Americans view sex in political discourse with weak stomachs even as women privately search for options to protect themselves from unintended circumstances. Based on this, it is evident that conservative pharmaceutical corporations are laden
30 with fear over the reaction of extremist pro-life groups, religious organizations and prominent members of the Republican Party to increased research and even successful marketing of contraceptive alternatives. The enormous market of consumers who would welcome convenient alternatives to the daily "pill", such as a patch, monthly hormone injections, or intrauterine devices, continue to wait much longer than necessary for such products on account of the in-
35 timidating presence of a minority of well-organized non-consumer groups dominating product availability. The solution to this paradox is not only to preach that corporations need to pursue the orthodoxy of their own free market rewards, but also to create open communication about the real sexual lifestyles of women and to organize women around a possible bounty of consumer choices by criticizing their opponents' self-appointed flag-planting missions to a
40 private moral high-ground.

1. The passage states that which of the following can be considered more important than a certain product's profitability?

    (A) corporation's safety
    (B) cost of development
    (C) managerial complications
    (D) supply chain risk
    (E) publicity

2. The implication of the author in the sentence (line 11): "*Still, there appears to be as many as 100 new contraceptives trapped between development and market*" is that

    (A) The corporations could bring these products to market but choose not to.
    (B) The products were not likely to be well received by consumers.
    (C) The products are not safe for wide distribution.
    (D) The products would bring a loss for corporations if they were all marketed simultaneously.
    (E) The products are too costly to manufacture.

3. The passage presents the decisions of pharmaceutical corporations and their marketing campaigns as a function of

    (A) corporate responsibility
    (B) canny marketing
    (C) risk taking
    (D) a lack of information
    (E) risk averseness

4. The logic behind the author's presumption that women are under-served by the birth control market is that

    (A) women have less disposable income than men do
    (B) women are unwilling to buy new contraceptive products
    (C) women are more likely than men to sue manufacturers
    (D) women are less uniform than men in their contraceptive needs
    (E) women are not swayed by advertising

5. With which of the following assessments of the pharmaceutical market would the author likely agree?

    (A) It must be regulated so that women will have all the choices they need.
    (B) It is not subject to the political influence of extra-market actors.
    (C) It is inherently biased against women.
    (D) It could provide women with many of the sources of contraceptives they seek.
    (E) It should be abandoned.

6. Which of the following would be a plausible step, in light of the passage, to increase the willingness of pharmaceutical companies to offer more contraceptive products to women?

    (A) Normalizing discussions on sex through televised discussions

    (B) Increased purchasing of available contraceptive products by women

    (C) Passing legislation that would have men take more responsibility for the consequences of sex

    (D) A demand that pharmaceutical companies lower their prices

    (E) Banning advertising of contraceptive products

7. In the sentence (line 23): "Being proactive about contraception is a safer course of action than relying on the benevolent consideration of their partner and uncertain availability of his wallet condom", the term "uncertain availability" most nearly means

    (A) likelihood

    (B) poor chance

    (C) voluntarism

    (D) good chance

    (E) reliability

8. Which of the following best describes the tone of the author?

    (A) exploratory

    (B) biased

    (C) neutral

    (D) appreciative

    (E) opinionated

Chapter 5

Answer Key

Passage 1

(1) C	(3) B	(5) C
(2) C	(4) A	

Passage 2

(1) D	(3) B	(5) D
(2) C	(4) C	

Passage 3

(1) C	(3) B	(5) B	(7) B
(2) E	(4) D	(6) A	

Passage 4

(1) D	(3) E	(5) B
(2) D	(4) A	

Passage 5

(1) E	(3) D	(5) D
(2) C	(4) A	(6) A

Passage 6

(1) D	(4) A	(7) C
(2) A	(5) E	(8) A
(3) C	(6) D	(9) B

Passage 7

(1) E	(3) D	(5) A	(7) B
(2) A	(4) E	(6) E	(8) C

Passage 8

(1) C	(3) C	(5) A	(7) D
(2) B	(4) E	(6) C	

Passage 9

(1) E	(3) A	(5) E	(7) C
(2) E	(4) C	(6) A	

Passage 10

(1) B	(3) C	(5) B	(7) C
(2) C	(4) C	(6) B	(8) A

Passage 11

(1) A	(3) D	(5) C	(7) B
(2) C	(4) A	(6) E	

Passage 12

(1) D	(3) C	(5) B	(7) D
(2) D	(4) C	(6) C	(8) C

Passage 13

(1) A	(3) C	(5) C	(7) D
(2) A	(4) A	(6) B	(8) E

Passage 14

(1) D	(3) D	(5) B	(7) C
(2) C	(4) D	(6) D	(8) D

Passage 15

(1) D	(3) E	(5) C	(7) E
(2) E	(4) D	(6) E	(8) C

Passage 16

(1) C	(3) A	(5) D	(7) E
(2) B	(4) C	(6) A	(8) B

Passage 17

(1) D	(3) D	(5) A	(7) D
(2) C	(4) C	(6) D	(8) C

Passage 18

(1) B	(3) D	(5) D	(7) C
(2) E	(4) C	(6) A	(8) D

Passage 19

(1) D	(3) C	(5) E	(7) B
(2) A	(4) D	(6) E	(8) A

Passage 20

(1) C	(3) B	(5) B	(7) D
(2) D	(4) C	(6) C	(8) C

Passage 21

(1) C	(3) E	(5) C	(7) E
(2) E	(4) B	(6) A	(8) E

Passage 22

(1) C	(3) C	(5) A	(7) A
(2) B	(4) A	(6) B	(8) B

Passage 23

(1) E	(3) E	(5) E	(7) C
(2) D	(4) D	(6) D	(8) C

Passage 24

(1) C	(3) C	(5) C
(2) D	(4) D	

Passage 25

(1) E	(3) E	(5) D	(7) A
(2) A	(4) D	(6) A	(8) E

Chapter 6
Solutions

6.1 Passage 1 (Sales force automation)

Understanding the Passage

This is a short passage of low difficulty level on business. A standard GMAT short passage asks you 3-4 questions, but we have asked you 5 questions in this passage. You should spend 2.5–3 minutes reading the passage and 60-75 seconds answering each question; so, in all, you should spend approximately 6 minutes on a short passage. For this passage, you should take approximately 8-9 minutes.

Companies don't fully succeed in holistic implementation of Sales Force Automation (SFA), because they miss the most important factor critical for success – the users' efficacy to fully utilize the capability of SFA. In setting up SFA system technology, the implementation team assumes the intended users have only low literacy in computer use proficiency. However, the users have computer literacy but lack technological knowledge about SFA. This leads the trainers to use unsuitable training techniques *meant for users with low computer literacy*. In reality, today's sales departments are mostly made up of users who have been exposed to computers, and are, therefore, *computer literate,* but who have never had to use them consistently and who struggle to grasp how much strategic value SFA will have *(therefore, they are not well-versed in optimum technology use)*. An SFA project's success hinges on creating a situation where both sales representatives and managers can reap the benefits of the SFA tools, but all too often they haven't relied on technology as a strategic tool to meet objectives. *[The author feels this aspect should be taken into account in the training programs to maximize the returns from SFA and use it optimally.]*

Their compensation and job performance are very quantifiable, based on how well they do against a set of revenue targets. Inevitably they tend to define SFA in terms of its usefulness handling the transactions they normally work on *[The sales teams cannot fully comprehend the extent to which they can utilize SFA and end up using it to only handle transactions]*. The SFA market has done a good job of selling the benefits of SFA tools to drive sales performance, but having convinced companies to purchase systems *[the SFA systems]*, there is intense pressure to achieve a strong return on investment *[for the companies who spend money to buy the SFA systems]*. To ensure a successful SFA implementation, companies need to set realistic expectations and consider issues that are unique when deploying the system. *[Thus, according to the author, what companies should do to ensure optimum use of SFA is set realistic targets and consider the company's characteristics in implementing the SFA system]*

Main Point: Poor implementation of SFA systems: incorrect approach, and how to correct it so that companies can better use SFA and reap its full benefits.

1. The question asks us to understand the main purpose of the paragraph. The author starts by straight away introducing the topic of the discussion – that companies don't implement SFA properly. He explains how the companies fail to do so – by ignoring the literacy level of users about computers. He goes on to explain how SFA can be properly implemented and used much better than it is today. All in all, he discusses the inadequate implementation of SFA and points out that if SFA is implemented and used properly, it can be used for meeting strategic goals.

   Let us analyze the options one by one.

   (A) This option is **incorrect** because this is one of the many possible concerns for the company but not the main purpose in writing this passage.

   (B) This option is **incorrect** because the author merely discusses advantages and possible benefits of SFA and not its disadvantages. The author does point out that companies are concerned about the cost factor (by discussing their worries with return on investment), but this concern is not his main purpose.

   (C) This is the **correct** answer. The author discusses the poor implementation and the recommended method for correct implementation of SFA so that companies can better use and implement SFA and reap its full benefits.

   (D) This option is **incorrect** because the author does not imply that the onus of training the users lies on the SFA market. Though the author brings the issue of lack of skills for using SFA, he does not criticize the SFA market for not having trained the users well enough in SFA.

   (E) This option is **incorrect** because the author points out the opposite of this. The author explains that SFA can be much more useful than it is now.

   The correct answer is C.

2. This is a question on specific detail.

   The question asks us to locate a specific detail in the passage, namely why traditional training approaches are inappropriate for SFA projects. The answer lies in the first three sentences of the passage, which state that companies miss out on succeeding at SFA projects because the implementation teams assume that the users are relatively illiterate in computer proficiency, but they are not. On the contrary, they lack skill from a technological aspect. This assumption causes the training programs not to be as effective as possible. The passage states that the trainers misjudge the computer literacy of the potential SFA users and consequently use the wrong training techniques.

   Let us analyze the options one by one.

   (A) This option is **incorrect** because the number of SFA users is not mentioned anywhere in the passage.

   (B) This option is **incorrect** because the passage does not state that the management teams lack experience in defining goals.

   (C) This is the **correct** answer. It matches our deductions.

(D)   This option is **incorrect** because the author suggests the opposite of this – that the users are more computer literate than they are thought to be.

(E)   This option is **incorrect** because the passage states that the users do use SFA for transactions, thus implying that they are capable of helping users to define transactional goals.

The correct answer is C.

3.   This is a question on specific inference.

We are asked to infer about SFA for its optimal use. We know that the author feels that the SFA is not utilized to its potential.

Let us analyze the options one by one.

(A)   This option is **incorrect** because it is too extreme. While the author is quite positive in his praise for SFA, we cannot infer that it would be "perfect" for reaching transactional goals. Also, the users currently already use SFA for transactions, and the author believes that this is not all SFA can only do.

(B)   This is the **correct** answer. The author does imply this in the last line of the first paragraph in which he states that SFA hasn't been used for strategic objectives.

(C)   This option is **incorrect** because it is too specific. The author mentions that SFA can yield more benefits but not that it can yield "quantifiable" goals for the "managers" only.

(D)   This option is **incorrect** because the author does not imply this at all. The author states that SFA can be used because a sales force has quantifiable revenue targets, but not that SFA can keep track of those "revenue targets".

(E)   This option is **incorrect** because the author does not say only experienced users can maximize its benefits, but rather properly trained ones can.

The correct answer is B.

4.   This is a question on specific inference.

The question asks us to infer about holistic implementation of SFA. The passage states that companies miss out on succeeding in SFA projects because the implementation teams assume that the users are illiterate in computer literacy, but they are not. They lack in technology. The passage states that the trainers misjudge the computer literacy as low of the potential SFA users and consequently use the wrong training techniques. Thus, it follows that SFA could be successfully implemented if the training programs did not assume the users to be illiterate in computer literacy, and correctly assess that they lack only in technology aspect, and trained them in a different way for using SFA to maximum benefit.

Let us analyze the options one by one.

(A) This is the **correct** answer. It matches our deductions that users need to be trained more than in basic ways.

(B) This option is **incorrect** because SFA goals haven't been discussed in the passage at all; only sales goals have been mentioned.

(C) This option is **incorrect** because the passage does not imply that SFA is not accepted by the staff, but does imply that users don't use SFA to its maximum.

(D) This option is **incorrect** because the literacy level of SFA trainers isn't in question, rather the method of training is.

(E) This option is **incorrect** because SFA isn't to be connected with either job performance or revenue goals. Rather, SFA can be used for strategic objectives.

The correct answer is A.

5. This is a question on specific inference.

The question asks us to find a specific inference about successful implementation of SFA. To maximize the benefit of SFA, training programs need to be changed. However, for successful implementation of SFA, the author, in the second paragraph and especially in the last line, mentions that SFA can be successfully implemented if realistic goals are set after a company identifies its unique situation and understands it. Thus, a company needs to assess itself and set achievable targets.

Let us analyze the options one by one.

(A) This option is **incorrect** because the training of training staff in not an issue; the issue is training the sales staff on the technological aspect of SFA.

(B) This option is **incorrect** because the author mentions that this is already being done with SFA and that this alone isn't enough. SFA should be used for more than just this.

(C) This is the **correct** answer. This matches our deductions.

(D) This option is **incorrect** because the author mentions this as explanation for why the companies use SFA for keeping track of the transactions. However, this is not how he suggests that the SFA will bring about a more positive outcome.

(E) This option is **incorrect** because no such thing is mentioned in the passage.

The correct answer is C.

6.2   Passage 2 (The WTO and sustainable development)

Understanding the Passage

This is a short passage of low difficulty level on business and economics. A standard GMAT short passage asks you 3-4 questions, but we have asked you 5 questions in this passage. You should spend 2.5-3 minutes reading the passage and 60-75 seconds answering each question; so, in all, you should spend approximately 6 minutes on a short passage. For this passage, you should take approximately 8-9 minutes.

Environmental concern and development are inseparably linked *[This is the author's opinion]*. Experience demonstrates that environmental standards and cleaner production are compatible with and supportive of economic growth *[Basically, it is possible to have economic growth/profits while being environmentally conscious]*. Healthy people and ecosystems are more productive *[According to the author, being eco-conscious leads to more productivity]*. This link between economic growth and environmental improvement is enshrined, together with the commitment to development, in the World Trade Organization's Preamble, which includes sustainable development as a basic objective of the trading system *[The WTO also agrees that economic growth is linked to environmental consciousness]*. In endorsing this concept, despite some reservations, WTO members unanimously recognized that trade and the economic growth the WTO helps to create must be fostered in the context of sustainable development, which integrates economic, social, and environmental policies *[Initially, some members did not want to but eventually did recognize that all trade and economic prosperity has to come only after being eco-conscious. This is why the WTO's Preamble endorses this concept]*. Economic growth, sustainable development, and opportunity for citizens are fundamental goals of every society *[These should be goals of every society]*. And the record of the past five decades clearly shows how the trading system has helped us reach some of these goals. [For five decades, we, the people, have strived to reach some of these goals, but have not succeeded in all.]

Since 1960, the WTO has negotiated a 90% drop in tariffs and non-tariff barriers to trade have also been dramatically reduced *[So, the WTO has managed to attain a lot of economic growth]*. Moreover, market access for agriculture and services will be further expanded upon conclusion of the next Uruguay Round *[Further growth will be achieved in the economic sphere]*. Thus, since 1960 trade has grown fifteen-fold; world economic production has quadrupled; and world per capita income has more than doubled *[All in all, economic growth and opportunity goals of the WTO have come to bear fruit]*. However, has the World Trade Organization done enough to promote sustainable development and protect the environment? *[The author questions whether the WTO has succeeded in achieving economic goals while protecting the environmental.]* In reference to the concept of sustainable development, the Brundtland Commission Report of 1987 stated "we must meet the needs of the present without compromising the ability of future generations to meet their own needs." *[The author inserts some report's quote here to describe what is meant exactly by "sustainable development", probably to imply that it has not been achieved.]* Have any laws been made to make sustainable development mandatory? *[Again, this is a rhetorical question to imply that the WTO has probably not worked in a concrete way towards sustainability goals.]* The answer is yet to be presented by the WTO. [Thus, the author believes that the WTO has not kept up its promises for sustainability development.] Taking into account state practice, treaty law, international case law, and relevant legal literature, sustainable development is not yet a norm of international law *[So, nowhere

is "sustainable development" mandatory or compulsory even though it is one of the main goals mentioned earlier]. Currently it reflects a policy goal of the international community *[It is given the status of only policy goal, but not mandatory law].* This method of taking a concept so important only as a precautionary guideline has brought the WTO's intentions regarding sustainable development into question *[The author believes that by not taking sustainable development importantly enough, because the WTO did not make it a mandatory law, the WTO's intentions about environmental consciousness are in doubt.].*

The author first introduces sustainable development and then explains the WTO's official position on it. Then data about the WTO's economic goals is given and the WTO's success at meeting them. The author then questions the WTO's lack of success at meeting sustainable development goals.

Main Point: While the WTO has met its trade and economic goals, it lacks in its environment goals.

1. This is a main purpose question from the general category.

    The question asks us to title the passage. For that, we must understand the purpose of the passage. The passage talks about the environment being linked to development. Then it introduces the WTO and its various functions, and its endorsement of the connection between sustainable development and economic growth. Later the passage explains how trade has grown dramatically because of the WTO's policies. However, in the second half of the second paragraph, the author raises questions about the WTO's environmental achievements. Thus, the author wishes to draw attention to the WTO's performance regarding sustainable development goals.

    Let us analyze each option one by one.

    (A) This answer is **incorrect** because it is too general and does not discuss the environmental concerns mentioned in the passage.

    (B) This answer is **incorrect** because it implies that the WTO has taken some actions to protect the environment, but the author implies otherwise.

    (C) This answer is **incorrect** because it's too general and does not even mention the WTO even though the author specifically discusses it.

    (D) This is the **correct** answer. It includes both the WTO and the environment, the two main areas in the passage.

    (E) This answer is **incorrect.** Though it correctly addresses the issue, it's too general and does not even mention the environment and the WTO, even though the author specifically discusses both.

    The correct answer is D.

2. This is a detail question.

The question asks us to look at a specific detail from the passage about the conditions under which the WTO endorsed the link between the environment and sustainable development. The answer to this question can be found in the first paragraph which states that the WTO accepts that care for the environment is compatible and interlinked with business and that sustainable development is one of its goals.

Let us analyze each option one by one.

(A)   This answer is **incorrect** because it is too general and does not specifically mention sustainable or environmental development.

(B)   This answer is **incorrect** because it is too extreme. The passage does not mention that the WTO committed itself only to environmental concerns.

(C)   This is **correct.** It matches our deductions. The WTO members also recognized that the environment and development are interlinked and so added sustainable development as one of the WTO's goals.

(D)   This answer is **incorrect** because there is no concept of temporary development discussed in the passage.

(E)   This answer is **incorrect** because the WTO did not accept sustainable development as a goal only by understanding healthy ecosystems, but by recognizing that environment and development are interlinked.

The correct answer is C.

3.   This is a function question from the general category.

To understand why the author presents that question, we must understand the point he is making. The author presents the given question and then defines sustainable development and presents another question. The gist of that entire part is that while the WTO is supposed to promote sustainable development, it hasn't. Thus, the role of the question in that paragraph is to introduce the idea that the WTO hasn't done enough for sustainable development.

Let us analyze each option one by one.

(A)   This answer is **incorrect** because the author does not question the WTO to assess its actions, but rather to point out its lack of action towards the environment.

(B)   This is the **correct** answer. This matches our deductions. The author does present the question to imply that the WTO hasn't kept up on its work towards sustainable development.

(C)   This answer is **incorrect** because the author does not suggest anything to imply that sustainable development is not possible.

(D)   This answer is **incorrect** because the author does not challenge the WTO, only its lack of action towards sustainable development.

(E)   This answer is **incorrect** because the author does not question the WTO generally on its actions, but rather on its lack of action towards the environment.

The correct answer is B.

4.   This is a specific inference question.

     It is a bit tricky because it asks us to find an option with which the author would **disagree.**
     Let us analyze each option one by one.

     (A)   This answer is **incorrect** because the author would agree with the statement that
              economic and environmental goals can be achieved together.

     (B)   This answer is **incorrect** because the author would agree with this statement as well
              because the author wants the WTO to take action towards sustainable development.

     (C)   This is the **correct** answer. The author would disagree with this statement. The
              author does not think that the WTO is not more motivated by business. In fact,
              the author thinks probably that the WTO is more motivated by business than by
              environmental concerns.

     (D)   This answer is **incorrect** because this is given in the passage by the author and he
              would agree with it.

     (E)   This answer is **incorrect** because the author would agree that the WTO has not
              been instrumental in protecting the environment.

     The correct answer is C.

5.   This is a specific inference question.

     This question asks us to locate a specific detail about the conclusion of the Uruguay
     Round and make an inference based on that. This is given in lines 13-15. These lines
     imply by the use of the word *moreover* that the reduction of trade barriers will be
     expanded during the Uruguay talks.

     Let us analyze each option one by one.

     (A)   This answer is **incorrect** because no environmental measures have been discussed.

     (B)   This answer is **incorrect** because the author does not discuss laws with respect to
              the Uruguay Round.

     (C)   This answer is **incorrect** because we cannot infer that new agreements will be
              formed.

     (D)   This is the **correct** answer. This matches our deductions.

     (E)   This answer is **incorrect** because it's too extreme. We cannot infer that "dramatic"
              growth will occur.

     The correct answer is D.

6.3 Passage 3 (Sourcing therapeutic proteins)

Understanding the Passage

This is a medium length passage of intermediate difficulty on medical science. A standard GMAT short passage asks you 3-4 questions, but we have asked you 5 questions in this passage. You should spend 2.5-3 minutes reading the passage and 60-75 seconds answering each question; so, in all, you should spend approximately 6 minutes on a short passage. For this passage, you should take approximately 13-14 minutes.

Protein therapeutics, rarely used earlier, are now more important, especially since their first therapy – human insulin–25 years ago. Protein therapeutics are very significant in every field of medicine, but still a bit new. Human proteins *(examples given)* are in great demand for the treatment of a variety of diseases. The human blood method is expensive and can have AIDS or hepatitis C contamination. Human cell culture costs are very high and the output is small. Bacteria or yeast proteins yield much larger quantities but the proteins produced are difficult to purify and lack the appropriate post-translational modifications that are needed. *[The gist is that human proteins are very important. There are various ways to harvest them, but the human blood method, the human cell culture method, and the bacterial method have major challenges]*

In contrast, human proteins produced in the milk of transgenic sheep, goats, and cattle have all the required things. Currently, research is going on to procure therapeutic proteins from transgenic animals (genetically modified organisms (GMO)). We can expect very high output and low cost. An advantage of producing transgenic animals: it uses less than half the number of experimental animals than pronuclear injection. Also, another advantage: possible to specify the sex of offspring and thereby reduce the time taken to generate a flock (producing a large number of animals). The main disadvantages of making therapeutic proteins in animals are 1) that it takes a long time to generate animals, 2) that proteins can't be harvested until lactation (secretion of milk) begins, and 3) that the trans-gene may affect the cow and disrupt a gene required for an important function. Despite these points, transgenic animals could provide an alternative source of therapeutic proteins to help meet these demands. *[The gist is that the best way to produce human proteins is from transgenic animals. It has two advantages over the pronuclear method. It has three disadvantages. However, despite those, we need protein therapeutics and the transgenic animal harvesting method.]*

From the above summary, we can see that the author explains why protein therapeutics are important now, the methods available to harvest human proteins, plus what the best method is, along with its advantages and disadvantages. However, the purpose is not merely to inform us about human proteins and transgenic animals, but also to recommend that this is the way going forward for how to deal with the increased demands of the medicinal industry.

Main Point: The importance of therapeutic proteins and the available alternative source (harvesting therapeutic proteins from transgenic animals).

1. This is a main purpose question from the general category.

    This question asks us to title the passage. Thus, it is a main purpose question.

    Let us analyze each option one by one.

(A) This answer is **incorrect** because the passage is not talking about proteins in general. The topic is clearly protein therapeutics and human proteins in particular. Moreover, transgenic animals are discussed as an alternate source, and arguably the best one, to procure human proteins.

(B) This answer is **incorrect** because while the author does explain that transgenic animals are the best sources for harvesting human proteins, his main purpose is not to explain only that. He wishes to explain how human proteins can be harvested in humans themselves, and transgenic animals, and why they are important.

(C) This is the **correct** answer. More than two thirds of the passage deals with harvesting human proteins and the advantages and disadvantages of those methods. Option C includes option B, while option B does not include C. If you have any confusion, you must choose option C, as it is broader in scope.

(D) This answer is **incorrect** because the author does not discuss **only protein** therapeutics, but also discusses **human proteins** and their harvesting methods.

(E) This answer is **incorrect** because the author does not discuss **only protein** therapeutics or its advantages and disadvantages, but discusses **human proteins** and their harvesting methods, and the advantages and disadvantages.

The correct answer is C.

2. This is a detail question.

    This question asks us to pinpoint a specific detail about the advantages of human proteins over proteins obtained from bacteria. This is mentioned in lines 8-11, which implies that human-derived proteins possess the necessary post-translational modifications. We want an option that lists an advantage that human proteins have, and that is not possessed by proteins obtained from bacteria.

    Let us analyze each option one by one.

(A) This answer is **incorrect** because this is not a disadvantage of proteins obtained from bacteria, but rather an advantage possessed by proteins obtained in that manner.

(B) This answer is **incorrect** because while we can infer that human proteins must be easier to purify than bacterial proteins (given in the passage), we cannot say that human proteins will be "exceedingly" pure.

(C) This answer is **incorrect** because the cost factor of bacterial proteins is not mentioned in the passage.

(D) This answer is **incorrect** because the time factor of bacterial proteins is not mentioned in the passage.

(E)   This is the **correct** answer. This is one of the advantages of human proteins over proteins obtained from bacteria (given in the passage).

The correct answer is E.

3.   This is a detail question.

We are asked which question can be answered from the information given in the passage.

Let us analyze each option one by one.

(A)   This answer is **incorrect** because the passage merely mentions that the output of proteins from human cell cultures is limited, but not why it is so.

(B)   This is the **correct** answer. The passage can answer why bacterial proteins are unsuitable because the passage clearly states that the protein from bacteria lacks the necessary modifications to be effective.

(C)   This answer is **incorrect** because how much protein is produced per liter is given but not how much by a flock. Hence, we cannot answer this question from the passage. To answer this, we would need to know the milk output of animals and the number of animals in a flock.

(D)   This answer is **incorrect** because no such distinction has been given in the passage.

(E)   This answer is **incorrect** because the passage only provides some diseases for which protein therapeutics have been used, but not all. Also, the passage does not specifically state that protein therapeutics are the only method that worked with those diseases.

The correct answer is B.

4.   The question is on specific inference. It is a bit tricky. We have to find information about protein therapeutics which, according to passage, is unsupported. Thus, we have to find the information that IS supported/true about protein therapeutics. This means that four options will present either false information, unsupported information, or out of scope information about protein therapeutics, and the right answer will present something true about protein therapeutics.

Let us analyze each option one by one.

(A)   This answer is **incorrect** because we need something true about protein therapeutics, and this option presents false information (that protein therapeutics can be used to treat AIDS and Hepatitis C). This is not given in the passage. On the contrary, the references to AIDS and Hepatitis C are used in relation to the risk of contamination from these diseases during the process of the purification of human proteins from blood. This option is a common trap laid for those students who do not read the passage in detail and only skim.

(B)   This answer is **incorrect** because again we need something true about protein therapeutics, and this option presents the unsupported information that protein therapeutics can cure diabetes. All we know is that we can produce human insulin, but not whether we can cure diabetes.

    (C)   This answer is **incorrect** because this option presents the false information that protein therapeutics cannot be produced in transgenic animals. In reality, the passage does discuss how protein therapeutics can be produced in transgenic animals.

    (D)   This is the **correct** answer. We know that protein therapeutics can produce human insulin. This is given in the passage (sentence 1/paragraph 1).

    (E)   This answer is **incorrect** because this option presents the unsupported information that protein therapeutics can treat any undefined condition. No such thing is mentioned in the passage.

The correct answer is D.

5.   This is a specific inference question.

The question asks us to infer what is true for animals produced by pronuclear injection. This is given in lines 18-21: "*An advantage of ... time taken to generate a flock.*" It gives reasons why transgenic animals are better than those produced by pronuclear injection.

An advantage of producing transgenic animals is it uses less than half the experimental animals than pronuclear injection does. Also, it is possible to specify the sex of offspring and thereby reduce the time taken to generate a flock.

Let us analyze each option one by one.

    (A)   This answer is **incorrect** because the reference of time is given for transgenic animals with reference to the possibility of specifying the sex of offspring and thereby reducing the time taken to generate a flock. This does not mean, however, that it takes twice the time to produce a pronuclear flock compared to a transgenic one.

    (B)   This is the **correct** answer. The lines quoted above state that one of the advantages of using transgenic animals over pronuclear is that we can predict the sex of transgenic ones, but we can't with the pronuclear ones.

    (C)   This answer is **incorrect** because this information is not true about transgenic animals. It is the other way around–an advantage of producing transgenic animals is it uses less than half the experimental animals than pronuclear injection does.

    (D)   This answer is **incorrect** because we cannot infer this about either transgenic or pronuclear animals.

    (E)   This answer is **incorrect** because this information is not available about either transgenic or pronuclear animals.

The correct answer is B.

6.   This is a specific inference question.

The question asks us to infer a statement with which the author would agree.

Let us analyze each option one by one.

(A)   This is the **correct** answer. The author would agree with this statement because in the last line of the passage he mentions that the demands of the medical industry can be met by protein therapeutics.

(B)   This answer is **incorrect** because we cannot necessarily say that the author thinks human proteins are the "best" way. If this were true, the author would not mention the disadvantages. This is too extreme an option.

(C)   This answer is **incorrect** because it is too extreme. We cannot say that the author thinks human proteins are the "only" way.

(D)   This answer is **incorrect** because it is too extreme. The author ends on a positive note regarding human proteins. Hence, he would not agree that protein therapeutics is unnecessary or unfeasible.

(E)   This answer is **incorrect** because we don't know how much importance the author would attach to protein therapeutics compared to every other medical discovery of the century.

The correct answer is A.

7.   The question is from the reasoning category. We have to find information to weaken the author's contention against proteins produced from human cell culture. The author contests human cell culture because he states that "*proteins can be produced in human cell culture but costs are very high and output small.*" Thus, any information that provides information against this will be our answer.

Let us analyze each option one by one.

(A)   This answer is **incorrect** because the author's contention is not that proteins from human cell culture are unpure, but that they are costly and low in output.

(B)   This is the **correct** answer. It goes against the author's main contention as discussed in the analysis given above.

(C)   This answer is **incorrect** because the author's contention is not that proteins from human cell culture are controversial or opposed by any groups' activists like animals right' activists for the use of transgenic animals, but that they are costly and low in output.

(D)   This answer is **inconclusive** because while it might take care of low costs (because the process deploys a minimum amount of equipment and takes half the time for production), it won't necessarily resolve the "low output" issue.

(E)   This answer is **incorrect** because the author's contention is not that proteins from human cell culture are contaminated or are not replicated correctly, but that they are costly and low in output.

The correct answer is B.

6.4   Passage 4 (Climate change due to volcanic eruptions)

Understanding the Passage

This is a short passage of high difficulty level on geology. A standard GMAT short passage asks you 3-4 questions, but we have asked you 5 questions in this passage. You should spend 2.5–3 minutes reading the passage and 60-75 seconds answering each question; so, in all, you should spend approximately 6 minutes on a short passage. For this passage, you should take approximately 8–9 minutes.

Previous studies on understanding the potential of Icelandic volcanic eruptions in modifying the environment have concentrated on the degree of induced climate change, but the complex interaction of the processes which control the atmospheric circulation patterns of the earth were imperfectly understood. Even with advanced equipment, they have proved difficult to model. *(There were previous studies which checked whether Icelandic volcanic eruptions have the potential to modify the environment. These studies concentrated on the degree of "induced" or brought-about climate change [as opposed to natural climate change]. However, even then, the complexities of the interaction processes that control the atmosphere were not fully understood. Even with advanced equipment, they were difficult to model into accurate conceptual details. The inference the author wants to drive home is that those studies would be, at best, limited, given the lack of understanding of the processes.)*

Documentary evidence suggests that during the Laki fissure eruption in 1783, severe acid damage to crops occurred in northern Europe, and acid pulses killed fish in Scotland.*(There is evidence that a volcanic eruption, in Laki [in Iceland], in 1783, acid probably caused crop damage and killed fish in Northern Europe, possibly modifying the environment.)* Although an induced climatic change was probably the primary mechanism responsible, the degree to which atmospheric circulation responds to volcanic forcinh is uncertain, so it is unsatisfactory to suggest that stress in the paleo-environmental record, associated with a volcanic eruption, has inevitably occurred in response to volcanic forcing of the climate. *(While we can say that it was not a natural climate change but an induced one that caused the damage, the degree to which the Laki volcano forced the change cannot be determined. So, we must not suggest that volcanic eruption forced the climate change and brought about a paleo-environmental (an environment at a period in the geological past) record change. Stress (power) [killing fish and damaging crops] was directly a result of that eruption).* The only volcanic eruptions which possess the theoretical ability to bring about climate change are those which emit substantial volumes of volatile gases. *(Not all, only some volcanic eruptions possess the ability to bring climate change. The ones that can change climate are those that emit substantial amounts of volatile gases.)* "Climate change theories" require that these be injected into the stratosphere and remain in the troposphere. *(Theories state that these emitted gases from such volcanic eruptions are injected into the stratosphere* (the second major layer of Earth's atmosphere, just above the troposphere) *and remain in the troposphere* (The troposphere is the lowest layer of Earth's atmosphere and the site of all weather on Earth.)). They must inevitably settle and be deposited on the surrounding sea and land rather than distant ecosystems.*(These gases will typically settle and be deposited on the surrounding sea of the volcanic eruptions and not in some distant land).* Despite plenty of excavations, such sedimentary evidence still eludes around the Laki central fissure. *(No sedimentation, the kind associated with the climate-changing volcanic eruptions, has been found around the Laki area. The inference being implied here is that it is*

unlikely Laki brought about the kind of climate change as is believed.)

In the above passage, the author starts by introducing the concept that volcanic eruptions are thought to cause induced climate change but immediately presents the fact that there's not enough evidence to say so because the degree of complex atmospheric interactions isn't understood yet. He further makes this point using the Laki eruption, which is believed to have caused damage in Northern Europe, and possibly brought about climate change. However, the author explains that if the Laki eruption had brought about climate change, there would be volcanic emissions that would have settled around the sea and land. Such deposits haven't been found yet, so it is likely that the Laki eruption is not fully responsible for the climate change.

Main Point: To prove that volcanic eruptions are not very likely to cause induced climate change, and definitely not to the degree believed.

1. This is a main purpose question from the general category.

   Let's analyze the options one by one.

   (A) This option is **incorrect** because the author is not concerned with how eruptions work, but rather what their effects are.

   (B) This option is **incorrect** because the author does not discuss various theories as the main purpose. He merely presents them to make one point only. This is not his main purpose.

   (C) This option is **incorrect** because the author does not provide any evidence towards explaining climate change in Northern Europe, but merely explains that there is lack of such.

   (D) This is the **correct** answer. This matches our deductions.

   (E) This option is **incorrect** because the author does not discuss any controversial hypothesis at all.

   The correct answer is D.

2. This is a detail question.

   The question asks us to locate some detail about previous studies of volcanic eruptions. This is mentioned in the first paragraph. There were previous studies to check whether Icelandic volcanic eruptions had the potential to modify the environment. However, the complexities of the interaction processes that control the atmosphere were not fully understood. Even with advanced equipment, they were difficult to model into accurate conceptual details.

   Let's analyze the options one by one.

   (A) This option is **incorrect** because we cannot infer that the findings were necessarily refuted. The author calls them into question but does not conclusively refute them.

(B)   This option is **incorrect** because the passage states that the eruptions were likely not responsible, rather than responsible, for the climate change.

(C)   This option is **incorrect** because the previous studies were more likely accepted by existing theories than not. We cannot necessarily say that they were rejected.

(D)   This is the **correct** answer. This matches our deductions.

(E)   This option is **incorrect** because the passage states that the eruptions were likely not responsible for the climate change.

The correct answer is D.

3.   This is a specific inference question.

We know that there is evidence that acid from a volcanic eruption in Laki in 1783 probably caused crop damage and killed fishes in Northern Europe, possibly modifying the environment. However, the degree to which the Laki volcano forced the change cannot be determined. So, we must not suggest that the volcanic eruption forced the climate change and brought about paleo-environmental stress [killing fish and damaging crops]. Also, no sedimentation has been found around the Laki area and thus there is no proof that Laki brought about the kind of climate change as is believed.

Let's analyze the options one by one.

(A)   This option is **incorrect** because no such thing is mentioned in the passage.

(B)   This option is **incorrect** because no such evidence is presented in the passage to infer this.

(C)   This option is **incorrect** because the passage does not provide information to specifically infer this. It merely states that Laki emissions deposits, if there are any, haven't been found yet.

(D)   This option is **incorrect** because this is the opposite of the implied inference. The author makes a case to suggest that the degree to which the eruption could affect change in the climate of Northern Europe is uncertain. The evidence in Laki also does not support it; hence, we cannot say that the eruption did so.

(E)   This is the **correct** answer. This matches our deductions.

The correct answer is E.

4.   This is a reasoning question on weakening the conclusion.

The question asks us to prove the author incorrect and prove that Icelandic eruptions did bring about induced climate change. We need to find evidence to prove that. The author bases his claim that the Icelandic eruption probably did **not** bring about induced climate change on the lack of sedimentation associated with the climate-changing volcanic eruptions around the Laki area. Thus, to prove that Icelandic eruptions did bring about induced climate change, we need to prove either that the Laki volcano emitted volatile gases that were injected into the stratosphere and troposphere that eventually got deposited in the surrounding land and sea. Such evidence would prove the author incorrect.

Let's analyze the options one by one.

(A)   This is the **correct** answer. This matches our deductions.

(B)   This option is **incorrect** because the author does not deny that the Laki eruptions caused environmental stress, but he disputes that such stress brought about induced climate change. Hence, this would not prove the author wrong.

(C)   This option is **incorrect** because this would not prove the author wrong. He does not dispute that fish and crops were affected. He disputes their link with climate change brought about by volcanic eruptions.

(D)   This option is **incorrect** because this is out of scope. Mere climate fluctuations do not necessarily prove the author wrong that volcanic eruption causing those fluctuations led to climate change. Climatic fluctuation is a temporary phenomenon, and climate change is permanent.

(E)   This option is **incorrect** because this is too generic. Environmental records of Europe will only show events but not necessarily prove that those events happened because of the volcanic eruption in Laki.

The correct answer is A.

5.   This is a function question from the general category.

We are asked to find the purpose of the first paragraph with respect to the second paragraph, i.e. what is the first paragraph explaining and what is the connection to the second paragraph. The second paragraph proves the point that the Icelandic eruption probably did **not** bring about induced climate change. The first paragraph discusses the belief that the Icelandic eruption did bring about induced climate change only to later say that there's not enough evidence to say so because the degree of complex atmospheric interactions isn't understood yet. Thus, the author makes a point in first paragraph and then explains it in detail in the second paragraph. So, the first paragraph served as a sort of introduction to the details in the second paragraph.

Let's analyze the options one by one.

(A)   This option is **incorrect** because the author does not discuss multiple theories at all.

(B)   This is the **correct** answer. This matches our deductions.

(C)   This option is **incorrect** because the author makes the opposite point that the climate change was not the result of the volcanic eruption completely.

(D)   This option is **incorrect** because this point is being made in the second paragraph. The first paragraph merely states this point but the second paragraph **proves** it. This is a tricky option.

(E)   This option is **incorrect** because the author implies the opposite of this in the entire passage.

The correct answer is B.

6.5   Passage 5 (Stock options in CEO pay)

Understanding the Passage

This is a short passage of intermediate difficulty level on business policy.

Defenders of runaway CEO pay argue that market forces are at work determining executive compensation levels and CEOs are rewarded for increasing their company's stock prices. *(CEO pay is runaway, i.e. shot up very high. However, there are defenders of this trend. These defenders argue that the rising pay is nothing but market forces at work. The CEOs should be paid highly because they increase their company's stock prices.)* But are America's CEOs entitled to such lucrative pay deals based on their performance? *(The author poses a rhetorical question asking whether CEOs actually deserve such lucrative deals, implying that he believes that the pay is too high.)* In 1998, the business press exploded with stories of pay for mediocrity *(In 1998, press started criticizing this trend of high pay for CEOs by stating that even mediocre CEOs who are not deserving are getting paid too much.)*: When it comes to executive pay, stock option grants appear to have the Midas touch*(CEOs and such executives are getting paid by mode of stock options. Stock options are as valuable as gold.)* . As the stock market has broken record after record, they have become an increasingly popular form of executive compensation. *(As the stock market is booming and breaking records, more and more CEOs are getting paid by stock options in the companies.)*

According to compensation analysts, stock options make up two-thirds of a CEO's pay, up from one-third in the 1960s. *(So, in 1960s, 1/3rd of a CEOs pay was through stock options, whereas now it is two-thirds, according to compensation analysts. Percentage share of stock options as part of CEO's pay seems to have risen dramatically.)* Instead of having to beat their competitors, CEOs with stock option-fueled compensation packages are graded on a curve: the rising stock market. *(Earlier, CEOs had to beat their competitors. Now, it seems that CEOs are graded against the stock market, given that their pay is linked to the stock market by way of stock options.)* As stock prices increase generally, even mediocre CEOs can realize large gains from their options. *(The stock prices always increase, as a general trend, even with no effort on the part of the CEO. Thus, even an average-performing CEO can earn lots of money through stock options without putting in much effort at all.)* Analysts estimate that only a quarter of option grants awarded to CEOs contain any sort of link to performance, such as premium-priced or indexed stock options. *(Analysts estimate that only a 25% of the stock options given to CEOs are actually linked to their performances. The remaining 75% of the stock options are just part of pay for being a CEO.)* But executive equity incentive plans can hurt shareholders. *(Such pay trends can hurt shareholders, according to the author.)* Recent research examined the largest U.S. companies by adjusting for the value of their executive's stock options. *(A study on the biggest companies in the U.S. was conducted by taking into account the value of their executive's stock options.)* The study found that 11 firms went from profit to loss, and 13 had their profits halved. *(The report found that 11 firms went into loss, and 13 companies had profits halved.)* In addition, the study found that the average potential dilution of shareholder value from stock options is 9.2 percent for S&P 500 companies. *(Also, this trend of paying CEOs in stock options diluted shareholder value by 9.2 percent for the top 500 companies.)*

The author starts by introducing the current trend in CEO pay–that pay is rising and is more and more composed of stock options. He then presents a rhetorical question asking whether

this is justified. He then presents statistics and research to prove that CEO pay is too high and is hurting the shareholders.

Main Point: To conclusively prove that CEOs should not be entitled to compensation through the mechanism of stock-options and that this trend will hurt the shareholders and the company.

1. This is a main purpose question from the general category.

    We have derived the main point already; let's analyze the options one by one.

    (A) This option is **incorrect** because the author does more than just explain CEO's stock option-linked compensation packages. He makes an effective case against them as part of a CEO's pay. Had the option been "to explain the **demerits of** CEOs stock option-fueled compensation packages", it would have been correct.

    (B) This option is **incorrect** because the author did not explicitly express that he has an issue with the excessive pay of CEOs. The author has an issue with the mechanism of payment–stock options. Perhaps the author is fine with the excessive pay if it is linked to profit of the company or another indicator rather than stock prices.

    (C) This option is **incorrect** because the author does not discuss lack of parity (equality) among CEO compensation packages. In fact, he implies that all CEOs, even the mediocre ones, get paid too highly.

    (D) This option is **incorrect** because the author does not argue against **bonuses**. He argues against excessive pay. This is a tricky option because the author does suggest that performance-linked pay is not as bad as pay given for stock market performance of the company. However, he does not argue as much against bonuses as against compensation packages.

    (E) This is the **correct** answer. This matches our deductions. He does criticize the rising pay of CEOs via stock options. He quotes examples of companies undergoing losses, and dilution of shareholder value.

    The correct answer is E.

2. This is a function question from the general category.

    Let us deduce what point the author makes around this phrase to understand why the author mentions it. The author uses the phrase "Midas touch" and states that the share option packages are extremely lucrative in nature because he talks about stock markets breaking records. Thus, he wants to emphasize that stock options are like "gold" and have the "Midas touch" because their value will appreciate greatly.

    Let's analyze the options one by one.

    (A) This option is **incorrect** because no historical economic situation has been discussed that involves "Midas". The author does compare compensation packages from today to those of the 1960s, but he does not mention "Midas touch" for that purpose.

(B) This option is **incorrect** because the author does not make any literary emphasis or comparison.

(C) This is the **correct** answer. This matches our deductions. The author does use the phrase to explain how lucrative the stock options are.

(D) This option is **incorrect** because the author does not criticize mediocre CEOs, but criticizes the fact that mediocre CEOs get paid as much as any other CEO.

(E) This option is **incorrect** because the author does not use of this phrase to prove that stock option compensation packages are absurd (illogical). He makes that point in the next paragraph.

The correct answer is C.

3. This is a detail question.

The author proves that stock option compensation packages are illogical in the second paragraph. Thus their flaws are mentioned in that paragraph. The author has many issues against the stock option compensation packages. He states that percentage share of stock options as part of CEOs pay has risen dramatically. It is wrong to pay CEOs through stock options because stock prices always increase as a general trend, even with no effort on the part of the CEO to further the company. Thus, even a mediocre CEO can earn lots of money through stock options without putting in much effort at all. He further states that only a quarter of the stock options given to CEOs are actually performance- linked. The remaining 75% of the stock options are just part of pay for being a CEO. Such pay trends can hurt shareholders. Also, paying CEOs in stock options diluted shareholder value by 9.2 percent for the top 500 companies. So, the author mainly discusses how CEOs stock-option compensation packages can undermine the value of shares.

Let's analyze the options one by one.

(A) This option is **incorrect** because this is not the author's reason for criticizing the stock option compensation packages. Rather, this is the defenders' reason for supporting stock option compensation packages.

(B) This option is **incorrect** because the author's main problem is not that stock options are becoming more and more popular, but that pay is rising too much and is not linked to performance. The option statement does not articulate the basis of the criticism.

(C) This option is **incorrect** because this is the opposite of what the author states. The author suggests that CEOs get paid for the stock price rising but have to put no effort into improving the company performance.

(D) This is the **correct** answer. This matches our deductions. The author mentions twice that shareholders get hurt and that potential dilution occurs because of stock option compensation packages.

(E) This option is **incorrect** because this is the opposite of what the author states. The author suggests that CEOs get paid for the stock price rising but have to put no effort into improving company performance. Thus, according to the author, the stock option compensation packages are not performance-based.

The correct answer is D.

4. This is a specific inference question.

    This question asks us to find an option regarding stock option compensation packages with which the author would agree.

    Let's analyze the options one by one.

    (A) This is the **correct** answer. The author would agree with this because this is the point the author has mainly made when he criticized stock option compensation packages. He states that it is wrong to pay CEOs through stock options because stock prices always increase as a general trend, even with no effort on the part of the CEO. Thus, even a mediocre CEO can earn lots of money through stock options without putting in much effort at all. He further states that only a quarter of the stock options given to CEOs are actually performance linked. The remaining 75% of the stock options are just part of pay for being a CEO. Thus, the author would agree that currently, companies consider their stock performance more important than actual performance.

    (B) This option is **incorrect** because the reference of two-thirds comes from the first sentence of the second paragraph: "*stock options make up two-thirds of a CEOs pay*" which is unrelated to the option statement. We have no way of knowing whether the amount of compensation packages has risen by two-thirds. All we know is that stock options made up one-third of CEO pay earlier but now make up two-thirds of CEO pay.

    (C) This option is **incorrect** because the author would not suggest this. While he may suggest that CEO's pay should be performance-linked, he wouldn't suggest that **all** of it be through premium-priced or indexed stock options.

    (D) This option is **incorrect** because while this option might be factually true, this is not the author's intention. This option implies that stock option compensation packages should not be awarded to CEOs when the company performs well in the markets. The author does not suggest that. He suggests that CEOs should be awarded for improving the company's performance and **not only** for a company's stock price rising, which is very likely anyway.

    (E) This option is **incorrect** because the passage does not suggest that stock option compensation packages enhance stock market figures. The passage suggests that due to rising stock prices, the CEOs benefit.

    The correct answer is A.

5. This is a tone question from the general category.

    This question asks us the author's attitude towards stock option compensation packages. We know that the author's statistics and research show that CEO pay is too high and is hurting shareholders. His main point seems to conclusively prove that CEOs are not entitled to such compensation and this trend will hurt the shareholders and

the company. Thus, his attitude seems very negative towards stock option compensation.

Let's analyze the options one by one.

(A) This option is **incorrect** because the author does not show only restrained (limited) criticism. He is fully against stock option compensation packages. He does not mention even a single point in favor of stock option compensation packages and hence we cannot say that he has limited criticism towards it.

(B) This option is **incorrect** because the author does not mention even a single point in favor of stock option compensation packages and hence we cannot say that he has at all any approval towards it.

(C) This option is **incorrect** because there is no disgust on the part of the author. He merely makes an unemotional case against stock option compensation packages.

(D) This is the **correct** answer. This is the author's tone because the author finds stock option compensation packages of today completely unacceptable and that's why he presents such a strong case against them.

(E) This option is **incorrect** because the author disapproves of stock option compensation packages but not in an unjustified manner. He presents proper research and statistics to make his case.

The correct answer is D.

6. This is a specific inference question.

The question asks us to find an option that can be inferred from the passage.

Let's analyze the options one by one.

(A) This is the **correct** answer. This can be inferred from the given passage. The passage states that in the 1960s, stock options made up only one-third of the CEO's pay. Today, they make up two-thirds of a CEO's pay. The author states that today the potential for shareholder value dilution because of CEO compensation packages is 9.2%, at two-thirds. Thus, it follows that, in the 1960s, at one-third, the potential for dilution because of CEO compensation packages was less.

(B) This option is **incorrect** because we cannot say that shareholders did not get hurt at all by companies in the 1960s. All we know is that in the 1960s, stock options made up only one-third of a CEO's pay. Today, they make up two-thirds of a CEO's pay. Thus, the potential for hurting shareholders through stock option compensation packages is greater today than it was in the 1960s.

(C) This option is **incorrect** because no such implication is made in the passage.

(D) This option is **incorrect** because while the author suggests that CEOs should be paid according to performance, he does not imply that the profits will be necessarily higher.

(E) This option is **incorrect** because It is the other way around. The passage rather suggests that "A CEO's pay should **NOT** be linked to the company's performance in the stock market."

The correct answer is A.

6.6   Passage 6 (Rising health care costs & medical malpractice)

Understanding the Passage

This is a short passage of intermediate difficulty level on business policy *(medical practices)*.

In 1990, a Harvard Medical Practice study cited the fact that 95,000 deaths a year in the U.S. are due to medical malpractice; an additional 700,000 individuals are subject to injury as a result of medical malpractice. These numbers are alarming. To hit our senses with the disproportionately high number of casualties due to medical malpractice, the author compares it with the casualties a jumbo jet would have caused had it crashed every day for a year. Despite this, barely 2,100 doctors a year are penalized in connection with a malpractice claim. [*The author implies that lot more than 2100 doctors are committing malpractice but they are not being charged or punished.*] Of those health care providers *(used to refer to "doctors & other health care professionals")* that do come under scrutiny and contempt, sadly the majority of them are subject to sanctions *(penalties)* on the grounds of substance abuse *(also known as "drug abuse")* or fraud, rather than medical malpractice [*meaning, malpractice goes either unnoticed or unpunished, possibly leading to more carelessness. The doctors committing malpractice get charged for different reasons, and not malpractice.*]. In the meantime, federal legislators are considering mechanisms to limit the claim amount a patient can get as compensation for damages incurred as a result of medical malpractice. [*However, legislators think that the amount of money a patient can win against a doctor accused of malpractice should be capped/limited, to reduce the cost of insurance overall.*]

Lawmakers hope that in capping jury awards *(Claim amount that a patient can win if he files a case against a doctor for malpractice)* to plaintiffs *(Claimants/patients)*, it may be possible to reduce rising health care costs. Since those costs are ultimately charged to patients in the form of insurance premiums, the reigning *(topmost/main)* logic implies that limits on claim amounts will save the patient money, and bring the cost of high quality healthcare within the reach of more Americans. [*The claim money that any patient/claimant wins against any doctor/hospital charged with malpractice is ultimately paid by insurance companies. These companies eventually make insurance more costly to pass on the high cost to the customer again.*] However, the soundness of this approach is in doubt when we consider that a congressional budget office report found that only 1% of national health care costs results from the expense of medical malpractice insurance premiums being passed on to the patient. [*Actual facts show that malpractice claim money costs only 1% of the health care costs.*] However, accidents, misdiagnosis, and conflicting prescriptions cost the nation nearly $60 billion a year. [*Actual malpractice costs more. So, the author wishes to imply that capping the claim money that a patient can win against a doctor for malpractice is pointless because it's not the real reason insurance premiums and healthcare is so costly. The real problem lies with the actual expenses caused by malpractice itself, and not cases suing for malpractice.*]

Even with these losses imposed on patients and on taxpayers yearly, less than 1/2 % of all civil cases pursued actually charge doctors with medical malpractice. [*The author implies that the malpractice issue is not being taken seriously enough, despite the loss and cost to patients.*] The 2000+ doctors who are penalized each year amount to hardly 1% of all acting health care providers. [*The author implies that even though only 1% of doctors are charged, there must be more committing malpractice, and they don't get charged or punished.*] Thus the amount of

money going back into the hands of victims is a relatively petty contribution to the overall cost of health care in America when compared to the cost of compensation for the harm of malpractice. *[So, even if some patient/claimant wins a big amount in a case of malpractice against some doctor, it is negligible compared to the actual cost to make up for the wrong caused by the malpractice.]* Rising health care costs may more predictably be reduced by improving the way in which the policies of the health care industry are laid and by removing untrustworthy doctors from practice. *[The author provides a recommendation on how to deal with doctors accused of malpractice and how to have a better healthcare industry.]*

The passage is about reducing the rising cost of healthcare in the U.S., and understanding its components. Federal legislators are considering a plan to peg down the claim amount as a result of medical malpractice; it can possibly reduce rising health care costs. However, this approach doubtful; a report found that only 1% of health care costs results from the expense of medical malpractice insurance premiums being passed on to the patient. The author concludes that rising health care costs may be reduced by sound health care policies and by removing untrustworthy doctors from practice.

Main Point: Disciplining doctors and formulating sound health care policies can more predictably reduce rising health care costs.

1. This is a main purpose question from the general category.

    We have already derived the main point; let's analyze the options one by one.

    (A) This option is **incorrect** because it only partially covers the scope of the passage. Moreover, "widespread policing" is too vague a term. This option does not even mention doctors' practices with regard to malpractice.

    (B) This option is **incorrect** because it is too generic, vague, and wide in scope. It does not even mention that the problem is "rising health care costs" and not just "health care costs".

    (C) This option is **incorrect** because the author pinpoints that one of the major sources of high health care costs is the practices of undisciplined doctors.

    (D) This is the **correct** answer. This option talks about the role of doctors and patients. It rightly addresses the issue that rising health care costs have more to do with the malpractice of doctors than with the behavior of patients. Additionally, the passage affirms that malpractice claims from patients have been shown to have only a minor impact on health care costs.

    (E) This option is **incorrect**. It is too narrow in scope and it does not address the main point of the passage at all.

    The correct answer is D.

2. This is a function question from the general category.

    The passage states that over 95,000 people die due to malpractice every year. Many times, we are not able to react to the degree of severity because the number-95,000

or, say, 950,000–does not have any shape. The author uses the example of casualties caused by a jumbo jet so that a reader can visualize the figure of 95,000. A jumbo jet with a capacity of 200-250 would have to crash 365 times to make 95,000 casualties. It is a dramatic way of telling us the severity.

With the above analysis, option A is the correct answer. Though option B is close, the purpose of comparing the number of malpractice victims to the number of jumbo jet accident casualties is missing; it merely states "what" the author says in the example but not "why" the author gave us that example. The question asks us not "what" the point is but "why" the author made that point.

The correct answer is A.

3.   This is a specific inference question.

Refer to paragraph 1 (line ??): "*fewer than 2,100 doctors a year are disciplined in connection with a malpractice claim*". The author implies that even though only 1% of doctors are charged, there must be more committing malpractice, and they don't get charged or punished. Also the conclusion recommends firing more doctors. So the inference is that too few doctors are penalized.

- **(A)** This option is **incorrect** because the passage did not mention that penalties are given out for the wrong reasons.
- **(B)** Similarly, this option is **incorrect** because the passage did not mention that penalties given out are not severe enough.
- **(C)** This is the **correct** answer. It follows our deductions.
- **(D)** Like option A and B, this option is **incorrect** because the passage did not mention that penalties are given out to wrong offenders.
- **(E)** This option is **incorrect**. It is a rephrased version of option B.

The correct answer is C.

4.   This is a specific inference question.

Option A is the correct answer because the passage states that a congressional report (refer to paragraph 2) found that malpractice claims account for only a minor portion (1%) of health care costs. Other options do not qualify to be inferred as they are either against the stated/implied facts (options B and C) or are out of scope of the passage (options D and E).

The correct answer is A.

5.   This is an inference question.

The passage speaks directly about the role of doctors in inflating the costs of healthcare through malpractice, and patients not having sufficient opportunity or ways to recoup those costs. A likely inference with which the author would agree is that the malpractice of doctors and the unwillingness of the authorities to charge such doctors is responsible for rising healthcare costs.

(A) This option is **incorrect** because the author does not intend to mean that insurance companies will deliberately try to inflate their rate of return on premiums.

(B) This option is **incorrect** because the author does not mention expensive treatments.

(C) Like option A and B, this option is **incorrect** because the author does not intend to imply that doctors are compelled to reduce their services in order to cover their own expenses. This is out of scope.

(D) This option is **incorrect** because the author does not even mention options for treatment.

(E) This is the **correct** answer. It follows our analysis.

The correct answer is E.

6. This is a function question from the general category.

Let us analyze both sentences:

Lines: 5-7: "*Despite the multitudes of people who die or suffer as a result of medical malpractice, fewer than 2,100 doctors a year are disciplined in connection with a malpractice claim*".

⇒ The take away message from the sentence is that more doctors must be penalized because of malpractice.

Lines: 9-11: "*These facts resurface at a time when federal legislators are considering measures to limit the monetary amount a patient can claim as compensation for damages incurred as a result of medical malpractice.*"

⇒ This sentence is in contradiction to the finding in the first sentence. It can better be summarized as "*Despite the findings of the first sentence, federal legislators are considering measures to limit the claim amount.*"

(A) This option is **incorrect** because had the findings from the first sentence been taken into consideration, the lawmakers would not have thought of putting a cap on jury awards. It goes against the implications made by the author.

(B) This option is **incorrect** because it is too general and does not discuss the essence of both sentences.

(C) This option is **incorrect** because it does not address the purpose.

(D)   This is the **correct** answer because the sentences address the contradiction between the policy-making of Congress in aiming to lower health care costs by restricting patient awards and the research of the congressional budget office that says malpractice claims account for a minor part of health care costs because a very small number of doctors that commit malpractice are charged or penalized.

(E)   Like option B, this option is **incorrect** because it is too general and does not take the essence of both sentences.

The correct answer is D.

7.   This is a reasoning based question on assumption.

Conclusion: Greater policing of doctors will reduce the incidence of malpractice and drive down costs.

Let us predict the assumption. Why does the author conclude that greater policing of doctors will reduce the incidence of malpractice and drive down costs? There is an underlying assumption here: greater policing will ensure that doctors err less and improve their performance, thereby reducing the cost. He thinks that the policing will have a deterrent effect. Let us see the options one by one.

(A)   This option is **incorrect** because even if most doctors are responsible, they can still commit malpractice. The issue at hand is to reduce negligence and improve performance so that malpractice can be reduced.

(B)   This option is **incorrect** because it does not address the issue of malpractice.

(C)   This is the **correct** answer. It matches our deduction.

(D)   This option is **incorrect** because it is opposite of the conclusion. If doctors will never protect one another from investigation in case one commits malpractice, then there is no need for greater policing, which is against the conclusion.

(E)   This option is **incorrect** because it addresses the issue of corruption and not malpractice.

The correct answer is C.

8.   This is an Inference question.

Read the sentence (lines 13-14): *"It is the hope of lawmakers in capping jury awards (claim amount) to plaintiffs (claimants) that it may be possible to reverse the tide of rising healthcare costs."*

In view of this sentence, option A is the most appropriate because the idea that jury awards should be reduced is connected to the idea that patients are claiming too much in the way of compensation.

The correct answer is A.

9. This is a tone question from the general category.

We have to choose an option that is the most inappropriate; it means that 4 options relate to the tone of the author and the correct option does not. Let us understand the tone of the author. The author presents the content in an analytical fashion. He discusses the facts, and sees the pros and cons of the issue. We also find that he is critical of the Congress policy of capping jury awards to the patients. His tone is critical and disapproving. The author describes the issue well, so there is a shade of descriptive tone too.

Now let us discuss each option.

(A) Distraught means upset and worried. The tone of the author is certainly distraught; he is upset and worried with the healthcare policy being discussed in its present form. So this option does relate to the tone of the author.

(B) Apathetic means indifferent and uninterested. The author seems to be very concerned about the issue of malpractice and is subjective in places. He is not apathetic to the issue. This is the **correct** answer.

(C) Infuriated means very angry. The author is certainly angry with the healthcare policy being discussed in its present form. So this option does relate to the tone of the author.

(D) Dire means extremely concerning. The tone of the author implies that ignoring the much wider role of doctors in malpractice will have dire consequences in the time to come. This option does relate to the tone of the author.

(E) Disparaging means criticizing, and critical. As discussed above, the passage does have traits of a disparaging tone. This option does relate to the tone of the author.

The correct answer is B.

6.7   Passage 7 (Whistleblower laws)

Understanding the Passage

This is a long passage of low difficulty level on business policy and law.

Whistleblower laws are meant to encourage employees to expose corruption and mismanagement at the work level. The author gives an example of the role of a whistleblower in a factory in the manufacturing sector where a person may physically pull or blow a whistle to halt production in order to stop a faulty production process.

The federal government has passed legislation to provide incentives, as well as protection, to government employees who observe their co-workers and managers following unlawful practices or exercising abuse of their position.

Increasingly, the term whistleblower has been associated with somebody who informs about trustworthy co-workers. [*So, the people who tell the authorities about some employee's misconduct or unlawful behavior get branded as being untrustworthy and disloyal towards their group.*] However, whistleblower laws seek to change this public impression. The author expresses regret about the fact that government bureaucracy and state-financed corporations can at times appear to operate above the law, ignoring the administration, avoiding the discipline of a formal review, and doing their business while largely being able to hide themselves from public scrutiny. Because of these possible ill-effects, it is especially important that courageous employees should stand up on behalf of the voters to whom these institutions are answerable and bring out in the open any wrongful conduct in such organizations. Since an employee who decides to report illegal or unreasonable behavior to the authorities regularly finds that he is harassed with intense inquiry, or even with made-up charges if he continues to stay at his place of employment, it is necessary that the act of exposing unethical performance be appealing enough so that any harassment posed by angry co-workers and vengeful bosses should not sway the whistleblower from revealing the wrong-doing. Due to this threat, whistleblower laws often provide the whistleblower with a percentage of the money considered 'saved' by his honesty. Moreover, a settlement amount or court award is often paid to the successful whistleblower to compensate for the risk he has carried in exposing the co-worker.

Additionally, the whistleblower is simultaneously given protection against undue dismissal and other vengeful acts that a corporation or department might privately take against the claimant. These incentives were meant to make whistleblower laws both a progressive reform and effective legislation, so much so that the incentive aspects of whistleblower laws have not only brought many nervous employees forward to report co-workers, but has also encouraged some to go into the business of spying on suspicious employers with an intent towards reporting them to government investigators and collecting their incentive once a decision is reached.

The passage discusses whistleblower laws. It highlights the challenges an employee could face if he decides to report a co-worker of wrong-doing. The co-worker could be vengeful and the whistleblower employee's institution could even harass him. Whistleblower laws encompass measures to induce more upright employees to come forward by way of protecting their interest through incentives, court-settlement awards, and employment preservation.

Main point: Potent whistleblower laws are all-encompassing.

1. This is a specific detail question from the general category.

    (A) This option is **incorrect** because it is the opposite of what is said in the passage.

    (B) Like option A, this option is **incorrect** because it is also the opposite of what is said in the passage. The meaning of this option is: Whistleblower laws were put in place to nurture the feeling that the whistleblower is disloyal, which is wrong per the passage.

    (C) This option is **incorrect** because whistleblower laws were not put in place to uncover all corrupt practices; it is an unrealistic and extreme expectation.

    (D) This option is **incorrect** because it is not stated in the passage that the direct aim of the new laws is to save money.

    (E) This is the **correct** answer. It is supported by the sentence (lines 19-23): "Since an employee who decides to report illegal or unreasonable behavior to the authorities regularly finds himself to be the subject of intense scrutiny, or even fabricated accusations, if he continues to stay at his place of employment, it is necessary to make the act of bringing unethical performance to light appealing enough to outweigh the disincentives posed by angry co-workers, punitive bosses, ..."

    The correct answer is E.

2. This is an inference question.

    (A) This is the **correct** answer. It is supported by the sentence (Lines 31-32): "These (pecuniary, meaning 'financial') incentives were meant to make whistleblower laws both a progressive reform, and effective legislation." Without these incentives, potential whistleblowers might be too scared of likely repercussions and not step forward at all.

    (B) This option is **incorrect** because it is irrelevant; the added measures in whistleblower laws are meant for employees, and not for corporations.

    (C) This option is **incorrect** because the added measures in whistleblowers laws with incentives and employment protection do not imply that many lawmakers were whistleblowers themselves at one point of time. It is irrelevant and out of scope.

    (D) This option is **incorrect** because it is written from the perspective of the co-worker who is reported for conducting disloyal behavior, when the implication should be drawn from whistleblower employee's perspective.

    (E) This option is **incorrect** because there is no basis to draw any inference like this. This is out of scope.

    The correct answer is A.

3. This is a detail question.

    Option D is the **correct** answer; it is supported by the sentence (Lines 13-16): "Government bureaucracy and state-financed corporations can at times appear to operate above

the law, outlasting administrations, *evading the discipline of elective review*, and oiling their machinery while largely hiding from the public eye." Other options are either too vague or general, or irrelevant.

The correct answer is D.

4. This is a specific detail question.

   (A) This option is **incorrect** because it is irrelevant; no such thing has been discussed in the passage.
   (B) This option is **incorrect** because no such thing has been discussed in the passage.
   (C) This option is **incorrect** because the question asks about the effectiveness of whistleblower laws, and not about how much they are realistic.
   (D) This option is **incorrect** because patriotism in relation to whistleblowers is not discussed in the passage.
   (E) This is the **correct** answer, as explained by the sentence (lines 31-36): "incentives were meant to make whistleblower laws both a progressive reform, and effective legislation, so much so that the lucrative prospects of being a whistleblower has not only brought many reluctant employees forward, but also has encouraged some to go into the business of poaching through phonebooks for dubious employers with an eye towards reporting them to government investigators and collecting their prize."

The correct answer is E.

5. This is an inference question.
   (A) This is the **correct** answer since the passage makes a distinction between legal reforms and effective whistleblower legislation to which lawmakers seek to attach financial inducements. The existence of ineffective legislation would imply that there have been laws passed but they have not had the full expected reach.
   (B) This option is **incorrect** because no such thing has been discussed in the passage.
   (C) This option is **incorrect** because it does not relate to the question asked.
   (D) This option is **incorrect** because it is irrelevant.
   (E) This option is **incorrect** because it is not relevant to the question asked.

The correct answer is A.

6. This is an inference question.

Option E is the correct answer since 'oiling their machinery' typically means keeping the day-to-day means of the business functioning. Even if you do not know the meaning of 'oiling the machinery', you can infer it from the context of the passage. Its meaning must be in the range of working for the interest of self. Other options do not qualify as correct.

The correct answer is E.

7. This is a tone question from general category.

Reading the passage, we can understand that the attitude of the author towards whistle-blower legislation is approving, or positive. Option B is the correct answer since all the other options designate a negative connotation to the author's attitude towards whistle-blower laws. The negative connotation is not supported by the passage. In addition, option B is supported by the sentences (Lines 13-19): "Government bureaucracy and state-financed corporations can at times.... Therefore, it is especially important to make it possible for courageous employees...." and the lines 31-36: "These incentives were meant.... but also have encouraged some to go into the business of poaching.... once a decision is reached."

The correct answer is B.

8. This is an inference question.

Option C is the best answer since the plaintiff in this case refers to the person suing the business or government to obtain a claim or compensation or to correct a practice that he asserts is wrong.

The correct answer is C.

6.8   Passage 8 (Rising European Union and the U.S.)

Understanding the Passage

This is a long passage of high difficulty level on business and economics.

The European Union's (EU) world market is growing exponentially. Only the E.U. has the economic power to challenge the United States over international trade policies, but the U.S. is reluctant about E.U. proposals, which address the issues of labor regulations, the opening of consumer forums, and concerns for the environmental. Interest groups asking for these developments have been ignored in the process over trans-Atlantic economic unification (spanning and crossing the Atlantic Ocean); those with an interest in these groups see a trend towards liberalizing the rules for corporate advantage in the economic co-ordination that has evolved between the United States and Europe. Much of the current communication between the United States and the European Union is focused on establishing an agreement that forms the rules of trans-Atlantic trade and, on the extent of trade conducted between the U.S. and Europe, is much greater than what is happening between any other pair of regions in the world.

The bone of contention between the United States and the European Union on this issue came up when the U.S., Mexico, and Canada joined together and made the agreement known as the North American Free Trade Agreement: NAFTA. NAFTA is meant to standardize industrial and labor regulations between the United States and its neighboring countries so that tariffs can be reduced, international transport encouraged, and corporate investment diversified. Though standards of production will raise the quality of production and the level of cooperation across the continent, it creates a hurdle and makes a contradiction to European expectations of international regulation. To tackle this problem, the E.U. has proposed TAFTA– the Trans-Atlantic Free Trade Agreement, but the United States has repeatedly hesitated regarding the TAFTA proposal as it seeks to protect its dominance in the Western Hemisphere (America, the western part of Europe, and Africa). The U.S. can dominate the region and protect its factories and corporations from comparable European production and demanding practices.

Many interest groups have raised their voices over this issue and accused the U.S of maneuvering, protectionism, uncaring deregulation, third world exploitation, and anti-competitive practices. The route to economic expansion is an important issue in both the U.S. and the European Union; some interest groups repeatedly oppose this just to safeguard their own interest in the region while ignoring better world order.

The passage is about the rising economic power of the E.U. and its proposal of trans-Atlantic economic unification. On the other hand, the U.S. has an agreement–NAFTA–with its neighboring counties. Though it is good, it is a barrier for the E.U. in trade. To further its own interests, the E.U. has proposed TAFTA–the Trans-Atlantic Free Trade Agreement–but the US is reluctant regarding this agreement as it presumes that its dominance in the western hemisphere would cease to exist.

Main point: The ambivalent feelings of the U.S. in joining up with the potent E.U.

1. This is a function question.

   (A) This option is **incorrect** because, though it is factually correct, the intent of the author is not to merely demonstrate the difference between the past E.U. and the present E.U. in the context of the passage. He shows the difference in the E.U.'s standing to prove the E.U.'s considerable presence.

   (B) This option is **incorrect** because the passage does not need to clarify the number of parties in trans-Atlantic trade since it is clear in the passage that there are only two parties being discussed.

   (C) This is the **correct** answer because the first sentence seeks to introduce one of the most important economic powers worldwide.

   (D) This option is **incorrect** because though it seems correct, it is not necessarily true and the author does not show any belligerence on the part of the E.U. in the passage.

   (E) This option is **incorrect** because it is not relevant to the question.

   The correct answer is C.

2. This is an inference question.

   (A) This option is **incorrect** because it suggests no progress can be made. Impasse means deadlock. The passage does not suggest that a deadlock has been reached; the dialogue is ongoing, but consensus could not be reached. Impasse would mean that nothing can go further.

   (B) This is the **correct** answer because the exchange between the U.S. and the E.U. is a persistent disagreement over a certain topic.

   (C) This option is **incorrect** because 'shuttle diplomacy' refers to an explicit political process which is not identified in the passage. It means using an impartial third party to discuss terms between two concerned parties.

   (D) This option is **incorrect** because though some groups have accused the U.S. of brinkmanship in paragraph 3, it is not in the context of 'heated dialogue'. Brinkmanship is the political maneuver of taking things to an extreme to force the other party to accede.

   (E) This option is **incorrect** because the 'heated dialogue' between the U.S. and the E.U. is not occurring in a lighter vein; there are serious ramifications to it.

   The correct answer is B.

3. This is an inference question.

   Option C is the best possible answer, supported by lines 20-23: "While bringing standards of production into alignment is a goal that ought to raise the quality of production and the level of cooperation across the continent, it also creates an opportunity to establish a standard contra to European expectations of international regulation." The E.U. fears that NAFTA's standards may be incompatible with that of Europe's, hence the E.U. proposed TAFTA.

Other options are either not worth considering because they are out of scope or they are not supported with justifiable reasoning.

The correct answer is C.

4.   This is an inference question.

The question means that from the perspective of the E.U., production and environmental standards should be higher than those of North America. If they are lower, it is disadvantageous to the E.U.. We have find the best reason out of the 5 options.

Option E is the correct answer because lower production and environmental standards, for example, could make doing business cheaper for U.S. companies than for other companies. The passage mentions "the United States is noncommittal on E.U. proposals calling for the alignment of labor regulations, the opening of consumer forums and the offer of an audience to environmental groups". The inferences given in other options cannot be made as no such things were mentioned in the passage. Also, the U.S. seems unwilling to agree to TAFTA because it wants to continue its dominance in the region. If it gives in to TAFTA, the E.U.'s higher standards will have to be met or business will go to the E.U..

The correct answer is E.

5.   This is an inference question.

Option A is the correct answer since 'callous' refers to being uncaring, and the passage notes that interests groups in Europe express concern about liberalization based only on corporate advantage in favor of U.S. industries.

The correct answer is A.

6.   This is an inference question.

Option C is the correct answer since the last sentence (line 32) of the passage states: "The route to economic expansion is a prominent issue in both the U.S. and the European Union, and some (groups) with a say in the matter repeat these protests as a screen (shield) for their own plans to tip the balance of economic advantage towards their own region at the expense of all other involved parties in the process of exploring for parity." Thus, the author believes that some groups in both the U.S. and the E.U. are "biased" toward maintaining their dominance in the region.

The correct answer is C.

7. This is an inference question.

Option D is the correct answer since the United States has hesitated regarding, but not rejected, TAFTA. Option C is incorrect because securing relations with Mexico and Canada does not upset trade relations with the European Union. Had the option been 'The U.S. willingness to only honor NAFTA', it would have been correct. Other options are out of scope or don't fit the "must be true" category.

The correct answer is D.

6.9   Passage 9 (In-fighting Indian princes and the rise of the British)

Understanding the Passage

This is a long passage of low difficulty level on history.

For 17th century Europeans, the history of Eastern empires was stereotyped. India's historical events were predictable customs of unrefined and stereotypical traditional stories. According to the traditional story, typically, the founder of an empire would be a brave soldier and a frantic conspirator who would topple corrupt scions of a more ancient empire. The founder's son might inherit some of his talent; but in two or three generations, descendants become immoral and corrupt and are dethroned by some new adventurer. *[Thus, in the minds of the British, whenever anyone is dethroned in Eastern empires, it is justified because, according to them, the person sitting on the throne is a descendent of a brave person but does not have the appropriate qualities to rule correctly and should be overthrown/removed from the throne.]* Thus an upright rebellion will dethrone a corrupt empire and subsequently be dethroned by another rebellion. *[This is how they rationalize creating and orchestrating rebellions to remove the existing rulers.]* This practice was ongoing. This led to the recurrence of civil war and anarchy at fixed intervals. Due to these anarchistic practices, Britain's rulers could visualize their might in the subcontinent. *[Using such tactics, the British were virtually in control because they removed the rulers who could potentially disagree with the British and put in such rulers who would end up being puppets in British hands, thereby ensuring British interests.]* The British wished to avoid the bloodshed periodically occurring during the toppling of an empire and this led them to gain the favor of India's local empires. *[They played a diplomatic game by removing the current ruler and backing a new ruler, and they thus avoided actual wars but gained favors from the newly installed ruler.]*

The British were able to impose a proxy rule over India by setting up native princes in positions of power. It is to be noted that Indian empires used to follow the law of "doctrines of lapse", which means that if the ruling king dies without any sons *(heirs)*, any of the related princes *(nephews)* could lay claim to the empire. The British used to support anyone of the princes, and help maintain his power as long as it was in their interests. *[If there are two possible candidates for the throne, they would support the one who would further their interests the most and put him on the throne.]* In this way the princes became practically obliged to cooperate with the British, and the result was two generations of trivial tyrant princes, protected by the British. These tyrant princes spent their lives in apathetic dishonesty, cruelty, and oppression. *[The rulers chosen by the British were always bad ones who could not be removed because they were protected by British might.]*

The passage is about how the British could enforce their rule over India, their strategy, and tactics. The British took advantage of in-fighting among princes to claim the empire once the leadership to it lapsed. The British used to support a prince and make him the king, and, by doing this, the new king would be obliged to the British. Unfortunately the king under the shadow of the British would become corrupt and cruel.

Main Point: In-fighting among the princes of the Indian Empire and tactics by the British to impose proxy rule in India.

1. This is an inference question.

    Option E is the best answer because the passage speaks of the British in the following way: "Their methods took advantage of existing "doctrines of lapse", and made use of what was already the declared law in cases of heredity. By intervening on behalf of one prince or another, both of whom may have been equally suited to claim the right to the throne in cases in which the rights to leadership lapsed, they put themselves in a position to support a leader they selected, and to maintain his power as long as it was in their interests. In this way the princes became practically obliged to cooperate with the British.". So, they ruled by proxy *(indirectly)* by making the ruler obliged to them. Thus, their proxy rule can be attributed to the "doctrine of lapse".

    Other options are not discussed in the passage and so cannot be necessarily inferred.

    The correct answer is E.

2. This is an inference question.

    (A) This option is **incorrect** because we cannot compare the situations prevailing before and after the British came to India. It is out of scope of the passage.

    (B) This option is **incorrect** because there is no implication made in the passage that British intervention in India now requires closer monitoring.

    (C) This option is **incorrect** because the reverse of this option is true. On the contrary, the author may disagree that British intervention in India was a positive influence on India. The scheming done by the British sustained their favorite, yet corrupt and incapable, kings in the monarchies for a long time. These rulers otherwise would have been dethroned by brave, upright rebellions.

    (D) This option is **incorrect** because it is too extreme and cannot be inferred from the passage.

    (E) This is the **correct** answer. The passage suggests that had the British not intervened, the cycle of change in power would have taken place at a fixed interval, and, at least periodically, India would have had a competent king followed by corrupt kings. But because of the British supporting their favorite, yet corrupt and incapable, kings, there was no change of leadership. Thus, British interference led to a necessarily bad king, whereas without British intervention, India would have had good kings sooner or later.

    The correct answer is E.

3. This is a tone question from the general category.

    (A) This is the **correct** answer because the author laments the constant decline of kings into "feeble inheritors"; he notes that feeble inheritors fostered by the British have done more bad than good for India.

    (B) This option is **incorrect** because the author endorses the belief that change of power by a rebellion is the remedy to get rid of cruel kings. He does not despair of it or give it up.

(C)   This option is **incorrect** because the author is not skeptical of the prevailing cycle of rule. He, in fact, acknowledges it.

(D)   This option is **incorrect** because 'matter of fact' is a neutral phrase. The author is certainly opinionated about the cycle of rule in Asia. He doesn't treat it merely neutrally.

(E)   This option is **incorrect** because we can't say that he necessarily approves of the cycle of rule. He acknowledges it as something that has worked out fairly well but that does not mean he likes it and approves of it. He may believe that there might be a better way. All we can say is that he certainly disapproves of British interference and that he accepts that the cycle of rule works better when left alone, but we can't say that he approves of it necessarily.

The correct answer is A.

4.   This is an inference question.

(A)   This option is **incorrect** because the British allowed princes to take over power, albeit the prince of their choice.

(B)   This option is **incorrect** because, according to the passage, the people were not supposed to choose their leader; it's the hereditary cycle of rule that choose the leader.

(C)   This is the **correct** answer because the last two sentences of the passage (line 21) endorse this: "The result was two generations of petty despots, insulated from the consequences of misrule by British bayonets. The despots spent their lives in listless debauchery, broken by paroxysms of cruelty and oppression". The British safeguarded their favorite, yet cruel, kings and did not let rebellions oust them, causing damage to the subcontinent. Thus, the rule continued because the Indian people did not have the sort of strength needed to overcome British power.

(D)   This option is **incorrect** because the passage did not talk about the demoralization of the Indian identity.

(E)   This option is **incorrect** because while this is the reason the despot rulers were put on the throne, it is not necessarily damaging. The British can exploit the doctrine of lapse and put a prince on the throne but this does not have to be damaging, if they had put a good ruler there. However, the British were greedy and sought to have an indirect rule over India, so they always chose the leaders with low morals. Thus, we can attribute the damage to the British attitude towards India or to their greed, but not necessarily to the way they put people in power.

The correct answer is C.

5.   This is an inference question.

Option E is the best option as it is exemplified by the British policy of coordinating with princes in need of support because their interest was to rule the Indian subcontinent by proxy and without bloodshed. Thus they cooperated when it was in their best interests to do so.

Other options are either not discussed in the passage or cannot necessarily be inferred.

The correct answer is E.

6. This is an inference question.

    (A) This is the **correct** answer because the British aided princes who were vulnerable and were competing with another prince. This action required little up front British influence in order to determine the outcome of the dispute, while making Britain the effective "kingmaker" in the region and allowing the British a great deal of influence later. This means that they had some amount of influence.

    (B) This option is **incorrect** because the British did not take over the leadership role themselves but put in rulers through whom they could rule by proxy.

    (C) This option is **incorrect** because the British were not helping the princes to discuss their dispute.

    (D) This option is **incorrect** because the British influence in the area was not impartial, but self-interested.

    (E) This option is **incorrect** because there were local candidates for leadership.

The correct answer is A.

7. This is a tone question from the general category.

    Option C is the correct answer as is demonstrated by the British decision to seek to advance their own interests in India when it was possible to do so during times of disorder. Nothing else is possible to be attributed to the British in the given passage from among the options.

The correct answer is C.

6.10   Passage 10 (The Belgian economy: from devastation to restoration)

Understanding the Passage

This is a medium length passage of medium difficulty level on business policy and economics.

For 200 years until WW I, the Wallonia area of Belgium was a technically advanced industrial region, while the Flanders area was predominantly agricultural. *[Both Wallonia and Flanders are in Belgium.]* After WW II this difference between Wallonia and Flanders faded because Belgium had its industrial infrastructure remain relatively intact, and this set the stage for rapid development, particularly in Flanders. The older and traditional industries in Wallonia began to lose their competitive edge during this period. However, because the world economy was growing, there were no immediate effects on Belgium's economy, at least not until 1973. Unfortunately, the oil price shocks between 1973 and 1979 and the resultant demand and supply equation of oil brought the Belgian economy into a period of protracted recession *(economic slump)*.

All this contributed to Wallonia losing its primacy and Flanders growing in importance for Belgium. In the 1980s and 1990s, the economic progress of the country started coming from Flanders. In the early 1980s, Belgium faced a difficult period of structural adjustment caused by declining demand for its traditional products, worsening economic performance, and neglected structural reform. Consequently, the recession from 1980-82 devastated Belgium in many ways–unemployment rose, social welfare costs increased, personal debt rose, the government deficit touched 13% of GDP, and national debt, although mostly held domestically, thrived. This was the time for quick and effective action. To fight this slump, in 1982 Prime Minister Martens' government formulated an economic recovery program to promote export-led growth by enhancing the competitiveness of Belgium's export industries. As a result, economic growth rose from 2% in 1984 to a peak of 4% in 1989. In May 1990, the government linked the Belgian currency, the franc, to the German currency, the mark. However, as German interest rates rose after 1990, Belgian rates subsequently increased and this resulted in a decline in the economic growth rate of Belgium again.

Belgium, otherwise a wealthy country, had spent more but collected fewer taxes for years. Belgium reacted to the 1973 and 1979 oil price hikes with poor macroeconomic policies: it absorbed the workers who were laid off in the private sector into the public sector and subsidized ailing industries–coal, steel, textiles, glass, and shipbuilding–in order to support the economy. But due to this, debt reached 121% of GNP by the end of the 1980s. However, thanks to Belgium's high personal savings rate, the Belgian Government managed to finance the deficit mainly from domestic savings. This minimized the damaging effects on the overall economy.

The passage is about the devastated economy of Belgium and how it rose after WWII. The Flanders region of Belgium led the growth of Belgium, but the oil price shock in 1973-73 pushed Belgium into an extended slump. During the early 80s, it faced many economic challenges from structural adjustment caused by low demand of its products and poor economic performance. In 1982, PM Martens started an economic recovery program led by export-oriented growth. Economic growth rose from 2% to 4% in 1989. In 1990, the government linked the Belgian currency (the franc) to the German currency (the mark), but the move resulted in a de-

cline in the economic growth rate. The author blames Belgium's damaged economy on the fact that Belgium reacted to the 1973 and 1979 oil price hikes with poor macroeconomic policies: it supported and subsidized ailing industries. Due to this, debt reached 121% of GNP by the end of the 80s. The author ends the passage on a positive note, pointing out that the Belgian economy could finance the deficit mainly from domestic savings it had accrued over the years, thus minimizing the damaging effects on the overall economy.

Main Point: Surmounting the challenges of the devastated Belgian economy through structural reforms after WWII.

1. This is a main point question from the general category.

   (A) This option is **incorrect** because the passage is not about Flanders and its rise to a leadership position in Belgium, it is about the Belgian economy.

   (B) This is the **correct** answer because the passage discusses the Belgian economy under structural readjustment. This option correctly addresses the challenges the Belgian economy had to face after WWII.

   (C) This option is **incorrect** because the passage is not about Flanders but is about the Belgium economy.

   (D) This option is **incorrect** because the passage only mentions P.M. Martens as influencing economic restructuring; it narrowly covers the scope of the passage.

   (E) This option is **incorrect** because the topic of the passage is not just the damage inflicted by the government.

   The correct answer is B.

2. This is a function question.

   (A) This option is **incorrect** because the passage is not about Flanders but is about the Belgian economy.

   (B) This option is **incorrect** because the passage does not demonstrate how all of Belgium could have followed Flanders's example in order to prevent economic hardship. Flanders' rise after the war was coincidental, and not a deliberate plan that brought success.

   (C) This is the **correct** answer because the success of Flanders in some sectors and the decline of Walloon in other sectors exemplify the change in the economy as a whole.

   (D) This option is **incorrect** because it is not demonstrated that Belgium was in a position to experience "runaway" economic growth. In fact, the damaged situation in the Belgian economy is discussed throughout the passage.

   (E) This option is **incorrect** because there is no single factor that drove down growth in the Belgian economy.

The correct answer is C.

3. This is a specific inference question.

    (A)   This option is **incorrect** because the oil price hikes were not a structural problem with the Belgian economy, but rather an outside event faced by the entire world.

    (B)   This option is **incorrect** because policymaking did not immediately change in response to the oil price hikes. Also, the author would not consider the eventual policy changes "an improvement" because he thinks that Belgium's response did not contain effective macroeconomic perspectives.

    (C)   This is the **correct** answer because the oil price hikes revealed the inherent weakness in the Belgian economic organization. Such weakness in the economy was present all along but was not being revealed until that point. This is comparable to the fable in which an emperor goes around without clothes and nobody dares to point it out, except a child. Thus, the analogy is that Belgium is analogous to the unclothed emperor and the oil price hikes are similar to the child who pointed out *(revealed)* that the emperor *(Belgium's economy)* had no clothes *(was weak)*.

    (D)   This option is **incorrect** because the precarious Belgian economic condition preceded the oil price hikes. The Belgian economy was not in a great shape before the oil price hikes. Only Flanders' rise and world economy kept it going.

    (E)   This option is **incorrect** because the passage does not represent the oil price hikes as an opportunity to turn to exports to spur growth.

The correct answer is C.

4. This is a function question.

    (A)   This option is **incorrect** because Martens is not treated in the passage as only a source of mismanagement. He is shown to have shored up Belgium's economy after the shock the oil price hikes wreaked on Belgium's economy.

    (B)   This option is **incorrect** because the passage does not consider Martens' efforts to be misspent. He managed to bring Belgium up a bit.

    (C)   This is the **correct** answer because the passage seeks to show that the progress Martens made was amid genuine economic difficulty even if it lacked a macroeconomic perspective.

    (D)   This option is **incorrect** because the passage does credit Martens with improving aspects of the Belgian economy. Also, the author does criticize Martens' lack of macroeconomic perspective.

    (E)   This option is **incorrect** because the Belgian economy did improve after a bad run.

The correct answer is C.

5. This is a tone question from the general category.

    (A)   This option is **incorrect** because the passage does not seek to apologize or paint poor actions in a good light.

(B) This is the **correct** answer because it provides a historical interpretation of the actions taken during a period.

(C) This option is **incorrect** because the passage does not seek to assert a political position or discuss a controversy.

(D) This option is **incorrect** because the passage does not seek to argue against an interpretation of the facts.

(E) This option is **incorrect** because the passage is better understood as a historical interpretation rather than all-encompassing account of events.

The correct answer is B.

6. This is an inference question.

(A) This option is **incorrect** because the passage mentions ways in which the government responded advantageously using its power.

(B) This is the **correct** answer because the passage suggests that it is economically inefficient to aid ailing industries. The author mentions that the subsidizing drove up the government's debt to 121% of GNP, suggesting that the author personally does not agree with this measure.

(C) This option is **incorrect** because the passage does not suggest the market can be ignored.

(D) This option is **incorrect** because the passage does not accuse the government of making decisions too slowly.

(E) This option is **incorrect** because the passage seeks to demonstrate the need to structure the economy in a way that is appropriate to minimize the effects of market fluctuation.

The correct answer is B.

7. This is an inference question.

(A) This option is **incorrect** because it is too broad, and unsubstantiated.

(B) This option is **incorrect** because the passage does not assert that economists are not pragmatists.

(C) This is the **correct** answer because the piece is a historical interpretation and makes assessments of the correct course of action after the fact, which is different from making decisions at the time of an issue.

(D) This option is **incorrect** because the author does assert that correct answers cannot be found in economics.

(E) This option is **incorrect** because the passage does not mention that the policy decisions were politically motivated.

The correct answer is C.

8. This is a tone question from the general category.

    (A) This is the **correct** answer because the passage acknowledges the advantages and disadvantages of high rates; the tone has shades of ambivalence. If the question asked us the tone towards "high personal savings alone" we could say that the passage is positively inclined towards it, but we cannot say it is either positive or negative about "high rates of interest".

    (B) This option is **incorrect** because the passage mentions an advantage of high interest rates, so the author is not skeptical about it.

    (C) Like option B, this option is **incorrect** because the passage sees some advantages to high interest rates, so the author does not see it threatening.

    (D) This option is tricky, but **incorrect**. It may seem correct except for the concern expressed by the author regarding slowing the Belgium economy.

    (E) This option is **incorrect** because the passage does not expect failure as the natural consequence of high interest rates, but acknowledges successes and difficulties.

The correct answer is A.

6.11 Passage 11 (Craving for fast food: who to blame – behavior or the brain?)

Understanding the Passage

This is a medium length passage of medium difficulty level on medical science and human behavior.

A finding by scientists has shown that consuming more "fast food" *(food with a high content of processed sugar, salt, and saturated fats)* can be addictive, just like other controlled substances *(heroin, narcotics, etc.).* According to researchers, fast food can trigger an addiction in the brain, causing it to ask for more fast food. *[Scientists conclude that fast food is addictive and the addiction demands regular feeding.].* Many scientists see a relationship between people's decisions to choose fast food as their preferred food and influencing factors in the environmental such as the wide availability of fast foods. *[Scientists believe that people want to eat fast food mainly because of permissive culture, environment, and easy availability of fast food]*; it leads to detrimental effects on human health and development. The researchers conclude that the brains of overeaters of fast foods experience some chemical changes triggering more appetite for the unhealthy food. *[The scientists believe that as one starts eating fast food regularly, the brain undergoes changes and craves more and more fast food.]*

If people continue to eat too much unhealthy food, it will initiate changes in the brain that raise the minimum level of eating the brain is usually satisfied with. *[Eating addictive stuff, or fast food, follows the law of diminishing returns, i.e. the amount that one needs to eat to get satisfied keeps increasing over time.]* Moreover, high consumption of fast foods stimulates opiate receptors in the brain *[opiate receptors are distributed widely in the brain; they act as natural pain relievers and eating fast food mimics this effect.).* Due to this, frequent and bigger doses of fast food feign some effects of opiates. *[Scientists contend that an uncontrolled amount of unhealthy food makes changes in the brain's response. The brain is only satisfied with bigger and more frequent feedings. Since the effect of fast food is similar to that of opiates, or pain relievers, people crave more to get the same psychotropic effect.].* Scientists performed an experiment on rats. They fed rats a sugar-rich diet; when they stopped the sugar-rich diet, they found that the rats showed the symptoms of withdrawal– shivering and chattering teeth. Their behavior was comparable to opiate addicts when the supply of opium is reduced to such addicts. When the rats were given the drugs that block opiate receptors *(natural pain relieving areas in the brain)*, the dopamine levels in their brains *(an area linked with the dynamics of reward–reward is used for "craving for more food" and responsible for keeping a person addicted)* looked similar to those in heroin addicts. The scientists concluded that obesity can be viewed as a disease beyond the control of those affected by it *(just as addiction is beyond the control of addicts).* *[Scientists contend that propensity to eat more unhealthy food and get fatter is not truly related to one's behavior, but rather to changes in the neurochemistry of the brain.]*

Lawyers argue that society has a responsibility to regulate food and educate people about the abuse of unhealthy foods. Fast food companies should be held accountable for the ill-effects arising from unhealthy food. Still, some scientists are skeptical about the degree to which some researchers attribute the addiction to unhealthy food as the cause of neurological disorder rather than people's behavior. *(Some skeptics think that it is not right to blame neurochemistry alone for fast food addiction. People choose to eat fast food and so choice should*

be factored in, too.) They contend that a habit and an addiction can be differentiated on qualitative parameters and not on quantitative parameters. *[These scientists think that some people habitually eat fast food but never overeat while others overeat fast food repeatedly, and this difference is not just the quantity of fast food consumed by both.]* The scientists think it's a qualitative difference, i.e. the qualities of these people differ. The ones who eat fast food regularly do not throw caution away and eat all they want but those who become addicted overrule common sense and eat more than is justified. These scientists think we cannot blame neurochemistry changes alone for differences between habitual fast food eaters and addicted overeaters.

The author cites a finding made by a few scientists claiming that unhealthy food, if consumed regularly and in large proportion, will make some neurological disorder in the brain, which in turn will ask for more food to satiate it. This leads to its ill-effects such as obesity. They contend that obesity may not be tackled only by exercising discipline in eating, as the brain will not be satisfied and will ask for more of such food. It needs to be treated like any other addiction disease. Some scientists are skeptical as to the degree of this claim.

Main Point: Addiction to unhealthy food is triggered more by the brain and less by undisciplined behavior, but some scientists remain unconvinced.

1. This is an inference question.

    (A) This is the **correct** answer because the passage demonstrates that people can be affected by environmental influences that create a cycle of addiction though they may not be aware that a chemical imbalance may have unconsciously affected their decision-making.

    (B) This option is **incorrect** because the scientists who see the relationship between decisions and environment note that it is not always possible to control surroundings once decision-making skills have been compromised.

    (C) This option is **incorrect** because the passage makes a distinction between being vulnerable to a cycle of addiction and having no responsibility over one's own behavior with an eating disorder. The passage does not suggest that overeaters are not responsible for their behavior. It just states that overeaters cannot control their impulse to overeat because their neurochemistry is affected. However, they still remain responsible for what's happening to them. They need to be treated like any other addict.

    (D) This option may be correct, but it is not affirmed in the passage. It's out of scope.

    (E) This option is **incorrect** because the passage does not say that overeaters are unable to overcome the difficulties of withdrawal. It does not even suggest that they try to withdraw from something.

    The correct answer is A.

2. This is reasoning based question on strengthening the argument.

    (A) This option is **incorrect** because the argument is vulnerable to criticism; even if obesity is a pre-existing condition in individuals, companies are still responsible

for protecting consumers from possible side effects that the consumers may experience because of a company's products.

(B)   This option is **incorrect** because corporations are expected to provide consumers with a safe product or to warn them of its dangers. Arguing that obese people must treat their disease with medication that blocks opiate receptors is akin to shunning the responsibility.

(C)   This is the **correct** answer because it eliminates the threat of an addiction caused by the product by establishing that obesity is a result of consumer habits, not addiction to products. This will prove that overeating is not a result of neurochemistry altering the effects of the company's products. This option will put the responsibility on the consumer *(by implying that moderation is a choice)* and free the company from the blame of making addictive products.

(D)   This option is **incorrect** because corporations are still liable for the unforeseen damage caused by their products, although they have found out that fast food causes chemical dependency in people. This will not free them from blame.

(E)   This option is **incorrect** because corporations must still provide safe food.

The correct answer is C.

3.   This is an inference question.

(A)   This option is **incorrect** because while it may be true, the purpose of the scientists, as presented in the passage, is not to argue about strict diets.

(B)   This option is **incorrect** because it is not necessarily true. Even those who are not obese can be equally vulnerable to the health hazards of chronic consumption of fast food. The passage does not support such a deduction.

(C)   This option is **incorrect** because one does not necessarily have to have a genetic predisposition to obesity in order to contract the disease. This is out of scope.

(D)   This is the **correct** answer because treating obesity as a disease allows people to understand that obese people suffer from their behavior in a way that people without the disease may not. There are factors other than solely individual behavior, such as chemical imbalance, that may be considered responsible for obesity. Scientists do think that environmental factors and neurochemistry changes are responsible for obesity.

(E)   This option is **incorrect** because it is not true and is not stated by the scientists mentioned in the passage.

The correct answer is D.

4.   This is a detail question.

(A)   This is the **correct** answer because the researchers object to the conclusions reached based on the evidence *(findings)* found by their colleagues. *(Refer to the first sentence of the passage.)* The skeptics believe that data may exist on neurochemistry being altered, but the extent to which individual choices determine obesity should not be discounted. Thus the skeptics disagree with the conclusion of the researchers.

(B) This option is **incorrect** because there is no mention in the passage that suggests that the researchers doubted the expertise of their colleagues. They certainly were skeptical about the findings presented by their colleagues.

(C) This option is **incorrect** because there is no mention of the proponents making any assumptions that the skeptics disagreed on.

(D) This option is **incorrect** because there is no mention of the method, or of the opponents' objection to it, in the passage.

(E) This option is **incorrect** because the researchers do not contest the validity of the data collected.

The correct answer is A.

5. This is a function question.

(A) This option is **incorrect** because the skeptics do not disagree that overeaters are addicted. However, they object to the blame for the addiction being laid solely on chemical changes, and not on individual choices.

(B) This option is **incorrect** because the scientists mentioned in the beginning of the passage acknowledge that there are several factors that contribute to a person's behavior.

(C) This is the **correct** answer because opponents view "qualitative" consumption choices to be primarily behavioral, and not primarily chemical problems. So, it follows that those skeptics would object to the assumption that addictive behavior has nothing to do with behavior and choices, and is dependent only on chemical imbalances in the brain.

(D) This option is **incorrect** because this assumption is not made in the passage.

(E) This option is **incorrect** because this assumption is not made in the passage.

The correct answer is C.

6. This is an inference question.

(A) This option is **incorrect** because dopamine makes rats happier as they pursue consumption *(reward)*, and therefore they feel encouraged to eat more. Refer to the latter part of the second paragraph: *"Later, by treating rats with drugs that block opiate receptors, scientists were able to lower the amount of dopamine in the nucleus acumen of rats' brains, an area linked with the dynamics of reward."* The word "reward" is used here for "more food". It can be inferred that by lowering the level of dopamine, the desire for more food reduces, so the role of dopamine would be to make one long for more food *(and to reward oneself)*.

(B) This option is **incorrect** because dopamine does not block opiates. The passage talked about opiate-blocking drugs that helped to lower dopamine levels.

(C) This option is **incorrect** because opiates are not replaced by dopamine.

(D) This option is **incorrect** because, on the contrary, dopamine is linked to the reward mechanism which activates when rats receive opiates.

(E) This is the **correct** answer since rats are encouraged to eat more. It follows from the deduction made in option A's explanation.

The correct answer is E.

7. This is a detail question.

(A) This option is **incorrect** because we cannot infer from the passage that the lawyers' position implies that the government lacks knowledge.

(B) This is the **correct** answer because the passage states that lawyers argue that there is a responsibility to regulate food and educate people about the abuse of "unhealthy foods" in a way that is comparable to society's control of opiates and narcotics. Corporations (fast food restaurants) that target this vulnerability (addiction to fast food) in human beings can then be held liable.

(C) This option is **incorrect** because lawyers are arguing that it is the responsibility of corporations, and not the market, to keep consumers informed, and to account for damage caused by their products.

(D) This option is **incorrect** because the lawyers do not assume governmental incompetence. Moreover, the lawyers wish to make fast food restaurants, and not the government, accountable for damaging public health.

(E) This option is **incorrect** because by placing the responsibility for a good diet on the individual, the lawyers' objective to make fast food restaurants liable will get diluted.

The correct answer is B.

6.12   Passage 12 (Masks & gas attacks during WW II)

Understanding the Passage

This is a short length passage of low difficulty level on wartime history.

World War II exposed America to the need for security of its citizens. Unlike in WW II, in WW I its citizens were never attacked.

The highest priority for the U.S. was the protection of children from possible attack. WW II had a history of participating nations attacking civilian areas. It was started by Germany on London, and then the Allied Forces retaliated with attacks on the German city of Dresden.

A leading concern for Britain and the U.S. was the exposure to gas attacks upon the youth population. Immediately after Pearl Harbor, thousands of military training masks were rushed to people living on the islands. However, these masks were unsuitable for protecting children. Hawaiian officials produced an expedient *(a temporary means to an end)* made up of bunny ears and a hood. The Sun Rubber Company designed a relatively acceptable mask based on the universal Walt Disney cartoon figure Mickey Mouse. The adoption of these masks made them popular among children and this in turn potentially reduced the element of fear of masks.

This measure would increase the chances of survival for youth; it was important to protect them because a large number of working age males were vulnerable to losing their lives fighting overseas.

The passage is about the mechanism of protecting the youth population of the U.S. from possible gas attacks during WW II. The author discusses the importance of protecting them, the challenges with masks, and the popularity and adoption of innovatively-designed masks for children.

Main Point: Challenges and a mechanism to protect youth from gas attacks during WW-II.

1.   This is a detail question.

     The first paragraph of the passage mentions that World War II exposed America to the need for security of its citizens. Unlike in WW II, in WW I, its citizens were never attacked. Option D is the only answer mentioned in the passage distinguishing World War I from World War II.

     Option E—The threat of nationalism from foreign aggressors—is extreme and cannot be inferred.

     The correct answer is D.

2. This is a function question.

    (A) This option is **incorrect** because there was no such intent (to destroy the civilian wartime infrastructure) reflected in the passage.

    (B) Like option A, this option is **incorrect** because there was no mention of reducing the number of potential reinforcements for dwindling armies in the passage.

    (C) This option is **incorrect** because nothing of this sort was stated in the passage.

    (D) This is the **correct** and the best answer as stated in the sentence (line 9): "Germany unleashed the lengthiest bombing campaign of the war on the people of London primarily to weaken British morale."

    (E) This option is **incorrect** because nothing of this sort was stated in the passage.

    The correct answer is D.

3. This is a function question.

    Option C is supported by line 23-27: "The popularity of these masks was dependent on internalizing their use in children ...This potentially reduced the element of fear. If the element of fear could be diminished, gas masks might be employed by their owners more quickly in the event of an attack, and also worn without interruption."

    The design of gas masks to look like Mickey Mouse was intended to encourage children to wear the masks and wear them properly so that they were safe against possible gas attacks.

    Other options are either not supported by the passage or are irrelevant.

    The correct answer is C.

4. This is a detail question.

    Option C is indicated by the sentence in the last paragraph (line 29): "All of this would increase the chances of survival of the youth population, of no small concern to a nation with large numbers of its working age males facing the perils of combat overseas."

    In other words, the measure of protecting children from possible gas attacks would increase the chances of survival of the youth population; it was important to protect youth because a large number of working age males were vulnerable to losing their lives fighting overseas.

    Option B is close but is not supported by the passage.

    Other options are either not supported by the passage or are irrelevant.

    The correct answer is C.

5. This is a main Point question from the general category.

We have derived the main point in the Understanding the Passage section.

Main Point: Challenges and a mechanism to protect youth from gas attacks during WW II.

Option B is the best answer since the passage primarily discusses the role of civilian terror tactics and the provisions needed to protect children from those tactics.

Other options are either not supported by the passage or are irrelevant.

The correct answer is B.

6. This is a detail question.

Option C is the correct answer since an expedient is something used as a temporary means to an end, and is helpful or useful in a particular situation.

The correct answer is C.

7. This is a function question.

Option D is correct since the passage states: "The popularity of these masks was dependent on internalizing their use in children by making their presence part of a perceived game. This potentially reduced the element of fear that the masks conveyed on their recipients. If the element of fear could be diminished, gas masks might be employed by their owners more quickly in the event of an attack ..."

Other options are either not supported by the passage or are irrelevant.

The correct answer is D.

8. This is an inference question.

(A) This option is **incorrect** because enemy propaganda as a danger is not discussed in the passage.

(B) Like option A, this option is **incorrect** because the youth of the civilian population itself is not the danger.

(C) This is **correct** since the point of providing gas masks in a familiar form is to allow civilians to make the correct decisions by being prepared to act correctly.

(D) This option is **incorrect** because it is not supported by the passage. Though the attack of Germany on Britain was meant to weaken British morale, the author did not ratify it as a significant avoidable danger of a wartime terror attack.

(E) This option is **incorrect** because it is not supported by the passage, and lack of warning of an attack is not an avoidable danger.

The correct answer is C.

6.13   Passage 13 (Lord Dalhousie's uniform rate of postage in India)

Understanding the Passage

This is a short passage of low difficulty level on the topic of business sociology.

Lord Dalhousie is credited with the creation of the modern postal system in India. He implemented the practice of levying a uniform rate of postage throughout India, irrespective of origin or destination.

Many critics ridiculed Dalhousie's idea. It was, they said, pushing Rowland Hill's scheme of penny postage for England to the extreme in India. They viewed it as a "reductio ad absurdum" of the reform that had been effected in Great Britain. [*It was termed as extreme as the area of India was far more than that of England implying uniform rate is devoid of any logic; it was absurd!*].

Lord Dalhousie was firm in his decision of levying the uniform rate of postage. Earlier there had been an argument over the payment for delivery of every letter, and the rural postman used to charge additional money to the recipient for his service. But Dalhousie's intention was that with the new simplistic system of postage stamps, petty bickering with postmen would cease to exist, and people would be assured of reliable service.

His postal system became a self-sustaining organization, from which the financial outlay for postal services could be recouped. The social results were even more important. It has been said that the half-penny postage system of Lord Dalhousie was more significant in bridging the gap between the various parts of India than earlier developments such as the telegraph, the railway, and other formal systems.

The passage is about the implementation of Lord Dalhousie's innovative but absurd-seeming postal scheme in India, which proposed to charge a uniform rate of postage throughout India, irrespective of origin or destination. The passage talks about its success owing to its simplicity and the social benefit it caused.

Main Point: The success of Lord Dalhousie's uniform rate of postage scheme in India.

1.   This is a detail question.

     Option A is the correct answer and is demonstrated by the description in the passage of perceived injustice which opponents saw in the new Indian post system. Lord Dalhousie implemented the scheme of levying a uniform rate of postage throughout India irrespective of origin or destination, which was ridiculed by many critics. It seemed absurd and unreasonable to charge for a letter going a long distance the same amount as for a letter going a short distance.

     Though option B deserves a thought, it can be inferred from the passage that the proposed postal scheme by Lord Dalhousie was not unproven – it was applicable in England, but looking at the vast geographical area of Indian, it looked rather unreasonable. Critics

were opposed not because it was unproven, but because it seemed illogical.

Other options are either not discussed in the passage or are irrelevant.

The correct answer is A.

2. This is a detail question.

   (A) This is the **correct** answer because in the last sentence (line 24) of the passage, it says that the half-penny postage scheme by Lord Dalhousie was more significant in bridging the gap between the various parts of India than earlier methods such as the telegraph, the railway, and other formal systems. It adds "The social results were even more important.". Thus, the system facilitated communication.

   (B) This option is **incorrect** because it is not mentioned in the passage.

   (C) This option is **incorrect** because though it was anticipated that the new postal system would be capable of stopping local postmen from squeezing extra fees from customers, it was not the prime benefit of the half-penny post scheme in India.

   (D) This option is **incorrect** because though it was anticipated that half-penny post scheme in India would be self-sustainable, and would not drain finances from British colony funds, it was not the prime benefit to India. The passage says "The social results were even more important.", thus option A is the correct answer.

   (E) This option is **incorrect** because it cannot be inferred from the passage. It is too extreme.

   The correct answer is A.

3. This is an inference question.

   (A) This option is **incorrect** because it is extreme and devoid of any solid reasoning.

   (B) This option is a close option, but **incorrect** because though the scheme succeeded in both places–England, which was small, and India, which was large, we cannot infer that if something works on a small scale, it should work on a large scale as well. The execution of the scheme also matters, which was not dealt with in detail in the passage.

   (C) This is the **correct** answer because the passage observes that benefits provided by uniform postage were the elimination of wrangling with local postman, and the creation of reliability. If the result of these changes in the system was increased postage, then the disorganization caused by the previous system may have been more costly than shipping a letter across India at a set rate, irrespective of cost. Thus, Dalhousie proved that charging uniform lower rates was a much better proposition in the longer term for the postal system than not.

   (D) This option is **incorrect** because it's out of scope.

   (E) This option is **incorrect** because we cannot infer this; there is no support to infer this.

The correct answer is C.

4. This is an inference question.

    (A) This is the **correct** answer because it can be deduced from the experience of Dalhousie in different roles in the administration and internal development of the region, as well as his willingness to disregard the criticism of traditional financiers, whom we might assume were using traditional methods of problem resolution. He didn't see India's vastness as a detriment to a scheme that had worked in a smaller place successfully.

    (B) This option is **incorrect** because there is no evidence to support this.

    (C) This option is **incorrect** because there is no evidence to support this.

    (D) This option is **incorrect** because it cannot necessarily be deduced.

    (E) This option is **incorrect** because though the objective of bridging the gap between different parts of India was achieved through the postal scheme, other objectives could have been met through the telegraph, the railway, and public instruction, which were of equal importance.

    The correct answer is A.

5. This is a detail question.

    Option C is the correct answer because "reductio ad absurdum" literally means to reduce something to an absurd degree, or to extend something to an absurd degree. However, if you are not sure about the meaning, you can still infer it from the context.

    Let us examine the sentence and infer the meaning. *"For these onlookers, Dalhousie's plan was not so much an extension of the English penny postage scheme, as a **reductio ad absurdum** of the reform that had been effected in Great Britain."*

    It is clear that critics found the idea of implementing the postal scheme as absurd simply due to its success in England. They were of the opinion that extending the same scheme to much larger geography was absurd! Clearly option C is the correct answer.

    The correct answer is C.

6. This is a detail question.

    Option B is the correct answer as indicated in the sentence (line 19) stating "The system was more reliable for the person mailing the letter, and encouraged **increased patronage.**"

    Other options are either not discussed in the passage or are irrelevant.

    The correct answer is B.

7. This is a detail question.

    Option D can be seen as the correct answer from the sentence (line 22) stating "The proof of his success was the renewal of the postal system as a self-sustaining organization rather than its continuance as a chronic drain on British colonial finances."

    Other options are either not discussed in the passage or are irrelevant.

    The correct answer is D.

8. This is an inference question.

    (A) This option is **incorrect** because, in fact, it is the other way around. Uniform rate of postage irrespective of distances shows that transaction costs may not increase substantially even in larger markets.

    (B) This option is **incorrect** because it is an extreme answer. We cannot infer this from the passage.

    (C) This option is **incorrect** because it is an extreme answer. We cannot infer this from the passage. Though there was mention of postmen wrangling over the charges to deliver letters and trying to squeeze some extra money from the recipient, calling them "always corrupt" is an extreme reaction.

    (D) This option is **incorrect** because it is an extreme answer. The passage does not have supporting evidence to infer that letters are the MOST efficient means of communication.

    (E) This is the **correct** answer because wrangling (disputing/bickering) with local postman appeared costly as it limited the reliability of the system. This unreliability decreased patronage and raised costs. However, when rates were standardized, patronage increased to the extent that the postal system became self-sustaining and did not need the British government's financial intervention. So, this can be inferred.

    The correct answer is E.

6.14   Passage 14 (New global economic order)

Understanding the Passage

This is a medium length passage of high difficulty level on the topic of global economies.

Many legislators perceive that the journey to economic prosperity in post-industrial economies is predetermined, that the nation needs to compete with its rival nations in betterment of information services in the economy. Bill Clinton did the same by leading the U.S. economy into information technology (IT) services. However, this idea that all post-industrial economies must follow this predictable path and the idea that there is a predictable path is incorrect (*according to the author*). The author implies two things: one, that there cannot be a pre-set, predictable path to economic progress, and two, that not all countries should pursue development in IT at the expense of the manufacturing sector. Following this idea will be detrimental to jobs within the nation and it will affect other nations negatively too. This idea misses one key fact: that countries never directly compete with one another (*economist Paul Krugman agrees with this idea*). The author believes that even rival countries are never competitors, and if a country undermines its manufacturing sector to favor the IT sector, it will hurt the balance of jobs that is necessary in its post-industrial economy. The author advocates a balance between manufacturing and IT jobs. To think that developing the IT sector is the way to have technological development is incorrect (*according to the author*). Sacrificing the manufacturing sector to improve IT, especially to compete with a rival nation *that has a good IT sector* would be foolish because it would wipe out the trade relationship that the nation has with its rival. (*The nation that used to have manufacturing strength must have exported goods to its "rival" nation that is better at IT. By reducing its manufacturing jobs, the nation is jeopardizing its trade with the "rival" nation, only to try to compete in IT, something that the other nation already has. Thus, by reducing manufacturing, any country would reduce its trade and leverage with other nations.*) The author seems to imply that if everyone tried to improve IT, who would manufacture goods?

Thus, innovation does not mean that there is a fixed path (*of growing the IT sector at the expense of the manufacturing sector*), especially if the nation's resources favor manufacturing and not IT. Innovation should be defined as building the economy in a way that utilizes the nation's resources to the optimum (*this is the author's implication*). In fact, given that everyone in the world is becoming technologically advanced, the best way to ensure economic development is to make sure that the country's human resources and their skills match what the country's resources are made of, and this will ensure maximum growth in the international market. [*An example of that would be: Suppose a country has a vast coastline [natural resource]. Matching the labour force with this resource would mean utilizing the coastline to the optimum by developing fisheries and docks thoroughly, instead of trying to make everyone an IT expert.*]. The author thinks that the standard of living within a country should not be judged by how many white collar workers (*professionals/office workers*) a nation has, but should be judged by how the economy matches the skills of its workers to its productive activities, and by how well it fulfills the demands of global markets. The author implies that the global markets don't need only IT services, and that a nation should focus on what its resources and people can provide best. In that manner, a country can ensure maximum global trading and economic development. He further adds that institutions and authorities in a country can help improve the skills of a national workforce while maintaining the economy independent

from other countries. Even if a country chooses not to develop its IT sectors, it would be not be dependent on the countries that have developed their own IT sectors. Though the author acknowledges that an information economy can also give a nation certain political, military, and status advantages over other nations, the relationships among nations must not strive for equalling their information processing sectors, since a global market has scope for things other than IT too.

The passage is about busting a myth that post-industrialization, nations must strive for economies based on Information technology even at the expense of the manufacturing sector, and compete with other nations–*considered a predictable growth path*. A renowned economist is of the opinion that nations are not rivals and one must not treat them as such because one country may depend on another for the supply of key resources and products. The author advocates a balance between manufacturing and IT jobs. To think that developing the IT sector is the only way to have technological development is incorrect.

Main Point: Sacrificing the manufacturing sector for an information technology economy just for the sake of developing IT is foolish.

1. This is a detail question.

    (A) This option is **incorrect** because this is not the primary problem mentioned about the idea of developing the IT sector. The author's main contention against developing IT is that hurting manufacturing in a post-industrial economy will hurt jobs and reduce optimum utilization of resources.

    (B) This option is **incorrect** because it is not a drawback accordingly to the legislators. On the contrary, in the first part of the first paragraph, the legislators opine that the growth is predictable with an information service sector economy, however the author does not agree with this notion.

    (C) This option is **incorrect** because though it was mentioned in the passage that (line 5): "*this perception, that there is a specific, and even predictable, direction growth must go in, and that it must be done at the expense of manufacturing industries,*", we can infer that the manufacturing sector will be discouraged, however we cannot necessarily infer that the output from the manufacturing sector will decline.

    (D) This is the **correct** answer, as shown by the statement (line 11): "*As such, quickly removing a manufacturing sector in order to encourage the growth of an information and service sector can unnecessarily remove jobs*".

    (E) This option is **incorrect** because it cannot be inferred from the passage.

    The correct answer is D.

2. This is a tone question from the general category.

    The passage mentions that Bill Clinton's comparison, (line 8) "*Moreover, it overlooks the fact that, as economist Paul Krugman favors saying, countries are not direct competitors with one another*". So, when Bill Clinton led the USA's economy into growth by developing IT sectors to overtake his competitors, the author considered that the wrong thing

to do. Thus it is best termed as inaccurate.

Closest to option C is option A– Premature; however it is incorrect as the author is very decisive in quoting the statement from economist Paul Krugman who quashes the myth that *countries are direct competitors with one another.*

The correct answer is C.

3. This is a detail question.

Refer to the last sentence of the first paragraph (line 16): "*…, especially if the goal is seen as economic growth at the expense of a perceived competitor, with whom one must continue to trade goods and purchase economic inputs.*"

Option D is the correct answer since the passage says that states cannot really be considered rivals because they must continue to trade with one another. This is one of the main reasons the author is against developing IT at the expense of the manufacturing sector.

Other options are either not discussed in the passage or are irrelevant.

The correct answer is D.

4. This is an inference question.

Option D is the best answer since the concluding sentence of the passage states (line 29): "*This (reliance on an information economy) does not assume that an information economy does not give a nation certain political, military and status advantages over other nations*".

This implies that military status is of significance and hence a country with significant military status would be treated as a competitor. This might be the reason various countries try to improve the IT sector, even at the expense of the manufacturing sector, i.e. a developed IT sector bestows political and military advantages upon the country.

Other options are either not discussed in the passage or are irrelevant.

The correct answer is D.

5. This is a detail question.

Refer to the mid portion of the last paragraph (line 26): "*Institutions within a country can help improve and direct the skills of a national workforce, while accommodating quality of life considerations, without an economy having to be at a disadvantage compared to a*

foreign managerial or information economy."

Option B is the best answer since the passage notes the importance of institutional factors in guiding economies.

Other options are either not discussed in the passage or are irrelevant.

The correct answer is B.

6. This is an inference question.

   (A) This option is **incorrect** because it is not supported by the passage, and it is an extreme option. Refer to the upper part of the first paragraph (line 5): "*However, this perception, that there is a specific, and even predictable, direction growth must go in, and that it must be done at the expense of manufacturing industries*". 'A predictable direction growth must go in' is a wishful statement made by Bill Clinton. We can conclude that the author does not think that growth is predictable with simply developing IT.

   (B) This option is **incorrect** because it is the opposite of what the passage suggests. Refer to the mid part of the first paragraph (line 2): "*This perception........overlooks the way in which social groups, productivity and technology interact.*". It clearly suggests that social groups must be taken into consideration in economic growth.

   (C) This option is **incorrect** because it is the opposite of what the passage suggests. The passage notes that even in post-industrial economies removing manufacturing jobs can be detrimental.

   (D) This is the **correct** answer because it is supported by the passage. Refer to the mid part of the first paragraph (line 11): "*As such, quickly removing a manufacturing sector in order to encourage the growth of an information and service sector can unnecessarily remove jobs from an economy and destroy the balance that is necessary, even in a post-industrial economy, between the manufacturing sector and the information processing sector.*" It clearly suggests that the manufacturing sector is the key sector in an economy, especially in a post-industrial economy because it helps to utilize the resources to the optimum.

   (E) This option is **incorrect** because it is not supported by the passage.

   The correct answer is D.

7. This is a main point question from the general category.

   The passage is written to criticize the common assumption that economies must eliminate manufacturing jobs in order to advance in a global world of post-industrial nations following a promising and lucrative information technology economy.

   We have already deduced the main point: "Sacrificing the manufacturing sector for an information technology economy just for the sake of developing IT is foolish."

The tone of the passage is critical. Let us view each option one by one.

(A) This option is **incorrect** because the passage does not talk about how to reinvent an economy.

(B) This option is **incorrect** because the passage does not talk about corporate competition among nation states.

(C) This is the **correct** answer. It clearly follows from the deduction we made.

(D) This option is **incorrect**. "Old is Gold and New is just Glitter" is also a metaphor; here, "Old" implies the manufacturing sector, and "New" implies an information economy. Calling the manufacturing sector gold implies that the passage advocates supporting only the manufacturing sector, while calling an information economy glitter implies that the passage feels that an information economy does not have any substance, that it will fizzle its glitter soon. However the passage does not suggest anything of this sort.

(E) This option is **incorrect** because the passage does not discuss how economies perish.

The correct answer is C.

8. This is a function question.

The passage seeks to criticize the common assumption that economies must eliminate manufacturing jobs in order to advance in a global world of post-industrial nations following an information technology economy. Thus, it seeks to challenge existing beliefs.

(A) This option is **incorrect** because the passage does not raise an issue to be resolved.

(B) Like option A, this option is **incorrect** because the passage does not address an issue to be resolved.

(C) This option is **incorrect**, though it is a tricky option, because the passage is not written to provide a set of directions to the issue. It is limited to criticizing the common assumption that economies must eliminate manufacturing jobs in order to advance in a global world of post-industrial nations.

(D) This is the **correct** answer because it follows the analysis we made earlier.

(E) This option is **incorrect** because the passage does not discuss the solutions.

The correct answer is D.

6.15 Passage 15 (Randomness in modern physics)

Understanding the Passage

This is medium length passage of high difficulty level on the topic of modern physics.

By the early twentieth century, scientist started becoming skeptical about Newton's clockwork universe theory [*Laws of physics*]. Newton's hypothesis that the universe follows a deterministic pattern of behavior [*that is, he proposed that every action of any part of the universe is determined and, by extension, can be predicted once all the factors are known*]. But today's scientists find the deterministic claim untrue when they analyze the behavior of atoms. To prove the randomness as a law of physics in the behavior of atoms, they performed an experiment on radioactive atoms. They picked two identical atoms of a radioactive isotope, uranium 238, and found that they began to decay at different times, even though there was no difference in their initial behavior. [*One of the important properties of radioactive elements is that they continuously decay and, by the completion of their half-life, their weight becomes half of the original weight. The scientists found that two identical atoms of the radioactive isotope uranium 238 began to decay at different times. This was against the hypothesis of 'Deterministic behavior of the universe' proposed by Newton.*] There was no observable reason that could explain the random pattern of decay in the radioactive atoms. Thus, it couldn't be "determined", as Newton had hypothesized.

The author states that the earth would be in big trouble if these atoms' behavior was predictable, as expected in the Newtonian world-view. He added that radioactivity [*Decaying of radioactive elements*] is an important source of heat for our planet, apart from heat from the sun. In reality, each atom begins to decay at a different time (random, not predetermined) to release its energy, resulting in a nice steady heating effect in the earth. The scientists claim that the earth would be a much colder planet if only sunlight heated it and not also radioactivity. [*This proves that both the sun and radioactivity heat up the earth*]. They add further that if radioactivity didn't heat the earth, there would probably be no volcanoes, the oceans would be in a solid state, and sea life would not exist. Thus, radioactivity and its heating effect are directly responsible for life on earth.

The scientists present the worst case scenario that if radioactivity were deterministic and not random, all the uranium 238 atoms in our planet would presumably take the same time to decay after starting at the same time. As a consequence, the huge amount of stored nuclear energy in the uranium would all be released simultaneously, blowing our whole planet to ashes. [*"Thy kingdom come" is a phrase in the Christian Lord's Prayer referring to the Kingdom of God, as in the end of time*]. They further claim that, in reality, we have only a general idea of the process of how our solar system was created. Some portion of the universe may have come from nuclear reactions in supernova explosions (A supernova is an astral explosion [*explosion of a star*] that briefly outshines an entire galaxy, radiating as much energy as the sun is expected to emit over its entire life span, before fading from view over several weeks or months.), another portion from intra-galactic supernova explosions, and others still from exotic events like the collisions of tiny white stars in the galaxy. [*The purpose of putting forth highly astronomical scientific information is to claim that the laws of physics follow certain randomness and are not deterministic because none of these events is predictable or determined in a set way. These events are random in nature, but necessary for the survival of life on*

earth.] It is called a new version of physics, incorporating certain kinds of randomness, like quantum physics. Quantum physics represented such a dramatic distinction from the previous deterministic tradition that every other theory that came before it is considered classical, even the theory of relativity. [*The author is not trying to prove all the classical theories wrong but is trying to prove that the assumption of all those theories that everything in the universe is determined is wrong. Randomness is required to make the universe function and to sustain life.*]

The author explains in detail about a new view of the laws of physics; it is called Quantum physics. Quantum physics was much in contrast to the Newtonian model of laws of physics, in which the deterministic and predictable nature of the universe was the doctrine. The author cited an experiment with radioactivity that proved that due to the randomness of the laws of physics, we survive on Earth. He sums up with an endorsement of Quantum physics.

Main Point: Laws of physics follow randomness and not determinism.

1. This is a main point question from the general category.

    We have already derived the main point. Only option D qualifies as the correct answer.

    Also, while option A may seem close, it is not. The author's purpose is not so much to debunk all the Newtonian laws as to prove that a deterministic assumption is wrong. Thus, the author does not want to prove Newton's physics irrelevant but just wants to eliminate the assumption that everything in the universe runs like clockwork and is determined.

    The correct answer is D.

2. This is a function question.

    We have discussed in the 'Understanding the passage' section that the experiment on understanding the decaying pattern of uranium 238 was to prove that even the same elements starting at the same point decay at different times, implying they do not follow deterministic behavior, but randomness. Thus, the example of radioactive atoms was to prove how behavior is random and not deterministic, thus option E is correct.

    The correct answer is E.

3. This is a detail question.

    (A) This option is **incorrect** because the experiment on identical radioactive isotopes was at first conducted by scientists, and Newton had no bearing on it. We cannot necessarily infer this.

    (B) This option is **incorrect** because understanding the chemical properties of radioactive isotopes was not the purpose of the experiment.

    (C)   This option is **incorrect** because discussing the physical events with radioactive isotopes was not the purpose of the experiment.

    (D)   This option is a tricky option, but **incorrect** because the experiment proved that even two identical radioactive isotopes would decay at different times, but not rates. Their rate of decay is the same. Also, their time of decay can be different, but does not have to be.

    (E)   This is the **correct** answer as discussed in option D.

The correct answer is E.

4.   This is a detail question.

Refer to the last sentence of the passages (line 26); option D is the correct answer because the passage states that everything preceding the age of "quantum physics" is in the deterministic tradition and is considered classical, even the theory of relativity. Thus, the theory is classical and along the lines of Newton's deterministic universe.

The correct answer is D.

5.   This is a detail question.

Refer the first sentence of the third paragraph (line 17): "But there would be an even worse consequence if radioactivity were deterministic: after a few billion years of peace, all the uranium 238 atoms in our planet would presumably pick the same moment to decay…blowing our whole planet to kingdom come." The meaning of the metaphor "blowing our whole planet to kingdom come" is 'destroying the earth'. Option C is the correct answer.

The correct answer is C.

6.   This is a main point question from the general category.

We have already derived the main point; however now we will discuss all the options.

    (A)   This option is **incorrect** because it is too specific to supernovas and the rise of life in the world. It does not mention physics at all.

    (B)   This option is **incorrect** because it would be for a broad review of the principles of classical physics in general. However, we are discussing only one underlying principle of classical physics – determinism.

    (C)   This option is **incorrect** because the passage does not say that quantum physics is the most basic principle in physics. Also, this option is too general and does not mention either determinism or randomness.

    (D)   This option is **incorrect** because the passage is not debating the merits of the classical and quantum models of physics; it is merely asserting the relevance of quantum physics over all previous models of physics.

(E) This is the **correct** answer because the passage deals with moving into a new era of physics by seeing how the old tenets of physics needed to be understood in terms of new principles.

The correct answer is E.

7. This is a tone question from the general category.

(A) This option is **incorrect** because the piece does not conform to the impartial, formal style of journalistic news reporting.

(B) This option is **incorrect** because the piece is a prepared argument.

(C) This option is **incorrect** because the piece does not urge a response or action.

(D) This option is **incorrect** because the passage is not trying to cover objectively a broad range of detailed knowledge in a formal style.

(E) This is the **correct** answer because the passage does present an explicative (descriptive/explanatory) argument.

The correct answer is E.

8. This is an inference question.

(A) This option is **incorrect** because on the contrary, it is the other way around; the passage advocates that quantum physics can be considered a correct interpretation of physical events.

(B) This option is **incorrect** because quantum physics is not presented by the passage as a supplement to Newtonian physics.

(C) This is the **correct** answer because the passage presents quantum physics as a new version of physics which interprets the world in a completely different way than previous analytical tools allowed.

(D) This option is **incorrect** because the author does not present quantum physics as the replacement for Newtonian physics; it has an independent identity. Quantum physics merely refutes one underlying principle – determinism.

(E) This option is **incorrect** for the same reasoning advocated in option D.

The correct answer is C.

6.16 Passage 16 (Synergetics)

Understanding the Passage

This is a lengthy passage of high difficulty level on the topic of neo-science.

Synergetics is an epistemology for interpreting concepts in life through geometric relationships. [*Synergetics is a study of knowledge for interpreting concepts of life using geometry. Epistemology is the study of knowledge and justifying what we know.*]

Buckminster Fuller, a multi-disciplinary scholar and inventor, coined the term synergetics to describe what he considered a "coordinate system" for the physical universe, summoning the language of the Cartesian coordinate plane with which mathematicians graph physical space. [*So, Buckminster Fuller is considered the inventor of synergetics. He describes synergetics as an explanation/portrayal of the universe and all its parts on a graph, like mathematicians use graphs to represent physical space.*] Synergetics has come to serve as a method for describing the behavior of whole systems whose behavior cannot be predicted from independent analyses of their parts. [*There are various things in the universe whose analyses don't make sense. Synergetics explains such phenomena by representing them as a holistic system that can explain these happenings in a comprehensive manner.*] In Fuller's conception of synergetics, this coordinate system, seeks to map not only the physical characteristics of the universe, but also the rationale structuring of mankind's heuristic interpretations of the world. [*So Fuller's system maps the physical, actual universe on a graph and also adds the interaction of mankind's understanding of the physical universe on the graph.*] The basis of Fullers' model is that all observable phenomena can be codified as interactive systems, and those systems can be principally understood as a geography of spherical networks comprised of interrelated points of interest. [*So, Fuller believes that all happenings are part of an interactive system, and different things/systems are interconnected with each other through some common points of interest, and all these comprise spherical/cyclical networks that can be charted on graphs.*] Those interrelationships then equate with the morphology of observable phenomena. [*Such interactions are then as visible as something physical in the world.*]

At its most discrete, Fuller understood a "system" as being the first division one could make of the universe. [*At its most basic, Fuller thinks that a universe can be divided into systems.*] That logic could then be applied to all things that existed. [*Each system has logic in the parts it contains.*] It follows that conceptual thoughts themselves are synergistic systems. [*Also, thoughts (they are part of any system containing people) are also systems in themselves.*] Not the least of his intentions was to have a better way of speaking about the dynamics of the universe by understanding the structure of thinking, man's tool for hashing through observation, and composing it in relational terms. [*One of his important intentions was to explain the workings of the universe by explaining the way and the manner in which humans think. This is important because thinking is man's tool for expressing in rational language what he sees and observes of the world. Thus, each man's thinking contains one universe – a system.*] This would then lead to a model that demonstrated the nature of the paradigms that enveloped thought. [*Explaining the thoughts would create a model that would explain the basis that created thoughts.*] If the known laws of the universe could be said to be bottled in thoughts, then Fuller sought better carafes in which to carry and relay the derived logic of empirical knowledge. [*Fuller believed that since all known laws can be expressed and kept as thoughts, explaining thoughts would*

explain the "why" of those laws itself. This is why he wanted a better way of expressing not just the thoughts, but the process of thinking itself. His carafe (a container, usually for liquids), metaphorically meant as a canvas or way of communication, was coordinate geometry.] His immediate language for contending with these ideas, and creating a fluid, interactive metaphor for the activities of observable phenomena (in the form of physical energy, or ideas, or knowledge) was what came to him most readily, geometry. [*His way of expressing all those models of thinking and laws and processes and weaving them into an interactive system that explained the universe was to use geometry.*] The unit of that geometry was the tetrahedron. It became the unit of his explanations. [*So, he chose tetrahedron to explain all such systems.*]

Ultimately, Fuller offers a science of sociological networks and the internal riggings of the mind in order to construct a system of rules for otherwise unruly occurrences. [*In sum, Fuller presents a methodological network to bring meaning to chaotic life and explain the seemingly random occurrences in the universe.*] His subject matter was the pattern of all activities. [He wanted to explain the basic pattern of all happenings and phenomena.] Synergetics sought to create an explanatory model for experiencing natural occurrences by pointing to the underlying order of activity that is universally in harmony with mathematic rationality. [*His models present an explanation of occurrences by threading in the underlying activities whose interactions caused them and he shows such patterns using mathematical logic.*]

The passage is on the topic of synergetics–neo-science. Buckminster Fuller is considered the inventor of synergetics. He describes synergetics as an explanation/portrayal of the universe and all its parts on a graph, like mathematicians use graphs to represent physical space. There are various things in the universe whose analyses don't make sense. Synergetics explains such phenomena by representing them as a holistic system that can explain these happenings in a comprehensive manner. Fuller conceptualized models for understanding and interpreting the universe with the help of systems, and he coined a geometric unit to explain all such systems–tetrahedron.

Main Point: Synergetics: a study of knowledge for interpreting concepts of life using geometry.

1. This is a detail question.

    Option C is the best option because synergetics is described in the first line of the passage as an epistemology for interpreting concepts in life through geometric relationships.

    It can be narrowly translated as "synergetics is the study of interpretation of knowledge".

    Other options were either not discussed in the passage or are out of scope.

    The correct answer is C.

2. This is a detail question.
    (A) This option is **incorrect** because synergetics is defined as the science of interpreting knowledge or concepts in life through geometric relationships; the passage never alludes to the point that it is a model for inventing information.

(B) This is the **correct** answer because it is "heuristic", which refers to a system of education under which the pupil is trained to find out things by himself or herself. It is supported in the passage in a couple of places. Refer to the last sentence of the passage (line 31): "Synergetics sought to create an explanatory model for experiencing natural occurrences". Also refer later to part of the second paragraph (line 11): "The basis of Fullers' model is that all observable phenomena can be codified as interactive systems, and those systems can be principally understood."

(C) This option is **incorrect** because it is too narrow, and, moreover, the first sentence of the last paragraph states (line 29): "Fuller offers a science of sociological networks." Calling it a social network is too general.

(D) This option is **incorrect** because synergetics is not a model for the routine application of knowledge, rather it is an exploratory model.

(E) This option is **incorrect** as it is irrelevant; we know that synergetics is heuristic as discussed in option B's explanation.

The correct answer is B.

3. This is a detail question.

(A) This is the **correct** answer because "morphology" refers to the study of the form of animals and plants, or the study of the form of words and the system of forms in a language, i.e. it is a study of what can be seen. Empirical also means what can be observed.

(B) This is **incorrect** because while synergetics itself may refer to the theoretical relationships of phenomena, the word "morphology" as used in the passage does not.

(C) This is **incorrect** because this is out of scope of the passage.

(D) This is **incorrect** because neither Fuller nor synergetics is concerned with categorizing or classifying. Instead, the idea is about expressing phenomena holistically as a whole system and not parts or categories.

(E) This is **incorrect** because neither synergetics nor the word morphology is concerned with naming or classifying.

The correct answer is A.

4. This is a detail question.

Option C is the correct answer because the passage describes a "system" as the first division of the universe, thus a "system" is a "subgroup".

Fuller doesn't express only thoughts through synergetics, and so not all "systems" can be called "conceptual thoughts".

Further, Fuller endeavors to make his "systems" a holistic representation, and not just pieces or parts. Thus, a "system" can't be just a "component" or "a series of related

mechanisms" both of which are not "holistic".

A "unit" can be, but is not necessarily an independent, whole system. So, we cannot call a "system" in Fuller's synergetics. Fuller's unit would be a tetrahedron.

Thus, a "system" is best described as "subgroup".

The correct answer is C.

5. Option D is the correct answer because the passage states that Fuller used geometry as his heuristic model, and the most basic unit of that model was the "tetrahedron" (refer line 27).

Other options are incorrect as "the system" itself is not the device for teaching synergetics as a model, rather the system is understood with the help of synergetics as a model for which Fuller conceptualized a unit–the tetrahedron.

Other options do not qualify to be discussed in the purview of "Fuller's most basic device".

The correct answer is D.

6. This is a detail question.

    (A) This is the **correct** answer because the passage notes that Fuller used synergetics (line 7) "as a method for describing the behavior of whole systems whose behavior cannot be predicted." It is also supported in the first sentence of the last paragraph (line 29): "Ultimately, Fuller offers a science of sociological networks and the internal riggings of the mind in order to construct a system of rules for otherwise unruly occurrences."

    (B) This option is **incorrect** because synergetics means to study the behavior of observable phenomena. It is supported in the latter part of the second paragraph (line 11): "The basis of Fullers' model is that all observable phenomena can be codified as interactive systems."

    (C) This option is **incorrect** because nothing about inexplicable relationships was quoted.

    (D) This option is **incorrect** because nothing of this sort was even discussed in the passages. These kinds of options are cleverly crafted by test makers so that you may fall for incorrectly-worded similar terminology if you hurriedly read the passage.

    (E) This option is **incorrect** because it too vague and unclear with respect to the scope of the passage.

The correct answer is A.

7. This is a detail question.

    Option E is the best answer. It is supported by a couple of sentences in the latter part of the third paragraph (line 23): "Fuller sought better carafes in which to carry and relay the derived logic of empirical knowledge. His immediate language for contending with these ideas, and creating a fluid, interactive metaphor for the activities of observable was what came to him most readily, geometry."

    The correct answer is E.

8. This is a tone question from the general category.

    This passage is certainly a hard one and the concept discussed in the passage sometimes become abstract and illusive. The passage is basically describing what synergetics is, along with information about its inventor, Fuller. It describes the neo-science field. At times, the content of the passage becomes hard to decipher, but throughout the passage, we find that the author tries to introduce and educate the reader on synergetics.

    Let us understand the options one by one.

    (A)   This option is **incorrect** because the author is not critical about the abstract concepts in synergetics. Though some content is illusive, it is not critical.

    (B)   This option is the **correct** answer; it follows from the analysis we made earlier.

    (C)   This option is a tricky, but **incorrect** because throughout the passage the author maintains the tone of describing or exploring something, and does not analyze synergetics in relation to other theories. Also, he does not present any evaluations of any analysis he made. The author is only concerned with being informative rather than judging and analyzing the content.

    (D)   This option is a tricky, but **incorrect** because the content of the passage is rather abstract, illusive, and distracting. It is not absorbing or worthy of holding the interest of the reader.

    (E)   This option is a tricky, but **incorrect** because in the context of the tone of the passage, "principled" (righteous/moral) is irrelevant.

    The correct answer is B.

6.17 Passage 17 (Sustainability of homo sapiens)

Understanding the Passage

This is a long passage of high difficulty level on the topic of biology.

Biomass is the total mass of all living members of a species. Considering all the species, human beings are one of the largest biomasses on earth [*Insects have the most biomass*]. They are the leading influence on earth's ecosystems, and, as a result of ecological processes, they inhabit most areas throughout the world. A species has a great chance of survival if its aggregate biomass is at the top compared with other species. Since the biomass of human beings is on top, they claim their territory *(habitats)*, and have control of resources. [*For a species to survive, it must compete with other species and have influence, thereby leveraging on sustainable resources*]. It might be short-sighted to belittle the success of an emerging species or breed for being small in number if it is evident that the members of the species are elegant and well-adjusted [*The author says that while the aggregate biomass is one of the determinants of the species' success, it is not wise to think less of species with less biomass if they have good adaptations that allow them to adjust well to the environment*]. A species' ability to adapt to their habitat in the ecosystem, yet being able to vary according to the needs of the environment, is considered very beneficial. Human beings have had nearly unparalleled success compared to other species in successful adaptation. As a result, human beings exist in huge numbers. It is a fact that human beings have remained in a generally undifferentiated form that allows them to rank highly as a single successful species. [*Human being did not branch out in many different sub-species; they adapted themselves well and remain Homo sapiens. Usually when a species changes, its habitat or the environment around it has changed, and the species is forced to adapt to the new surroundings and often adapts and changes so much that it is no longer like the earlier species, and becomes a new variant.*]

Compared to other species, human beings are considered unique, as they retain their form as they travel from environment to environment. [*Other species, if adapted successfully, may lose their form.*] Despite challenges in the environment and adapting to new environments, human beings have been able to adjust their behavior sufficiently to avoid having nature make such extensive piecemeal adjustments to them that entirely distinct workable alternatives of the same model occupy the new space. [*It means that humans withstood nature's default adjustment of splitting a species into similar yet different variants of surviving species.*] And with these adjustments, other species such as dinosaurs transmogrified to pigeons, primitive fish to amphibians and then eventually to whales, even Homo sapiens *(human begins)* partially to Neanderthals (a similar yet different species of human) for a time. [*All these are examples of when nature stepped in to help a species to adapt to survive better and the final result was drastically different from the original one.*]

Surviving and extinct variants of each species had to co-exist alongside their parental species [*Original species and newly-adapted and developed species live side-by-side*]. Many surviving species, with successful reproduction with other members, move into another ecosystem. Following this, each variant species was considered a different species from its parent species [*Each variant becomes nearly completely different from the original ones – and probably can no longer mate with the original species*]. In this way, the exchange of genes among members occurred across the globe, and a new species takes on a scientifically unique identity at dif-

ferent times and in different places. But humans remain a distinct species [*compared to other species, humans did not branch out to many variant species*] not because they are the first to exist in so many habitats and take advantage of so many resources, but for the reason that they have become one of the relatively few species to inhabitat different parts of the world in great numbers while being able to exchange genetic material [*sexual reproduction*] with others from their group, even if they had been largely geographically isolated from other groups over many generations. [*Humans are different because while they populated different habitats all over the world, unlike other species they did not undergo such drastic changes that they could not continue to mate with other human beings from different places. So, human beings are one of the most successful species ever.*]

Main Point: Survival of the supreme species Homo sapiens.

1. This is a detail question.

    Option D is the correct answer supported by the sentences given in the first part of paragraph 1 (lines 4-7): "*It can be said the most rudimentary measure of the **success of the species** is its position near the top of the aggregate biomass scale... For human beings, it is a reflection of **their claim on territory, and their consumption of resources as a species.**"*

    Option A is classic case of mixing up words. The passage states "*It can be said the most rudimentary measure of the success of the species is **its position near the top of the aggregate biomass scale**", and <u>not at the top of the food chain</u>.*

    Other options are either not stated in the passage or are inconclusive.

    The correct answer is D.

2. This is a detail question.
    (A) This option is **incorrect** because, on the contrary, the passage states otherwise. The second sentence of the second paragraph (line 17) states "*Human beings are considered unique as **they retain their form** as they travel from environment to environment."*

    (B) This option is **incorrect** because though the passage mentions that even Homo sapiens partially yielded to Neanderthals for a time through piecemeal adjustments, it does not make human beings unique in their colonization of the Earth. What makes human colonization unique, and unlike that of other species, is that while spreading to different habitats they did not adapt to the extent of becoming different from the original species. Most species change and adapt so much when they move to new habitats that they no longer resemble the original species.

    (C) This is the **correct** answer. It is supported by (line 17): "***Humans thus remain distinct** (unique) not **because** they are the first to exist in so many habitats, and take advantage of so many resources, but in that **they** have become one of the relatively few organisms to **accomplish widespread population of different habitats while***

being able to exchange genetic material with others from their group, even if they had been largely geographically isolated over many generations." This implies that unlike other species, humans could withstand splitting into different groups yet were able to habituate themselves densely in diversified habitats. Thus, they survived as one species despite their dispersal all over the world, and did not get differentiated and fragmented into different sub-species.

(D)   This option is **incorrect** because though it is correct that human beings are one of the highest ranked organisms on the biomass scale, it does not make human beings unique with respect to the colonization aspect. Also, insects are ranked higher than human beings on the biomass scale.

(E)   This option is **incorrect** because this is opposite of the fact given in the passage. Refer to the last part of the last paragraph (line 17); the gist is: Humans thus remain distinct (unique)... because... they accomplish widespread population of different habitats while being able to exchange genetic material with others from their group, even if they had been largely geographically isolated over many generations.

The correct answer is C.

3.   This is a detail question.

Option D is the correct answer. Since human beings had the ability to adjust themselves according to their environment, they could withstand the genetic splitting into different species. It is supported by: *"Still, human beings have been able to adjust their behavior sufficiently to avoid having nature make such extensive piecemeal adjustments to them that entirely distinct workable alternatives of the same model occupy the new space."* It means that humans withstood nature's default adjustment of splitting a species into a similar yet different variant of a surviving species by adjusting their behavior to suit the environment in which they were put.

Other options are either not stated in the passage or are not supported.

The correct answer is D.

4. This is a detail question.

   (A) This option is **incorrect** because it is not mentioned in the passage.

   (B) This option is **incorrect** because it is also not mentioned in the passage. How densely any species is populated is not mentioned.

   (C) This is the **correct** answer since the passage notes that it is the *"widespread population of different habitats (population size) while being able to exchange genetic material with others from their group"* which the passage notes as 'distinct' in terms of success over other species. That is how biomass is defined and success of a species is how much biomass it has accumulated.

   (D) This option is **incorrect** because the passage mentions that genetic code is dispersed around the world for any given species, but the ability of that species to retain its genetic code is one of the criteria for success and not merely the global dispersion of its genetic code.

   (E) This option is **incorrect** because as shown by the sentences *"It might be short-sighted to belittle the success of an emerging species or breed for being small in number if it is evident that the members of the species are elegant and well-adjusted. However, the ability to adapt one's habitat to the largest ecosystem, while still **retaining the flexibility to deal with local demands on the population may be considered high art in the annals of successful adaptation.**"* There are two factors to be taken into account for success, one: the ability to adapt, and two: being flexible in dealing with local demands of the population. Thus, the degree of adaptation to its environment by itself cannot be quantified as success.

   The correct answer is C.

5. This is a detail question.

   The passages measures success through many parameters: species biomass (insects on the top, and humans near the top), capability to claim territory and consume resources, and adaptation in different environments. Option A is the correct answer since the passage discusses the effect of ecological change driving species into different habitats, which is related to geographic dispersion.

   Other options are either not mentioned or are not inferable from the passage.

   The correct answer is A.

6. This is a detail question.

   Option D is the correct answer since the passage discusses the fact that some species had to co-exist alongside their predecessors or previous forms.

   The correct answer is D.

7.   This is a function question.

Option D is the correct answer because the passage discusses the movement of human genetic material as human beings migrated across the earth. Refer to the last part of the last paragraph; the gist is: *"Humans thus remain distinct (unique)... because... they accomplish widespread population of different habitats while being able to **exchange genetic material <u>(or, migration of species)</u> with others from their group, even if they had been largely geographically isolated** over many generations."*

Other options are either not mentioned or are not inferable from the passage.

The correct answer is D.

8.   This is a detail question.

Option C is the correct answer since the passage is a detailed, fact-driven, objective, and impartial discussion of a topic. It is neither biased nor critical of the facts presented in the passage. It isn't vague or harshly critical (polemical) either. Thus, it can be best expressed as balanced.

The correct answer is C.

6.18   Passage 18 (Punctuated equilibrium updates Darwin)

Understanding the Passage

This is lengthy passage of high difficulty level on the topic of biology.

Darwin's theory of the Origin of Species deals with the topic of evolution and the formation of new species. It has been widely analyzed and more theories stemming from it are being discussed. According to the theory of Origin of Species, the fitness of species within a specific environment is the determining factor for the success or failure of a new species, and it provides some of the organisms of a species a competitive advantage over others. As a result, some members of a species were able to multiply, while others slowly were beaten for food, territory, security, and the opportunity to reproduce. [*In a nut shell, the theory of Origin of Species lays importance on the fitness of the species to survive and reproduce. Accordingly, unfit species would slowly become extinct as they lose the competition for food and territory with fit species.*]

Darwin's theory of the natural adaptation of species was subjected to further analysis focusing on the precise processes that transform competitive advantage into the formation of new species. The concept of punctuated equilibrium is one such reinterpretation. [*The theory of punctuated equilibrium views Darwin's theory as simplistic and too natural; it has a different take on Darwin's theory of adaptation.*]

Punctuated equilibrium is a theory similar to Darwinian logic, but it raises specific inquiries about the formation of new species rather than simply looking only at how fitness plays a pivotal role in forming a new species. According to Darwin, if one organism contains all the elements of its breed of organisms, but also some uncommon advantageous trait, it will successfully reproduce. This process continues as long as their mating makes them more fit for prevailing environments, eventually leading to the formation of a new species. But punctuated equilibrium takes another approach to the conditions necessary for the formation of new species.

Punctuated equilibrium is critical of Darwin's process of reproduction and causation, finding it to be overly determined, or simplistic. According to the theory of punctuated equilibrium, any comparatively advantageous traits absorbed by members of a species would be redistributed among a large number of members of the species, and it would be impossible to observe the continuous and subtle variation among the members until one observes them after a long duration of time or in isolation. [*"the tiny Galapagos Islands" are small isolated islands where Darwin made his observations that led him to formulate the Origin of Species. Thus, it would be impossible for a few individuals with some favorable variations to create a new species altogether over time.*] Punctuated equilibrium corrects Darwin's theory by stating that the sudden emergence of a species with more fitness than its former species would not usually occur until there is a disastrous event. [*This is in contrast to Darwin's theory, which suggests that differentiation among species occurs gradually as some individuals acquire favorable adaptations and successfully reproduce in abundance to form a new species; punctuated equilibrium says an external factor such as a disastrous environment is necessary to induce the permanent differentiation among species.*] It further emphasizes that the comparative advantage only leads to the formation of a new species if the conditions in which it occurs are catastrophic or ecologically

devastating for the species as a whole, such as massive geographic reformations (for example, the flooding of the Mediterranean basin). [*Conditions must always be sufficiently harsh to induce speciation-formation of a new species.*] This creates a timescale for speciation that is better represented by a pendulum swing in one swift motion than by seeping growth and petty attrition of a Darwinian refrain spread out over successive generations. [*This means that species are formed suddenly when conditions become harsh. This transition is best represented by the swing of a pendulum where on the one side is the original species and as the pendulum swings to the other side, and conditions change suddenly, a new species is formed. This is in contrast to the Darwinian model, in which the timescale would be very gradual, and species would change almost imperceptibly, over time, accruing one change at a time in some generations. Thus, it would take many generations to make a new species and thus the graph would be a gradual slope.*]

The passage is about Darwin's theory of the Origin of Species, which deals with the evolution and the formation of new species. According to it, the fitness of species within a specific environment is the determining factor for the success or failure of a new species. However, the theory of punctuated equilibrium sees Darwin's adaptation theory to be over simplistic and too natural. According to the theory of punctuated equilibrium, an external factor such as disastrous environment is necessary to induce the permanent differentiation among species, in contrast to the Darwinian theory which suggests that speciation is a very gradual process that happens as organisms accrue minor changes over successive generations.

Main Point: Darwin's simplistic theory of Origin of Species and an update based on the theory of punctuated equilibrium.

1. This is a main point question from the general category.

    (A) This option is **incorrect** because proponents of punctuated equilibrium do not say fitness is not an issue.

    (B) This is the **correct** answer because the passage seeks to introduce a more refined interpretation of the development of fitness in a species while using the same source as its basis for the surrounding science. Punctuated equilibrium probes the fitness factor further and looks at it through another dimension.

    (C) This option is **incorrect**. Second line Darwinists are referred to as proponents of punctuated equilibrium-the evolutionary reformers. According to the option, the fitness is a secondary issue to the proponents of punctuated equilibrium, whereas according to the passage, it is not.

    (D) This option is **incorrect** because the passage does not present the material as putting a model that is broken back together , but as refining the model with a different approach.

    (E) This option is **incorrect** because the passage does not portray the inaccuracies in Darwin's theory as being the result of dishonesty.

    The correct answer is B.

2. This is a detail question.

    (A) This option is **incorrect** because it is out of the scope of the passage. The passage does not talk about anything of this sort.

    (B) This option is **incorrect** because it is out of scope. The passage is concerned with the evolution of species and not extinction.

    (C) This option is **incorrect** because it is out of the scope of the passage.

    (D) This option is **incorrect** because punctuated equilibrium does not simply fill in unexplained aspects of Darwinian evolution; rather, it explains the process of speciation in a contrasting way to the Darwinian model.

    (E) This is the **correct** answer because Darwin considers transformations (mutations) responsible for evolving differentiated species, while punctuated equilibrium considers ecological disasters responsible for that.

    It is supported by *"Punctuated Equilibrium updates Darwin by noting that the sudden emergence of a differentiation, endowing an organism with more fitness than the rest of its species, would not usually give that organism or its descendants a significant degree of independence in the absence of disastrous conditions. For the evolution reformers, this comparative advantage only leads to speciation if the conditions in which it occurs are cataclysmic for the species as a whole."*

    The correct answer is E.

3. This is an inference question.

    (A) This option is **incorrect** because there is no mention in the passage of the fossil record.

    (B) This option is **incorrect** because the passage does not state or imply that Darwinists do not consider the role of ecological disasters.

    (C) This option is **incorrect** because it does not bear on the difference between Darwinists and Punctuated Equilibriumists. The statement "species is a relative term for a collection of individual gene permutations" itself is does not state the difference between two theories.

    (D) This is the **correct** answer because Punctuated Equilibriumists observe that Darwinist principles function based on drastic changes in nature, but not on changes "by seeping growth and petty attrition (slow change)." Thus, their primary objection is that the Darwinian model of gradual change accruing over generations would lead to speciation in a controlled and protected environment, such as the one in the Galapagos Islands. However, on a greater scale, as in the real world (an unprotected, uncontrolled environment), such small changes would be absorbed and unnoticeable. Thus, in an actual scenario, speciation would happen only in the case of drastic environmental changes.

    (E) This option is **incorrect** because it is not mentioned in the passage.

The correct answer is D.

4. This is a detail question.

    (A) This option is **incorrect** since the passage does not present Punctuated Equilibrium as an extension of Darwin, but as an adjustment to Darwin.

    (B) This option is **incorrect** because Punctuated Equilibrium is not a concise version of Darwinism but rather an altered version.

    (C) This is the **correct** answer since the passage asserts, "Punctuated Equilibrium updates Darwin..."; it rather supplements Darwin's theory with an outlook on other aspect without moving out of the periphery of the theory.

    (D) This option is **incorrect** because Punctuated Equilibrium incorporates aspects of Darwinism.

    (E) This option is **incorrect** because Punctuated Equilibrium does not seek to be an extension of Darwinism but a correction of it.

    The correct answer is C.

5. This is a tone question from the general category.

    Option D is the best answer since the passage notes that Darwinism is correct but only in a small environment under controlled conditions. The passage asserts that punctuated equilibrium asks 'specific questions' regarding evolution that Darwinism does not ask, and thus would regard Darwinism as less detailed or more simplistic. Also, the proponents of punctuated equilibrium call Darwin's model too simplistic.

    The correct answer is D.

6. This is a detail question.

    Option A is the best answer since the passage asserts that speciation happens under 'cataclysmic' conditions or conditions of 'unexpected ecological devastation' which may be understood to be turbulent and something for which a species could not prepare –sudden and unpredictable.

    The correct answer is A.

7. This is an application question.

    All the options listed talk about new traits found in the members of species or their disappearance. According to the theory of punctuated equilibrium, catastrophic conditions would lead to the formation of new species or bring about differentiable or major change. Thus, those changes that seem to have no drastic environmental triggers would be considered less explicable by proponents.

Option C is the correct answer since the other options represent sudden changes in ecological conditions which would trigger species-wide change.

The correct answer is C.

8. This is a detail question.

    Let us take the reference: *"For the evolution reformers, this comparative advantage only leads to a speciation event if the conditions in which it occurs are cataclysmic for the species as a whole, including massive geographic reformations (such as the flooding of the Mediterranean basin) or **unexpected** ecological devastation."*

    (A) This option is **incorrect** because the passage implies unexpected ecological devastation yields comparative advantage to a species, and an epidemic does not serve the purpose.

    (B) This option is **incorrect** because the piece "For the evolution...." already talked about massive geographic reformations, so it is expected that it would talk about an aspect other than "massive".

    (C) This option is **incorrect** because "immediate" does not fit well with ecological devastation.

    (D) This is the **correct** answer since the passage seeks to communicate the inability of a species to prepare for an event. Thus, the word "unexpected" implies "sudden and unpredictable", which is "unforeseen".

    (E) This option is **incorrect** because "At once" does not fit well with ecological devastation.

    The correct answer is D.

6.19   Passage 19 (Abortion law)

Understanding the Passage

This is a medium length passage of low difficulty level on the topic of socio-economics.

The debate on the legalization of abortion in America has been advocated on the grounds of human rights and freedom of choice. The supporters of these views want lawmakers to alter any legislation pertaining to abortion. Moreover, economists also want lawmakers to alter any legislation pertaining to abortion by looking at the issue from some practical point of view. While it is important to note that the life of any unborn child matters, the economic relevance of bringing up an unwanted child and depriving him of an adequate life-style must also be considered when looking at legislation pertaining to abortion. [*Apart from looking at the abortion issue on moral grounds, it should also be looked at from an economics point of view.*]

However, researchers have pointed out that there is a correlation between the Roe vs. Wade abortion empowerment legislation and reported crime statistics twenty years after an unwanted child is born. They suggest that when abortion is not allowed, the crime rate increases. This conclusion is based on findings that within a few years of Roe vs. Wade's abortion legislation, up to 25% of all pregnancies in the United States resulted in abortions. Also, they observe that crime rates between 1985 and 1997 declined. The researchers note that due to the implementation of abortion legislation, a significant number of illegitimate children were not born, and this led to a decrease in crime during this time frame. It mentions a 20 year period because it is the age at which most wrongdoers engage in the majority of any society's illegal activity. Since those illegitimate children are relatively inexperienced (and thus don't get gainful employment), lack moral values, are deprived of societal support and adequate opportunities to grow from, they are more prone to violence and rebelliousness compared to women or adult males. The researchers realize that abortion by a woman is a practical and sensible step if she is not prepared to care for an unwanted child. Raising an illegitimate child is a great challenge. This in turn deprives the child of adequate resources to grow, and exposes him to the likelihood of illegal conduct in society.

A low crime rate signifies that giving a choice to a woman when to have a baby is a welcome move. Another aspect to the abortion debate is that crime is financially costly to taxpayers. According to one estimate, taxpayers would lose as much as $30 billion annually because of crimes committed by teen-aged illegitimate children who had not been aborted, thereby creating an even higher crime rate. Though ideologists have been arguing against abortion, legislators must look into abortion reform from all aspects so that they can reach a rational decision, especially from an economic angle.

The passage is about reforms aimed at abortion legislation. Though the demand to legalize abortion has been argued from a moral point of view–human rights and freedom of choice, there is another aspect discussed in the passage–economics (the cost society pays due to letting unwanted children be brought up in society.). The passage argues that illegitimate and unprivileged teenaged children indulge in crimes and society has to pay dearly for it. To sum up, the author advocates that legislators look into this aspect while reforming abortion law.

Main Point: Reform abortion law: it's time to look at it from a financial and safety point of view.

1. This is a detail question.

    Option D is the best option since the passage claims the difficulty lawmakers have with contending with the abortion debate problem relates to their inability to see past ideologies (moral issues), while the benefit offered by the researchers is information on the practical results of abortion for society (a lower crime rate, and annual savings as high as $30 billion).

    While option A is too general and vague, other options do not qualify to be in the reckoning.

    The correct answer is D.

2. This is a tone question from the general category.

    While reading the passage, we find that the author is clearly of the opinion that reform on abortion legislation must take place. Apart from lawmakers being influenced from the point of view of human rights and freedom of choice, he cites the economic aspect–the cost and crime due to abortions that do happen. There are indicators in the passage that imply that the author is in favor of the reforms such as *"As the **ideological arguments** over abortion **refuse to abate**, it may be time for **hamstrung legislators** to consider new sources of information **to simplify their decisions** about reopening the question of abortion reform and government aid."* Option A is the correct answer.

    The closest option could be journalistic, however it is incorrect because he is not merely reporting various aspects and facts. He is not unbiased (as journalism is supposed to be) but is in favor of reforms in abortion laws and conveys such ideas implicitly. He is quite clearly not a disinterested party given the last sentence, *"it may be time for hamstrung legislators to consider new sources of information to simplify their decisions about reopening the question of abortion reform and government aid"*; he suggests that action be taken on this from a practical point of view. A journalistic argument will not present an opinion but merely present the various aspects.

    However, the author quite clearly wants us to be persuaded about reform in abortion laws. Thus, he is "persuasive" in his passage.

    The correct answer is A.

3. This is a strengthen the argument question from the reasoning question category.

    Let us understand the claim of the researchers.

    Claim: There is an economic cost society has to pay (an annual cost to the tune of $30 billion because of crime committed by illegitimate teen-aged children) due to

anti-abortion.

Let us look through each option one by one and see which option supports or strengthens the claim made by the researchers.

(A)   This option is **incorrect** because it is irrelevant. The researchers are concerned about the crime committed by illegitimate and unprivileged teenaged children, and not by white-collar workers (professionals and office workers).

(B)   This option is **incorrect** because the aspect of the economy is out of scope; the economic cost arising from an issue and the economy itself are two different things.

(C)   This is the **correct** answer since reduced crime at an earlier stage in states which first legalized abortion could show that the birth of unwanted babies in other areas is correlated with higher crime in those areas for the length of time that abortion was illegal in those states. This will directly support the researchers' claims that allowing abortion reduces crime rates.

(D)   This option is **incorrect** because it is irrelevant.

(E)   This option is **incorrect** because it would instead weaken the claim.

The correct answer is C.

4.   This is an inference question.

Option D is the correct answer since the passage claims that anti-abortion legislation results in higher crime because mothers are unable to care for babies they are legally compelled to have. It is suggested that mothers do not want babies they are not ready to raise in part because they are incapable of raising them. Also, the researchers who claim that unwanted pregnancies lead to increases in crime specify that such crimes are conducted by males, and not females. Thus, those researchers assume that the un-aborted babies are more likely to be males than females, and that these males, when not properly cared for by their unwilling mothers, will resort to crimes in their adolescence or early youth.

Other options are either irrelevant or not discussed in the passage.

The correct answer is D.

5.   This is a function Question.

(A)   This option is **incorrect** because the author clearly supports the position of the researchers for reforms in abortion legislation.

(B)   This option is **incorrect** because it is irrelevant.

(C)   This option is **incorrect** because the author does not seem to weigh any of the position vis-a-vis others.

(D)   This option is **incorrect** because it is an extreme option. Though the author assumes that moral debates on economic issues like abortion cannot solely help in formulating legislation, it does not mean that they cannot help in any way in formulating legislation.

(E)   This is the **correct** answer because the passage notes that the abortion debate has ideological contentions that do not abate, and a simpler method of resolving the problem may be useful.

The correct answer is E.

6.   This is a function question.

Let us look at the given piece: *"As the ideological arguments over abortion refuse to abate, it may be time for hamstrung legislators to consider new sources of information to simplify their decision about reopening the question of abortion reform and government aid."*

Let us understand the gist: The author is against the position taken up by ideologists–anti-abortion proponents. He seems to be trying to persuade restrained legislators to consider the pro-abortion position and reach a decision on abortion reform and government aid using persuasive economic data. Thus, his main purpose seems to be to get some useful legislation made and for the debate to end.

(A)   This option is **incorrect** because it is irrelevant.

(B)   This option is **incorrect** because it is the other way around. The author seeks to simplify the abortion debate.

(C)   This option is **incorrect** because it is irrelevant.

(D)   This option is **incorrect** because it is the other way around. The author is against the position taken up by ideologists–anti-abortion proponents, and wants the debate to rather end sooner than later.

(E)   This is the **correct** answer. It falls in line with what we analyzed earlier.

The correct answer is E.

7.   This is an inference Question.

(A)   This option is **incorrect** because it is not necessarily true, since it is only abortions of **unwanted babies** that researchers assert can be reasonably correlated with lower crime.

(B)   This is the **correct** answer because it clearly articulates what researchers imply: Crime decreases and money is saved when women have freedom of choice not to give birth to unwanted children.

(C)   This option is **incorrect** because population growth is not equated with crime or the birth of unwanted babies.

(D)   This option is **incorrect** because the passage does not mention the role of non-violent females as a practical consideration in the abortion debate.

(E)   This option is **incorrect** because it is the opposite of the researchers' conclusion.

The correct answer is B.

8. This is a main point question from the general category.

    Let us look at the piece where the word "suboptimal" is used. *"Going forward with an unwanted pregnancy presumably confers on the woman too great a challenge in raising a child she is poorly prepared for, and provides the child with an upbringing that is **suboptimal**, making him more vulnerable to be party to illegal conduct."*

    Option A—Inadequate—is the correct answer since the passage communicates a condition in which children are not being provided a sufficient standard of living to assure quality of life and are poorly prepared to decline illicit opportunities for gain.

    While almost perfect, economically advantaged, and second best do not have negative undertones, inefficient is an incorrect substitute in the present context.

    The correct answer is A.

6.20   Passage 20 (Surveillance)

Understanding the Passage

This is a medium length passage of medium difficulty level on the topic of law and policy.

Secretly observing suspects has always been a tool in investigation activities over the years, but the most important difference between modern practices of surveillance and traditional practices is that in the past, the everyday routine of the accused and his social behavior were monitored, whereas currently almost everyone who is considered even remotely suspicious or likely to commit a crime is subjected to intense and unrelenting scrutiny without being aware of it. [*The author seems critical of the fact that in modern day surveillance, according to him, the extent of surveillance on the suspects is a breach of privacy.*] No less foreboding is analysis through calculations of regression and methods of associated comparison that broadens scientifically the range of 'suspicious' behavior in order to justify the oversight of new types of actors, and an increased number of actors. [*The author asserts that analyzing suspect's behavior based on his past activities and on his associations to try to estimate the current scenario is a dangerous trend. When scrutinizing a person's behavior, there may be nothing wrong with what he is currently doing, but the analysis shows that he had negative associations in his past or was close to committing a crime in the past. This is the justification that governmental agencies use to survey more and more people, bringing those people under their expanding definition of "suspicious". The author is highly critical of this behavior on the part of the government.*] These abilities are being incorporated into a policy about which the public is not aware, and one which is outside the scope of current legislation. [*People are not aware of these new trends of unscrupulous surveillance; moreover it is outside the scope of current legislation, that is, it would be considered illegal if someone other than the government were doing so.*]

Given that most people regard themselves as 'law abiding,' and that the avoidance of crime, drug abuse and other quality of life infractions rates highly in citizens' priorities, the development of improved surveillance systems is widely seen as a benign invasion that improves policing. [*Most people see themselves as 'law abiding' citizens, and though they view the increased surveillance on their life as an invasion of their privacy, they consider that it is done with noble intentions.*] In a famous incident in the UK, two young men were put under surveillance (because they had appeared suspicious as per the analyses) and were discovered to be the culprits in the murder of a young boy; following this, people in the UK began to feel that surveillance served a purpose. Since then, the most widespread use of surveillance cameras has occurred in the UK. The impracticality of, and lack of interest in, prosecuting every transgression caught by the system obscures its threat to individual liberty. [*Most people feel that it is nearly impossible to track every person's each and every activity and so feel that the invasion on their privacy is minimal.*] But while this may keep the disadvantages of surveillance from bringing people to vocal dissent [*since they feel their privacy is not really being invaded, they do not protest against the huge increase in surveillance*], what should be raised in the public consciousness is that what surveillance changes is the amount of leverage a minority of actors (authorities, bureaucrats, or system managers) have over the general population [*but they are not aware that this surveillance is impacting the negotiating/defending powers that any individual or group has against the government*]. In any encounter in which one individual must confront the state, the state achieves an advantage by having so many more 'leads' on the individual with which to use bullying tactics, and by engaging in non-judicial activities such

as Secret Service searches, the disbanding of rallies, and the detention of political and foreign activists. [*The state resorts to bullying tactics and non-judicial activities such as Secret Service searches on individuals to frame charges against them; the state can even exercise the same on political figures and foreign activists. Thus, using surveillance, any governmental authority can establish that any person "seems" suspicious and then go on to intimidate that person, even if no actual proof of any wrongdoing is present.*]

Compiling a file of criminal activities engaged in by a subject under surveillance is routine. But there can also be an insinuation of an activity that a government uses politically to undermine the position of a subject. [*Though keeping a record of criminal activities of people is routine, at times the authorities use the surveillance records to imply that someone has done something wrong without any actual proof of anything at all.*] That action changes the direction of prosecution, reiterating the importance of, and the reasoning behind, such safeguards as the Miranda acts, designed to protect suspects from incriminating themselves in the absence of their lawyer. [*Due to these kinds of practices, the intention of prosecution takes the wrong course, and the very purpose of the Miranda acts (which are designed to prevent suspects from incriminating themselves in the absence of their lawyer) is lost because just doing anything can be construed as suspicious by the government and held against the person, thereby restricting the person's freedom and rights.*] The greatest danger is that the rules of criminal justice can be controlled by a bureaucratic, authoritarian organization to prolong detention and to control the flow of information under conditions of the confinement of a subject, in order to improve the ability of investigators to aid the prosecution. [*The greatest danger of these practices is that the rules of criminal justice can be controlled and influenced by authorities; these authorities unduly harass suspects and try to manipulate the case in order to aid the prosecution by using the surveillance records to delay the freeing of the persons and keeping them in jail, etc. to help the police and prosecuting lawyers in making a better case.*] The monopoly which public bureaucracies have on prosecution and investigation allows them to use or disregard official rules in ways that are not transparent to a defendant. [*These new trends of unscrupulous surveillance do not pay respect to the official rules and, sadly, it is not known to the accused that they are being cheated on account of this, since effectively it is the government breaking the rules, and the public isn't aware of such thing.*] It has been shown that increasing the level of surveillance in the public arena does not improve the ability to identify offenders, but improves the ability of the government to operate extra-judicially. This offers authorities the opportunity of manufacturing opportunities for themselves to control behavior in ways that are beyond redress. [*On the contrary, it has been noticed that increasing the level of surveillance on the public does not improve the state's ability to identify offenders, but it unjustifiably improves the ability of the government to operate above the law and force people into legal battles against which the people have barely any defenses.*]

The passage is about government and authorities exercising extra-judicial power in the guise of increased surveillance on people. They influence the case against the defendants. By way of increased surveillance, the authorities invade the privacy of people. The author is clearly against the current trend. The innocent people are not aware of the fact that the state does not have any right to infringe upon their lives and make use of evidence collected through unauthorized means against them.

Main Point: The state exercising extra-judicial power in the guise of increased surveillance on people and influencing prosecution.

1. This is a main point question from the general category.

    This is a main point question. We have extracted the main point already. The passage notes that the biggest danger posed by the government regarding defendants is its ability to aid the prosecution in ways which are outside the realm of legal review.

    Let us review each option one by one.

    (A) This option is **incorrect**. Though it is correct that the author is concerned about the ability of the state to record the activity of everybody, it is not the main concern. The repercussions arising from the ability to record the activity of everybody is the main concern– the ability of the government to influence prosecution.

    (B) This option is **incorrect**. Like option A, though it is correct that the author is concerned that people are unaware about the surveillance performed on them, it is not the main concern. The repercussions arising from the ability to record the activity of everybody is the main concern– the ability of the government to influence prosecution.

    (C) This is the **correct** answer. It follows the analysis we made earlier.

    (D) This option is **incorrect**. It is a concern of tertiary importance.

    (E) This option is **incorrect**. Like option D, it is a concern of tertiary importance.

    The correct answer is C.

2. This is a detail question.

    (A) This option is **incorrect**. The passage does not exactly support this. Though people view increased surveillance as a benign invasion, it does not function as consent from them. They do see it as an invasion, though benign.

    (B) This option is **incorrect**. On the contrary, people view increased surveillance as a benign invasion.

    (C) This option is **incorrect** because the passage states that otherwise most people are largely law-abiding.

    (D) This is the **correct** answer since it is supported by the statement that people are unaware of all aspects of the policy of government surveillance and how it can be used to manipulate legal battles between individuals and the state.

    (E) Like option A, the passage does not exactly support this. Though people view increased surveillance as a benign invasion, it does not mean that they find it beneficial to them. At best, they may think of it as a necessary evil.

    The correct answer is D.

3. This is a detail question.

    Option B is the correct answer since the passage notes that the power of the government in the area of prosecution lies in its ability to work around safeguards and to manipulate

bureaucracy against a suspect's legal rights. The passage also shows concerns over the ability of the government to influence prosecution. The passage states that the increased surveillance does not aid in tracking down more criminals.

Option A is close but incorrect because the author implies that the surveillance is being used unfairly against citizens who are suspects, not just against criminals. Thus, we cannot infer option A.

Other options are either not stated in the passage or are not inferable.

The correct answer is B.

4.   This is an inference question.

Option C is the correct answer. It is supported in the passage by the statement: "*the state achieves an advantage by having so many more 'leads' on the individual with which to use bullying tactics, and by engaging in non-judicial activities.*" It implies that the state partially operates outside the law.

Option A not does not qualify to be inferable because, though the author is concerned about the extra-judicial power of the state, it does not mean that the government should be able to police itself to avoid overstepping its powers. However it can be inferred that government should not resort to unreasonable surveillance. In fact, the author seems to prove that the government has not been able to correct itself, and has resorted to using this illegal means to get control over suspects.

Other options are either non-inferable or are irrelevant.

The correct answer is C.

5.   This is a detail question.

Option B is the correct answer. It is supported by the statement that the state improves its ability to "operate extra-judicially" and act in ways that are without redress. Also, the author calls the "state-actors, government authorities" the minorities, that is, a small part of the population. He accuses the minority of using surveillance to infringe upon the rights of the unaware public.

Other options are either not stated in the passage or are not inferable.

The correct answer is B.

6. This is an inference question.

   (A) This option is **incorrect** because though after the UK boy's murder case most people in the UK approved of increased surveillance on them, it is invalidated by the author. He believes that the public is unaware of the real danger of increased surveillance by the government.

   (B) This option is **incorrect**. As discussed in option A, the use of surveillance is invalidated by the author.

   (C) This is the **correct** answer because the passage mentions the murder case as an example of the 'perception' of the public in regard to the benefits of surveillance in contrast to the reality of the state being able to improve its ability to prosecute the defendants it has caught. The author then goes on to explain why increased surveillance is not for the best. So, clearly, the author feels that the catching of the murderers is not a good enough reason for the government to resort to such surveillance.

   (D) This option is **incorrect** because we cannot infer this.

   (E) This option is **incorrect** because it is the opposite of what the author implies. The author feels that the increased surveillance does not help identify and track more criminals but is used by the state to intimidate and incriminate helpless citizens. Thus, the author is more likely to think that the case in which two murderers were apprehended is a one-off incident and not a reproducible result.

   The correct answer is C.

7. This is a function question.

   (A) This option is **incorrect** because it is too general and does not talk about the specific issue of surveillance.

   (B) This option is **incorrect** because it is not inferable.

   (C) This option is **incorrect**. Though the law would indirectly give defendants the opportunity to explain their side of the story better, the purpose of the law is not to achieve this.

   (D) This is the **correct** answer. It is supported by the statement that the ability of the government to change the direction of the prosecution or to improve the prosecution reinforces the need for safeguards protecting suspects from abuses in the process of investigation and trial. The author states that increased surveillance is used by the government to aid the prosecution and that it makes laws like the Miranda acts useless. Thus, laws like the Miranda acts must have been intended to limit the power of the government to aid the prosecution against citizens.

   (E) This option is **incorrect** because it is irrelevant.

   The correct answer is D.

8. This is a detail question.

   (A) This option is **incorrect** because we cannot construe that unjustifiably increased surveillance will render unreasonable punishment to offenders.

(B) This option is **incorrect** because it is not inferable.

(C) This is the **correct** answer. It is mentioned in the passage where it shows the relationship between the monopoly over prosecution and investigation and the ability that this monopoly gives to authorities to disregard official rules and manipulate the defendant. Increased surveillance without public permission and use of that to intimidate the citizen and detain him are examples of the government using its monopoly to help the prosecution.

(D) This option is **incorrect**. It is not mentioned in the passage.

(E) This option is **incorrect**. Like option D, it is not mentioned in the passage.

The correct answer is C.

6.21   Passage 21 (Reforms in the European education system)

Understanding the Passage

This is a long passage of low difficulty level on the topic of education systems.

European universities are increasingly adapting to global standards of education. The need to adapt to global standards stems from the fact that multinational corporations recruit human resources that are versatile, and not limited to a country and culture in terms of experience. German engineering schools have understood this dynamic better and are transforming themselves to the compelling need. Engineering schools elsewhere in Europe were shortsighted in assuming that engineering programs were immune to any upheaval from outside as they exclusively focused on engineering content. This shortsightedness is a clear example of how educational systems are governed by the coursework provided.

Professional schools must be concerned with their myopic attitude towards their courses. Some corporations and many international educators across engineering fields have observed some gap between students' core competencies and current needs. The main concerns of the German university system are that the courses are isolated and devoid of any interaction among the courses. Another important issue is that too few courses are taught in English. Due to the lack of availability of English courses in German engineering schools, too few international students opt for German programs. Another drawback is that if German engineering students seek to change the course midway, they feel disadvantaged. This is because they have limited experience in taking courses in other German universities, and taking engineering courses abroad is a rare possibility. Moreover, if these students were to transfer to another school, much of their course credits (points accumulated though previous programs) would not count towards a future degree in a different program, meaning they would have to start from the beginning in any new course. For these reasons, engineering education is being analyzed by all segments of society– businessmen, educators, and government officials.

To address the issue, engineering administrators have started developing course curriculum to suit the global and ever dynamic needs of students. These issues have jointly led educators to identify the need for a new Magna Carta of universities in order to turn their awareness into solutions. The outcome of this collective attention is the Bologna Declaration. [*The Magna Carta Universitatum is a document to celebrate university traditions and encourage bonds amongst European universities, though it also serves as a universal inspiration and is open to universities throughout the world. It was proposed by the University of Bologna in 1986, and has been signed by 755 universities from 80 countries*] Its recommendations are fourfold:

(1) Establish a system of comparable degrees (degrees that can be related to other international degrees) so that students can compete for other international programs.

(2) Adopt a two-tier, internationally acknowledged and widely popular system of schooling– undergraduate and graduate programs.

(3) Establish a standard credit system for classroom work.

(4) Find a way to ensure the quality of programs offered Europe-wide.

These improvements not only increase the international marketability of students, but they also increase the flexibility of students in case they choose to change direction during their university years.

The passage is about the transformation taking place in the European education system to equip students to adapt to the international education system and international market. The passage discusses the status quo in the European education system by looking at the situation in German universities–how German students face challenges with non-standardized courses offered by their universities, how a lack of courses based on the English language hampers the attractiveness of these schools for foreign students in Germany, and how compelling pressure from multiple corners–multinational corporations, international educators, and other bodies – has forced Germany to adapt to international standards.

Main Point: Reformation in the European education system to adapt to the international education system and international market.

1. This is an inference question.

    (A) This option is **incorrect** because as per the information given in passage, we cannot infer that sociology programs do not have the same difficulties as other programs.

    (B) This option is **incorrect** because nothing of this sort was mentioned in the passage.

    (C) This is the **correct** answer because the passage notes that German engineering programs are a good choice for the change because they operate according to a logic which says that they do not need to pay heed to external conditions. Thus, a discipline such as sociology, which studies a range of social conditions, would be less useful as an example, since it will pay attention to external conditions and accordingly adapt.

    (D) This option is **incorrect** because it is devoid of any logic.

    (E) This option is **incorrect** because nothing of this sort was mentioned in the passage.

    The correct answer is C.

2. This is detail question.

    Option E is the correct answer because the passage states that a major problem with the lack of instruction in English in engineering courses is that it makes it harder for students from abroad to take courses in German universities. It is supported by the passage (line 20): *"The lack of availability of English courses in German engineering schools contributes to there being a paucity of international students in German programs."* Other options are out of scope of the passage.

    The correct answer is E.

3. This is a detail question.

    The sentence is (line 27): *"For these reasons, engineering education has come under well-lit scrutiny by businessmen, educators, and government officials."*

    Option E is the correct answer because it duplicates the adjectival nature of the phrase which relays a notion of observation enacted through diligent examination by many interested parties. Also, the fact that the sentence includes diverse people like businessmen, educators, and government officials shows that the issue is being examined from multiple aspects.

    The correct answer is E.

4. This is a detail question.

    The passage uses the word "paucity" in the following sentence (line 21): *"The lack of availability of English courses in German engineering schools contributes to there being a paucity of international students in German programs."* The critics are concerned about a significantly smaller number of international students in German programs.

    Option B is the correct answer because "paucity" means a smallness of number or quantity.

    The correct answer is B.

5. This is an inference question.

    Option C is the correct answer since the passage asserts that the vocational inflexibility in the German education system makes it difficult for German students to be mobile outside the system. The author advocates that students must have liberty to even change the direction of their course. Thus, the author feels that courses should be flexible enough to allow students to interact with other disciplines, and even switch to another field if they wish so.

    Option A, B, and D are not discussed in the passage. Regarding option E, the author does not mean that by advocating to provide flexibility in choosing courses, and by incorporating courses in English, that students should be encouraged to work outside of their national origins. It implies that students must have flexibility in choosing their career effectively and nothing should impede that.

    The correct answer is C.

6. This is a detail question.

We listed the Bologna Declaration's recommendations in the Understanding the Passage section; in short the four recommendations were:

(1) Establish a system of comparable degrees

(2) Adopt a two tier system of schooling–undergraduate and graduate programs

(3) Establish a standard credit system for classroom work

(4) Find a way to ensure the quality of programs offered Europe-wide

(A) This is the **correct** answer as it encompasses all four declarations made in Bologna.

(B) This option is **incorrect** because nothing of this sort was under the purview of the Bologna Declaration.

(C) Like option B, this option is **incorrect** because nothing of this sort was under the purview of the Bologna Declaration.

(D) This option is tricky, but **incorrect** because the Bologna Declaration does not enlist this objective. Its main objective is to standardize the educational system in Europe as agreed upon by the concerned parties.

(E) This option is **incorrect** because it is irrelevant.

The correct answer is A.

7. This is an inference question.

We have to choose an option that articulates the author's concern about "the unlikelihood of engineering students ever changing their course of study".

(A) This option is **incorrect** because the author states otherwise.

(B) Like option B, this option is **incorrect** because the author states otherwise.

(C) This option is **incorrect** because nothing of this sort is inferable.

(D) This option is tricky, but **incorrect** because the author does not imply that engineering schools need to be concerned with the potential in other fields of study. Other fields may have potential, but so does the engineering field. The author advocates that if students wish to opt out of engineering courses, they must have flexibility in doing so.

(E) This is the **correct** answer because it correctly expresses the concern.

The correct answer is E.

8. This is a detail question.

The reference to 'mobile' was made in the first part of the first paragraph (line 2): "*European universities must answer the perceived needs of **multinational corporations**, as these firms aspire to draw on an employee base that is borderless, and highly **mobile**.*"

Option E is the correct answer because some of the main actors with an interest in re-evaluating the German education system are large corporations in need of having access to a wide labor pool, and students who seek to increase their options in the workforce. Other options are out of the scope of the passage.

The correct answer is E.

6.22   Passage 22 (The U.S.'s Nuclear Energy Program)

Understanding the Passage

This is a long passage of low difficulty level on the topic of nuclear energy.

In 1957, the U.S. invested in mining the atom to make it useful as a source of energy, and for engineering and military revolution. Up to that point, atomic energy was utilized for the development of more powerful weapons of mass destruction, warships, and submersibles. The U.S. Atomic Energy Commission (AEC) took the initiative to develop peaceful applications of modern nuclear power (a source of abundant energy for domestic use). Moreover, under the guise of noble intentions, scientists could carry out other development, primarily to manufacture Cold War armaments. The AEC later named the partly noble and partly treacherous program the "Plowshare Program"–implying noble intentions.

In Aug 1958, the AEC selected Ogotoruk Creek as the site for the detonation of an atomic bomb *(A gulf was chosen to test an atomic bomb)*. The rationale behind testing an atomic bomb was political and practical. The AEC had decided to disguise the discussion of nuclear weapons by pairing nuclear arms with civil engineering. They reasoned that if nuclear energy could prove to be a boon to civil engineering, then using nuclear energy for Cold War purposes – such as making nuclear weapons – and nuclear ground testing could be portrayed positively and the public's negative opinion towards these things could be reduced. The AEC played clever and named their plan "Operation Plowshare". The name "Plowshare" was deliberately chosen as it referred to the holy prose–"beat their swords into plowshares". [*It is a concept in which military weapons or technologies are converted for peaceful civilian applications. The plowshare is often used to symbolize creative tools that benefit mankind, as opposed to destructive tools of war, symbolized by the sword, a similar sharp metal tool with an arguably opposite use–that of plowing the earth and farming.*] The AEC presented atomic technology as an engineering wonder, the driver of future development in the U.S..

Russia's successful launch of the Sputnik I satellite into space panicked the U.S. To outdo Russia, America's scientific and engineering team proposed an "earth excavation" program to demonstrate the U.S.'s impressive and beneficial applications of America's existing nuclear capabilities. It advised detonating a 2.4 megaton atomic device on the northwest coast of Alaska. The supposed purpose was to create a deep water hole to facilitate the shipping of coal, timber, and oil from one part to another. The detonation had the apparently noble intention of developing Alaska's coastal state. This proposal was accepted by the AEC, who named it 'Project Chariot'. The plan was marketed to Alaska's financial community and lawmakers, but they remained unconvinced of the plan's commercial viability. The AEC then attempted to sell the plan to the U.S. Congress as a unique opportunity to impress the Congress with what nuclear energy could do for the country. However, a local unit objected to the plan and wrote to the President about not continuing with the plan as they were skeptical about heavy metals leaking into the ground and water, and about radiation in the environment. Due to this, Project Chariot was dumped and replaced by less visible projects (thus less under public scrutiny) and these projects would be revealed to the common public many decades later.

Main Point: The highs and the lows of the U.S.'s maiden nuclear energy program.

1. This is a detail question.

   Option C is the correct answer because the passage mentions that the AEC sought to "bowdlerize" (line 14) (censor) the contemporary discussion on nuclear weapons. The implication is that they wanted to increase the positive comments regarding nuclear weapons by naming it "Operation Plowshare"–implying a program of noble intentions, and reduce the public's negative sentiments against it.

   Options A, B, and E are out of scope and option D is opposite of what is meant after naming the program "Operation Plowshare".

   The correct answer is C.

2. This is a detail question.

   The phrase is used here: *"Their preferred advice was to detonate a 2.4 megaton atomic device on the northwest coast of Alaska, to create a deep water hole facilitating the shipping of coal, timber, and oil, while developing Alaska's coast, with **obvious benefits for the 48 mainland U.S. states.**"* The detonation was meant to provide much better access to coal, timer, and oil (resources) with the use of an under-water tunnel.

   Option B is the best answer because the sentence refers to the development of Alaska's coast.

   The correct answer is B.

3. This is a detail question.

   Option C is the best answer since the passage discusses the AEC conducting a "reconnaissance" (inspection) of the area, a physical scan by reconnaissance personnel on location.

   Option D is close, but incorrect as the passage does not mention anything about cartographic research and topographical comparisons for the selection of the creek. So, we cannot assume that option D is necessarily true.

   The correct answer is C.

4. This is an inference question.

   (A) This is the **correct** answer because if scientists interested in Sputnik's successful launch wanted to engage in "one-upmanship", it can be assumed that the statement being made about the Sputnik accomplishment is the thing which these actors consider important. The American scientists felt the need to retaliate (as a reply)

by showing America's superiority in nuclear science. Thus, the American scientists clearly viewed Sputnik I as a political claim by the Russians on the world stage, as part of the one-upmanship game in the Cold War era.

(B) This option is **incorrect** because the scientists were not limited to regarding Sputnik I as merely a scientific achievement; they did engage in "one-upmanship" with a counter nuclear program.

(C) With the same reasoning as cited in option B, this option is **incorrect**.

(D) This option is **incorrect** because the scientists did regard Sputnik I seriously (not as specious [fake] showmanship). They did engage in "one-upmanship" with a counter nuclear program.

(E) This option is **incorrect** because nothing of this sort can be inferred from the passage.

The correct answer is A.

5. This is a tone question from the general category.

Option A is the correct answer because the AEC was seeking to improve the reputation of nuclear weapons. This implies that the American public had a negative perception of nuclear weapons and testing. The AEC felt that teaming nuclear arms with civil engineering could dilute the intense public skepticism towards above ground nuclear testing. This implies that people in general were doubtful (skeptical) about nuclear weapons testing and held it in a negative light.

The correct answer is A.

6. This is a detail question.

(A) This option is **incorrect** because it is not evident from the passage that President Kennedy disapproved of the project.

(B) This is the **correct** answer because the passage notes that the AEC shut down the program because they had reconsidered the reaction their project would earn them, thus implying that they would not be able to carry pro-nuclear favor from continuing their program and thus should not continue "Operation Plowshare" by pursuing Project Chariot. This is also evidenced by the great number of negative reactions they received, thus dashing the AEC's hope of whitewashing the nuclear programs issue.

(C) This option is **incorrect** because only after being termed commercially unviable was the project sent to the president for consideration.

(D) This option is **incorrect** because nothing of this sort was discussed in the passage.

(E) This option is **incorrect** because it cannot necessarily be inferred from the passage. We know that there are negative opinions expressed by detractors of the programs, but not necessarily that they indulged in politics.

The correct answer is B.

7.   This is a tone question from the general category.

Option A is the correct answer because the inventors of "Operation Plowshare" were politically motivated in "spinning" the perception of nuclear weapons with positive images,
and thus were seeking politically savvy (shrewd and clever) methods of influencing the
discussion on nuclear weapons.

The correct answer is A.

8.   This is an application question from the reasoning category.

We discussed in the "Understanding the Passage" section that the AEC played clever and
named their plan "Operation Plowshare". The name "Plowshare" was deliberately chosen
as it referred to the holy prose–**"beat their swords into plowshares"**. [*It is a concept in
which military weapons or technologies are converted for peaceful civilian applications.
**The plowshare is often used to symbolize creative tools that benefit mankind, as
opposed to destructive tools of war, symbolized by the sword, a similar sharp metal
tool with an arguably opposite use.** Thus, a plowshare refers to using a negative, or evil,
object, such as a sword and turning it into an object of good, such as a plow, meant to
yield good deeds like farming.*]

From the above analysis, it is evident that "beat their swords into plowshares" means
"turn evil (sword: a destructive tool) into good (plowshare: a useful tool):".

The correct answer is B.

6.23   Passage 23 (Mechanized production systems in Europe)

Understanding the Passage

This is a long passage of medium difficulty level on the topic of business and processes.

During the 1870s, industrializing nations went through radical technological challenges. However these nations followed drastically different approaches to leverage on their productive capacity and carry on industrial development. Manufacturing companies decided that their best bet was to rationalize the production process and thus weighed the pros and cons of mechanization of production. However, such mechanization debates had no clear winning side and were subject to numerous debates.

Though many industries in many countries anticipated some benefits from mechanization (production with the help of machines and a mass production process using assembly lines rather than only manual input, i.e. labor making each article personally), the rationality of increasing production while reducing production costs was still debated. The mechanization side of the debate was not winning with a clear margin.

German printing and textile firms showed why industrialization was not a cut and dried process (a simple process that is followed according to a plan, set procedure, or formula). *[It implies that there is no standard procedure to augment industrialization and such a decision cannot be taken lightly].* In the meantime, German and Austrian companies transitioned to mechanical production from hand-work of printed cotton handkerchiefs (handcrafted articles).

These great handcrafted articles made by certain regional manufacturers let them make their mark in the international market. Few German firms obtained the ability to double and triple production while reducing their work force; however, there were some risks in adopting mechanization. While this new mechanized order did bring a substantial drop in the total remuneration of labor (reduced salary costs), it also significantly lowered the sale price and raised risks of overproduction. *[Though machination reduces labor cost, it usually results in mass production, resulting in overproduction. Such developments lead to a fall in sale prices, and can also cause demand to fall because of oversupply.]* Head over heels *['Head over heels' is now most often used as part of 'head over heels in love'. When first coined, it wasn't used that way though, and referred exclusively to **being temporarily the wrong way up**. It is one of many similar phrases that we use to describe **things that are not in their usual state - 'upside-down', 'topsy-turvy'**, etc.]* (Topsy-turvy) production of items *[excessive production of items]* did not pay attention to the ability of the market to absorb such overproduction, and this resulted in negative impressions about products on the market. *[The author implies that when companies rushed into mechanization, replaced labor, and started producing items at double the speed, they did not pay attention to the market (specifically the demand and other factors that factored into the demand). This oversupply and lack of attention to the market brought about negative impressions about those products (which would result in falling demand)].*

The failure of double-printed 'Turkish bonnets' (a kind of skull cap) in the marketplace is an example of why fast and cheap production techniques are not necessarily the best means of production for established manufacturers. The market experienced a sudden unpredictable drop in the demand for these bonnets. Before manufacturers could react to the changed

preferences of customers (due to mass production through mechanized process), a large inventory was already there in the market with no takers for the same, resulting in huge losses. The crisis was aggravated due to a monetary crisis in eastern markets. This led to unrest in the industry, and stakeholders started contemplating the efficacy of the new production order.

Only a few regions adopted mechanization because the sentiment towards it was skeptical. The American production system was solely based on standardization, mechanization, and mass production and it did not seem to face the problems that others had, and the American system had drawn European attention to standardized production, which did offer an increase in profits while reducing labor costs and control unpredictability in production. The lessons from the case of the 'Turkish bonnets' imply that the American system of production, since its inception, overlooked some pitfalls arising from standardization, mechanization, and mass production techniques. However, the American system was abreast of the conditions of the world market and was not untouched by them. Unlike printing and textile firms in Germany and Turkey, manufacturers of watches in Switzerland, of scarves in Germany, and weavers in Glarus did not adopt the new mechanized American system. This differential adoption of the manufacturing process *(in which some adopted mechanization and some did not)* brought about "class formation" *[mechanized classes and unmechanized ones]* and caused class disparity. It also resulted in capital rigidity *(when there are two choices with no obvious better one, instead of choosing one of the two choices, the investors choose neither and capital is either frozen or unavailable–capital rigidity).* This class disparity and capital rigidity would become built-in pressure points on the American economy *(that is, eventually the American economy would face these challenges as well).* Also due to these challenges, many European producers could not develop a consistent, reproducible system of mechanization. *[This incomplete adoption of mechanization prevented Europe from developing a uniform production method.]*

Main Point: Europe's response to mechanization in the industrialization process.

1. This is a main Point question from the general category.

    We have already derived the main point of the passages. Option E is the correct answer because the passage discusses the pros and cons of strategies of industrialization.

    Option E is the correct answer because the passage discusses varied responses from European companies to industrialization. "Some were camphor and some were wet wood" is used as a metaphor which implies that a few companies were like camphor (camphor catches fire instantly), meaning that a few German and a few Austrian companies adopted industrialization quickly while Switzerland and Glarus were like wet wood, implying that they did not adopt industrialization (wet wood has a hard time catching fire)".

    Other options are either too narrow in scope or are irrelevant.

    The correct answer is E.

2. This is an inference question.

(A) This option is **incorrect** because nothing of this sort (related to a national war machine) was even discussed in the passage.

(B) Like option A, this option is **incorrect** because nothing of this sort (related to processed sugar) was even discussed in the passage.

(C) This option is **incorrect** because we cannot infer that the author would agree that industries must exercise protectionism, implying no need to change and interfere in the markets to protect domestic companies. The author advocates that industries must evaluate whether industrialization or mechanization is beneficial for them or not. If it benefits an industry, the industry must follow it.

(D) This is the **correct** answer because the passage discusses the risk of overproduction in the middle of the second paragraph (line 15): *"But risks accompanied this methodology-presented risks of **overproduction.**"*

(E) This option is **incorrect** because as discussed in option D, the author is concerned about overproduction.

The correct answer is D.

3. This is a detail question.

Option E is the correct answer because the passage shows that a monetary crisis in eastern markets caused problems in the industry. It was cited in the example of "Turkish bonnets". The problem was exacerbated when demand fell and preferences changed. So, the author used the example of the bonnet market in Turkey to explain how local markets and preferences can be unfavorable for industrialization.

Other options are not relevant to the question.

The correct answer is E.

4.   This is a detail question.

Option D is the correct answer since the section of the passage discussing bonnets, which were produced using standardized mass production techniques, refers to over-production as a major problem the producers faced.

Option E is incorrect as the alienation of the workforce resulted due to low demand and high supply of bonnets. It is not the threat posed by standardization.

The correct answer is D.

5.   This is a function question.

   (A)   This option is **incorrect** because on the contrary, overproduction of bonnets, un-matched with the preferences of customers, had a poor sale.

   (B)   This option is **incorrect** because it is the other way around. The example of the bonnet emphasizes that it is relevant to discuss technological advances in indus-trialization keeping in mind market conditions.

   (C)   This option is **incorrect** because we cannot necessarily infer this.

   (D)   This option is **incorrect** because it is the other way around. The example of the bonnet emphasizes that it is important to conduct market research. Turkish bonnet makers had to pay the price for ignoring this aspect.

   (E)   This is the **correct** answer because it is demonstrated by the drop in demand. The producers should have reacted to this change by reducing production of items that were no longer sought after. Instead, technological advances gave them the opportunity to increase production but decreased their reaction rate, and, as a result, they were left with a big inventory while the demand dropped.

The correct answer is E.

6.   This is an inference question.

Option D is the correct answer because the last part of the passage states (line 32): *"the American system was not uniquely immune to the conditions of the world market. Manufacturers of watches in Switzerland, of scarves in Germany and weavers in 19th century Glarus were reserved about their approval of change."* This implies that America faced problems in standardizing industrialization. Not all European manufacturers went for standardized industrialization because they were aware of these potential dangers.

Other options do not qualify to be correct.

The correct answer is D.

7.   This is an inference question.

(A)   This option is **incorrect** because the opinion of self-interested parties was not discussed in the passage.

(B)   This option is **incorrect** because the passage does not discuss the impact on socialized countries.

(C)   This is the **correct** answer because through the example of the bonnet, the passage states that technological improvements can create economic difficulties as well, something that was unanticipated initially.

(D)   This option is **incorrect** because competitive pressure from industrializing nations is not discussed in the passage.

(E)   This option is **incorrect** because social agendas are out of the scope of the passage.

The correct answer is C.

8.   This is a main Point question from the general category.

We have already derived the main point of the passage: "Pros and cons of the evolution of industrialization in Europe."

We will discuss each option one by one.

(A)   This option is **incorrect** because it focuses more on America, while the passage focuses on comparing industrial models.

(B)   This option is **incorrect** because it would be a good title for a passage discussing different examples of industry in detail, rather than comparing the pros and cons of industrial models.

(C)   This is the **correct** answer because the passage discusses uneven responses from European companies to industrialization. "A few German and a few Austrian companies adopted industrialization quickly while Switzerland and Glarus did not adopt industrialization."

(D)   Like option A, this option is **incorrect** because it focuses more on America than on industrial models.

(E)   This option is **incorrect** because it would be an appropriate title for a passage discussing the advantages of industrial rationalization, rather than discussing the advantages and disadvantages of standardization for different industries.

The correct answer is C.

6.24   Passage 24 (Gangsta rap)

Understanding the Passage

This is a long passage of medium difficulty level on the topic of society and culture.

Gangsta rap is a form of gangster lifestyle rap music; its lyrics are based on violence, pleasure-seeking behavior, and hatred against women. Usually Gangsta rap is found on the American West Coast, but the term "Hip-hop" is broader and encompasses a mixture of many styles. It is unclear whether the violence in gangsta rap is actually based on real violent incidents. *[the discussion of graphic violence and a "don't-care-about-society's-rules" attitude are trademarks of gangsta rap].* When such traits were packaged with smooth technical production, it helped West Coast rap to distinguish itself within Hip Hop music.*[Hip Hop music is a mixture of different styles.]*

Gangsta rap made California famous in music circles by demonstrating that it could be the birthplace of music with lyrics that are based on societal issues prevalent in African-American society. With great music, it made its mark on people. Traditionally, rap was rooted on the East Coast, but Gangsta rap differentiated itself from East Coast rap with the use of commercial production style. (Los Angeles had an extensive music post-production industry making wide use of synthesizers). The combination of Los Angeles' advanced technical production methods and lyrics based on socio-economic and racial messages branded Gangsta rap as a uniquely West Coast style of music. Gangsta rappers had an impatient and militant attitude which arose from the bitter experiences of facing disadvantage and racism. However this helped them to be differentiated from the East Coast artists.

Initially all West Coast rap was branded as Gangsta rap, but audiences appreciated Gangsta rap as a distinguished form of rap music. This made it possible for Hip Hop to solidify its foothold in American music.

The evolution of Hip Hop music occurred among the economically lower class in smaller downtown areas of the American East Coast. Previously, this style of music, with a heavy emphasis on rhyming and high decibel beat, had been universally identified as Hip Hop. But this identity was challenged by the rap group N.W.A.'s Straight Outta Compton's different style. Compton's aggressive, minimalist sound were much different from the traditional conventions of rap. Compton's lyrics were based on living on excesses and merciless criticism of American society. It is alleged that American society exploited American blacks who were always at a disadvantage, and these unfair realities were reflected in the group's songs. This led to a very different style of Hip Hop, something which could not be classified into what was traditionally considered Hip Hop.

Despite such hate messages towards American society and the highly commercial production style of this music, Gangsta rap became a commercial hit. However, rap fanatics who valued conventional Hip Hop for its authenticity and popularity respected Gangsta rap music despite its being heavily dominated by smooth, modern production techniques (something that traditional Hip Hop had stayed away from). These rappers started attracting a huge fan base, expanding into the mainstream while maintaining its traditional fan base. One of the artists, Dr. Dre, used funky music that had originated in disco. He mixed it with a "canned beat"

(a heavy sound that was popular in California) with which he blanketed his message (lyrics) which made him reach the general public. The combination helped Hip Hop to appeal to a more varied audience. This helped listeners to appreciate Gangsta rap's lyricism and musical production style on its own terms rather than solely measuring it against the yardstick of East Coast rap. Once West Coast rap was acknowledged as a unique style, fans were able to compare the quality of East Coast and West Coast rap.

Main Point: The evolution of the American West Coast's maverick Gangsta rap.

1. This is a main Point question from the general category.

   (A) This option is **incorrect** because the passage discusses rhyming as a characteristic of traditional rap; it is not the main reason Gangsta rap became commercially successful.

   (B) This option is **incorrect** because though Gangsta rap's appeal to rap aficionados is acknowledged in the passage, rap aficionados were only a portion of the music's ultimate audience.

   (C) This is the **correct** answer because Gangsta rap became successful by integrating both these factors–commercial production techniques and biting social observations–into its music.

   (D) This option is **incorrect** because it is not mentioned in the passage.

   (E) This option is **incorrect** because the passage does not discuss the work done by vocalists in post-production.

   The correct answer is C.

2. This is a detail question.

   (A) This option is **incorrect** because the passage does not mention that audiences were confused by gangsta rap.

   (B) This option is **incorrect** because the passage does not mention any disconnect between critical and commercial success for gangsta rap.

   (C) This option is **incorrect** because the passage does not talk of gangsta rap as only black art. Lyrics were based on problems faced by blacks but that does not mean that the genre was exclusively made up of black artists.

   (D) This is the **correct** answer because the passage mentions that the imagery of violence "enabled West Coast rap to distinguish itself within Hip Hop music" and develop into a complete genre by itself.

   (E) This option is **incorrect** because it was the coupling of indulgence and social activism which resulted in the "gangsta rap" moniker.

   The correct answer is D.

3. This is a detail question.

    (A) This option is **incorrect** because gangsta rap was a part of Hip Hop; it differentiated itself within Hip Hop but did not contrast with Hip Hop.

    (B) This option is **incorrect** because the passage does not discuss the alienation of audiences.

    (C) This is the **correct** answer. Refer to the first paragraph (line 3): *"While it is unclear whether the violence in gangsta rap-,when packaged with **smooth technical production, enabled West Coast rap to distinguish itself within Hip Hop music.**"* It is clear that it made it possible to discuss gangsta rap as a new style.

    (D) This option is **incorrect** because gangsta rap appealed to a more heterogeneous audience and achieved commercial success.

    (E) This option is **incorrect** because the street credibility of gangsta rap was maintained despite its use of slick production techniques.

    The correct answer is C.

4. This is a tone question from the general category.

    (A) This option is **incorrect** because the author does not argue for or against gangsta rap; he is not judgmental or opinionated.

    (B) This option is **incorrect** because the author does not view the hedonism and misogyny of gangsta rap merely as tools to achieve the purpose of gangsta rap. He does not suggest any such thing.

    (C) This option is **incorrect** because though the author questions whether these aspects of gangsta rap have a real basis, he does not question the sincerity of their use in songs.

    (D) This is the **correct** answer because the author dispassionately acknowledges a relationship between these aspects of gangsta rap and its rise.

    (E) This option is **incorrect** because it is too general a statement.

    The correct answer is D.

5. This is an inference question.

    (A) This option is **incorrect** because it is not supported by the passage.

    (B) This option is **incorrect** because it is not supported by the passage.

    (C) This is the **correct** answer because the passage indicates that the music industry in L.A. was long established and made use of such methods, thus it can be concluded that this style had been popularly received and was useful in establishing "Gangsta Rap" as a popular medium. Also, the passage gives the example of Dr. Dre using canned beats despite their origins in disco because he knew it was familiar for the audience and a good vehicle for his message.

    (D) This option is **incorrect** because it makes a connection between synthesized beats and corporate oversight that is not supported by the passage.

    (E) This option is **incorrect** because it is not mentioned in the passage.

    The correct answer is C.

6.25   Passage 25 (Women's contraceptives)

Understanding the Passage

This is a long passage of medium difficulty level on the topic of health and wellness.

When an organization launches a product, the number of potential consumers is an important aspect to assess the potential of profits. However, it is not the only variable that needs to be taken into consideration. Even though a given product may be very useful and people could be willing to buy it, the effect of that product on a corporation's image and the public's goodwill towards that product is not a guarantee to make it commercially successful. *[It is contrary to normal belief that if a product is desirable and people at large long for it that when it makes great sales, a company's image will increase in direct proportion.]* Some corporations use loss-leader products to increase the profits of unrelated products through their benefits to branding. *[A loss leader is a pricing strategy where a product is sold at a much lower price to stimulate other sales of more profitable goods or services. For example, in some countries where the advertising of liquor products is restricted, companies advertise and sell music CDs with the same brand name as a popular brand of liquor at throw-away prices with the hidden objective of promoting their liquor brand.]* Corporations are equally aware of the fact that successful products which can hurt the company's image will hurt the sales of other products, and thereby the corporation may fail to grow in a market due to political interference from pressure groups that have political clout.

The above phenomenon is observed in the American contraceptive industry. Research indicates that women need more choices of contraceptives. Despite dire need, corporations deliberately do not launch many contraceptives on the market and leave them hanging in the R&D phase. The corporations' ploy not to launch a variety of female contraceptives shows that females are neglected and not treated on par with male consumers. Unlike men, who have a single, relatively simple, and effective measure of contraception, women have varied needs so many alternatives must be made available to them to suit their lifestyles, sexual appetites, and personal habits.

Unlike men, it is women are at risk of an unwanted pregnancy, so they are more worried about protecting themselves from the result of their sexual relations. For a woman, it is better to be prepared with her own contraceptive than to rely on her male partner's likelihood of carrying a condom with him. Despite the fact that women have pressing needs, Americans do not wish to talk about sex as a routine thing. This makes women search for options privately to protect themselves from unintended circumstances (i.e. unwanted pregnancy). Based on this, conservative pharmaceutical corporations do not make and market innovatively designed female contraceptives as they are scared about the reactions and political influence of anti-contraceptive extremist pro-life groups, religious organizations, and prominent members of the Republican party. Such political groups can affect a corporation's success with other products or even make it politically difficult for the corporation to exist freely in the market. Women are deprived of many innovatively designed contraceptives due to the intimidating presence of a minority of well-organized non-consumer groups determining product availability *[Women do not get the contraceptive choices that they should because the conservative groups who are pro-life and such political organizations control the political power and indirectly keep the companies from releasing the products through intimidation].* The solution

to this paradox *[the paradox is that there is a demand that is not met with apt products.]* is not only to preach that corporations need to pursue the orthodoxy of their own free market rewards *[that means one should not just say that free-market ideology is best, but should also practice free-market ideology in which the market demands **only** determine what products a company makes and provides]*. *[Thus,]* corporations must also create an open environment to talk about the real sexual lifestyles of women, and make available for women products of their choice while ignoring the pressure groups–extremist pro-life groups, religious organizations,and prominent members of the Republican party.

Main Point: The unavailability of varied choices of female contraceptives despite a dire need.

1. This is a detail question.

    Option E is the correct answer since the passage notes that while loss leader products are valuable for the branding (publicity) of surrogate products though they lose money, corporations are wary of profitable products that have negative effects on other products, which is why many companies don't provide contraceptives even though there is a huge demand for such products (because they fear the negative publicity associated with it).

    The correct answer is E.

2. This is an inference question.

    (A) This is the **correct** answer, as can be seen from the phrase (line 14): *"The unwillingness of corporations to supply female consumers with their products of choice"*.

    (B) This option is **incorrect** because it is contradicted by the fact that it is women's "products of choice" of which they are being deprived. Also, the passage implies that the corporations don't bring out the contraceptives because they fear the negative publicity, despite a great demand for such products. Thus, it is given that the consumers (women) would receive the products well.

    (C) This option is **incorrect** because it is not mentioned in the passage.

    (D) This option is **incorrect** because it assumes more than what is written in the passage. It is not necessarily true. The passage merely states that the contraceptives may cause losses in other products of the same company because of negative publicity and not because of the reason mentioned in the option.

    (E) This option is **incorrect** because it is not mentioned in the passage.

    The correct answer is A.

3. This is an inference question.

    Option E is the correct answer. It is supported by the sentence (line 29): *"Based on this, it is evident that conservative pharmaceutical corporations are laden with fear over the reaction of extremist pro-life groups, religious organizations, and prominent*

members of the Republican Party to increased research and even successful marketing of contraceptive alternatives."

Pharmaceutical corporations feel that it is a risk to introduce and market new products, as they fear the reaction from pressure groups. And because of their unwillingness to bear that risk (i.e. they are averse to risk), the products never enter the market even though there is a demand for such products.

The correct answer is E.

4. This is an inference question.

    Option D is the correct answer because it can be derived from the sentences (line 17): *"women are afforded a cornucopia (many) of alternatives which suit their **lifestyles, sexual appetites, and personal habits**. However, for women's sake, this patchwork of options should never be viewed as too varied or as colorful enough."* Thus, the author feels that, owing to women's physiological differences, women need plenty of contraceptive choices, and there aren't enough on the market.

    Other options are not supported by the passage.

    The correct answer is D.

5. This is an inference question.

    (A) This option is **incorrect** because it is not mentioned in the passage. In fact, the author propagates free-market ideology in the end.

    (B) This option is **incorrect** because it is the opposite view of the author. The author agrees that political influence from those such as Republicans and others stifle the market of much needed contraceptives.

    (C) This option is **incorrect** because it is not mentioned in the passage.

    (D) This is the **correct** answer since it can be accounted for by the sentence (line 32): *"The enormous market of consumers who would welcome convenient alternatives to –continue to wait much longer than necessary for such products on account of the intimidating presence of a minority of well-organized non-consumer groups."* The author advocates that women are deprived of varied contraceptives because corporations are scared of the backlash and negative publicity.

    (E) This option is **incorrect** because it is not mentioned in the passage.

    The correct answer is D.

6. This is a detail question.

(A) This is the **correct** answer since the passage is concerned with the inability of Americans to discuss sex in a natural way. This allows anti-contraceptive groups to have a more vocal and organized presence that prevents more contraceptive products from entering the market.

(B) This option is **incorrect** because increased purchasing of current products may not encourage corporations to diversify.

(C) This option is **incorrect** because if men took more responsibility for sex it would presumably be less risky for women to be sexually active, given that the passage indicates that one reason women need an array of contraceptive options is because it is unsafe to rely on their partners for contraceptive availability.

(D) This option is **incorrect** since it would discourage companies from offering more products.

(E) Like option D, this option is **incorrect** since it would discourage companies from offering more products.

The correct answer is A.

7. This is a detail question.

(A) This is the **correct** answer since the phrase refers to the possibility that the man may have a contraception alternative. The author wants to say that "being proactively safe is better than depending on the **possibility** (not impossibility) of a wallet condom." Thus, "likelihood" is the best choice.

(B) This option is **incorrect** because the phrase intends to convey uncertainty, but not a particular degree of uncertainty.

(C) This option is **incorrect** because it is completely out of place.

(D) Like option B, this option is **incorrect** because the phrase intends to convey uncertainty, but not a particular degree of uncertainty.

(E) This option is **incorrect** because reliability refers to the quality of the contraceptive and not just whether it is available or not.

The correct answer is A.

8. This is a tone question from the general category.

(A) This option is **incorrect** because the author does not explore new things. He merely presents the observations and negative consequences for women with a solid but judgmental reasoning.

(B) This option is **incorrect** because the author presents the observations and difficulties of women with a solid reasoning. He is not unduly biased towards women's needs. He supported the cause with facts and figures.

(C) This option is **incorrect** because the author does express his opinion and is aggrieved due to ignorance of women's dire need.

(D) This option is **incorrect** because the author is rather critical of the current scenario.

(E) This is the **correct** answer because as discussed in the other options, the author is opinionated. He presents a case and discusses all its aspects and firmly and explicitly mentions his opinions on the matter that the companies are not right in delaying contraceptives and that the pressure groups are to blame.

The correct answer is E.

Chapter 7

Talk to Us

Have a Question?

Please email your questions to info@manhattanreview.com. We will be happy to answer you. Your questions can be related to a concept, an application of a concept, an explanation of a question, a suggestion for an alternate approach, or anything else you wish to ask regarding the GMAT.
Please mention the page number when quoting from the book.

GMAC – Quants Resources

· *Official Guide 2017*: It is the best resource to prepare for the GMAT. It is a complete GMAT book. It comes with a Diagnostic test, which helps you measure your capability beforehand. It features Verbal, Quantitative, and Integrated Reasoning questions types. The book contains an access code to avail GMATPrep Software, Online Question Bank and Exclusive Video.

· *GMATPrep Software*: If you buy the OG, you get a free online resource from the GMAC—the testmaker. Apart from practice questions and explanation, it also has two genuine Computer Adaptive tests; you can also buy four additional CATs and few practice questions upon the payment.

Manhattan Admissions

**You are a unique candidate with unique experience.
We help you to sell your story to the admissions committee.**

Manhattan Admissions is an educational consulting firm that guides academic candidates through the complex process of applying to the world's top educational programs. We work with applicants from around the world to ensure that they represent their personal advantages and strength well and get our clients admitted to the world's best business schools, graduate programs and colleges.

We will guide you through the whole admissions process:

» Personal Assessment and School Selection
» Definition of your Application Strategy
» Help in Structuring your Application Essays
» Unlimited Rounds of Improvement
» Letter of Recommendation Advice
» Interview Preparation and Mock Sessions
» Scholarship Consulting

To schedule a free 30-minute consulting and candidacy evaluation session or read more about our services, please visit or call:

 www.manhattanadmissions.com 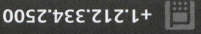 +1.212.334.2500